Not Scattered or Confused

Not Scattered or Confused

Rethinking the Urban World
of the Hebrew Bible

Mark McEntire

WESTMINSTER
JOHN KNOX PRESS
LOUISVILLE · KENTUCKY

© 2019 Mark McEntire

First edition
Published by Westminster John Knox Press
Louisville, Kentucky

19 20 21 22 23 24 25 26 27 28—10 9 8 7 6 5 4 3 2 1

Unless otherwise indicated, Scripture quotations are from the New Revised Standard Version of the Bible and are copyright © 1989 by the Division of Christian Education of the National Council of the Churches of Christ in the U.S.A. and are used by permission.

Book design by Sharon Adams
Cover design by Eric Walljasper

Library of Congress Cataloging-in-Publication Data

Names: McEntire, Mark Harold, 1960– author.
Title: Not scattered or confused : rethinking the urban world of the Hebrew Bible / Mark McEntire.
Description: First edition. | Louisville, Kentucky : Westminster John Knox Press, [2019] | Includes bibliographical references and indexes. | Identifiers: LCCN 2019002008 (print) | LCCN 2019016103 (ebook) | ISBN 9781611649635 (ebk.) | ISBN 9780664262938 (pbk. : alk. paper)
Subjects: LCSH: Cities and towns in the Bible. | Bible. Old Testament—Criticism, interpretation, etc.
Classification: LCC BS1199.C55 (ebook) | LCC BS1199.C55 M34 2019 (print) | DDC 221.8/30776—dc23
LC record available at https://lccn.loc.gov/2019002008

Contents

Preface

A confession is in order first. I live in a rapidly growing city, about a mile from the center of town, and I love it. I grew up in a religious tradition that was, at best, suspicious of urban contexts. At worst, cities were dens of iniquity, to be avoided whenever possible.

Solitude often dominates our perceptions of the Hebrew Bible. Abraham and Moses do their most important work on lonely mountaintops. The ideal human existence seems to be life in an isolated garden. Heroes like Jacob, Joseph, and David spend their formative years in the company of sheep. In American Christianity the most popular biblical text has become a poem in which readers envision themselves alone with God in green pastures beside ponds. Such lives and settings could hardly have produced the kinds of texts that fill the Hebrew Bible. Even the initially isolated characters of the biblical story move towards cities and a way of life that resembled the lives of the writers of the biblical books. These writers reached into the lonely, quiet places of ancient traditions and brought the stories and characters to themselves and their ways of life in urban settings. These polar ways of existence create a tension in the text that deserves more attention in our reading habits.

This shift in reading begins with an understanding of who the writers of the biblical books were and how these urban scribes worked with traditions that were sometimes anti-urban in order to shape a story more favorable to their way of life. Such tensions within the text may correspond to the dilemma of many modern readers who live in cities but are attached to religious traditions that value "natural" settings and their pastoral images over constructed places with massive buildings and crowded streets.

Looking at the texts of ancient Israel through this lens has led to some surprising results. I arrived at a few conclusions about the sources used to compose the biblical books and the way they were used that will likely prove controversial. I had not seen these possibilities before I began reading the texts with this particular concern. I did not expect the book of Jubilees to emerge as vital for understanding the literary and theological processes explained in this book: the more this project developed, the more important Jubilees became. My conclusions stop short of what some may desire. This is not a comprehensive, biblical theology of the city. The texts are too vast and variegated for such a construction. Neither does it lead to a specific urban spirituality, though I think it indicates the need for one or more; an end product like this is outside the scope of my expertise and ability. There is much more work of many kinds to be done on this subject. The work that follows—rethinking the urban world of the Hebrew Bible—required even more interdisciplinary input than I expected and runs up against my own limitations at a number of points. I hope others, better equipped, can advance further conclusions.

The pages that follow explore texts both inside and outside the Bible to discover their various ideas about cities and the people who live in them. This exploration will lead to questions about the connections between the presentation of cities and the lives of the scribes who shaped them and, finally, to the concerns of persons living in modern cities, like me.

Acknowledgments

It is difficult to say when a project like this began. In 2006 I presented a paper at the Annual Meeting of the Society of Biblical Literature called "Portraying a Distant Past: Literary Effects in Genesis 1–11," and many ideas that were in nascent form in that paper are in chapter 2 of this work. If what follows has been in the making for at least a dozen years, then it is not possible to remember and acknowledge all those it has bumped into along the way. In earlier and different forms, attempts to shape these ideas into a book have met with painful rejection; so I have to thank Bob Ratcliff at Westminster John Knox Press for his generous receptivity as my ideas came into this present form. My colleagues and students at Belmont University have given me their patient attention as I have rambled my way toward clearer thinking about many elements that fill these pages, and I am grateful for the place they make for me in their midst. While this book is a reflection on living in crowded places, the task required solitude, the magnitude of which is only possible with a careful guardian like Marie. Gratitude for help must be accompanied by a plea for forgiveness for all that I surely neglected along the way while I did this work.

1

Building the World

The earth is filling up with humans. Our population is headed toward ten billion and may pass twelve billion before the growth rate begins to slow. The development of human civilization has reached a point where its future will need more deliberate thought and planning. Our dominance over the planet has reached a level that has caused many scientists to declare the end of the Holocene epoch and the beginning of an eighth epoch of the Cenozoic era, the Anthropocene epoch. In *Half-Earth: Our Planet's Fight for Life*, eminent biologist Edward O. Wilson has written most forcefully about the unsustainability of human expansion on the planet; and Wilson's book spawned the Half-Earth Project. The premise is that human beings need to collect themselves onto half, or less, of the planet's surface and leave the remaining half for other species. The necessary cognitive shift that would make such an effort possible is daunting and lies primarily outside of the sciences. In Wilson's words, "We would be wise to find our way out of the fever swamp of dogmatic religious belief and inept philosophical thought through which we still wander."[1] Wilson is not unopposed in the scientific community, as many argue that we should embrace the Anthropocene as our epoch, even with its resulting mass extinctions and radical alterations of the earth's climate. Wilson called this "extreme Anthropocene worldview" the "most dangerous," and he documented the reasons for such an accusation.[2] The irony of an epoch named for our human species is that we are not well adapted to survive in it. Humans are creatures of the Holocene.

The biblical tradition is filled with cities: Enoch, Babel, Ur, Haran, Sodom, Gomorrah, Bethel, Jericho, Hebron, Nineveh, Damascus, Samaria, and Jerusalem. Most often they function as settings for the stories the texts tell, but sometimes the fate of cities, real or symbolic, becomes a central concern of the text. They become characters in their own right. The determination of layers of development in the Bible and the connection of those layers to specific historical concerns can become problematic if pressed for too much precision, but a general sense of the historical contexts out of which the biblical traditions emerged is certain enough. A broad historical picture, along with the use of literary tools necessary to connect these texts to particular concerns, may allow for reasonable conclusions about the development of ideas in ancient Israel.[3] The combination of historical and literary approaches currently coalescing in the field of biblical studies offers possibilities for looking at the portrayal of cities in new ways. The central question of this volume is how the understandings of cities and urban life in biblical texts shift in response to the changes in the culture that produced those texts. An important set of questions about the reading of the Bible naturally follows questions about its production. If the view of cities and urban life in the literary collection called the Bible is the result of changes over the long period of its production, then readers are encountering a diversity of views on this subject. Any particular text may be isolated to support a particular perspective, but what might we conclude about our own urban lives from an examination of our changing views of urban life in ancient Israel?

The central question of this book requires a multidisciplinary approach, even if the primary work involved is interpreting ancient texts. Beginning the task, therefore, requires defining and describing several ideas that will frequently impinge upon the interpretive work to follow. It is necessary to look at the definition of the central word, "city," even if no single, fixed definition is achievable. While it would be convenient to assume that a purely philological approach—attempting to look only at how the relevant words are used by the ancient writers—would suffice, the assumptions of modern readers about that word will always be present. There is an entire contemporary field of study called urban theory, which attempts to understand what cities are and how they operate. While the primary focus of urban theory is on modern cities, the observations such study yields can bring insight to the exploration of ancient cities in ancient texts.

The goal of this book is to ask what the biblical text reveals about the views of cities in ancient Israel and how reading such texts in the ancient and modern worlds might shape the experiences of readers, but the corpus of literature of ancient Israel, out of which the biblical books emerged, was a much larger collection than the texts of the Bible. Placing the literature that will receive greater attention within the broader collection is a careful process, and better tools for performing this task have been emerging rapidly. The full "library" of Second Temple Judaism is coming into clearer view. The overlapping study of scribal cultures and their practices during the Second Temple period is expanding, and a useful portrait has developed. Scholarship is no closer to being able to name the writers of these books, but it has produced a more thorough picture of something more important than the names of writers: that is, the kinds of people who wrote these books. Examining scribal culture leads to questions about audience, because asking who wrote these books invites questions about who they wrote them for. Finally, some prominent efforts to address the city and urbanization, particularly within the Christian theological tradition, exert a powerful influence on the discussion and must be brought into view, even if their conclusions are misguided or outdated. This introductory chapter expands on these issues in order to develop an adequate foundation for the discussion of textual traditions in the chapters to follow.

A study like this one will prompt a recurring objection about the anachronistic imposition of modern ideas upon ancient cultures. This is an objection that demands a careful hearing, and the progress of the study should be guided by the limits it can establish. Nevertheless, a rigid adherence to such cautions also leads to a warped perspective. Using questions about orality and literacy, Paul Evans has demonstrated that there is a danger of moving too far in the other direction, one he has labelled the "exoticization" of ancient cultures. The assumption that there is a divide between modern and ancient societies that modern interpreters cannot cross creates a skewed perspective. In short, assuming ancient people were a lot like us or assuming they were nothing like us are two erroneous ditches between which modern interpreters should choose to steer.[4]

UNDERSTANDING A CITY
AND DEFINING CITIES IN THE BIBLE

In 1977 Frank Frick published a bold and innovative work called *The City in Ancient Israel*. Part of this work was an early effort to bring insights from the social sciences to the task of interpreting the Bible. The subdiscipline of sociology called "urban studies" or "urban theory" began in the early twentieth century, so it had several decades of work and development behind it at the time of Frick's writing, and he sought to make use of the best insights from this field of study. Urban theory is necessarily an interdisciplinary effort. Many find its origin in the work of sociologists like Max Weber and Georg Simmel, but this was not the primary focus of their work. A more thorough approach to cities appeared in the work of Walter Benjamin, but Benjamin was a philosopher, and his study of the city was primarily a tool to develop a philosophy of history. The person who most clearly established a modern field of urban theory was probably Henri Lefebvre, who published most of his work through the middle of the twentieth century. One of the enduring issues in the discipline of urban theory, embodied in Lefebvre's work, is the extent to which a theorist can be committed to a particular position on what cities should be. The list of scholars here reveals a portrait of the development of urban theory founded in Continental European scholarship and closely related to Marxist approaches to politics and economics. This led to a particular understanding of what cities are for, and a sense that they should function deliberately, that they should be designed rather than just allowed to develop.[5]

Frick began his discussion with the work of Louis Wirth and Robert Ezra Park, both urban sociologists who were members of the Chicago school during the first few decades of the twentieth century. Thus, the views underlying his work were American and decidedly capitalist. The Chicago school was characterized by a commitment to the use of observation and data to bring about the improvement of the city. The urban way of life inevitably led to social problems that needed solving. At the time of Frick's writing, the insights of the social sciences were just beginning to make their way into the field of biblical studies. The extent to which contemporary observations could be mapped back onto the cultures that produced the biblical literature is uncertain, and the danger of anachronistic thinking is always present.[6] Frick seems to have recognized this problem in his choice to highlight Gideon Sjoberg's work *The Preindustrial City*. While transferring modern observations back onto biblical cultures has severe limits, some of the problems could be diminished by observing contemporary cities that are less different from ancient ones. The field of biblical studies itself has gone through a massive paradigm shift since Frick's publication. Use of the social sciences in biblical interpretation is broad and still growing, and literary approaches have swept through and transformed the field. After two or three decades of fragmentation, new ways of reading appear to be coalescing that make use of a variety of approaches simultaneously, a situation that allows for looking at city building, urban life, and references to cities as entities both symbolic and real in the literature of ancient Israel in a more comprehensive way.

Another way to minimize anachronism may be to look at cities through a lens not necessarily related to modern industrialization or technology. The work of Richard Florida has focused attention on a "creative class" and its role in the new urbanization of America in the twenty-first century. Florida began with the assertion that creativity is a social phenomenon rather than an individual one, and it requires the kind of environment that a city with a diverse population provides.[7] Even in the modern world, with the supposed interconnectivity provided by instant technology, the importance of place has persisted. Just at the time when technology was supposed to have had a flat-tening effect on population distribution, cities around the world have experi-enced explosive growth. According to Florida, "Cities are not just containers for smart people; they are the enabling infrastructure where connections take place, networks are built, and innovative combinations are consummated."[8] Perhaps the most interesting question we can ask of this perspective is how much postindustrial cities might be like preindustrial cities with regard to creativity.

Urbanism in America has changed significantly over the past few decades. During the nineteenth century and most of the twentieth century, cities were the centers of commerce and industrial production. The "white flight" that followed the civil rights movement and integration of public schools in America resulted in cities losing many of their residents, who preferred to live in suburbs and commute into the city to work. City and suburb became racial dividing lines. Late in the twentieth century and into the early part of the twenty-first, the situation began to shift again as many people, especially young professionals, began to move back into the central parts of many American cities. The process of "gentrification" that this movement produced appears to have many positive economic effects as cities explode with growth and businesses follow; but there are devastating impacts for others, once again involving racial and ethnic disparities. Those who had remained in the cities, predominately members of racial and ethnic minority groups, are being pushed out of housing, and the new housing market offers them no affordable options for relocation.[9] The irony of this development is that it may increase the homogeneity of city populations, thus diminishing the matrix for creativity it seeks, but the full outcome remains to be seen.

The new urbanism in American cities is perhaps best evaluated by Flori-da's work. He explains the rapid return to urban life by defining the kinds of people who were relocating:

> Creativity involves distinct habits of mind and patterns of behavior that must be cultivated on both an individual basis and in the surrounding society. The creative ethos pervades everything from our workplace culture to our values and communities, reshapes the way we see our-selves as economic and social actors, and molds the core of our very identities. It reflects norms and values that both nurture creativity and reinforce its role. Furthermore, it requires a supportive environment—a broad array of social, cultural, and economic stimuli.[10]

The environment necessary to foster creativity is best provided by cities. One important element in the modern expression of creativity is a lack of clear boundaries between work and leisure. For those living in suburbs, the commute and the nature of work provide such a boundary, but for a creative class living and working in the same context, such boundaries are limited or absent. The development of modern cities involves a reshaping of life and work and the environment in which they take place.[11]

Richard Florida has been influenced significantly by the work of Jane Jacobs, nearer to the middle of the twentieth century. In *The Death and Life of Great American Cities* (1961) and *The Economy of Cities* (1969) Jacobs envisioned an economy driven by creativity, requiring the right kind of context—the urban neighborhood—to bring together the resources to generate creativity, what she called "the need for concentration."[12] The discussion below of cities in ancient Israel and its surrounding regions will make it apparent that safety was the primary driving force behind their development. Secondarily, the desire to centralize and control religious ritual played a significant role in the development of ancient Israelite cities. Providing the resources for creativity was not their reason for being, but it may be reasonable to assume that it was a byproduct of city building. The population concentrations provided a context for creativity, a principle that seems likely to have transcended the divide between modern and ancient cultures.

Within the field of urban theory there is difficulty assigning a clear definition to "city." Such clarity may be even more elusive for the related terminology in ancient texts. The pertinent terminology in Biblical Hebrew creates some difficulty for examining cities in the text. Biblical Hebrew has one primary word for such a cluster of human population—'îr. The word appears more than one thousand times in the Tanakh, with a tremendous range of meaning, and its etymology is unclear. The origins of the word may not be essential to understanding many of its uses and may even lead to false assumptions, since uses of a word can drift over many centuries. Nevertheless, a brief examination of etymology might provide a starting point for understanding that process. It is common in the study of Biblical Hebrew vocabulary to look for a verbal root for nouns. One suggestion for 'îr is a verb that appears in the Hebrew Bible and other Semitic literature that means "surround" or "protect." Another possibility connects 'îr to a hill or mountain. The ancient tendencies to build walls around cities and to locate them on elevated places (*acropolis* in Greek) make both of these suggestions logical. Either possibility or a combination of them points to a central idea of a city as a place of relative safety and security. This origin is a long way from what we mean by "city" in the modern world, but it could have been an idea still present even in the latest references in the Hebrew Bible. The irony that in the modern world cities are frequently portrayed as places of greatest danger will require examination at several points to follow.

The grammatical function of 'îr is puzzling in two ways. First, when the noun becomes plural it not only adds a plural ending, but also its spelling changes slightly. This has led to the proposal that a somewhat different word that only appears in the Bible as part of place names like Aroer in Deuteronomy 4:48 and Ar of Moab in Numbers 21:28 might be the source of the plural form. Second, while 'îr functions consistently as a feminine noun in Biblical Hebrew grammar, the plural ending it takes is the one characteristic of masculine nouns.[13] This irregularity points to long and diverse use of a term and increases the possibilities that its use varied significantly from time to time and place to place. The result is that readers need to read particular texts with a flexible meaning for 'îr and let those literary contexts help shape the meaning of the word.

The many different uses of 'îr create additional challenges. The extremes may be visible in two particular appearances. The book of Jonah calls Nineveh a city four times and asserts a population of 120,000 in 4:11.[14] Three of the four uses modify 'îr with the adjective *gadol* (great or large), so the narrator may be acknowledging that Nineveh lies at the extreme of this category and may go beyond what 'îr alone can describe. There may be an attempt to define the physical size of Nineveh in 3:3. Some interpreters read the phrase as something like "a three days walk across," but the meaning is difficult to determine. The nature of the book of Jonah also creates the possibility that any size or population numbers are hyperbolic. Nineveh was likely the largest city in the region, and its near mythic proportions may have been one of the reasons the writer of Jonah chose it for the setting of the story, but the enmity with which Israelites viewed the Assyrians and their central city, most visible in the book of Nahum, is probably more important to the story of Jonah. Most of the book of Ruth takes place in and around Bethlehem, and it identifies Bethlehem as a city ('îr) four times. It is difficult to describe the appropriate size of Bethlehem, or what is assumed by the narrator of Ruth, but it would have been nothing like Nineveh. The time of the writing of Ruth and the chronological setting in which the narrator places the story are many centuries apart; so should we look for the size of Bethlehem in the eleventh century (setting) or the fifth century (writing)? There is minimal evidence from either time period, but Bethlehem was most likely a small farming town in both.[15] The fourth chapter of Ruth indicates a setting it describes as "the gate" of Bethlehem, which seems to be a social gathering place that becomes the scene in which Boaz collects "ten men from the elders of the city" as witnesses to his negotiations with the other potential redeemer. So, the narrator is portraying something larger than a village of a few families but also one that has this kind of nonprofessional legal system. The Bible's use of the same word to describe both Nineveh and Bethlehem leaves a great deal of space in between for understanding any other use of the word.[16]

A second Hebrew word *hṣr* is sometimes translated as "village" but more frequently designates the "court" or "courtyard" of the tabernacle or temple (Exod. 38:9 or 1 Kgs. 8:64). A palace could also have a court, as in Esther 5:2. The challenges of understanding these terms in relation to human settlements are apparent in a text like Leviticus 25:29–31:

> If anyone sells a dwelling house in a walled city ['*îr*], it may be redeemed until a year has elapsed since its sale; the right of redemption shall be one year. If it is not redeemed before a full year has elapsed, a house that is in a walled city shall pass in perpetuity to the purchaser, throughout the generations; it shall not be released in the jubilee. But houses in villages [*hṣr*] that have no walls around them shall be classed as open country; they may be redeemed and they shall be released in the jubilee.

There are two ways to read and think about the distinctions in this passage. It may provide the clear distinction between the two categories—an '*îr* has walls and a *hṣr* does not. But if that was the accepted definition, then why did an explicit description of the presence or absence of walls need to accompany the use of these terms? Another possibility lies in uses like those throughout Joshua 13–21, where the phrase "cities with their villages" appears more than two dozen times. In these texts a village (*hṣr*) is related to a larger settlement ('*îr*) like a satellite. This description yields a relative comparison and does not present a fixed definition of a city, but it hints at ideas of function and organization as distinctive. The modern phenomenon of suburbs comes to mind here. These places are the result of growth and "sprawl" around central cities and find their identity in the central city. Modern analysis has identified them with terms like "new towns" and "edge cities."[17] The Joshua 13–21 land allotment passages are obviously the product of a much later time when population growth in Israel could have begun to produce a similar phenomenon, and a different word may have been required to designate a primary city as opposed to those gathered around it, even if the latter began to take on physical characteristics of the former. Finally, while cities ('*îr*) with names are abundant in the biblical literature, villages (*hṣr*) with names are rare. One exception is the list of five named villages in 1 Chronicles 4:32. They are all five described as pre-Davidic villages belonging to the tribe of Simeon, so they may not have been places familiar to the writers or readers of Chronicles. The land assigned to Simeon in the book of Joshua was in the wilderness, the Negeb region south of Judah, where large settlements would have been less likely. The disappearance of Simeon from the list of tribes in the Blessing of Moses in Deuteronomy 33 may indicate that a separate identity for this tribe eventually ended, a situation that fits with the assignment of a wilderness dwelling place. It may be that smaller settlements like these had names at some point, but the biblical writers did not find identifying them by names useful. Putting these last two possibilities together produces an interesting possibility. A village was a settlement related to a larger one, a city, and the name of the city it was related to was more important to its identity than its own name. This draws attention back to the modern suburb analogy, where that type of central-city identity is often the case. Large cities in the United States often exhibit what political scientists call "collar counties," which are very different demographically and culturally from the cities they surround. They depend on the economic opportunity provided by the city, but often act as havens from what residents might consider the negative aspects of a city. Persons living in those places still identify the name of the central city as their home, rather than the fairly anonymous suburb.

The Bible also uses the term *mibtsar* on a few dozen occasions. By itself the word means a fortification of some kind. The verb from which it is derived means to make something inaccessible. About half of the uses of this word appear as a qualification of *'îr*, which may create some confusion. For example, 2 Kings 17:9 accuses the Israelites of "building high places in all their cities" (*'îr*), followed by the prepositional phrase "from watchtower to fortified city" (*'îr mibtsar*). This could be taken to mean that *'îr* has a range of meaning that would include unfortified settlements, but the *mibtsar* may indicate something beyond ordinary walls and gates. It could denote a city that included military installations.

The origins of Israel and its traditions that appear in the biblical literature lie on the chronological boundary between the Bronze and Iron Ages, so the question of continuity versus discontinuity between the Late Bronze Age and the Early Iron Age in Canaan will arise at numerous points in this study. The observable remains of Bronze Age cities in the Levant are relatively limited, but several existed, usually built in circular or oval shapes on tells with fortifications. Therefore, some planning was involved in the development of cities. Hazor was by far the largest city of that period in the Levant that has been excavated. It was about eighty hectares in area, but the later Israelite city built on the sites seems to have been much smaller. Jacob Baumgarten has argued that the larger cities of Late Bronze Age Canaan were primarily residential, and the main activity was agriculture. There do not appear to have been specific areas designed for artisans or craftspeople. Larger cities contained multiple temples to different gods, while smaller cities had one temple near the center. Baumgarten emphasized that city planning and development were shaped by a combination of topography, traditional ideas, and technological innovation. There was considerable growth and development of cities in this area in the last few centuries of the Bronze Age, but the collapse of the political system here and more broadly in the Mediterranean world created a significant disruption.[18] This disruption appears to be the matrix out of which Israel emerged, so the question of continuity of urban development is critical to establishing Israel's identity.

The evaluation of architecture from the first two centuries of the Iron Age by Zeev Herzog yields a wide variety of settlement types and patterns. The period he calls Iron II, the tenth through sixth centuries, shows significant development and the classification coalesces into four types. In this era "capital cities" like Samaria and Jerusalem emerged. Major administrative cities exhibited a distinctly lower percentage of residential area because they consisted mostly of public structures, so their population was lower. In the Iron II period such cities existed at Megiddo and Lachish. Secondary administrative cities, like Beer-sheba, were carefully planned, perhaps built from the beginning for their administrative purpose. Despite a high percentage of space devoted to public buildings, the careful planning allowed for significantly higher population density than the major administrative cities. Finally, provincial towns, such as Tell Beit Mirsim and Beth Shemesh, were still fortified with walls but were almost entirely residential. A less deliberate plan meant that they had a lower population density.[19] A more recent synthesis is in the work of William Dever, who classified a six-tier hierarchy of sites: capitals, administrative centers, cities, towns, villages, and forts. These categories are based on a combination of size and function. The designation of capitals, administrative centers, and forts would be based on function, while cities, towns, and villages are differentiated primarily by size. Dever lists the settlements in Israel and Judah that would have fit into each category with an approximation of their population during the period of the two monarchies.[20] Presumably, cities from this period would have played a significant role in forming the ways that writers and early readers of the biblical books thought of cities. The wide variety demonstrated in these four types might explain why the biblical books can refer to such different types of settlements as cities.

Broader archaeological information may help to clarify the terminology in biblical texts, or at least provide some sense of what the writers and audience would have assumed about a city. John Rogerson has estimated that ancient Nineveh was a little more than two thousand hectares (about eight square miles). Eighth-century Jerusalem was likely a little less than 2 percent of that size. Biblical Israelite cities like Gibeon, Samaria, Shiloh, and Shechem would have been even smaller.[21] This difference between modern perceptions and ancient realities requires careful attention and constant reminders. C.

De Geus has attempted to describe a walk through an Iron Age Israelite city based on archaeological information. The type of city he presumes to describe is walled, and his description begins with the walls and gates around the perimeter of the city. Not all of the details are significant here, but the major features he described may help to develop a portrait of a biblical city. During the ninth and eighth centuries which are the focus of his work, De Geus concluded that only Samaria qualified as a true city, and he preferred the term "town" for all other settlements in Israel and Judah, even if the Bible refers to them all as 'îr. Many of these settlements were fortified, and their walls, magnified by the tendency to build them on mounds, made them formidable. In De Geus's words, "An Iron Age town was built to impress. It held sway over the area around."[22] The modern sense of specialization readers might associate with cities is not the foremost feature of such a model. Still, De Geus took the criteria Frick used and developed a list of ten features exhibited by a town. These included some specialists who did not spend most of their time on food production, a reasonable quantity of artistic works, evidence of some administration, payments to the town by those who lived outside of it, some monumental building, and signs of a class structure within the society.[23] While elements of the centralization of knowledge and economics are obvious in this list, power is the predominate feature.

Volkmar Fritz's description of the development of cities in ancient Israel during the Iron Age is useful despite its overt ideological tendencies. The massive disruption of civilizations in the Levant, along with those in all of the surrounding areas at the end of the Bronze Age, meant that the growth and development of cities from about the eleventh century had to begin along new lines. The degree to which the new growth was a continuation of the older system or an entirely new innovation is a matter of dispute. Fritz contended that the new form of territorial state that began to emerge during this period required a new conception of the city: "The establishment of cities in ancient Israel is an expression of political will and not the consequence of the continuation of an existing form of settlement."[24] The factors he uses to distinguish the needs of the new form of state—security, administration, accommodating population growth—hardly seem unique, though, casting doubt on his conclusions about discontinuity.

The religious aspect of cities is important in their structure, and even more so in literature about them. Mark Smith has documented the ways in which the Bible and other literature from the region portray the association of gods with places. While ancient traditions most often associated gods with mountains, the trend in the Levant and surrounding areas was toward association with cities. This accompanied the rise of territorial kingdoms and the building of temples in capital cities. "In a sense, cities were temples writ large. At the core of this conceptualization of the city was a corresponding notion about the temple's central importance: The fate of the one was not uncommonly the fate of the other, in historical reality, cultural perception, and literary representation."[25] The identification of these three aspects and their individual significance and an awareness of how they are connected are central to the discussion of cities throughout this study. Smith observed, for example, the use of public space in cities as the site of communal celebration and lament in 2 Samuel 1:20 and Amos 5:16. These spaces also served as the places where news was communally received and interpreted, so that shared identity was formed there.[26] Events in a certain place, the understanding of those events in other times and places, and writing and reading about those events are intertwined, and the spaces that held those events helped to form them. The preceding discussion of cities offers more of a collage than a portrait, a situation not unlike the modern world. Still, the complex description of ancient cities may provide a useful background against which to look at ancient texts that use them as settings and characters.

A little more than a decade ago Dieter Georgi produced a book that he understood to be the culmination of his career as a New Testament scholar. It turned out to be so because he died while *The City in the Valley: Biblical Interpretation and Urban Theology* was in production. He began the work with a robust response to what he observed as an unwarranted pessimism about the state of cities. The kind of renewal depicted in Florida's work was already apparent to him.[27] Georgi's work primarily concerned the Christian New Testament and the development of theological understandings of urbanism. He saw a powerful sense of "urban concern" within Christianity's early development that was eclipsed by later theological trends, particularly in the work of Augustine and the long story of its impact on Christian thought. The remainder of this work is not a version of Georgi's work, applied to the Hebrew Bible, though that would be a laudable effort; but my work will come back into conversation with his from time to time.

THE EXTENT OF THE LITERATURE

While the focus in this book will be on understanding the traditions that are in the Hebrew Bible, current scholarship is also making us more aware every day that the literature of the Bible is just part of a much larger literary world within Second Temple Judaism, and that the writers of all these texts, including those in the Bible, did not operate with our modern sense of textual boundaries and finality. If the world of ideas in which the writers of the biblical books operated included a much broader collection of literature, then the other texts available to us are also vital to our effort to imagine that world. This presents a difficult challenge, because it is too easy to see the literature not in the Bible as mere context for understanding that which is in the canon. Even referring to them as "nonbiblical" or "outside the Bible" defines them in relation to the biblical collection. Some of this terminological difficulty seems unavoidable because we have inherited the idea of a limited canon, but it is important to keep such challenges in view while exploring ancient Jewish literature and asking it a particular set of questions. Eva Mroczek has proposed the concept of a "mental book shelf" where the books are not arranged hierarchically or concentrically. The books which ended up in the Bible sit on that shelf among others that look very much like them and would not have been clearly distinguished in antiquity.[28]

The literary works available to us from this period come from a wide variety of perspectives and offer particular views of cities and urban life. Our greater awareness of the broad range of literature and the worlds that produced it raises even more questions about how the experience of the writers and their identity as urban persons might have influenced the way they portrayed cities and urban life in the texts that they wrote. There seems little doubt that works like Jubilees and 1 Enoch and the books of Maccabees were also the products of urban dwellers. The difficult task for a study like this is to interpret biblical texts alongside and in the midst of those which are not in the Bible without giving the biblical texts an undue sense of priority or centrality in understanding the past, while acknowledging that they have played a greater role in shaping Western culture, including modern perceptions of ancient life. To the greatest extent possible, the developing view of cities and urban life will be based on the perspectives of all available texts. The book of Jubilees plays the most significant role of any book not in the Tanakh and is the primary focus of chapter 8 of this book. The formation of literature in these settings and the growing role of literature as the bearer of tradition through time point to the significance of scribal activity and communities.

SCRIBAL CULTURE AND
LITERACY IN THE ANCIENT WORLD

The viewpoints expressed in texts of the ancient world are those of scribal communities about whom helpful descriptions have developed over the last couple of decades. The books of the Bible have most often been the focus of this work, but it seems most logical to assume a similar pattern of development for all of the literature in ancient Israel. The biblical books are most accessible to us and have been the subject of the most intense critical scrutiny, yielding the large amounts of internal evidence that point to the process of their development. William Schniedewind's *How the Bible Became a Book* examines the stages of this development and describes the kind of scribal milieu in which the Bible may have formed. Like all such schemes, it begins with the obvious assumption that Israelite traditions originated in oral form and that the capacity for writing extensive texts developed later and changed the nature of transmission. Two things about such a transition are essential to remember. First, it would have been very slow. Because few people could read and because written texts would have been rare, oral performance and dissemination of material would have continued for centuries after written alternatives appeared. Second, literacy and orality were not discrete ways of working with tradition and often functioned together in various ways.[29] Schniedewind argued for a somewhat earlier date for this transition than many, insisting that significant writing of biblical traditions occurred in the late monarchy, beginning in the late eighth century. One important part of his position is the conclusion that Israelite scribal activity was largely continuous with the Canaanite activity that preceded it.[30] This assumption has been called into question by Brian Schmidt, who has tried to demonstrate a gap in literary production of about fifty years during the ninth century. He has located four important monumental inscriptions that appeared in the Levant during the late ninth century: the Mesha Stele from Moab, the Deir Alla inscription, the Tel Dan inscription, and the Ammon Citadel. The sudden appearance of this many texts from about the same time highlights what Schmidt portrayed as a gap in literary development for much of the ninth century, likely because of military conflict and political instability. A more stable situation eventually made possible both increased urban development and the scribal activity that would have gone with it.[31] Questions still remain about the audience of such texts. Schmidt's four exemplars all have a monumental aspect to them, which likely means that the content of their writing and the ability of persons to read it were only part of their function. They were also displays of power, and that power was dependent upon a scribal class that could produce such writing.

The social and economic status of this emerging scribal class may be a significant issue, along with the ways that they would have been perceived by other members of the society. To some they would have been what Roland Boer has called "nonproducers." Part of the life of nonproducers was the need and goal to extract capital from producers. Such an arrangement is inherently conflictual. While scribes would have been among nonproducers, they did not necessarily possess the full status of estate-holders and royal court members who employed them.[32] Scribes appear to have had the power to shape the national story through their work, which could also have been the opportunity to define their role within it to their advantage.

The dispute surrounding the location(s) of scribal activity in ancient Israel is based on a combination of evidence, logical reasoning, and assumptions. The most important question for this study is the degree of centralization of writing. Did it take place primarily in urban settings? At or near one extreme is the assumption that writing remained closely connected to the palace throughout much of the period of the Israelite monarchy.[33] This is not the same as arguing that scribal activity was primarily urban. It could have been urban without royal sponsorship. The extension of royal power into less urban locations would have pushed the practice of writing into those places. The counterclaim that writing was extremely decentralized is often based on the widespread presence of the bizarrely named "abecedaries." These inscriptions composed simply of a written alphabet are typically assumed to be evidence of people learning to write. One particular inscription of this type that has received significant attention is the Zayit Stone, a late tenth–early ninth century inscription uncovered in 2005 at a tell about fifty kilometers southwest of Jerusalem. The presence of this stone in such a place is often taken as early evidence of widespread writing in the southern Levant, even in places far from a major city.[34] The presence of inscriptions like this was taken by Seth Sanders as evidence that writing took place in a variety of settings and was not entirely centralized.[35] While this may be correct, the more important question is what kind of writing might have taken place in such settings. The written alphabets are the most rudimentary possible type of writing. Even if they are evidence of persons learning to write, such writing would not necessarily have enabled anything more than the production of mundane documents like commercial receipts.[36] The creativity required to produce lengthy, complex works of literature only begins with the basic mechanics of learning the alphabet. Writing lengthy works of literature requires skills and resources far more advanced. Daniel Fleming takes all of this evidence and constructs an argument against the centralized development of literary traditions in ancient Israel.[37] I agree with Fleming's conclusions that writing was not entirely under the control of the palace, allowing for the development of traditions that portrayed the monarchy negatively. Such a conclusion should not be extended, however, to assume that a high level of literary production could have taken place most anywhere. Groups of scribes working together, enjoying the kind of interaction that could raise learning and literary production to the level exhibited in biblical books would seem to require an urban setting and significant resources. Activity like this need not have been restricted to the palace and the temple, but these are the two most obvious institutions that could have provided these kinds of resources. Imagining the scribes responsible for producing the books of the Bible and other similar literature in ancient Israel, at their various stages of development, as urban persons is difficult to escape. The influence of their social setting and ways of life on how they viewed the world would have seeped into the work they produced. This is not a conclusion that can be definitively proven, but every step leading to it bears a high level of probability. The chapters that follow this one examine how the literature of ancient Israel presented cities and the people who lived in them through the lens of the conclusion that the scribes who produced the literature in its preserved forms were urban people. When they wrote about cities, they were writing about the kind of context in which they lived. Even if some of the traditions with which they worked offered a different perspective on urban life, these traditions were reshaped by scribes who viewed urban life positively. Moreover, if their primary audience was composed of persons largely like themselves, then the motivation to present such a view of cities would have been magnified. Therefore, questions about who could read these kinds of text are also important.

Literacy has become a subject of keen interest in the study of ancient Israel, in large part because it is assumed to be a key factor in understanding how the biblical literature emerged. Knowing who could have read literature like the biblical books would point toward their potential audience. Even if the literature was produced to be read or performed by scribes for a larger audience, such reading events presume a concentrated population. If reading was restricted almost entirely to the professional scribal class, then the writers of such books may have been a relatively small group producing literature almost exclusively for each other. A limited audience for literature like these books would have been almost entirely an urban audience. A scene in the book of Nehemiah has received a lot of attention because it is a rare portrayal of public reading in ancient Jewish literature. It is impossible to say whether the portrayal in Nehemiah 8, in which Ezra reads the Mosaic law all morning to a crowd gathered at the Water Gate in Jerusalem, reflects a historical event. The scene has obvious literary and ideological purposes in the book of Nehemiah. A combination of the narrative in Nehemiah and historical evidence from outside the Bible may lead to a conclusion that if such a scene took place, it included a relatively small audience. The inhabitants of Jerusalem it envisions are primarily those returning from Babylon, who would have been descendants of the elite urban dwellers who had been deported. This subject will receive more detailed attention in chapter 7. For now, it seems best to conclude that what the story in Nehemiah 8 can tell us about literacy in postexilic Judah is limited, but what it may tell us about how the scribes who produced it understood themselves and their social roles is more significant.

A lot of interest in the subject of literacy has surrounded a particular item among the documents called the Lachish Letters, which were found and published in the 1930s. The one designated "Letter Number 3" discusses the subject of literacy. It seems to be written by a junior military officer to his senior officer, who has accused him of not being able to read a letter. In response, the younger man argues vehemently that he is capable of reading all of the correspondence sent to him. Looking at such a conversation from late in the period of Judah's monarchy, perhaps in the early sixth century, is fascinating. Logic might lead us in two different directions. The idea that a junior military officer would possess the ability to read and write letters of this sophistication points some readers to the conclusion that literacy had become widespread at the time.[38] The tone of the letter and its subject could just as easily point in the opposite direction, though. The assumptions of the senior officer and vivid protest of the junior officer may indicate that it was extremely rare for a person of that station to be literate at the time. The conclusion that this particular person was an aberration seems more likely.[39] The argument about this is important, but it only sheds limited light on the production and consumption of complex literature like the books of the Bible, because it is an isolated case.

Walter Aufrecht has argued that the invention and refinement of the alphabet was a force moving human civilization forward as much as pottery or metallurgy. The implications of this claim are vital for understanding the developing civilization of Late Bronze and Early Iron Age Canaan. A trained scribal class was a necessity for an urban society. Epigraphic evidence demonstrates the development of scribalism and the parallel development of urban culture.[40] It is difficult to imagine a growing city, particularly one with administrative tasks, functioning without the services of trained scribes. Likewise, a scribal class would require the resources that urban living would make available. The movement from logograms to syllabaries to a true alphabet made reading and writing in the ancient world easier.[41] Nevertheless, Christopher Rollston has offered ample evidence that such a development was not necessarily accompanied by growth in literacy rates leading to a situation in which a significant portion of the population in ancient Israel would have been able to read.[42] Rollston's conclusions are also in line with the thorough investigation of this question by Ian Young. Young was cautious in his conclusions because of the limited evidence, but his investigation of the question led to the statement that "The evidence at our disposal has been interpreted to give no hint that the 'ordinary' Israelite had any literate abilities at all."[43] Though written artifacts from the time of the height of the Israelite monarchies are found in more widespread locations, Horsley has quelled assumptions about increased literacy. "The increase in the number of inscriptions and simple records in eighth-century Israel and Judah attest a growth of central administration rather than an increase in the general rate of literacy."[44] The available evidence and logical conclusions that follow it lead to the conclusion that works of complex literature were written by, and primarily for, a relatively small group of elite, urban scribes.

THE CITY IN CHRISTIAN THEOLOGY

It is impossible to begin a work like this one without paying some attention to some influential works that may fall into the general category of Christian theology and which specifically address the portrayal of cities in the Bible. St. Augustine lived and worked in the city of Hippo in North Africa, and is often used as a convenient boundary for the end of antiquity. He wrote during the late fourth and early fifth centuries of the Common Era and is the kind of figure whose influence can hardly be overstated. One of his two most influential works was *The City of God*, a massive volume divided into twenty-two books. The first half of this work primarily addresses the fall of Rome and accusations that Christians were responsible for the tragic circumstances that befell "the Eternal City." The second half of the work is more significant for the present study, because Augustine used his interpretation of the Old Testament to develop an understanding of the two cities, an earthly city and a heavenly city, that could transcend the historical fate of an individual city like Rome. He grounded this dualism in his portrait of the good and evil angels in books 11 and 12 of *City of God*. Though the city functions primarily as a metaphor in Augustine's thought, the designation of the earthly city as a symbol of evil has had an impact on Christian thought for one and a half millennia. In his essay "Should Augustine Have the Last Word on Urban Theology?," Dieter Georgi championed a new concern for urban theology that resisted the influence of Augustine: "Augustine's individualizing and deurbanizing interpretation of 2 Cor 3 and other essential Pauline texts has followed and strengthened a compromise the post-Pauline generation felt compelled to make."[45] The failure of the Parousia to end the Roman Empire forced an internalization and individualization of the Christian faith that moved away from social and political engagement. For Georgi this was a "falsifying mutation of the Pauline message of universal justification and reconciliation" and a "perversion into an individualistic, ghettoized teaching of sin and forgiveness [that] completely covered the corporate dimension that had been critically addressed to the concrete urban community."[46] A new urban theology would require the undoing of Augustine's influence, particularly the sentimental sense of Christian pilgrimage as an individual experience, and a redevelopment of the "sojourning people of God" as an "urban reality."[47]

Two of the most significant modern works appeared in the middle of the twentieth century, Jacques Ellul's *The Meaning of the City* and Harvey Cox's *The Secular City*. Ellul is a difficult figure to define, and his work is equally enigmatic. He published this book in French in 1951 with the title *Sans feu ni lieu: Signification biblique de la Grande Ville.* The English translation appeared in 1970, with a very different title. The first part of the French title is a saying that might not have come through into English well in a literal translation such as "without fire or place." The phrase points to one of Ellul's biases about city life as lacking in a sense of belonging. More problematic is Ellul's approach to the Bible, one that relies upon a Christian supersessionist reading. He gives careful attention to the description of a redeemed city in the vision of a restored Jerusalem and temple in Ezekiel 40–48 but finds it full of specifically Christian imagery. His equation of the trees in 47:11–12 with the Edenic tree of life looks somewhat odd, but seeing this tree as the cross of Jesus distorts the passage beyond recognition. This can have nothing to do with how the composers of the book and their original audience understood the vision, or with their understanding of cities.[48]

One important way in which Ellul's work is compatible with this one is his sense of movement in the biblical understanding of cities. He recognized, in the early portions of the Bible in particular, some negative perspectives on city building. Ellul's own theological presuppositions, however, impinge on his reading of the text, creating internal conflicts within his work. For example, his conclusions about Cain's city building include this statement: "For God's Eden he substitutes his own, for the goal given to his life by God, he substitutes a goal chosen by himself—just as he substituted his own security for God's. Such is the act by which Cain takes his destiny on his own shoulders, refusing the hand of God in his life."[49] Ellul's reading of the Bible reveals a naiveté that allows assumptions not in the text to invade his exegesis. The root cause of the problems in this approach is clear in a passage within his discussion of Cain's city building:

> What appears to be remarkable in this brief and rich declaration of Scripture is that it is true no matter what position one adopts toward the Bible. If it is God's revelation, here is what God thinks of the affair. It is God giving us his appraisal of man's action and the profound meaning of the construction of the city. And we must accept it all for history, for this is how God sees this story. And we must believe that God's appraisal is truer than the scientific knowledge we may obtain.
>
> If the Scriptures are only an historical text, dependent on older documents, themselves dependent on myths created at the dawn of consciousness, our texts are also meaningful because they tell us what man wanted to do when he created the city, what he was hoping to conquer, what he thought to establish.

Both of the supposedly polar options Ellul described here treat the Bible as univocal, as if it contains one position on a subject like city building and urban life. Both views also ignore the political purposes for which the various parts of the Bible were produced. The idea of scribes in particular political contexts making use of older traditions in order to build a narrative to function within their own time seems entirely foreign to either view he expresses. His hypothetical "man" in the second option sounds like a collective human enterprise that has a singular intent. The Bible is a layered text, presenting multiple perspectives, and the authors themselves were far less likely to have been builders of the cities they inhabited and more likely a product of the city-building process.

Esteemed theologian and Bible reader Harvey Cox presented a robust portrait of a Christian religion for an emerging age in his 1965 classic, *The Secular City: Secularization and Urbanization in Theological Perspective.* Cox found the origin of this movement in the Hebrew Bible itself, describing Genesis 1 as "a form of 'atheistic propaganda' . . . designed to teach the Hebrews that the magical vision, by which nature is seen as a semidivine force, has no basis in fact."[50] While this view seems overstated, it still looks correct in terms of direction. Cox wrote this during an era that emphasized a distinct discontinuity between Israelite tradition and the surrounding cultures of Mesopotamia, the Mediterranean world, and North Africa. The separation of God from nature was not happening only in ancient Israel. Similarly, for Cox the exodus story acted as a "desacralization of politics" and Sinai a "deconsecration of values."[51] The social upheaval of the period in which Cox wrote *The Secular City* demanded a transition in Christian thought, and his is an important attempt, one which he continued to update for decades, including his *Religion in the Secular City: Toward a Postmodern Theology* in 1985 and *The Future of Faith* in 2009.

What we think the Bible "thinks" about cities matters. Even the positive expressions of the city in the Hebrew Bible, which later chapters will demonstrate most often come in depictions of Jerusalem, are dimmed in the New Testament when it becomes the place of Jesus' execution. In the book of Revelation Jerusalem must be replaced by its heavenly expression. The story and writings of Paul may appear to be anti-urban, because of the rejection Paul faced in Athens (Acts 17) and in his depiction of Corinth as a place of strife and idolatry, but the New Testament portrays Paul in cities. They are the only places where his work makes sense. In contemporary Christianity, urban life often receives negative assessments based on assumptions about the people who live there. The hymn by Catherine Cameron called "God, Who Stretched the Spangled Heavens" is a good example. Most of the song presents positive images of nature as divine creation, but the peculiar second stanza offers a harsh contrast, emphasizing the pride of cities. It depicts endless rows of buildings with "blank, unfeeling" windows, and people who are "lonely" and who "drift unnoticed." Even worse, these people are "lost to purpose and to meaning scarcely caring where they go."[52] The idea here is that cities resist God in their pride and create an environment that is inherently unhealthy for people whom God has created. This bias against city life is enhanced by the assumption that the "purple mountain's majesty" and "the fruited plain" are the natural divine environment in which humans may flourish. "America the Beautiful," and the original poem by Katharine Lee Bates on which it is based, make a reference to urban life in the less familiar fourth stanza, but it is odd in at least two ways. The "alabaster cities" do not seem like a fit description for American urban landscapes, particularly those Bates would have encountered on her journey through the Midwest to get to Pikes Peak where she wrote the poem. There is some indication that the city she had in vision was an artificial one constructed for the World's Fair exhibition in Chicago.[53] In addition, the reference to "human tears" is puzzling. Does the song envision the city as a place of suffering and torment? In contemporary American culture the association of biblical religion with the rural or small-town "heartland" is unavoidable. The other side of this association is the assumption that something about urban life is a poor fit with, or even antagonistic to, biblical religion and its traditions. The pages that follow demonstrate that the biblical literature and other ancient Israelite literature from the same period hold a complex mix of traditions that look at urban life in a variety of ways and use its portrayal for multiple purposes. The movement, however, is inevitably toward cities and a way of understanding them as positive settings.

PLAN OF THE BOOK

The Primeval Narrative sets the tone for the entire Hebrew Bible, as it is now configured. This framing is particularly pronounced with regard to the Bible's view of cities. The first eleven chapters of Genesis are intensely concerned with this issue, so the second chapter of this book will examine Genesis 1–11 in greater detail than will be the case for the remainder of the Bible in the chapters that follow. The discussion seeks to unravel the conflicted perspectives on the origin and purpose of human life and the nature of human communities. With this framework fully delineated, the next few chapters will follow the biblical narrative, observing the ways that cities and urban characters enter into the story and asking what this might reveal about ancient Israel's understandings of its own origin and identity. The texts in Genesis 1–11 still exert an influence on contemporary readers that exceeds texts' relative size. Looking at them through the lens of ancient Israel's complex relationship to urbanization can offer important perspective for contemporary readers seeking to navigate similar processes and settings. The great ancestors of Israel are not portrayed in Genesis as urban people, but they frequently interact with cities and the people who live in them. Chapter 3 will examine these interactions to determine how Israel understood its past and used those traditions to establish and maintain a national identity during the periods when they were producing the biblical literature. These figures also function, rightly or wrongly, as heroes and role models for contemporary readers. Examining their encounters with urban settings and people in a broader context of competing traditions provides greater nuance for such reading. The story necessarily changes when Israel acquires its own land and begins to build itself as a nation. Chapter 4 begins in Egypt and follows the exodus story. While this may look only like a foreign setting, the legal material that dominates the remainder of the Torah and the complex, interwoven traditions about how the Israelites came to Canaan reveal important understandings about the kind of society they understood themselves to be at the time the texts were produced and when they were incorporated into the biblical books.

As the biblical plot moves toward the building of nations—Israel and Judah—the consolidation of power requires the centralization of settings. Chapter 5 examines the presentation of the monarchy and the roles that various cities, particularly Samaria and Jerusalem, play in the text and what this reveals about the writers' views of urban life. The construction of these Israelite cities led to defeat and destruction, of course. Chapter 6 examines how the stories of destruction, dispersal, and exile show cities and their inhabitants as the targets of imperial invasion, in spite of their status as divine abodes. Destruction and exile are not the end of the biblical plot. A process of restoration also appears in a variety of texts. The restoration is always centered on the rebuilding of Jerusalem and its temple and the reestablishment of centralized religious institutions, so a city is at the core of the story. Chapter 7 asks important questions about how the literature related to the restoration sees Jerusalem and how it makes use of the story of rebuilding and re-urbanization of the Persian province of Yehud.

Chapter 8 moves in a very different direction by examining noncanonical literature, particularly the book of Jubilees. While the books of the Bible preserve texts that may have an anti-urban ideology and combine them with other traditions in order to reshape them and mitigate that perspective, the writer of Jubilees was more apt to remove those anti-urban traditions, or change them entirely, in order to remove any trace of anti-urban bias. The discussion in chapter 8 examines this radically new way of telling Israel's story and asks why someone would have produced it.

It might not be possible to reiterate too many times the central difficulty a study like this one faces. There are many versions of the story it analyzes and evaluates, and they fall into two quite different groups. First, there are multiple versions of the story of Israel within the composite document called the Bible, some of which have been woven together in ways difficult to separate. The primary function of these stories is ideological and theological. They seek to define a group of people at the time of their telling and writing. They use their version of the past to help shape the present. This does not mean that they cannot contain pieces of useful historical information. The second group of stories, or versions of the story, is modern and consists of the attempts to reconstruct the past based on textual and archaeological evidence. Their primary goal is to determine what happened in the past. This does not mean that such stories are unaffected by political, ideological, and theological concerns. While arguments for keeping these two groups of stories apart are important, there are advantages to looking at them together. Understanding what likely happened in the past may provide important clues about how the literature attempted to shape the story; and at some point this literature became influential and actually began affecting events outside the text, something that continues to happen up to this day in communities where these texts hold significant, even sacred, status.

2

In the Shadow of Nimrod

The Primeval Story and the Mythic Origins of Cities

The biblical framework for thinking about ways of life and their settings is established in the early chapters of Genesis, as the narrative builds the world in which subsequent events will occur. Genesis 1–11 in the Hebrew Bible is part of a long line of development of traditions. This chapter examines that development by looking at Genesis 1–11 as a point near the center of that process. Three essential texts stand on either side of it as critical points in the growth of what I call the Primeval Tradition, the various stories, lists, and poems that precede the traditions of the ancestors in ancient Israel. Most of the narrative material in Genesis 1–11 comes from what source critics of the Pentateuch call the Yahwist (J) source, which is the subject of this chapter, because it is part of Genesis, and Genesis provides our only access to it. The remainder of Genesis 1–11 is from the Priestly (P) source, which includes a creation account, a flood story, and a lot of genealogical material. The current book of Genesis also provides our only access to this source. Genesis 1–11 was then a major source for a later literary work called Jubilees, which presents the narrative bounded by Genesis 1 and Exodus.[1] The version of the Primeval Tradition and of the origins of Israel in the book of Jubilees is the subject of chapter 8.

This study operates from the conclusion that Genesis 1:1–11:27 (hereafter, Genesis 1–11) is a complete and coherent literary work on its own, one which I also refer to as the Primeval Story in Genesis.[2] The version found in Genesis is one expression of the Primeval Tradition, along with the expressions found in the J and P sources separately and those found in other literary works like 1 Enoch, Jubilees, and the Genesis Apocryphon. Though many of the components of Genesis 1–11 originated in older sources, and the final form may have been consciously developed as part of the book Genesis, the nature of the literature is so distinct from Genesis 12–50 that independent treatment is warranted. This chapter makes use of the procedures of source criticism to reconstruct an earlier versions of the Primeval Tradition (J and P), but that process will follow and interact with a reading of its final form.[3]

THE DISTINCTIVE NATURE OF GENESIS 1–11

By all accounts Genesis contains a diverse set of materials. Traditional methods of biblical interpretation, such as source criticism and form criticism, have made significant progress in talking about the types of literature in this corpus, the possible settings from which the units may have emerged, and how each unit may be connected to other literary units in the Pentateuch that share similar language, theology, and ideology. These methods declined in influence during the last decades of the twentieth century, as other approaches focusing on the literary features of the final form of the text arose within the field of biblical studies. One of the most powerful aspects of the newer approaches, often called "synchronic" or "literary," is the way they have led us to understand that texts construct narrative worlds, and the relationship of this idea to Genesis 1–11 is the primary subject of this section. It would be a mistake, though, to dismiss a method like source criticism, which is currently undergoing a significant revival within biblical studies. The implications of this revival for the Primeval Story is the subject of the section below on the composition of Genesis 1–11. The older notion of a clear line of demarcation between historical methods and literary methods or between diachronic and synchronic methods is dissolving. One reason a revival of source-critical methods has been possible is the return to its literary roots and the incorporation of what interpreters have learned from newer methods like narrative criticism. An elegant description of this appears in Ronald Hendel's reassertion of the existence of the source called the Yahwist (J), in opposition to those who had declared J dead.[4] In response to the position that there is no "discernible J style," Hendel observed that "this position may have been credible a generation ago, when literary study of biblical narrative was virtually nonexistent. But I submit that it is not credible today, when there are many lucid descriptions of the literary art of biblical prose."[5] The discussion of source criticism and the composition of Genesis 1–11 will be more intelligible after an initial exploration of the way the narrative operates.

Genesis 1–11 develops a unique narrative world, one which is obviously different from the world of our experience, and to which it must take us if its issues are to be addressed.[6] It is filled with odd names, very long human life spans, indeterminate geography, strange creatures and plants, and a direct connection between heaven and earth, all of which serve to develop a setting in the distant past that is mysterious and strange to modern readers. What if the ability to contribute to this sense of dislocation was one of the reasons for choosing certain materials and shaping them in particular ways? What effect might these features have had on early readers of Genesis, perhaps in the sixth or fifth centuries BCE? Did they feel as out of place as we do when reading it? The answer to this last question must be affirmative to at least some degree. The distinct shift in the nature of the narrative world beginning at Genesis 12, or more precisely 11:27, supports the idea that Genesis 1–11 deliberately builds a world that feels strange and distant in terms of its settings, characters, events, and use of time. The very different world of Genesis 12–50 must be the one closer to the experience of the earliest readers of the book. Genesis 1–11 makes use of literary devices that serve to put distance between the reader and the narrative world of the text, and this was probably true of the readers for whom it was originally written.

An important narrative element that enters the text immediately is the geography of this narrative world or, better yet, its lack of geography. Genesis 1 has no geographic specificity of any kind; its location is simply "the heavens and the earth." On the other hand, 2:10–14 describes the location of Eden as the place where the Tigris, Euphrates, and Blue Nile (Gihon) rivers flow from a single source. The rivers seem to indicate the broadest extent of Israel's geographical awareness, from Mesopotamia to Cush/Ethiopia.[7] Eden's location is a geographical impossibility, and does not exist in the world of any reader, ancient or modern. Eden is everywhere and nowhere at the same time, a perfect place to hide paradise.

Outside of Eden, Genesis 1–11 develops four distinct sets of narrative events, which are linked by genealogies: (1) the lives of Cain and Abel, leading up to the murder of Abel; (2) the flood, including the preparation of the ark and its contents by Noah; (3) the emergence from the ark and subsequent life of Noah and his family; and (4) the story of the people of Babel. The first two sets of events have no recognizable location at all, and the only reference to a place of any kind is the mysterious city Cain builds in 4:17, and names for his son Enoch. The city called Enoch is a surprising narrative element, though, and it stands in stark relief against the background of its context, so it demands specific attention and is the subject of the discussion later in this chapter. The third and fourth sets of events listed above have nebulous geographical settings, which are named in 8:4 and 11:2. Ararat is a group of mountains in the modern nation of Turkey, not a single peak, and nobody can say for certain which had the name first, the mountain in the Genesis story or the group of mountains that go by that name today. Shinar, in 11:2, likely refers to a region in Mesopotamia, but is also imprecise.[8] The vague geography of Genesis 1–11 gives way to a sudden emergence of precision, as the Ancestral Story begins, and every event is provided a location readers can locate on a map.

The other primary kind of text in Genesis 1–11, along with the stories described above, is genealogy. While readers often assume that genealogies are simply lists of names with birth and death notices, they occasionally exhibit some narrative development. Perhaps the most famous of these is the little story of Enoch in 5:21–24. Two elements of the Enoch text have made it the object of fascination, the perceived repentance of Enoch after the birth of Methuselah (v. 22) and the "taking" of Enoch by God that replaces a death notice.[9] No geographical setting appears in this or any other part of Genesis 5, though. The genealogy commonly known as the "Table of Nations" in Genesis 10, however, begins addressing geography to some extent, but the names of places are fused with the names of people in what looks like a genealogical list, and a clear geography still does not emerge. The ideological placement of Canaan (10:6) at the greatest possible genealogical distance from the ancestors of Israel is more important than geographical location. The expanded entry concerning Nimrod in 10:8–11 continues to compress the known world of the ancient Israelites, linking Cush/Ethiopia with the ancient cities of Mesopotamia—Babel, Erech, Accad, Nineveh, and others. (The peculiarity of the Nimrod text places it at the center of the discussion in a subsequent section of this chapter.)

After settings, the next narrative element to emerge in Genesis 1–11 is characters, and this is another place where the literature is sparse. The characters in Genesis 1–11 are remarkably undeveloped. Outside of the personages mentioned only within genealogical material, there are twelve human characters in the Primeval Story, only eight of whom are named, seven men and one woman.[10] Of those eight, only four utter any speech. Compared to the highly developed characters in the ancestral material of Genesis 12–50, like Sarah, Abraham, Hagar, Jacob, Rachel, Leah, and Joseph, the characters of the Primeval Story are mere silhouettes. We know little or nothing of their feelings, motivations, hopes, or dreams. Even a character so central to this part of Genesis and so massive in biblical tradition as Noah speaks only a single time, in 9:25–27. Those who speak the most—Eve, Adam, and Cain—speak only with God. In the Hebrew text of Genesis 1–11, none of these human characters ever speaks directly to another human being.[11] There are a few occasions when human speech is directed at other humans, but it never rises to the level of dialogue. Within the genealogy of Cain, Lamech addresses his poetic speech to his wives, but this is hardly a case of human characters in dialogue with one another, as Lamech makes a poetic declaration about himself to his wives that elicits no response. Noah's curse in 9:25–27 has no clear addressee, and the single, collective character in the Babel account speaks or thinks to itself in 11:4. Once again, like it did with geography, the movement in Genesis from the Primeval Story to the Ancestral Story involves a focusing effect, as the shadowy, distant characters of the former are replaced by the sharply distinguished and highly developed characters in the latter, who are revealed to the reader in intimate fashion. It seems safe to assume that whether the earliest readers of Genesis lived in the seventh, sixth, or fifth centuries, the pastoral semi-nomads of the Ancestral Story would have looked familiar to them, but it seems unlikely that the nine-hundred-year-old cultural founders of Genesis 1–11 would have generated such a sense of familiarity.

The changes in the portrayal of the divine character within Genesis, and within the entire Tanakh, are toward a more distant, hidden, and subtle figure.[12] A related issue that illustrates the distinct nature of the narrative world in Genesis 1–11 is the way it describes divine-human interaction. The shift that takes place in this feature as the book of Genesis progresses has been well documented.[13] In the Primeval Story the divine character speaks with Adam, Eve, the serpent, Cain, and Noah. None of these cases is portrayed as an unusual occurrence. They are not sudden, surprising divine visitations, and could hardly be described in form-critical terms as theophanies. God does not have to go down to earth or travel to meet these characters. There is no mediating "Angel of the LORD," as is common in other parts of the Tanakh, nor is there any theophanic fanfare. The abode of God and the abode of humanity are so closely connected that God simply begins talking to these characters. The portrait developed in 6:1–4 also implies regular contact between the "sons of God" and humans. Only in 11:5, as the Primeval Story approaches its end, is YHWH required to "go down" in order to interact with the human world.[14] In contrast, as the Ancestral Story proceeds, divine-human conversations are replaced by the more formal divine visitations experienced by Abraham, Hagar, Sarah, Isaac, and Jacob. These visitations are then replaced by the dreams Jacob and Joseph experience.[15] Jacob's divine experience is a combination of waking theophanies and dreams, while Joseph only has dreams, and these dreams are symbolic experiences requiring interpretation, not conversations with God inside the dreams.

In all of the features described above, Genesis 1–11 stands apart not only from other biblical literature but also from Genesis 12–50. The vague geography of Genesis 1–11 is replaced by a very specific geography in Genesis 12–50 that any modern reader can follow with a map of Canaan, and the original readers likely knew this geography. The flat characters of Genesis 1–11 yield the stage to some of the most carefully developed and memorable characters in all of ancient literature, particularly Abraham, Jacob, and Joseph, but even a secondary character like Hagar is portrayed in a much fuller fashion than any characters in Genesis 1–11. The changing way in which the divine character is portrayed also distinguishes Genesis 1–11 from the remainder of the book.[16] All of these features, and others, serve to build a distinctive world, one that is not only removed from the world of modern readers, but also from the lives of ancient readers. The remainder of this chapter will be concerned with what happens in that narrative world and how the story being told is related to this particular way of developing its components.

Careful reading reveals several texts in the Primeval Story that look odd, both in their intrinsic nature and in their placement within the whole. Genesis 4:17–24; 6:1–4; 10:8–11; and 11:1–9 all have to do with a way of life characterized by settlement, city building, and fame. The strange nature of this collection of texts creates the possibility that addressing the way of life they point to is an important part of the development of the primeval traditions. After this introduction, succeeding sections of this chapter offer a reading of the major parts of Genesis 1–11 with thorough attention to the role texts like 4:17–24; 6:1–4; 10:8–11; and 11:1–9 play in the plot. The resulting discussion will demonstrate that the plot of J and the plot of Genesis 1–11 present a polemic against city building and technology, the signature elements of empire, but not in the same way. The J source understands city building as an activity in opposition to YHWH, which YHWH seeks to prevent at all costs. The final form of Genesis 1–11 is more determined to put distance between an urban, technological way of life and the genealogical line leading to the great ancestors of the Israelites.

THE COMPOSITION OF GENESIS 1–11

There is not adequate space here for a full review of the history of scholarship on the composition of the book of Genesis, much less the entire Pentateuch. Such a review can be found in many places.[17] The Documentary Hypothesis that became the centerpiece of scholarship on the Pentateuch for about a century had been declared dead in some quarters, and at least relegated to the periphery in others, but these were both overstatements to differing degrees.[18] The rejuvenation of the Documentary Hypothesis now taking place within the study of the Pentateuch, sometimes labeled "neo-documentarian," is not only compatible with the approach to reading Genesis 1–11 in this study but may also offer essential resources to assist it.[19] The strongest adherents of the revival of this idea have moved back to a place prior to what now appears to be some of its wrong turns and dead ends, insisting that the Documentary Hypothesis is a literary response to a literary problem, the frequent narrative incoherence of the final form of the Pentateuch. The simplest literary solution to this problem is that four originally independent sources were combined by a single redactor in order to form the Pentateuch in essentially the form we now have.

The Primeval Story is a place where the combination of sources seems to have operated in a fairly simple manner, because, of the four classical sources, J, E, P, and D, only two are present.[20] The primary point of disagreement would be whether to label almost all of the material as P and J, or to use the labels P and non-P, leaving open the possibility that redactors added significant portions of the material, either from their own hands or from other, independent traditions.[21] Despite the differences between these two approaches, they are both responding to the same narrative difficulties. In the words of Joel Baden, "I have argued here for placing the historical claims of the narrative at the forefront of the analysis. . . ." Baden goes on to explain that "The mark of an author is his creation of and adherence to a distinctive and definable set of historical claims: who did what, when, where, and how. Where these claims are contradictory, we must consider that a different author is at work."[22] I would agree with this analysis, except for the use of the words "history" and "historical." The writers of texts in Genesis 1–11 were telling stories, and their process and intent are so far from what our modern word "history" describes that it is confusing to insert that term. What Baden has identified, setting, characters, events, and plot, are the standard elements of a narrative of any kind, and they help to construct a narrative world. The narrative world of Genesis 1–11 is the result of a combination of J and P, and it is best understood both by examining the final form of Genesis 1–11 and the materials that were used to construct it. Jan Gertz has responded to the same kind of narrative discontinuities in the final form of the text of Genesis 1–11, and would agree on most of the identifications of P material, but has argued for greater heterogeneity among the non-P texts.[23] This claim helps to highlight the disagreement between the two groups sometimes labeled "documentarians" and "supplementarians." The argument tends to operate with the assumption that for one group to be right the other one must be wrong. On the contrary, the supplementary process could describe the production of the sources, which the redactor of Genesis brought so fully and completely into the book that their internal workings, including their composition process, are still largely visible. Using the label "Yahwist" does not mean that the source was produced by a single author at one time. It had its own composition history as well. A generally accepted view of the source division of Genesis 1–11 looks like this:

P	J
1:1–2:4a	2:4b–4:26
5:1–32	6:1–8
6:9–22	7:1–5
7:6–10	7:11–17
7:18–21	7:22–23
7:24–8:5	8:6–12
8:13–19	8:20–22
9:1–17	9:18–27
9:28–10:7	10:8–19, 21
10:20, 22–23	10:24–30
10:31–32	11:1–9
11:10–27	11:28–30

My reading of Genesis 1–11 can function with either of these ways of understanding its composition or a combination of the two. The one major question that neither of them can address adequately is the presence of two powerful points of connection between Genesis 1 and 11:1–9, the first and last narratives in the present form of the book, and texts which appear to have come from two different sources. One of the connections is the use of first-person plural language in divine speech at 1:26 and 11:7, a feature shared with those two texts only by 3:23. The connection of the Babel story to both of the creation narratives, through the use of the rare divine first-person plural, arises at several points in the discussion below. The other point of contact is the scattering of the humans across the earth in 11:8, which looks like the involuntary fulfillment of the divine command to fill the earth in 1:28. There are equally strong connections between the Babel story in 11:1–9 and the Adam and Eve story in Genesis 2–3, so it looks as if the final narrative of the Primeval Story reflects both creation narratives at its beginning. These features are treated at greater length in subsequent chapters of this book.

ODD TEXTS IN GENESIS 1–11

The discussion of the nature of Genesis 1–11 above has already begun to highlight some of the stranger texts within it. Some of these need more extensive introduction here before they are taken up within the more sequential discussion of Genesis 1–11 that follows, because they have a significant effect on the shape of the whole chapter. Some might argue that all of the texts in this part of the Bible are odd, but some are easily stranger than others, particularly in the way they fail to fit the plot or even disrupt it. The first odd text is Genesis 4:17–24, which is primarily a genealogy of Cain but contains other strange elements as well. Initially the presence of this text raises two questions: First, why would there be a genealogy of Cain in Genesis at all? Since God banished Cain, and his descendants will be wiped out by the flood, why does Cain's family get any attention in a text that has the ultimate goal of introducing the origins of the people of Israel? The second, compound question is, Why does Cain's genealogy sit beside a larger and necessary one, the genealogy of Adam through Seth that leads to Noah, and why do the two of them have so much in common? Theodore Mullen has insisted that "any theory that attempts to explain the composition of the primeval history must be able to account for the existence of two varying, and somewhat internally contradictory genealogies in such clear literary proximity to each other."[24] The juxtaposition of the two genealogies may serve as an effective place to test the idea that the creation of a particular kind of narrative world was a significant factor in the composition of Genesis 1–11. Mullen and others have observed many similarities in form and content between Genesis 4:17–24 and 5:1–31, but beyond the mere presence of Cain's genealogy and its parallels with the genealogy that follows it, there are elements within 4:17–24 that are strange, surprising, and beautiful. The members of Cain's genealogical line are the most creative and innovative people in the Bible, the inventors of urban dwelling, music, animal husbandry, and metalworking. Why are such accomplishments associated with a cursed line of human beings?

A second unexpected text in Genesis is the strange story of the "sons of God" in 6:1–4. Interpretation of this text has often been preoccupied with where it came from and whether it was a fragment of some larger tradition, particularly in relation to 1 Enoch 1–36, rather than asking what such a text does for Genesis 1–11. When interpreters have asked the latter question, a common type of answer has been that 6:1–4 contributes to the portrait of sin and rebellion that makes the flood necessary, and this would appear to have been the assumption of whoever developed the chapter and verse numbers in the book of Genesis, but the story of the "sons of God" would seem to mitigate the blame heaped on humans in 6:5–13, an observation that demands a better explanation for the presence of 6:1–4. One element the text adds to Genesis 1–11 is a sense of connection between heaven and earth, a distinctive feature of this narrative world that differentiates it from the world of the readers of Genesis, ancient or modern. The connection between heaven and earth is not completely cut off at the end of Genesis 1–11, because there is still a way for God and two angels to get to earth to meet with Abraham and Sarah in Genesis 18. By the time Jacob gets to Bethel in Genesis 28, the connection will only be present in his dream, but perhaps the divine character did make it to earth one more time to wrestle with Jacob in Genesis 32.[25] Genesis 6:1–4 is part of the discussion below, where the description of the Nephilim, who are the hybrid divine-human creatures produced by the illicit unions in the story, as "men of a name" in 6:4 connects the passage to others in Genesis 1–11.

A third odd passage is in the midst of the genealogy in Genesis 10, which is often called the "Table of Nations"; but such a label provides a false sense of regularity and organization to this diverse collection of materials. Genesis 10:8–11 describes a character named Nimrod, who is a descendant of the accursed Ham, yet the text glorifies him as both "A mighty hunter before YHWH" and a great city builder. Upon initial inspection, 10:8–11 possesses some significant difficulties. The narrative form of the text interrupts the genealogy of Ham, and the cities Nimrod builds, such as Nineveh and Accad, are associated with ancient Mesopotamia; but the ancestors surrounding him in the genealogy, such as Cush, Egypt, and Put, are associated with Africa. The conflict between the internal, Mesopotamian geography of 10:8–11 and the African geography of its immediate context in the Hamitic genealogy is a problem interpreters have long recognized. The history of the discussion has been well summarized by Yigal Levine, but Levine's resolution depends upon the identification of Nimrod with Sargon, the ancient King of Kish, and the biblical writers' confusion of Mesopotamian Kish with African Cush.[26] Such an explanation is possible, but any interpretation that depends on the ignorance of the biblical writers is always dissatisfying and should be the course of last resort. Modupẹ Oduyọye has offered a different possibility by linking the Nimrod legend in Genesis with similar legendary material from northern and western Africa. The result is a powerful mythological figure who can transcend the boundaries of geography.[27] Nimrod straddles the entire world known to the ancient Israelites, and his placement in Ham's genealogy puts distance between all that he represents and the Shem genealogy that will produce the ancestors of Israel. One aspect of the text that may have been missed in previous discussions is its sense of movement. Does Nimrod abandon his "mighty hunter" status, an identity endorsed by YHWH, for his city-builder role, one about which Genesis 1–11 is suspicious at best?

The final odd text that demands some explanation is the well-known "Tower of Babel" story in Genesis 11:1–9. For the most part, I will avoid this common designation because it incorrectly identifies the tower as the central element of the story and obscures two of its more important features. First, these people are not just building a tower, but an entire city, a city linked by its name and its location, the land of Shinar, to the city-building activity of Nimrod. Second, while later tradition would assign a motive to these people—that they were trying to make their way into heaven—their motive in 11:4 is to "make a name" for themselves, a status that links them to the "men of a name" in Genesis 6:1–4 and Cain's son Enoch for whom the first city was named. The Babel story does not fit naturally into the plot of Genesis 1–11.[28] If 11:1–9 is assigned to the J source, which is the most common identification, then all of these odd texts would appear to come from that source, so it is possible that whatever meaning they initially conveyed together already existed in the earlier document. If this is the case, then the writer(s) of Genesis, in the process of combining the J and P sources, left the force of that meaning unchanged, diminished it, or magnified it. Determining which of these three options best describes the process that happened awaits the conclusion of this chapter.

The texts reviewed here are misfits in Genesis 1–11, and whether that was caused by the nature of their source or the patterns of their use in the composition of the book of Genesis, their presence requires thorough investigation. If we were to apply the narrative theory of Seymour Chatman, which identifies narrative events as kernels and satellites within a plot, depending on whether they are essential or nonessential to the structure of that plot, only the Babel story would seem to have any chance of qualifying as a kernel.[29] In ways these texts even seem to disrupt or confuse the plot. Genesis 11:1–9 allows for a restarting of the Shem genealogy, but the problem there could have been resolved by omitting one of the two. These claims might be untrue, however, if the narrative purpose of the author is something more than merely connecting Abram and Sarai back to the creation of the world. All of these texts will receive more detailed treatment below, especially in relation to their immediate surroundings. For now it is important to observe that they form an arc within this literature that is concerned with city building and technology, a way of life that threatens to extinguish other ways as surely as Cain killed Abel. But why is this first portion of the Hebrew Scriptures so opposed to a particular way of life? The Israelites may have understood their ancestors, like Abraham and Jacob, to be pastoral nomads, but they eventually became urban themselves and tradition claims their heroic king David built their great city, Jerusalem. The tense relationship between Israelite tradition and urban life erupts in the opening chapters of the Torah and it will remain tense to the very end of the Tanakh, and in the broader literary world of which these texts were a part. The examination of Genesis 1–11 is more careful and thorough than the treatment of any other part of the biblical text in this book because a response to city building and urban life is the Primeval Story's central theme, and Genesis 1–11 establishes a foundation for understanding the views of urban life in all the literature of ancient Israel.

GENESIS 1 AS INTRODUCTION TO THE PRIMEVAL STORY AND THE HUMAN PLACE IN THE WORLD

The first chapter of Genesis was almost certainly written by a different author than Genesis 2–4, but it is much more difficult to determine whether someone consciously wrote the first chapter to open the book of Genesis. Source criticism has reliably linked Genesis 1 to the P source, which provided about half the material for the Primeval Story. The primary dispute is whether P wrote with an awareness of the other major source, J. If P was the redactor, who combined his own material with the J material that already existed, then Genesis 1 is a conscious introduction to all of Genesis 1–11. Such a view has difficulties, however, like the confusing combination of the J and P flood stories into a single story in Genesis 6–8. On the other hand, if P and J originally existed as independent sources that a third person we can call the redactor of Genesis 1–11 combined, then connections between Genesis 1 and subsequent J material require more difficult explanations. The presence of a flood story in each of the sources, however, demonstrates that they could have arisen independently of one another and still shared some common elements and ideas. Even if J and P were independent, they still came out of the same general region and out of cultures that shared common experiences. They were written in the same language, even if in two slightly different regional or chronological forms. So, similarities or points of connection do not prove literary dependence.

The discussion of Genesis 1 here requires awareness of its form and patterns, so translation and format are intertwined and essential to observing its meaning. This is a particular case of such significance that discussion of differences from standard translations will not suffice, and a full presentation of my own translation is necessary. I have constructed the translation of Genesis 1 in the common format of poetry. While the broad, modern categories of prose and poetry do not always fit ancient texts with precision, Genesis 1 is closer to poetry than to prose. One of the central aspects of Genesis 1, of which this study will make use, is its regular, rhythmic nature, an aspect more visible when the text appears in the form of a poem.[30] The full translation is in appendix 1.

Regardless of whether the original writer intended the text we now call Genesis 1 to be poetry or prose, or whether writers at the time even thought of those categories in a way similar to us, the rhythmic quality of the text is unmistakable. This is not just a question of form but also of content and meaning. The world God creates in Genesis 1 is rhythmic and orderly, with everything in its place. One primary point of the narrative is that human life should reflect this rhythm, and what keeps the rhythm intact is keeping the seventh day as the Sabbath. The movement and rhythm of the story builds through the first half of the sixth day, which establishes the order and context for human civilization. The growing intensity is visible in the increasing length and complexity of the corresponding stanzas. The poetic translation demonstrates that the seventh day is different, but still has its own rhythm. Goodness builds in intensity as well, until the full work at the end of the sixth day is "very good."

Traditions about creation are much more diverse in the Tanakh than many readers are aware. Mark Smith has categorized this diversity and produced a compelling argument that the writer of Genesis 1 was aware of the diversity and sought to synthesize the various theological approaches to creation. Smith identifies creation texts based on three different emphases: (1) divine power, (2) divine wisdom, and (3) and divine presence.[31] The first of these models is entangled with the idea of divine conflict, which was a common element in ancient Near Eastern creation traditions outside of Israel, and is still visible in a text like Psalm 74. The conflict is necessarily absent from Genesis 1 because of its extreme monotheism. Even the great monsters of the chaotic deep in a text like Psalm 74 become unnamed products of the fifth day in Genesis 1, so divine power is not as overt in Genesis 1.[32] Nevertheless, the rhythm of the text demonstrates the power and precision of the divine ability to impose order. The second model places emphasis on divine skill in creating the world, and this feature also emerges in Genesis 1. There are many points of contact between Genesis 1 and Psalm 104, which is perhaps the ultimate expression of creation as an act of divine wisdom and skill. The key difference between the two texts is that the command to subdue creation, which humans receive from God in Genesis 1, is absent from Psalm 104.[33] The elevation of humanity above the rest of creation as its ruler is more closely connected to the third model of divine presence, which Smith finds most clearly expressed in Psalm 8. The identification of humans as the divine image or representation in Genesis 1 would seem to require human rule over the creation, if God is portrayed as the ultimate ruler, whose name is "majestic in all the earth" as in Psalm 8.[34] The creation of humanity as a mediator mutes, but does not eliminate, the significance of divine presence. The three aspects of creation do not appear in Genesis 1 in equal measure, as divine skill seems to be the prevailing theme, but they are all there. If Genesis 1 combines elements of all of three creation models in a context of transcendent monotheism, then the move toward human beings as the pinnacle of the works of creation, second only to the climactic establishment of the Sabbath itself, seems inevitable, and the sixth day of the creation sequence requires more careful scrutiny.

The development of the text toward the sixth day can be observed in simple terms of quantity by counting the lines in the poetic translation. The portion of the text addressing human civilization is in verses 26–31, but at least two factors deflect attention from the definition the text provides for human civilization. The first is the justifiable theological preoccupation with the meaning of the divine image, a concern that will be only secondary in the discussion here. A second barrier to seeing a description of human civilization is the unjustifiable blending of this text with Genesis 2:4b–25, including the common assumption that God only creates two people in 1:27. Careful attention to the rhythmic development of the world in all of Genesis 1, as well as to the grammar of this specific part, should protect readers from such an assumption. The world that grows in complexity throughout the expanding story requires a multiplicity of humans to match the multiplicity of everything else.

The opening words of 1:26 are the second of three repetitions of "God said . . ." in the account of the sixth day and the eighth of nine in the six-day account. The sixth day is not the first occasion of more than one divine speech introduced in this manner on the same day, as day three has already included two divine speeches to introduce both the dry ground (v. 9) and the plants that grow upon it (v. 11).[35] The second divine speech on day six considers the addition of human beings (v. 26) to the other land animals (vv. 24–25). The statement does not yet create the human beings, but proposes the idea among those to whom God refers as "us." This is one of just three examples of first-person plural divine language in Genesis 1–11, along with the statement at the end of the Eden account in 3:22 and the one in the Babel story at 11:7. A later section of this chapter examines the third of these texts and its relation to Genesis 1 more extensively, but it is important to recognize from the beginning that the two texts share some important features and form a narrative bracket around Genesis 1–11, which allows Genesis to proceed toward Abraham with the genealogy that begins at 11:10. On the other hand, the divine statement in 3:22 creates significant tension with 1:27. In 3:22, YHWH Elohim says, "Look, the humans have become like one of us, knowing good and evil, and now they might reach out their hand and take also from the tree of life and eat and live perpetually" (translations of Genesis 1–11 throughout this chapter are my own). The portraits of the human characters do not match. In Genesis 2–3 the humans are not "like God" until they eat from the tree; and once they attain that likeness, it is not good, but a threat to God, a very different view of humanity from the one in 1:26–31.

In 1:27, when God creates the humans, the narrator switches back to the singular "his image," and this switch is part of what has focused the understanding of the divine image on some kind of quality contained within individual human beings. The initial reference, however, is the plural construction, "our image," which points to an aspect of communal organization in the divine image. After centuries of various proposals concerning the meaning of the divine plural, contemporary scholarship has reached a near consensus that it refers to the heavenly court that appears explicitly in other places in the Tanakh, such as Genesis 6:1–4, Job 1–2, and Psalm 82:1, and throughout other ancient Israelite literature. This creates the possibility that the divine image includes the association of multiple individuals with the assignment of roles and tasks, indicating that the seeds of civilization lie within the creation of human beings, according to the perspective of Genesis 1. Living and working together are part of the divine likeness and the divine intent for humanity. Before God creates the human beings in 1:27, the divine speech in verse 26b begins to speak of their purpose, and it is a collective one. The plural verb form that opens verse 26b is difficult to interpret. Modern discussions sometimes become entangled in arguments attempting to relate this text to the contemporary environmental crisis. As important as this issue is, it should not distract from recognizing this role for humans is plural and gives birth to the idea of human civilization in the Tanakh. The verb is plural in form even before the sexual differentiation of humans as "male and female" in the next verse, meaning that God is proposing the creation of many human beings to go with the many plants and animals of various kinds already made. Whatever the verb means, the role is established before the humans are created, and the need for human beings within creation is to rule over it. The root of the verb appears a few more than two dozen times in the Tanakh with some variation in meaning, but by far the most common sense is to rule over or control something. The action is often harsh in nature, such as in Leviticus 26:17, Numbers 24:19, and Isaiah 14:6, and typically takes human beings as a direct object, with royal figures often acting as the subject.[36] The most apparent meaning is that human beings are to rule over the rest of creation as they would slaves, servants, or subjects, to their own benefit. This does not mean human beings bear no responsibility for the healthy maintenance of the rest of creation, just as kings do for their realms, but the imposition of a modern understanding of environmental care is foreign to the language of the text. The development of human civilization will require the exploitation of resources provided by the earth. The coming conflict with Genesis 3:22 grows more intense here. Whatever the "knowledge of good and evil" in Genesis 2–3 means, it seems impossible that humans could rule over the entire creation without it; yet the humans in Genesis 1 receive it, including the God-likeness it produces, at the point of their creation, and God evaluates the situation as "very good." There is tension between P and J concerning whether human knowledge is necessary and good or something improperly acquired and dangerous.

God creates human beings in Genesis 1, without any specification of number other than plurality, and gives humans charge of the created order, specifically dominion over animals. Aside from this, no other human activity is mentioned except for eating, but the command concerning eating creates a number of problems. Genesis 1:29 says, "And God said, 'Look, I give to you all plants bearing seed, which are upon the face of the earth, and all the trees which the fruit of the tree is on them bearing seed. They shall be food for you.'" Why does the divine speech about human diet only refer to plants here, presuming a diet that would have been very difficult for pastoral nomads? There are perhaps four reasonable explanations for this. First, if Genesis 1 is a Priestly text, then eating animals is a complex issue that it could hardly address without getting entangled in dietary laws, which would be out of place both in terms of the narrative logic of the Pentateuch and the literary form of Genesis 1. This proposal is consistent with the common understanding of the two sources of the flood story, where P's version avoids the subject of clean and unclean animals with which the J version of the flood story becomes involved. A second way of understanding why the writers of Genesis 1 would have inserted such a challenging dietary command is that they were aware of the story in Genesis 2–3 and did not wish to create tension with the divine command concerning human diet in 2:15–16, which would seem to be restricted to plant life. The idea that the human diet is restricted this way in the entire J narrative seems unlikely, however, given the use of animal skins for clothing in 3:21, the herding of livestock by Abel in 4:2, and the use of animals as offerings in 4:4. The second explanation is closely connected to a third one, which uses the covenant with Noah in Genesis 9:1–7 as a bracket along with 1:28–30 to postulate a period of vegetarianism in Genesis's portrayal of human existence.[37] There are good reasons to connect these two texts when they are viewed in isolation from their surroundings, the most significant of which is the repeated command to "Be fruitful and multiply and fill the earth" that accompanies both divine statements. In 1:28–30, God only gives plants for food, and in 9:1–7, God adds animals to the human diet, with what sounds like a clear reference back to the earlier command of 1:29 in 9:3. There are problems created by an application of this idea that is too strict or literal. The command about eating plants in Genesis 1 is also given to all of the other animals in creation, and there is no mention of what other animals are to eat in Genesis 9. The idea of God commanding nonhuman animals concerning what they can eat is odd, and becomes even more odd with the observation that some animals are purely carnivorous by nature. The idea of a vegetarian period in the history of humans and all other animals outside of the world of the text is untenable. Inside the world of the text there are the same problems mentioned above: that humans are herding animals and using animal skins for clothing, which makes the assumption that humans are not eating meat between these two texts difficult to apply to the whole of Genesis 1–11, though it makes more sense in a pure P Primeval Story.

The best solution to this question is a careful modification of the third solution. The narrative logic of Genesis 1–11 faces an enormous problem created by its longest narrative, the flood story that is at its center. For one of the sources used in the Genesis flood narrative, the P source, the story simply will not work if animals are eating other animals, so Genesis 1–11 contains a depiction of a narrative world in which a diet of only plants is possible for human beings. One of the well-known conflicts within the flood story is the one concerning the number of animals. In 6:19–22 (P), Elohim commands Noah to take just two of each animal on the ark. The Priestly source made this idea work by using the framework created by the placement of 1:28–30 and 9:1–7 and making the eating of other animals a postdiluvian practice. On the other hand, in 7:1–3 (J) YHWH commands Noah to take seven pairs of the clean animals onto the ark. This is often explained as a way to provide animals for sacrificial rituals after the flood, and Noah does perform one such ritual in 8:20–21, but this would not require seven pairs of each clean animal. It seems more natural to assume that in the J flood story these clean animals provide food for the humans and the other carnivorous animals in the ark. Neither version of the flood story, nor the combination of them we now find in Genesis, shows us life inside the ark during the flood, but the assumption of the J narratives seems to be that humans and other animals eat meat on the ark.

As this study moves through the world of Genesis 1–11, observing carefully those texts that are relevant to the conflict between settled, city-building life and pastoral nomadism, it will become apparent that the conflict is not a concern for the Priestly source. Therefore, the assumption in Genesis 1:28–30 of a human diet that would have required settled agriculture and a means of food distribution is not a problem for this source; and this conclusion brings us back to the command to be fruitful and multiply and fill the earth, which originates in 1:28 and must be repeated after the flood in 9:1. The command is the closest statement available to an overt description of human civilization in Genesis 1, so it is this statement, and its accompanying assumption about the human diet, that require interrogation in order to determine what portrait of civilization it assumes; but we must also place the statement into the full context of Genesis 1. As demonstrated above, the world Genesis 1 imagines is carefully ordered, and the principle that orders creation, the seven-day cycle ending in Sabbath, is transferred to the presumed human civilization that reflects the created order through the command that appears many times in later portions of the Torah for humans not to work on the Sabbath. Genesis 1 would have had no need to state this transferal to human work in more explicit terms, because its audience would have already known it. God does not explain the analogy, but it awaits communication in later P legal material. The apparent discomfort with this delay on the part of the writer of Jubilees, resulting in an expanded version of Sabbath law that includes the application to human work in its own in Jubilees 2:17–33, is an important issue in chapter 8. Throughout the Torah the kind of work that ceases in observance of Sabbath is agricultural work (e.g., Lev. 25:4). Genesis 1 presumes a human civilization developed around settled life and agriculture, and this kind of civilization, carried out to fulfill God's command to "rule over," is declared by God to be good.

There is significant evidence that the description of the world in Genesis 1 is intimately related to the temple in Jerusalem. Joseph Blenkinsopp uses the literary features called the "solemn-conclusion formula" and the "execution formula," both prominent in Genesis 1, to connect it to the building of the tabernacle in Exodus 25–40 and the development of tribal boundaries in the land allotment in Joshua 13–22.[38] If such a connection is present, then the assumption of settled, urban life is at the foundation of the world portrayed in Genesis 1, but it is not visible at the surface of the text. The command God gives to the humans to "fill" the earth in 1:28 need not be understood as a prohibition against settling and gathering in cities, and the connection between this command and the divine "spreading" or "dispersal" of the humans in 11:8 will need exploration at multiple points in this study. In the final form of Genesis 1–11, the divine dispersal in 11:8 may seem to be an act of judgment against a human race that refuses to obey the command in 1:28. Such a reading makes use of texts from two different sources, P and J, but it could have been this precise connection, observed by many later readers, that guided the redactor of Genesis to place the texts in this way. The dispersal would have created the necessary landscape for the entrance of Israel's ancestors, Abram and Sarai, to move into the narrative. This is one of many places in Genesis 1–11 where tension exists between the final form of the text and the source material, and it raises important questions about the freedom of the redactor to try to resolve such tensions. The presence of these points of tension seems to indicate the redactor was not free simply to eliminate difficult texts but was free to make lesser adjustments, such as changing the order of the stories in the sources, so that they could serve a different purpose in Genesis 1–11. This issue will await further observations about the portrayal of human civilization in Genesis 1–11.

Genesis 1:1–2:4a says very little, explicitly, about the nature of human civilization, and it would have seemed odd for it to do so when only describing the beginning of the world; but the reading above demonstrates that a portrait of human civilization can be inferred from what this text says. The priestly creation account presumes a human community that has spread throughout the earth and exercised control over it, using the land and using animals for work in an orderly and productive fashion that depends on settled agriculture and a system of distributing its produce effectively in order to support a world filled with humans. One of the challenges facing the reading of Genesis 1–11 described here is how to understand texts that oppose city building as part of the sacred literature of a group, the Israelites, who eventually became significantly settled and urban. This may help to explain why Genesis 1 says so little overtly about human civilization, but an explanation of the tension will await a later discussion in this chapter.

THE STORY OF HUMANITY BEFORE THE FLOOD

The initial problem most readers might have with the opening of the story of Adam and Eve in Genesis 2:4b is that it is both a beginning and not a beginning. Even if the persons who divided the chapters and verses had gotten it right, it would still be the second chapter of Genesis, and reading it would demand some way of understanding how it relates to the preceding material. Source criticism has solved one part of the problem of why two such starkly different creation stories exist in Genesis by assigning them to different origins. The question historical-critical methods do not handle as well is why the author of the book might have placed them side by side in such a way. The discussion of Genesis 1 has already cautioned against the easy assumptions that Genesis 2 is an expansion of day six and Adam and Eve correspond to the misreading of two humans, rather than two kinds of humans, created in 1:27.[39] Chapter 8 of this book contains an examination of the ancient work called Jubilees, but it is significant to note here that Jubilees mixes elements of Genesis 1 and Genesis 2 in its account of creation. The choice the redactor of Genesis made was not the only possible way to include both.

One productive solution is viewing the Genesis 2–3 narrative as fitting inside the grander scope of Genesis 1, within the narrative world developed by Genesis 1–11. The stories intersect at the end of Genesis 3, when Adam and Eve leave the garden and move into the larger world, complete with other people, created in Genesis 1. This solves problems recognized by interpreters for millennia, such as who Cain and Seth would have married and who Cain was afraid would kill him (4:16). It also raises interesting additional questions about what Adam and Eve carry with them into the larger world that they enter when leaving the garden. One benefit Genesis 2–3 brings to the larger story is the presence of named characters, in whom the reader already has significant investment. This resolves perhaps the greatest weakness Genesis 1 has as a creation narrative on its own: its lack of specific characters to follow.

The earlier presentation of Genesis 1 demonstrated that it is very much like a poem, and poems do not usually excel at character development. Genesis 2–3 also offers an explanation of how a world that the divine character evaluated as so completely good throughout Genesis 1 can have become so corrupted by 6:12, both texts commonly associated with the Priestly source. Adam and Eve carry the results of the curses pronounced upon the snake and the ground in 3:14–19, but they carry something else with them as well, the knowledge they gained from eating the special fruit. This realization requires a more careful look at what happened in the garden concerning the "tree of knowledge, good and evil."

There have been more ways of understanding the fruit from the tree of knowledge of good and evil than anyone can count. Some have understood "good and evil" to be a merism, two contrasting words serving to bracket everything in between, thus, simply a way of saying "all knowledge." If read in a more straightforward manner, however, the tree creates significant tension with the divine description of creation in Genesis 1 as entirely "good." Why does YHWH plant the possibility for something other than good in the garden? Because of the dominance of the "original sin" concept within the history of Christian interpretation of this passage, the possibility that the effect of eating from the tree will be a balance between benefit and cost has been underexplored. The text offers little straightforward information and much confusion. The tree of knowledge makes its first appearance in 2:9, along with another tree, the "tree of life." The narrator specifically describes the location of the tree of life, "in the midst of the garden" but does not locate the tree of knowledge. It has merely been an assumption of many readers that the two trees stand together in the center. The language of 2:9 is also ambiguous about whether the two named trees are like all of the others planted in 2:9, in terms of being "pleasing to look at and good for food." The reader must wait until 3:6 to discover, through the perception of Eve, that the fruit from the tree of knowledge possesses such qualities. The story in Genesis 2 diverts the reader's attention from the trees and their fruit immediately by explaining the mythical geography and geology of Eden in verses 10–14.[40] Attention to the tree returns at verse 16 with the divine command to the man about eating. The first statement provides the man with permission to eat "from every tree of the garden," and the prohibition against eating from the tree of knowledge, good and evil, may seem like a reconsideration of the initial command. The reason for this limitation is clearly expressed but raises its own questions. YHWH Elohim warns the man that "on the day you eat from it you will surely die." The most apparent questions are: What is the purpose of the tree and its fruit, if not to be eaten? And why does YHWH Elohim place in the garden a tree that will kill the humans and make it accessible to them?

In addition, the absence of a command not to eat from the tree of life leaves the reader wondering if the human does eat from that tree and whether it has an effect related to its name. Would fruit from the tree of life be an antidote for fruit from a tree causing death? If the name of the first tree and the divine warning about the second tree are put together, then YHWH Elohim has planted a tree of life and tree of death in the garden, and knowledge goes with death.

The text diverts the reader's attention from the tree again after 2:17, this time using the story of the creation of the animals, leading to the "building" of the woman to be a companion for the man. Readers have seen the tree twice and then been led to look away, but the tree's presence is impossible to forget. The woman's arrival in the story at verse 22, after the divine command and warning concerning the tree of knowledge, may cause readers to wonder if she is aware of the rule. If the woman is built from a part of the man, does she share the consciousness of things that have happened before the separation? Readers need not wait long for some kind of an answer to such questions, because the serpent interrogates the woman about the divine command in 3:2. The pattern of her answer reflects the pattern of the divine command very closely, as her opening statement in 3:2 matches God's speech in 2:16b. Once again, the limitation that follows qualifies the earlier statement, but the woman's speech in 3:3 diverges from the divine command in 2:17 in two ways. First, she identifies the forbidden tree differently, calling it "the tree that is in the middle of the garden," the location given to the tree of life in 2:9, so the tree to which she refers is unclear. Second, the woman extends the command against eating from the fruit of the tree to include not touching it. The snake's response in 3:4–5 seemingly clarifies the discussion by describing the result of the eating, first in the negative terms, "you will not die," and then in positive ones, "your eyes will be opened, and you will be like God, knowing good and evil." The snake is speaking of the tree of knowledge. The mysterious aspect of the snake's speech is the use of second-person plural language to address his audience. Even though 3:1b had informed us the snake was talking to the woman, the Hebrew verb forms and pronouns he uses to address her are all plural, which becomes most conspicuous in 3:5 when four such forms appear: "On the day you (pl.) eat from it your (pl.) eyes shall be opened, and you (pl.) shall become like gods, knowers (pl.) of good and evil." It is not until 3:6b that we learn the man has been with the woman all along, and this may explain the plural address, but it is also possible that the snake is telling Eve about the implications of her eating for the entire human race.

The discussion above already referred to the question about the qualities of the fruit from the two named trees and pointed ahead to the description in 3:6. It is the narrator who speaks here of the qualities of the fruit from Eve's perspective, and says three things about it. The first description, that it is "good for food," matches the general description of all the trees in the garden in 2:9, and the second description, "pleasing to the eyes," is very close to the previous one. These two alone are enough to raise questions not only about the purpose of a forbidden tree, but why its fruit would be edible and attractive. If the fruit of this tree is not for human consumption, then what is it for? The addition of the third description, that "the tree was desired to make skillful," creates even more difficulties. The word in 3:6 is a causative infinitive often translated as "to make wise," and this word is frequently associated with the more common root word for wise, but carries a somewhat different connotation, which may include insight, success, or skillfulness. This raises questions about what Eve and Adam received by eating the fruit. Inside the garden, the only noticeable effect is their awareness of their nakedness. In Genesis 3:5 the snake says eating the fruit will make them "like God(s)," and YHWH Elohim confirms this in 3:22. The divine appearance in 3:8 overwhelms curiosity about the nature of the fruit and its appearance, though, and ideas about divine punishment dominate interpretation of Genesis 3.

Five texts in Genesis 1–11 include divine punishment: (1) the casting of Adam and Eve out of the garden, (2) the banishment of Cain, (3) the limiting of life spans in the wake of the "sons of God" affair, (4) the flood, and (5) the dispersal and confusion of languages at Babel. The punishment sequence is prominent enough that it has become part of a common way of reading Genesis 1–11 as a cycle of sin-punishment-redemption.[41] One of the many problems with construing the Primeval Story as a cycle of sin and punishment is that such interpretations rarely asked careful questions about what God is punishing, other than a general sense of human wickedness, or what the goal of such punishment was, other than upholding some sense of divine authority. Two ideas emerge most clearly from this collection of texts. First, God is punishing, and perhaps trying to prevent, human violence. Banishing Cain and the divine statement about flooding the earth in 6:11 point toward such an understanding of the cause of divine punishment, though it is not clear in either case how the punishment will prevent such behavior in the future, and it does not. Second, punishment is a response to the human tendency to settle, centralize, and "make a name" for themselves. These practices, which I label together as city building, appear in the stories of Cain, the Sons of God, Nimrod, and Babel. The opening of this chapter identified the four city-building/fame stories in Genesis 1–11 with the J source. Subsequent sections will address each of these texts in more detail. Eventually, reconstructing the J source and looking at how these texts would have related to each other in that form will become necessary, but that task awaits further development of the individual texts.

Before moving on it is important to note that the idea of work for humans is already present in the garden, but the nature of the work needs careful attention. Along with the placement of the man in the garden and the instructions about eating, the narrator says YHWH Elohim places the man in the garden "to serve it and keep it" in 2:15. It has become common to translate the first verb in this phrase as "till." The Hebrew root is the same one in the phrase at the end of 2:5, that "there was not a man to work the ground." The use of "till" in 2:5 goes back to the King James Version, and looks more appropriate with "the ground" as direct object, rather than the garden. The use of "till" in either case creates difficulties, though, because in modern English it implies plowing, an action unsuitable for a garden full of fruit trees. The root is flexible in its meaning, and often dependent on context. Without a context, the common translations are "work" or "serve." Genesis 2–3 never shows Adam or Eve working the ground, so Cain becomes the first visible "worker of the ground" in 4:2, where the language matches the statement of lack in 2:5. Thus Cain is the worker of the ground 2:5 looks for and does not find. Does this mean the garden story in 2:8–3:23 is a narrative detour between the absence of a man to work the ground and the production of one? Such a description does not mean the garden narrative is unnecessary, because it explains too many elements of the story around it. It explains why workers of the ground are born to human parents through a painful and difficult process and why the working of the ground is difficult and sometimes unsuccessful. More importantly, it explains how the first worker of the ground gained the knowledge and skill to do it. The acquisition of this knowledge is more significant in the J narrative, where Cain was the ancestor of all the human race, who passed on the knowledge of human civilization, a force with which YHWH would have to contend with growing severity. The final form of Genesis does not erase the idea that the knowledge necessary for developing human civilization passed from Adam and Eve to Cain, but mutes it by making Cain's genealogical line a dead end, deriving Noah from the line of Seth.

Once Genesis 4 connects punishment to civilization, the punishment of Adam and Eve in Genesis 3 looks different. The cursing of the snake and the ground in 3:14–19 has results that will affect Adam and Eve in their lives outside of the garden. Adam and Eve will have difficulty producing a large family, according to 3:16, an activity which would be unnecessary were they to remain in the garden, and 3:17–18 indicates they will have difficulty producing ample food for a large, settled family. Because the punishment concerns life outside the garden, it is necessary to ask to what extent the disobedience concerns life outside the garden. When YHWH Elohim banishes Adam and Eve from the garden, YHWH Elohim does not take away from them whatever they gained by eating the forbidden fruit. If the infraction is not merely the act of eating fruit but the results it produces—gaining knowledge and skill—then they will continue in the act of disobedience by continuing to possess and use this knowledge and skill.

The story in Genesis 2–3 may assume some kind of "backstory" about a great tree in a primal garden.[42] Such an image arises at other places in the Tanakh, perhaps most significantly in Ezekiel 31 where Egypt and Assyria are compared to a mythic tree that began its life in the garden of Eden.[43] It is impossible to claim with any certainty a pattern of literary dependence between these texts, and it is easy to assume that the story in Genesis 2–3 is older than the oracle in Ezekiel, but the dearth of references to Adam and Eve in the Tanakh has led many interpreters to assume many biblical writers were unaware of the Eden story until a relatively late date. This argument is bolstered by the sudden appearance of many references to Adam and Eve in literature of the Hellenistic period, including "deuterocanonical" literature like Sirach, Tobit, and 2 Esdras; pseudepigraphical works like Jubilees and 1 Enoch; and books of the Christian New Testament like Romans and 1 Corinthians. The lack of a clear sense of literary dependence points to the possibility of a common source, a story of a primordial garden that could have been part of the common reservoir of tradition taken up by the writers of Genesis 2–3 and Ezekiel 31.[44] The connection between Genesis 2–3 and a prophetic oracle of judgment pronounced against great empires raises some important questions. From where did the notion of empire as a violation of an Edenic ideal come? Is this a connection developed by the writer of Ezekiel 31, or could it have been present in the backstory that also lies behind Genesis 2–3? If so, then the J source may display an anti-city bias very early and may view the transgression of Adam and Eve as an act entangled with city and empire building.

Before looking more closely at Cain's city-building life, an examination of the more familiar first life of Cain in 4:1–16 is necessary. The story of the first murder breeds endless interpretation, as it should. There is not adequate space here to evaluate it thoroughly in every aspect, but some features of the story are vital to the argument of this chapter.[45] The meaning of Eve's mysterious claim in 4:1b is difficult to fathom, in part because of its indecipherable grammar. A literal rendering yields something like: "I have acquired/produced/made/ begotten a man with YHWH." That her statement seems celebratory, no matter how it is translated, should be no surprise, since she has overcome the barrier this deity whom she invokes erected for her childbearing task in 3:17. The Hebrew verb qnh (acquire) is used about eighty times in the Tanakh, and the majority of the occurrences have to do with acquisition, typically financial in nature. There are also a dozen or so uses where the acquisition is not financial and the object is a person or other entity brought into relation with the subject. Most of these occurrences are in the wisdom literature, where wisdom itself is among the things that can be acquired.[46] There are three texts in which a meaning along the lines of "create, form, or make" is commonly recognized (Deut. 32:6; Ps. 139:13; and Prov. 8:22), and God is the subject in each of these.[47] E. Lipiński rejects the idea of "create" as a meaning in these texts and argues for "beget," though the difference is not quite clear, and, more significantly, he included Genesis 4:1 as a fourth example of this kind of usage.[48] David Bokovoy argues, based on biblical and ancient Near Eastern uses, that *qnh* should be translated as "procreate" here and reflects an ancient sense that the deity is "an active creative agent in the mysterious process of human conception."[49] The obvious use of a play on words between this verb and Cain's name points away from attempts to be too strict or precise about its meaning. Eve's use of *qnh* with herself as the subject is a declaration of her own creative capacity and that of the human race, and this capacity resides in Cain. She makes no such declaration concerning the birth of Abel. Genesis 4 contains no specific reference to the passing on of the knowledge Adam and Eve gained at such a high price in the garden, but Eve's reaction to Cain as, at least in part, her own creation may alert readers to that possibility as the story continues.

Along with the difficult verb, Genesis 4:1b also contains an ambiguous and difficult use of the preposition that precedes the divine name, one that most often means "with." Some English translations interpret the prepositional phrase to mean "with the help of YHWH," and there is nothing internal to the sentence to prevent such a reading, but it contradicts the divine statement in 3:16 when God declares the intent to make childbirth more difficult. It is also possible that Eve is comparing her production of Cain with YHWH's creation of Adam. She, along with YHWH, is one who has created a man.[50] Such a reading would explain Eve's puzzling use of "man" rather than "child" or "son," each of which would be more fitting if she was speaking of the act of procreation or begetting. A celebratory declaration by Eve that she has done something like God had done would also be a fulfillment of the statement of the snake in 3:5 that eating the fruit would make her "like God." The interpretation of 4:1b remains difficult and uncertain, but, however one reads it, the statement of Eve marks Cain as unique.

The quick succession from the birth of the two sons to the description of their occupations leaves completely unanswered any questions about how they made their way into these occupations, or even how old the two are at the time the conflict between them arises or how long the conflict lasts.[51] The movement of the two brothers in such different directions in terms of ways of living makes little sense in any kind of literal reading, and the text does not indicate directly which of these ways their parents had followed, but the divine speech in 3:17–18 sounds like it is assigning them to an impoverished life of settled agriculture. Perhaps it is not surprising that one of their sons would choose animal herding instead, but if the dietary limitations in 1:29 are understood in rigid fashion in a reading of the final form of Genesis, then it is unclear what Abel the shepherd would have eaten.[52] Sedentary farming and pastoral nomadism most likely did not represent exclusive ways of life. Jeffrey Szuchman cautions against using such definitions because of their overlapping nature,[53] and Thomas Thompson demonstrates that there was not a straight-line development from nomadism to sedentary existence. Rather, in the second millennium there seems to have been a movement back and forth between predominance of the two, along with a hybrid model called "transhumance," which involved seasonal movement between sedentary locations. Pastoral nomadism, according to Thompson, was often a response to extreme conditions, especially drought, which made settled agriculture impossible.[54] At the time the earliest traditions in Genesis would have been in their formation process, many people did some of both, or alternated between them, depending on weather conditions. Nevertheless, as legendary archetypes Cain and Abel may represent exclusive use of one way of life. The persistent question is why Genesis 4 tells us about them. The absence of Cain and Abel from the remainder of the biblical tradition is stunning. It seems entirely possible that later biblical writers simply did not know what to make of them.[55]

There have been many attempts to explain the reason for Cain's supposed rejection by YHWH.[56] The inability to locate a satisfactory answer should lead us away from the simple notion of acceptance and rejection as a way of understanding the presentation of the differing fates of Cain and Abel. Claus Westermann's solution to this interpretive problem still makes the most sense and is based on his understanding of "look upon" in 4:4–5. The language of blessing is an indication that Abel enjoyed success and prosperity while Cain did not. The differences in success experienced by the brothers could be interpreted as a distinction caused, directly or indirectly, by divine favor.[57] YHWH's language to Cain in 4:7 indicates a possibility that Cain might gain approval in the future, but such a prospect is connected to some idea of sin that is not clearly defined. The sin crouching at the door may include the desire to murder Abel, but if the sin overcomes Cain, then it may also include his subsequent actions, including building a city.[58]

There is little wonder that Cain might fail to achieve success, because he finds himself in the occupation and way of life specifically made difficult by the divine curse of the ground in 3:17–19.[59] Nevertheless, the fact that Cain ended up in the occupation that seems designated for Adam, even if in such dire terms, is another subtle factor in the text, along with Eve's declaration in

4:1, that Cain inherits whatever his parents have become at this point in the story. The original purpose for which YHWH God made the humans in 3:15, "to till and keep" the garden, is still connected to their purpose in expulsion, "to till the ground (adamah)," and it is connected to the man's identity as adam.[60] The task of "keeping" the garden now falls to the flaming sword that YHWH places at its entrance in 3:24. Thus Cain is just a "tiller" of the soil (4:2) like his parents. How Abel could be a shepherd long before such an occupation was invented by a sixth-generation descendant of Cain's (4:20) is an enduring mystery of this part of Genesis.

The actual murder in Genesis 4 receives very little attention in the text. Intense and puzzling conversations between Cain and YHWH surround the brief report in 4:8.[61] This scant attention and the meaning of Abel's name, "vaporous" or "fleeting," make it seem that his murder is merely the occasion for all of the interaction between YHWH and Cain. If Abel receives an abundance of God's blessing, then Cain receives an abundance of God's attention. Cain proves more capable than his parents, who were intimidated into silence by the divine pronouncement of their punishment, when he negotiates the terms of his own, though 4:13–16 alone does not fully indicate the extent to which he has future plans.

Genesis 4:17–24 looks like an entirely unnecessary and unexpected text. YHWH has cursed and banished Cain, and in the material that follows, Adam and Eve have a third son, Seth, through whose genealogical line the book of Genesis traces the remainder of its story. Furthermore, the claim that the flood killed all humans except for Noah and his family would bring to an end the survival of Cain's lineage. It is possible for a reader to assume that one of the three wives of Noah's sons descended from Cain, but the text provides no information about this one way or the other, and Genesis defines family lines through the male members; so any sense of Cain's family line continuing after the flood is absent from the story. Moreover, the success of Cain in this genealogy contradicts his punishment in 4:11. City building is not the same activity as settled agriculture, but it certainly depends on it, since there is no way to feed the population of a city without the fertility of the ground surrounding it.[62] Nevertheless, Cain succeeds as a city builder, and perhaps we are to understand that this was the only way of life left open to him after his punishment; but if this is so, then city building is a way of life first associated with a person who is cursed from the ground because he commits the first murder. The connections between fratricide and city building are difficult to ignore. The most obvious parallel is the murder of Remus by Romulus, leading to the building of Rome. Does the murder release Cain from a rivalry, allowing him to move on successfully?[63] Daniel Lowery points out that the Cain genealogy links the murders of Abel and Lamech's unnamed victim and concluded that the context enhances the negative portrayal of Cain's family, but Lowery resists the possibility that there is a negative portrayal of civilization here. This resistance, like that of some other interpreters, comes primarily on logical grounds that the writers and audience of Genesis, who want to connect themselves to Abel and Seth, instead of Cain, would also have made use of the advancements of civilization. Objections like this may miss the point that texts and their audiences can participate in the portrayal of archetypal figures, while being fully aware that life outside of the text is more nuanced.

There are many points of connection between Cain's genealogy and the genealogy of Adam through Seth in 5:1–32,[64] including the similarity of many of the names (see table 2.1), the narrative expansion of the seventh member, and the segmentation of the genealogy at the final generation.[65]

Table 2.1
A Comparison of Two Genealogical Lines

4:1, 17–22 (J)	5:1–32 (P)
Adam (Eve)	Adam
Cain	Seth
Enoch	Enosh
Irad	Kenan
Mehujael	Mahalel
Methushael	Jared
Lamech	Enoch
Jabal, Jubal, Tubal-Cain, Naamah	Methuselah Lamech
	Noah
	Shem, Ham, Japheth

It is just as important, however, to observe the differences between the two genealogies. As Modupẹ Oduyọye has illustrated, one of the odd things that happens in the genealogy of Cain is the apparent incorporation of the genealogy of Abel, specifically with the inclusion of Yabal, the tent-dwelling herdsman, and Yubal, the musician.[66] The remnants of Abel's pastoral ways are still here but are ominously bracketed by the technologies of city building, represented by Cain and Enoch, and metalworking, represented by Tubal-Cain.[67] The genealogy in 4:17–26, which has typically been identified as J material by source critics, revives the sheepherder, who had been killed by the agriculturalist in 4:1–16. As noted above, it also creates difficulties by locating the origins of sheepherding many generations later than Abel. The primal conflict between the two ways of life has not been fully settled, but they are merged together.

The Adam/Seth genealogy in Genesis 5, commonly identified as P material, leaves out the names seemingly related to Abel, Yabal and Yubal, and the name related to Cain, Tubal-Cain, and rehabilitates Enoch and Lamech. Instead of being a synonym for the first city, Enoch represents the expanded seventh member of this genealogy and is an example of godliness, while Lamech is the father of Noah, who brings rest, rather than a vengeful killer. The Enoch within the Seth genealogy is the most famous of these figures for two reasons, the first of which is his apparent immortality. The end of his genealogical report in 5:24 states that "God took him." The first Enoch, the son of Cain, achieves a different kind of immortality when the first city is named for him in 4:17. The Enoch in Seth's genealogy is also famous as a model of repentance, because 5:22 implies that he had not "walked with God" before the birth of his son Methuselah, but did so afterward.[68] There is no hint in Genesis 5 about what Enoch needs to repent for, but could it be his connection to city building revealed in the prior genealogy? Together, these two genealogies are negotiating conflicts between archetypal modes of being, and the genealogy of Cain and the names listed within it keep taking the story back, in circular fashion, to the conflict between Cain and Abel in 4:1–16. If Noah, the great survivor of the deluge, has been taken from the genealogy of Cain and placed into the genealogy of Adam/Seth, the furious activity of cultural development which Cain embodies has been replaced by the quiet and comforting ways of YHWH worship, exemplified by Seth, Enoch, and Noah, son of the very different Lamech. If the standard source division is correct, J had no problem with Noah and all humanity after him being descended from Cain.

The stories of great conflicts between ways of life take place in an "other-world," a world that the stories also help to construct in Genesis 1–11. Edmund Leach has described the setting of the Cain and Abel story as an "Other Time which is fitted to an Other World inhabited by Other Creatures who are not altogether men."[69] The conflict, at least in an ideological sense, must be settled in some other world because, while the Israelites would seem to be at least suspicious of civilization and technology, they cannot survive without them. Paula McNutt has described this "ambivalence" about a character like Cain, who is a suitably ambivalent character himself. Cain is a "culture hero" at the same time that he is something of a villain.[70] Cain and Abel both accomplish important tasks in establishing ways of life, as the J genealogy in 4:17–26 reports, then they are effectively removed from the Israelite lineage by the murder story and the P genealogy in 5:1–31. The opposition between these two genealogies will not be fully resolved in the flood account. They work

together even while there is tension between them. Oduyoye recognized that
the ways of Abel reemerge in the sons of Eber (10:21–25), the "passers-by,"
who are in perpetual conflict with the settling, technological, city-building
sons of Cain.[71]

The discussion above of the presence of a person named Lamech in
both of the genealogies can now receive full attention. In the genealogy
of Cain, Lamech becomes the most important figure, because with him
the genealogy becomes segmented, and four of his offspring—three
sons and one daughter—receive names. In the "Book of the Toledoth of
Adam" (Gen. 5), Lamech is the father of Noah, and it is with Noah that
the genealogy becomes segmented by naming three sons in 5:31. Lamech
is also emphasized here as the only person who speaks in this genealogy,
doing so to name his son and explain the meaning of his name in 5:29. This
means that Lamech is a speaker at the end of each genealogy, and his violent
speech in 4:23–24 stands in contrast to a speech about peace and comfort in
5:29.[72] If the small speech of Lamech about Noah is a fragment of J material
inserted into the "Book of the Generations of Adam," where else could it
have been in J other than along with the speech of Lamech in 4:23–24? It is
easier to imagine 5:29 as an insertion from the redactor, as Friedman argues,
but the origins of the birth saying are impossible to determine with any
certainty.[73] If these are two versions of a genealogy with common origins,
then the P version operates as a rehabilitation of the character of Lamech to
make him the father of Noah. Noah, on the other hand, as he is presented
after the flood in 9:20, looks more like a settler and cultural innovator, more
like the son of the Lamech descended from Cain than the one descended
from Seth. Christoph Levin observes that the biblical story, particularly its
J components that resemble the Utnapishtim story in the *Epic of Gilgamesh*
in so many ways, fails to follow the older account by having Noah rescue
"the craftsmen" by taking them into the ark as Utnapishtim did.[74] The most
controversial conclusion of this line of argument would be that Noah was
initially, in J, a descendant of Cain. In the final form of Genesis Noah does
not need to rescue the craftsmen or cultural founders, because he is one of
them. The next section discusses in more detail the way he perpetuates the
founding of civilization through his own particular skill, wine making, and
becomes the great-grandfather of the greatest city builder, Nimrod, who
in earlier tradition was a descendant of the sons of God, who apparently
survived the flood. The claim that J understood Noah to be a descendant
of Cain looks more than plausible, since the book of Genesis contains no
surviving evidence of J's awareness of Seth. Likewise, it contains no surviving
evidence of P's awareness of Cain and Abel.[75]

NIMROD THE CITY BUILDER

The introduction to the flood story in Genesis 6 is vague about the nature of the problem that YHWH attempts to solve with the deluge. The J flood narrative describes "wickedness" and "evil" in 6:5, though the description of evil identifies only an internal "inclination" of humans, rather than any outward actions. The P version of the flood story claims the earth is "corrupt" and "filled with violence." The justifications for the flood are complicated by the proximity of the strange text in Genesis 6:1–4. Like the genealogy of Cain, the presence of the "sons of God" story looks like a diversion. The description of the demigod figures called the Nephilim does not easily fit the narrative logic of Genesis 1–11 because they should all die in the flood and become irrelevant.[76] The "Watchers" tradition appears in expanded form in other places and may indicate that the brief text in Genesis was part of a larger story; but it is also possible that the terse, cryptic account in Genesis inspired the larger accounts. If the latter is true, then only this small story matters for the reading of Genesis 1–11. If a larger tradition existed, the writer may have used the fragment to call to mind a larger story for readers who would have known it, but it seems unlikely that the writer would use such a small fragment to point toward a tradition as vast as the one presented in 1 Enoch, for example. If true, such a literary move would also raise the challenging possibility that additional parts of Genesis 1–11 are just small fragments pointing to larger traditions about which we may not even know. Would the writer of Genesis have made such a literary move just once? The discussion of 6:1–4 here makes no assumptions about a larger tradition behind it, because to do so would be too speculative.[77] The important questions concern the role this text plays in Genesis 1–11 and its connections to other texts in Genesis.

Those responsible for dividing the book of Genesis into chapters apparently believed the "sons of God" story was more closely related to the flood narrative than to the genealogy of Adam that precedes it. Genesis 6:1–4 may contribute to the general sense of wickedness that leads to the flood, but its inclusion might remove some of the blame from human beings. One element it adds to the narrative development of the whole book of Genesis is a claim that this episode is the reason why YHWH chooses to shorten human life spans, so the great ancestors of Israel do not live as long as the primeval human beings. English translations often obscure another important element of the text in 6:4. A clumsy, literal translation would look something like this:

> The Nephilim were on the earth in those days, and also afterward, when the Sons of God came unto the daughters of men and they bore children. These are the *Gibborrim* of old, the men of the name.

The common translation of the final phrase as something like "men of renown" does not demonstrate the connection between these characters and the naming of the first city for the son of Cain, Enoch, in 4:17, and the effort of the people of Babel to "make a name" for themselves in 11:4. The tendency to translate *gibborrim* as "mighty ones" or "heroes" misses the connection between these characters and Nimrod, who was the first *gibbor* according to 10:8. The link this word creates is the reason for beginning the present exploration of Nimrod with a discussion of Genesis 6:1–4. The *gibborim*, city building, and fame (making a name) form the connections among the four odd texts that are at the core of this chapter.[78] The progression to Nimrod, however, will need to wait until after a brief discussion of some issues in the flood narrative and the story of Noah's family that lie between 6:1–4 and 10:8–12.

When the flood ends, the narrative of Genesis begins to explain how the world became populated again by the family of Noah. In the final form of Genesis, the story of Noah and his sons in 9:18–28 is an important introduction to the genealogy that performs this task because it explains some of the arrangements of people and places. Before looking at the development of the whole book in this section, it may be instructive to imagine how the sources might have looked. Most attempts to delineate J and P in this part of Genesis approximate the following pattern:

J	P
8:20–22	9:1–17
9:18–27	9:28–10:7
10:8–19	10:20[79]
10:21	10:22–23
10:24–30	10:31–32
11:1–9	11:10–26[80]

The P narrative here, consisting mostly of genealogies, portrays the rapid growth and dispersal of human beings after the flood, under the categories of Noah's three sons. The J narrative would have presented a somewhat different picture of a human community that stayed together, so that Japheth could "live in the tents of Shem" (9:27) and they could both enslave Canaan's descendants. If the source division above is correct, then one difficulty for the writer of Genesis would have been the presence of two or three genealogies of Shem, one or two of which participated in the three-part division of the world and another that carried the story forward to Terah and Abram. The first genealogy in 10:21 and 24–30 (J) identifies Joktan as the significant son of Eber and stops, while the second in verses 22–23 (P?) follows Aram for one more generation, and the third (P) in 11:10–26 moves from Eber through Peleg to get to Terah. The J source would also have had less material between the story of Nimrod and the Babel story, raising the possibility that they might have been connected, an idea that the discussion below explores more. The final form of Genesis inserts the story of Nimrod into the genealogy of Ham in Genesis 10.

Genesis 10 is often called the "Table of Nations" because it introduces geography and ethnicity to the book of Genesis, even though the geography is still vague and difficult to follow at points. The final form organizes the genealogy under the sons of Noah in the Japheth-Ham-Shem order, with the accursed youngest son in the middle, possessing the longest section of the three. The Ham genealogy, and particularly the large presence of Nimrod within it, will be at the center of the discussion as it progresses, but the strange inclusion of Canaan in the Ham genealogy and the preference for Shem over his brothers require some explanation first. The entire book of Genesis demonstrates a consistent preference for younger brothers, from Abel and Seth to Jacob and Joseph. The book of Genesis never clearly in one place states the birth order of the sons of Noah, but the order can be pieced together from a variety of partial references. Genesis 5:32 presents the sons for the first time as "Shem, Ham, and Japheth," and it is most obvious to assume this is the birth order from oldest to youngest. The next two references to the three sons, 6:10 and 7:13, put the names in the same order, and the names do not appear again until the introduction of the drunkenness story in 9:18, which repeats the same order. Difficulty arises when 9:24 calls Ham Noah's "youngest son." The beginning of the Table of Nations in 10:1 repeats the Shem-Ham-Japheth order, but their genealogies that follow are in the opposite order. A desire to place Shem, the genealogical line that leads to Abram and the Israelites, last in order to set up the texts that follow may explain the reversal. The final piece is the statement in 10:21 that Shem is the older brother of Japheth, so in order of age they are Shem-Japheth-Ham. The presence of Ham's genealogy in Genesis is not a mystery in the same way that Cain's is. If one purpose of Genesis 10 is to provide an ethnography of the world after the flood that demonstrates the relationship between the Israelites and other people groups, then including Ham's line is necessary. Its relative size, compared to Japheth's and Shem's, is more difficult to understand. Closer examination reveals the genealogy of Ham is trying to do things the others are not, and the description of Nimrod in 10:6–8 is at the center of the effort. Inserting the Nimrod narrative, along with the descendants of Canaan, into the genealogy of Ham places ethnic distance between this people and the way of life they represent and the Israelite descendants of Shem.

The story of Noah's drunkenness helps to explain the unexpected favor for the oldest son, a choice that runs against the grain of the book of Genesis. The opening of the story presents at least one risk that has already been acknowledged. The description of Noah as the first planter of a vineyard and first winemaker makes it possible for readers to recognize him as a fitting child of the other Lamech, the one descended from Cain, who produced so many other children who were cultural innovators. The story also raises two very difficult questions for nearly everyone who reads it. What does Ham do that is so awful to deserve the curse that follows and why does the curse fall upon Ham's son, Canaan? The solution to both questions lies in a reading that receives surprising resistance from many interpreters. In other places in the Pentateuch, most notably Leviticus 18, "seeing the nakedness" is a euphemism for having sexual relations, particularly forbidden relations with a family member. The most telling verses are 18:7–8, which equates the nakedness of the father with sexual relations with the father's wife. Such a reading would explain what Ham did, not simply stumbling upon his unclothed father, but having sexual relations with his father's wife, possibly his own mother, and why the curse falls on Canaan, the product of this illicit union. The close parallel story of Lot and his daughters in Genesis 19, which also ends with the sons produced by incestuous unions named as eponymous ancestors of Israel's enemies, Moab and Ammon, further enhances the plausibility of such a reading. Noah may have escaped the curse of Cain by being transferred to the other Lamech in the line of Seth, but one of his sons and his descendants get pulled back in. The burden of the forbidden fruit, passed from Adam and Eve to Cain and picked up again by progeny of the Watchers, is now carried by Ham and his descendants, and the central focus of this genealogical line is Nimrod.

The description of Nimrod in Genesis 10:8–12 is confusing in many ways. Part of the tension results from the apparent combination of sources. The Table of Nations appears to be a P document in terms of framework, but 10:8–12 is one of several insertions from J.[81] Nimrod is a grandson of Ham and nephew of Canaan, but the ethnographic nature of Genesis 10 cautions against taking family relationships too literally. There has been some dispute about the meaning of his "Cushite" identity. Cush and some of the other names in the Ham genealogy are associated with Africa, but this is difficult to understand in relation to the credit the text gives to Nimrod for building cities in Mesopotamia. There are many elements of this text that become entangled with Genesis 2, and this is an important key to its interpretation. The four rivers of Eden are often identified with Mesopotamia, which is obviously correct for the Tigris and Euphrates, but the Gihon, which "surrounds all the land of Cush," seems to describe the Blue Nile. Some interpreters resist the African identification because it places Mesopotamian rivers with an African river, which is geographically impossible, but that may be exactly the point the text is trying to make about the garden of Eden.[82] It includes the farthest rivers in each direction about which ancient Israelites would have known, so it is geographically everywhere, which also means it is geographically nowhere. Eden is not a place that fits into the world of human habitation and to which humans might go. Likewise, Nimrod transcends boundaries and stands astride all of the known world, from west to east.

The order in which the text presents Nimrod's two identities may be significant too. He begins as a Cushite (African) *Gibbor*, a great hunter who enjoys the recognition and approval of YHWH, Israel's God, and he ends as a Mesopotamian city builder, the founder of great imperial cities like Babylon and Nineveh, which symbolize the oppressive powers that always threatened Israel. The previous section explored some of the evidence for competing ways of life in the ancient Near East and found the line between nomadism and settlement in the lives of ancient people was not always a clear one. Real people moved back and forth between the two ways of life. Unlike the archetypal figures of Cain and Abel, who each represent just one way of life, Nimrod can represent two, but the little story of his life in 10:8–12 portrays a movement toward settled, city life.[83] Some interpreters choose to associate Nimrod entirely with Mesopotamia, and only express puzzlement at his inclusion in the genealogy of Ham.[84] Others identify 10:8–12 as likely a fragment from a large epic about Nimrod.[85] It is curious that the other place where many interpreters make such a suggestion is at 6:1–4, the other text in Genesis 1–11 that involves *gibborim*. The discussion of 6:1–4 identified the problems created by assumptions that texts in Genesis 1–11 are small fragments of large traditions that early readers would have known. While this might be true, it is difficult to proceed to interpret the present text on that basis, because the nature of such an outside referent is too hypothetical. It is also too difficult to see why the writer of Genesis would have made such a move, given that the Nimrod text disrupts the text and raises difficulties. Whether Genesis 10:8–12 is part of some larger tradition, or a J text added to a P genealogy, or both, Nimrod cannot be a descendant of Ham through Cush.[86] His placement in Ham's genealogy connects the many examples of successful city building associated with him to the line of Ham, like city building and technological innovation are connected to Cain in 4:17.

Nimrod's building of Babel in the land of Shinar projects forward in the book of Genesis and connects him to the Babel story in 11:1–9. It is intriguing to think about how these two texts might have been related to one another in the J source. The material between them can all be assigned to P, and the absence of a king in the Babel story is a curious feature. If the writer of Genesis pulled the Nimrod tradition away from the Babel story in order to insert it into the genealogy of Ham from P, one of the results was to link the problematic practice of city building with the cursed branch of Noah's genealogy, the line of Ham. Such a move would reflect the redactor's pre-flood movement of Noah away from the city-building tendencies of Cain's genealogy. Both times the redactor separated the genealogical line leading to Israel from those who live settled, urban lives. The question such an observation raises is why the separation happens twice. The redactor of Genesis 1–11 separates Noah from Cain and city building only to have urbanization reappear on a much grander scale just two generations after the flood.

The combination of J and P into Genesis also raises questions about how a Shemite like Terah and his family would have found themselves in Ur of the Chaldeans. P places the family of Terah in Ur, while J begins the story of Abram in Haran. The long genealogy of Shem in 11:10–26 provides the time for significant displacement and movement of peoples. The source of this genealogy is a matter of dispute. It looks like a P genealogy in many ways, and it is in conflict with J's genealogy of Shem concerning which son of Eber it follows, Joktan (10:26) or Peleg (11:19), but it also conflicts with the brief genealogy of Shem in 10:22–23, which chooses Aram from the sons of Shem rather than Arpachshad (11:10). Friedman assigned 11:10–26 to the author/ redactor of Genesis or a distinct third source available to that person.[87] The redactor harmonized the traditions as much as possible and created time and space for the movement of this family to the Persian Gulf region. The links between 11:10–26 and 5:1–31 are too strong to ignore, and these combined genealogies connect Adam to Abram. A mediating position might be that the P source inherited more than one set of genealogies. If we are to understand the Shemites as part of the Babel group, Terah and Abram are now many generations removed from the tendencies toward power and fame. Further discussion of the genealogy of Shem, particularly as it relates to the Babel story, will have to await the next section.

The observations in this chapter move the argument along to the text in Genesis 1–11 with the most challenging placement: the Babel story in 11:1–9. The story has significant internal tensions, but its relation to material both before and after presents the most significant challenge. Previous sections have given attention to texts in Genesis 1–11 that portray city building and the seeking of fame. Cain first embodied these behaviors explicitly when he built the first city and named it for his son, Enoch. Cain's genealogy in Genesis 4 comes to a mysterious end, reporting no deaths and ending with the children of Lamech, whom it portrays as cultural founders.[88] The mysterious offspring of the "Sons of God" in 6:1–4 perpetuated the problem of fame by becoming "men of a name," and YHWH responded by placing limits on the life spans of humans. The text also calls these offspring *gibborim*, and they survive the flood in their reflection named Nimrod, who becomes famous for his hunting prowess and who also takes up the city-builder identity of Cain, multiplying this identity to massive proportions. As the earlier discussion noted, the author of Genesis may have separated the Nimrod text in 10:8–12 from close contact with the Babel story in 11:1–9 in order to place Nimrod in the genealogy of Ham. It is impossible to know precisely how the Nimrod story and Babel story were related to each other in the J source, but the texts had to have been closer together there than in the final form of Genesis. The lack of any named, identifiable characters in the Babel story makes Nimrod's absence conspicuous. The mention of Shinar and Babel in 10:8–12 and 11:1–9 invites readers to imagine Nimrod present in the latter text.

In the final form of Genesis, the Babel story sits in the midst of two or three different genealogies of Shem. The first one, in 10:21–31, connects Shem directly to Eber in the opening verse, and states for the first time unequivocally that Shem is the eldest son of Noah. The genealogy proceeds, naming multiple sons in each generation, eventually arriving at Eber, whom it identifies as the father of two sons, Peleg and Joktan. The brief list in 10:22–23, which selects Aram rather than Arpachshad from among Shem's sons, may be a separate genealogical fragment, an insertion from P into a larger J text.[89] Like the names in the earlier genealogies of Japheth and Ham, some are recognizable names of nations or groups of people, which would explain, at least in part, why none of these genealogies present death notices or lengths of life spans. The genealogy ends as it develops the family of Joktan and places them in "the hill country of the east." The genealogy of Ham ends in 10:20 with the statement "These are the children of Ham, for their families, for their languages, in their lands, in their nations." The prior genealogy of Japheth ends in similar fashion in 10:5, but the text appears to have been corrupted. The present text produces a translation something like, "From these the coastlands spread, the nations in their lands, each to its own language, to their families in their nations." Shem's genealogy ends in 10:31 with a statement identical to the one about Ham's family in 10:20. The summary statement in 10:32 refers to all the sons of Noah, again describing their families, nations, and languages, reporting that they "spread out on the earth after the flood." This statement fulfills the command of God in Genesis 1 that humans should fill the earth, and the sudden appearance of 11:1–9 is somewhat surprising, a sense that is heightened by the presence of another Shem genealogy beginning at 11:10. It is possible that the Babel story is a response to a question that 10:32 might generate, such as "How did all this spreading out happen?" or "Why did people start speaking so many different languages?" Such a function would highlight the etiological nature of 11:1–9, but should not overshadow its participation in the judgment against city building in the Primeval Narrative. Another way of looking at the role of 11:1–9 will be possible after a closer look at the internal features in the text below.

The Shem genealogy in 11:10–26, which has no parallels for Ham and Japheth, looks much more like earlier genealogies in Genesis, particularly the *Sefer Toledoth Adam* ("The Book of the Generations of Adam") in Genesis 5, in which each unit provides one name per generation, the age of that figure when the continuing son is born, and the age at death. Each unit ends with an acknowledgment that the person "had other sons and daughters," but these receive no names. Eber appears in the third generation after Shem, but only one son of his is named, Peleg. The Joktan character from the previous Shem genealogy, who seemed to be the son of interest in that generation, receives no mention. The genealogy of Shem in 11:10–26 looks like a natural continuation of the *Sefer Toledoth Adam* in 5:1–31, producing a full genealogy that moves from Adam to Abram. If this is the case, then there is a lot of diverse material interrupting the grand genealogy, including other genealogies, expanded stories of Noah's family, and the Babel story.

One question that is always difficult to answer about an ancient text like the Primeval Story is whether its original readers would have been bothered by a lack of realism in the same way modern readers are. Genesis 6:11 makes the charge that the earth is "filled with violence," which could not be true unless the earth is filled with people. Even if the "earth" that the ancients were aware of is quite small, stretching from North Africa to Western Asia, filling it with violence would take some time. Genesis 5 provides 1,556 years for this to happen, but would that kind of realism have mattered to its author and first audience? If it did, then we have a reason for the placement of this genealogy and the long life spans it reports. The persons gathered at Babel seem to have resolved the problem of violence by agreeing to put their energy into cooperative work on a common task, but this time YHWH is displeased or threatened by the result, and puts an end to their effort by scattering them and confusing their language. By the time Abram and Sarai reach the land of Canaan in Genesis 12, there is already an established kingdom of Egypt, with a pharaoh, which they know about as a more reliably fertile place. So, when the famine strikes in 12:10, they travel there for relief. This is a lot of progress since the days of eight people emerging from an ark in 8:18. The genealogy of Shem in 11:10–26 provides about four hundred years for this progress.[90] Again, one cannot be sure what kind of realism would have been expected by the earliest audience of Genesis, but the Babel story offers an extra boost of divine momentum to the spreading of the human race.

THE PEOPLE OF BABEL AND THEIR CITY

The story of building Babel is brief and dense, requiring some careful unpacking. As mentioned in earlier sections, Genesis 1–11 contains very little dialogue between human characters. If the reader is to see, however, that humans speaking understandably to each other is a problem, then the portrayal of some speech seems necessary. The beginning of the story provides the necessary dialogue, not in the form of one specific character talking to another, but in general speech among the group members. The people say two things, the first of which is in verse 3: "Come, let us make bricks and burn them fully." The humans' speech to each other is awkward, but successful. The narrator reports in the next verse that they have produced bricks that can be used like stones, and they know how to stick them together with tar or bitumen. Brick making is not a craft that has been described earlier in Genesis, so these people appear to be cultural innovators like the family of Cain. Their second comment to each other is lengthier and more complex in verse 4: "Come let us build for ourselves a city and a tower, and its top shall be in the sky, and let us make for ourselves a name, lest we disperse upon the surface of all the earth." The text is vague about the nature of the tower, and readers' attempts to interpret it more precisely are heavily dependent on similar texts in Mesopotamian literature. The text contains no hint, either in the planning of the people or in YHWH's reaction, that they are engaging in idolatry.[91] There is no specific mention of what they might build in the first conversation, though the materials and knowledge are present. Contrary to the popular assumption that the purpose of these people is to invade heaven, the text is clear that their purpose is fame. It is somewhat more difficult to say exactly what they fear. Many translations make the verb "dispersed" or "scattered" sound passive, but it is not. The J source uses the same verb in the *niphal* stem in 10:18 to describe the dispersal of the Canaanites, and that use may be passive, but the lack of an agent makes a reflexive meaning more reasonable: "they dispersed themselves." The verbs in 11:8 and 11:9, when YHWH enacts the dispersal, are both causative forms with the people of Babel as direct object.[92] In 11:4 the people are afraid not of something that might be done to them but of the choices they will have to make. Their hope is that the city will keep them together, allowing them to avoid a life of nomadism. The description by the narrator in verse 8 reverses this: "And YHWH scattered them from there, upon the face of all the earth, and they ceased to build the city." The building of the city, which the group hoped would keep them together, results in scattering. Their desire for fame, "making a name," is fulfilled by the fascination with the story that has persisted for thousands of years.

In the context of Genesis 1–11, the purpose of YHWH in preventing the building of the city is difficult to determine. Babel is only one of several cities Nimrod builds, according to 10:8–12. If Genesis 1–11 is a condemnation or judgment of city building, then why is it acceptable for Nimrod's other cities to be successful? Many interpreters have recognized that there are multiple motifs in the Babel story that do not naturally go together and are uneven in the text, so there is a possibility they have independent origins. There are also duplications, including the double divine descent, the two building projects, and the two results of the divine action—scattering of the people and confusion of language. The first result, scattering, reflects the initial concern of the people in 11:4, but the confusion of languages only appears at the end of the story. The latter looks more obviously etiological in nature and may be imposed upon an earlier story that is about scattering. The text mentions the tower twice, both times along with the city, and mentions the city alone once. In this combination of motifs, the city building looks more foundational to the story and the tower secondary. When these two conclusions are combined, the story looks to be more concerned with scattering city dwellers than with confusing languages or disposing of an idolatrous tower. If scattering urban people is the primary concern, then the next step is to ask what such an act has to do with the genealogical material related to Shem that surrounds it.

One common way of thinking about the Babel story has been to assume the writer of Genesis placed it among the genealogies of Shem in order to adjudicate between them; but what if the purpose of the writer was something close to the opposite? Could the genealogies of Shem be packed around the Babel story in order to explain or contain it? To begin exploring this question it is important to consider whether the descendants of Shem, or Shem himself, are among the people of Babel. There are some points of confusion and overlap between the J genealogy of Ham and the P genealogy of Shem, the most significant of which is the presence of Asshur (Assyria) in each of them (10:11 and 10:22). One way to try to resolve this problem is by working with the grammar of 10:11, which says: "From that land Asshur went out, and he built Nineveh and Rehobot-ir and Kalah." In this context, though, it seems likely that Asshur is a place name, the biblical name for Assyria, which contained the cities of Nineveh and Kalah, so placing a preposition on it, producing "He went out to Asshur and built . . . ," would make good sense. This reading would assume that Nimrod is still the subject, and could either assume that the Hebrew preposition was omitted from the text at some point or that it was simply assumed within the verb and should be supplied in English. The latter seems more likely, and similar uses are attested elsewhere.[93] This would still leave the oddity of a person in Shem's genealogy with "Asshur/Assyria" as a name, but at least there would not be a duplicate name. Another possibility is that Nimrod belongs in the genealogy of Shem, which would put the two occurrences of Asshur in the same section. The movement of Nimrod into the Ham genealogy would leave the family of Shem associated with just one city, Babel, a failed attempt. Nimrod is a dangerous figure because he builds successful cities, except for Babel. Despite the failure of Babel, however, Nimrod survives as city builder, just as he survives the flood as a *gibbor*. The genealogies of Shem surround and contained the failed city, explaining it as a renewal of a nonurban way of life, including nomadism.

Further evaluation of the relationship between Shem's lineage and the Babel story requires returning to the source division of the section. One likely way of dividing it is as follows:

J	P
10:21	10:22–23
10:24–30	10:31–32
11:1–9	11:10–26

If this source division is correct, then the redactor of Genesis had three conflicting genealogies of Shem, one from J and either two from P or one from P and one from the separate genealogical source beginning with the *Sefer Toledoth Adam*. In J the important son of Shem is Arpachshad, whose genealogy leads to Joktan and stops. In the initial P genealogy (10:22–23) the important son is Elam. In the longer third genealogy (11:10–26), which looks like a continuation of 5:1–31, Arpachshad is the important son, but his genealogy moves through Peleg, not Joktan, to get to Abram. The Babel story may function in the plot to account for some confusion and redistribution of people but leads to the question of who readers are supposed to see present at Babel, according to J and according to the redactor of Genesis. The group appears mysteriously in 11:2, in the form of plural pronouns and verbs with no explicit subjects, but there is no antecedent in 11:1 that fits the mysterious "they" in the following verse. In the final form of Genesis "they" could be the "families of Noah's sons" from 10:32. The answer for J, the source of the Babel story, is more complicated, because 10:31–32 is a P text. In J, "they" of 11:2 could be the family of Shem in 10:24–30, if we imagine J with its elements in the same order in which they appear in Genesis. If the order was different there may be multiple possibilities, but the most logical is the people of the civilization described in the Nimrod account in 10:8–12. These people are already located in Shinar, and Babel is among the cities Nimrod built. A previous section already developed this idea, but it will help to repeat here the possibility that the Nimrod account was the introduction to the Babel story in J. A separate question is whether Nimrod is related to Shem. This would be difficult to accept in the J source, however, which is at least as much opposed to city building as Genesis, probably more.

The impasse here requires a more radical solution. Source critics always divide the present text into earlier sources, but rarely do they overtly reassemble the earlier source as a document. The primary criterion demanding resolution by the Documentary Hypothesis, particularly in its contemporary manifestation, is the narrative incoherence of the Pentateuch's final form. A necessary corollary to this initial observation is that the reconstructed sources should exhibit narrative coherence. Does the J source achieve such coherence if the pieces from Genesis are extracted then placed in the same sequence, or does it work better if the story of Babel preceded the flood in J? Placing the Nimrod story and the Babel story immediately after 6:1–4 solves a multitude of problems. First, it makes 6:1–4 look less like an isolated fragment. Instead, it introduces the origin of Nimrod, the great *gibbor*. Second, in the final form of Genesis the dispersal of humans in 11:8 to fulfill the divine command to fill the earth in 1:28 uses a J text to fulfill a P purpose. The redactor of Genesis may well have done this, but it does not explain the scattering for the purposes of J. The divine statement in 6:5 implies a dispersed human population. In J the purpose of scattering, if the Babel story followed the "sons of God" story and the Nimrod narrative, would be to decrease the influence of the illegitimate progeny, like Nimrod, who lead the humans to build cities. Third, the actions of God in the reordered J source would follow a more coherent sequence. God curses the ground and expels Adam and Eve from the garden for eating the fruit, curses and banishes Cain for killing Abel, limits the life spans of humans because of their interaction with the sons of God, scatters the builders of Babel, then floods the earth because humans had filled it with evil. Fourth, the new order explains the threat of the tower and the dispersal only of Babel among the cities of Nimrod. Towers might allow humans to survive the coming flood. While this seems an unlikely scenario for a single tower, the ability to build towers might pose more of a threat. The confusion of languages would then make survival of the flood more difficult. When YHWH says, "Nothing that they propose to do will now be impossible for them," the statement now has something more specific in view, which is human ability to survive the flood. This last point is the most troubling because it would mean that the divine being already had at least the possibility of the flood in mind when scattering the people of Babel.

This study of Genesis 1–11 began with observations about four odd texts in this part of Genesis that do not fit easily in the text. All four of the texts speak of fame and city building. The attempt to understand those four texts moved to a conclusion I did not originally expect: that in the J source the four city-building texts were all close together in a sequence significantly different from their order and placement in the final form of Genesis. My own translation of a reconstructed J source, containing the narrative portions now in Genesis 4–11, is in appendix 2.

The reconstructed J text puts city building front and center. God's attempt to halt the progress of settled living and the technology that goes with it progresses sequentially until the flood becomes the final solution. Some additional effects of the sequence above merit further attention. The mysterious appearance of Naamah in 4:22 has been a mystery. She may be there for several reasons, but if the "Sons of God" story was more closely connected to the Cain genealogy in J, then the acknowledgment of a daughter for the first time in Genesis helps 6:2 and its reference to "daughters of humans" make more sense. The connection of the genealogy of Cain to the Sons of God and their half-human offspring would explain why the latter would accelerate the city-building work of Cain and his descendants. The Babel story can now function more clearly as an expansion of the story of the building of Babel by Nimrod. The scattering of the people in Babel resulted in the building of multiple cities. The placement of Babel before the flood then allows the divine attempts to control human impulses to progress, because the lesser measure, scattering and confusion, comes first.

Two large additional questions await resolution in the following discussion. First, with J rearranged as above, how might we go back and understand the events in the garden, where the J narrative of humanity began? If city building was the central issue in J and remained an important issue in Genesis 1–11 because of all that J contributed to it, is city building the primary issue in the Eden story? Second, with the Nimrod narrative and the Babel story moved back before the flood, what did the J story after the flood look like? Little would be left before the appearance of Abram other than the Shem genealogy. With that part of the J story reformulated in the way the writer of Genesis may have received it, what else might we conclude about why the writer made the choices that led to the book of Genesis we have?

The opposition to city building and technology in Genesis stands in stark contrast to Mesopotamian traditions. Daniel Lowery has identified three central aspects of the "Mesopotamian theology of the city." These are the claim that the tools for city building are divine gifts to humanity, that the earth was "empty and uninhabitable" before the divine gift of civilization, and that humans were "barbaric, purposeless, and lost" before the development of cities and urban life.[94] In every way, Genesis disagrees with this theology. City building and technology are skills that humans acquire illegitimately and use in opposition to God. The earth was empty and uninhabitable in the beginning, but it was God's creative work that cured this condition and the spreading of humans throughout the earth, rather than gathering in cities, that would maintain it. Through the archetypal figures of Cain and Nimrod, Genesis portrays cities as barbaric and murderous, and these traditions all come into Genesis from the J source. The first city is named for Enoch, so his name is perpetuated beyond his own life. He is the first person for whom a name is made, an achievement to which the discussion will need to return as it recurs in places like 6:4 and 11:4.

Two individuals are cursed in Genesis 1–11, Cain (4:11) and Canaan (9:25). The parents of both of these individuals have a problematic interaction with fruit, and both are also entangled with settled farming. There is no apparent connection between the etymology of these two names, which look less alike in Hebrew than in English, but they are ultimately connected by city building. In Genesis Nimrod, Canaan's nephew, demonstrates that the flood has failed to put an end to humanity's city-building tendencies. The story of Ham and the drunken Noah (9:18–28) pushes the Canaanites genealogically as far away from the Israelites as possible, and this may be its primary purpose, but it also serves to push city building away from the Israelite tradition.[95] The limitations placed on Adam and Eve by the divine curse have their apparent effect when their second son must become a sheepherder rather than settling and farming with the rest of the family. Nevertheless, the limitations do not prevail as Cain, despite a more direct curse supposedly disrupting his relationship to the ground, is able to build a city, something he could not do without a significant level of agricultural productivity. Thus, Cain has the knowledge to overcome divine banishment and curse and create civilization. Is this the knowledge gained by his parents in the garden and passed on to him? In the J source it seems to be. Banishment and divine curse cannot stop the growth of human civilization, which is injected with even more vigor by the Sons of God. The redactor of Genesis could not remove this survival from the text, but could only keep relocating it away from the ancestors of the Israelites by relating Noah to Seth and making Nimrod a descendant of Ham.

READING GENESIS 1–11 IN AN URBAN WORLD

The initial concern of this chapter was the emphasis on city building, settled life, and technology in Genesis 1–11. As the exploration of the relevant texts progressed, it became clearer that ancient Israel produced multiple accounts of the primeval world, each with a different perspective on settled, urban life. To conclude, I return to each of the traditions in succession to summarize its view of the primeval world through the lens of urbanism. Those in Israel who produced literature were almost certainly urban dwellers, and the portion of Israel's culture reflected in literary production became dominated by urban life as the nation developed. Persistent traditions, however, grounded Israel's beginnings in the life of nomadic herders. Negotiating the tension between stories of ethnic origins and the reality of present ways of living formed the struggle of national identity waged by these writers. While no single, simple portrait of a nomadic sheepherder emerges from the period during which the biblical traditions were forming, people living in this way would have been on the margins of the societies that produced the traditions found in Genesis. The people with the resources to produce complex literature and their prospective audiences would not have been on the margins of society, but at the center of cultural power. Still, this is a relative evaluation, because Judah was a marginal entity on the world stage before, during, and after the exile.

The J source of the Pentateuch provided almost all the major narrative components of the Primeval Story in Genesis 1–11, an observation especially true of the components portraying city building and other features accompanying it, like agriculture, technology, and fame. The beginning of the chapter identified four texts from J that participate in its depiction of city building, each of which is an odd fit in Genesis 1–11. Examination of those four passages eventually led to a proposal for reordering them. The argument for changing the order of these four texts in a reconstruction of J began with an observation seldom made: that source division often simply assumes the elements in the earlier sources fell in the same order as they currently appear in the books of the Pentateuch. Contemporary expressions of the Documentary Hypothesis correctly identify narrative incoherence as the primary characteristic of the Pentateuch demanding source analysis. If this is true, then narrative coherence must be the primary criterion for reassembling the sources. To say it from the other direction, if the source documents are allowed to be narratively incoherent, then there was no need to divide the final form of Genesis in the first place. The present order of the J elements presents several problems. The jump from limiting life spans in the wake of the "Sons of God" event to killing all of humanity with a flood is too severe and abrupt. If the elements stay in their present order, then the Sons of God story is almost as isolated in J as it is in Genesis. The Cush-Nimrod line after the flood appears out of nowhere, and if one assumes J agreed with P that Cush was the son of Ham, then Nimrod was building massive cities just two generations after the deluge. The need for another divine action at Babel so soon after the flood is strange, and it is not so severe. These problems and others may be resolved by reconstructing J, placing the Nimrod narrative after the Sons of God story, followed by the Babel story, then the flood. In this order, the divine interventions in the world are of steadily increasing severity. The Sons of God story explains the presence of a *gibbor* like Nimrod. Both the Nimrod and Babel accounts fit into a coherent plotline in this presentation of J.

The reordering of J leaves one more unresolved issue this study has not fully addressed yet, the appearance of J after the flood. The remainder of the J material would develop out of the story of Noah's sons as demonstrated in appendix 3. The J genealogical material is fragmentary in Genesis, and one could assume it had more, but the redactor left it out; but once such omissions are granted, then there would seem to be no boundaries for them, and reconstructing the source becomes impossible. The genealogical material in J provides everything the J story of Abram needs. Though there is no complete genealogical connection, Abram is a descendant of Shem, and Shem's descendants are in their places.[96] The story of Abram in J takes place in Canaan and Egypt, and the origins of these two places and their people are present. In J, YHWH has done everything possible to rid the world of cities and their dominance to clear the way for a wandering herder like Abram to appear in the world and make his way.

The majority of the P source was genealogical, but it contained closely related texts about creation and the flood. Both of these stories contained connections to the tabernacle, the temple, and to Jerusalem. They did not express the anti-city bias of J, and the nature of the contents of P made it suitable as a framework into which the contents of J could be placed. When the redactor of Genesis came along, it is fair to assume he had at least two major problems to resolve. First, he had the P material, perhaps already including the genealogies in Genesis 5 and 11:11–27, and needed to integrate these with the J source.[97] Aside from two creation narratives and two flood stories to combine, he also had a difficult collection of genealogical materials to integrate. Second, if the J source looked like the one I have proposed, the redactor had a collection of stories that were severe in their anti-city-building stance, and needed to be tempered and modified for his urban audience. Genesis 5 provided a way to separate Noah from the genealogy of Cain, which also placed distance between Noah and the descendants of Cain who had created human culture. The most obvious implication of J—that Adam and Eve acquired the knowledge of settled human culture by eating the fruit and carried that knowledge out of the garden to give it to Cain—was disguised by the addition of Genesis 1 and Genesis 5 around the story of Adam and Eve's family. Genesis 1 presumed agricultural production and settled life from the beginning as part of the good creation, and Genesis 5 gave human history a path separate from Cain and his family. The separation left behind two hints:

the inexplicable presence of Cain's genealogy in Genesis and Noah's own innovative act of planting the first vineyard.

In order to make God's judgment on city building less destructive and final, the redactor moved the Babel story to a position after the flood, a move that also required moving the Nimrod narrative, because of their shared interest in the origins of Babel. The redactor placed Nimrod within the genealogy of Ham, a move that again put distance between the genealogical line leading to Israel and the worst excesses of settled life and city building. Genesis 11:11–27 allowed time for descendants of Shem to make their way to Ur, so that the P account of Terah and Abram could begin there. The movement of Nimrod and Babel left one telltale sign behind in pre-flood Genesis, the Sons of God story in 6:1–4 that looks fragmentary and isolated because it no longer provides the origin of Nimrod, the great *gibbor*. In post-flood Genesis, the redaction created three difficulties. First, the Nimrod narrative does not fit easily within the Ham genealogy, because it differs in form from everything around it. Second, there is a confusing array of genealogical material related to Shem. Third, the Babel story sits in the middle of the Shem genealogies, unable fully to explain them or be explained by them. The one factor that makes the plot of Genesis 1–11 still manageable, if confusing, is the creation of a space for the emergence of Abram as a wandering, nomadic sheepherder, even if among the scattered remnants of Babel rather than the cleaner aftermath of the flood. The knowledge and ability to build cities is still present, even if its application is limited because of communication problems.

The analysis of the redaction of Genesis above does not resolve all of the present problems, but it leaves fewer behind than others. Like all attempts, it has difficulty with two aspects of the redactor's work. First, why was the redactor able to use the source materials together in such different ways at different places? The redactor laid the two creation accounts side by side but wove the two flood stories together to make a single narrative. Both moves created the kind of narrative incoherence that has generated the Documentary Hypothesis. Second, why did the redactor not leave out or change even some very small details in order to mitigate the incoherence? The best response anyone can give to such a question is that the incoherent elements that puzzle modern readers were of less concern, or none at all, to readers of that time. Modern urban readers, like the writers and early readers of Genesis, might find difficulty in reading a story that looks upon their way of life negatively. The writer of Genesis has tempered, but not removed, the problem. Later ways of expressing the primeval tradition, along with later readers of Genesis, including modern readers, would find ways to diminish the anti-urban bias further. Perhaps the most obvious example is the accusation that the people of Babel were attempting to invade heaven. The examination of other ancient

Israelite texts that follows will look for continuing ways that they negotiate the complex relationship between the traditions they use and the ways of life of their writers and readers.

The beginning of chapter 1 observes the problems generated by the earth's massive population, which will continue to grow for at least another century. Resolutions to these problems will require a more careful and deliberate move toward urban concentration. While most parts of the world are well on their way to this goal, there is also resistance in many places, and that resistance is often tied to traditional ways of thinking about humanity as nonurban, some of which even demonize urban ways of life. The ways in which the writers of the book of Genesis renegotiated such biases in their own traditions may be visible in a careful reading of the texts in Genesis 1–11, like the one I have presented above. These ideas will become clearer as the next chapter proceeds to look at the ancestral traditions in the remainder of the book of Genesis through the same lens.

3

Not in Ur Anymore

The Israelite Ancestors Encounter Urban Life

The origin of the Israelite ancestors is murky in Genesis, and it seems likely that the author intended exactly such a perception. The previous chapter demonstrated a bias against city building and urban life within the J source's version of the Primeval Tradition. The P material in Genesis 1–11 does not express this attitude, and the combination of the two sources by the writer of Genesis diluted the anti-city tone of J without removing it. The survey of interaction between the great ancestors of Israel and cities in this chapter leads to a comparison to determine whether the same bias toward cities is in the sources of Genesis and continues in the whole book. Genesis 12–50, including the J material within it, does not contain the same high concentration of texts concerned with city building that Genesis 1–11 contains, so the evaluation will be broader in scope.

The major urban interactions in Genesis 12–50 are

12:10–20	The journey of Abram and Sarai in Egypt (entirely J)
14:1–24	The abduction of Lot and resulting war (separate unidentified source)
18:16–19:29	The destruction of Sodom and Gomorrah (entirely J except for 19:29)
20:1–18	The journey of Abraham and Sarah in Gerar (entirely E)
26:1–33	The journey of Isaac and Rebekah in Gerar and continuing conflict (entirely J)
34:1–31	The conflict between Jacob's family and Shechem (entirely J)
39–50	Joseph and the rest of Jacob's family in Egypt (mixture of J, E, and P)

The most deliberate and coherent examination of the ways of life of the Israelite ancestors in Genesis is the third chapter of Theodore Hiebert's *The Yahwist's Landscape*. This is a subject difficult to analyze because the archaeological evidence is meager, while the abundant portraits in the text come from a much later time and have many purposes other than telling readers what the lives of Abraham, Sarah, Hagar, Isaac, Rebekah, Jacob, Rachel, Leah, Bilhah, and Zilpah were like. Hiebert correctly identified the overemphasis on nomadic herding in much scholarship on the ancestral period. Based on archaeological information, he presents a more complex view of life in ancient Canaan, one in which sedentary agriculture and nomadic herding were connected. Even individual persons likely moved back and forth between these activities, depending on seasonal conditions and longer-term changes in climate. The portrait of the ancestors in Genesis places them most often in locations in the central hill county where this type of mixed agriculture would have been effective. Once Hiebert brought sedentary agriculture into the discussion, it was not difficult to find examples, particularly in J texts, of the ancestors growing grain and eating food associated with settled agriculture.[1] The Yahwist's view of the ancestors is of great importance because this source comprises the largest quantity of Genesis 12–50. For J the story of the ancestors is central, while the P source emphasizes Mount Sinai and uses the ancestors primarily to help introduce the idea of covenant.[2]

The below examination of texts shows that when the ancestors entered or lived in cities their experience was often difficult, involving captivity, violence, or the threat of violence. Hiebert points out that the ancestors are often portrayed in what readers of Genesis would identify as urban locations. If, however, we remove the dangerous interactions with Egypt, Sodom, and Gerar, along with the singular instance of violent conflict in Shechem, then the other instances typically put the ancestors in these urban locations for one specific purpose: to build altars. The visits of Abraham, Isaac, and Jacob to places like Shechem, Hebron, Bethel, and Beersheba are not included in the above list of urban encounters because there are no cities in view in the texts and no other characters. The original readers of the J source and Genesis would have recognized such places as cities, but they do not look like cities when the ancestors visit them. Whether shrines or the cities around them come first is impossible to say, in part because the two must go together, and their development is interdependent. Even if a shrine is established in an existing city, the presence of a religious site and the apparatus that develops around it will alter the setting. There are no portrayals of the ancestors remaining in these places and continuing to use the altars they build to worship YHWH. Of course the entire presentation of the ancestors is more concerned with the time and purpose of the writer. Genesis and its sources affirm the legitimacy of these worship sites in their own time by placing the ancestors there long ago. So, the only visible aspect of these later urban settings upon which the ancestors stamp their presence is their religious shrines.[3]

The two largest sources of material in the ancestral story, the J and P sources, understood Abram/Abraham to have come from two different places, Haran and Ur, respectively. The sources agree that Abram came from an important city, but these two cities are at nearly opposite ends of the great Euphrates River, many hundreds of miles apart. The redaction of Genesis managed to make the sojourn of Terah's family look like a two-stage process, one that began in Ur, paused for some time in Haran, where Terah died, then continued with Abram, Sarai, and Lot traveling southward into Canaan. What the two sources have in common is the connection between the family and influential Mesopotamian cities, though at opposite ends of that region. It may have taken two tries, but Abram and Sarai appear to be following the divine preference for leaving an urban setting for a less settled life. Other Abram traditions are more specific about the circumstances of the family's departure from Ur. The book of Jubilees (11:12–15) and the ancient midrashic commentary Genesis Rabbah (38) report that Abram burned the idols of Ur in his zeal against idol worship, and this event precipitated the family's move to Haran. Both texts seem to be explaining the early death of Abram's brother who was named Haran. In Jubilees, Haran is burned to death trying to save the idols from the fire, while in Genesis Rabbah he is thrown into the fire for declaring his belief in Abram's God. Genesis Rabbah also places Abram in an argument with Nimrod, the great city builder. In these other sources, Abram's conflict is not with urban life itself, but with the idol worship common in some cities. This feature connects with the desire to place the patriarchs in later Israelite shrine-cities, building altars for YHWH.

THE URBAN ENCOUNTERS OF THE ANCESTORS

The places where Abram and Sarai arrive in Canaan, and settle for a time to build altars, have the names of cities, but no cities are visible in the stories. There is no reference to buildings, other people, or any of the elements of civilization. During the initial journey through Canaan in Genesis 12:4–9, no other characters appear. The land might seem empty but for the narrator's reminder to his distant readers in 12:6 that "At that time the Canaanites were in the land." The rapid departure of Abram and Sarai from Canaan is surprising.

The inability of the land to support them raises questions about its promise, and displays a relative lack of infrastructure. In contrast, the ability of Egypt to support foreign travelers at such a time depends on two characteristics of the place. One of these is the nature of the Nile River, which provided irrigation for the territories through which it flowed even in times of local or regional drought. Simon Schama describes the Nile as the opposite of the Jordan, particularly in Christian tradition. Israel's river was purifying, and sometimes angry, like the God of Israel, while the Nile was associated with abundance and luxury.[4] Even the positive aspect of the Nile that saves the great ancestors of the Bible from famine could be negative because of its ability to tempt and entrap. The story of Joseph could be used to illustrate these possibilities. The other feature, demonstrated in the Joseph story later in Genesis, is the massive, organized storage of surplus food possible in an administrative center. So, the survival of Abram and Sarai, when they leave Canaan in Genesis 12, depends on the general nature of a city, and this particular city's geography. Genesis does not hide this idea, but does not make it obvious either. The story does not describe Abram and Sarai acquiring or eating food. Of much greater interest is the danger posed by the city, especially one associated with an empire like Egypt. The danger is one they require divine help to escape. The enriching of Abram and Sarai, at the expense of Pharaoh, is a curious feature of the story. The similar story of Abraham and Sarah in Gerar in Genesis 20 makes the wife-sister deception look like a refined scam the couple operated with divine assistance.[5] Two competing ideas concerning the relationship of the ancestors to cities are at play in this story and the story that dominates Genesis 14. Were the great ancestors independent of cities and their resources, needing nothing from them, or were they, even in times of dependence on cities, able to get the best of the empire and its leaders, with divine assistance? Because the ancestral traditions come from multiple sources, with different attitudes toward cities and their inhabitants, there are likely to be multiple perspectives on such questions in this literature.

The material in Genesis 14 will enter into the subsequent discussion, and its mysterious nature requires some discussion at the outset. The language of this text, including some of the divine designations, makes it an uneasy fit for any of the standard sources.[6] Among the unique aspects of the texts are the depiction of Abram as a powerful chieftain, leading an army of hundreds of men, and the designation of him as "Abram the Hebrew." This raises two possibilities and also serves as a useful example of how the two primary understandings about the composition of the Pentateuch—the documentary approach and the supplementary approach—are not mutually exclusive. A text like Genesis 14 may have been either an older tradition incorporated into the J source, thus one that did not fit its own style, or it could have been an additional piece of tradition used by the redactor or writer of Genesis beyond the three sources that make up almost all the book. Genesis 14 appears to have its own distinct agenda, as well as style, which marks it off as separate from the other source material. J. A. Emerton proposed a very early date for Genesis 14, perhaps even in the Davidic era, based on his understanding of priestly disputes in that period, which the Melchizedek story may have been adjudicating. This early date can no longer hold up, but Emerton's scheme is an example of a proposal that incorporates Genesis 14 with the J source prior to the final composition of Genesis and the Pentateuch. Volker Glissmann has proposed, based on structure and style, that Genesis 14 is a diaspora novella, directed toward the concerns of the Babylonian Golah community. Abram models positive interaction with foreigners, including kings, but does not allow himself to become overly entangled with them.[7] Benjamin Ziemer placed Genesis 14 in the Persian Period, as part of a program to maintain the preeminence of Jerusalem and explain the relegation of the trans-Jordan territory to the Ammonites and Moabites.[8] The late dates of the latter two proposals do not make incorporation into the J source prior to the redaction of Genesis impossible, but less likely because of the compressed time period in which multiple stages of redaction would have had to take place. The analysis below will indicate that the view of the Israelite ancestors' relationships with urban kings in Genesis 14 is different from that in the J source, but both resist close ties or dependence.

The character named Lot receives sporadic treatment in the book of Genesis, but his role in stories involving cities makes him central to the discussion here. Genesis 11:27 introduces him as the son of Haran, and 11:31 reports that he accompanied the family led by his grandfather Terah out of Ur to the city of Haran. Genesis 12:4 then reports that Lot accompanied Abram and Sarai in their southward journey into Canaan. Lot vanishes from the text during the sojourn in Egypt and reappears in Genesis 13 when his shepherds come into conflict with those of Abram. The conflict leads to an agreement that the two men will separate so that their herds will have adequate space to pasture. After the resolution, 13:12 places Lot among the cities of the plain, which included Sodom, but this verse describes him still living in a tent, so he does not yet look like a city dweller. During the strange story in Genesis 14, which includes the kidnapping of Lot, verse 12 describes him living "in Sodom." When that story concludes, Lot disappears from the text until chapter 19, when he plays his role in the story of the destruction of Sodom. The two angels who had visited Abraham and Sarah earlier travel to Sodom, and Lot greets them when they approach the city gate. He offers them hospitality, and, according to 19:3, the two angels, who appear as men, are staying with Lot in his house when the mob surrounds the structure and demands that Lot send them out. So, in the plot of Genesis, Lot had become a city dweller between chapters 13 and 19, but the sporadic nature of the text does not make it clear when or how this transformation happens. Once God determines to destroy Sodom, Abraham is able to negotiate the safeguarding of Lot and his family during the destruction, a story to which the discussion returns below.

An awareness of the eventual transformation of Lot into an urban person makes the negotiation between Abram and the king of Sodom after the war story in Genesis 14 even more fascinating. Abram and the king of Sodom meet in 14:17–24, a gathering that also includes Melchizedek, who is identified as a "priest of God Most High," and this latter aspect tends to dominate perceptions and interpretations of the text.[9] After Abram makes his gift to Melchizedek, though, the king of Sodom offers Abram some of the spoils taken during the war. Abram refuses the loot with a strange response in which he states, "I have sworn to the LORD, God Most High, maker of heaven and earth, that I would not take a thread nor a sandal-thong or anything that is yours, so that you might not say, 'I have made Abram rich'" (vv. 22–23). Abram resists any association with the king of Sodom that involves financial reward. There are at least two ways to understand the utterance that Abram does not want the king to be able to make, depending on the identity of the audience to whom the king might say it. First, Abram might not want to be indebted to the king in any way that would make him susceptible to the pressures of loyalty, if the king might request Abram's assistance in the future based on a past favor. The other possibility is that Abram has some sort of reputation he wants to maintain, one that the king could destroy by making this statement to other people. If the latter is the case, then does that reputation consist of independence from royal figures, lack of attachment to urban life, or a position of neutrality amidst local powers? Does the text presume, and the story of Lot demonstrate, that the city exerts a force difficult to resist? Those who become entangled with cities, as Lot may have once he pitched his tent in their midst, get pulled into their grasp. Abram, on the other hand, refuses the material goods produced by the city and refuses to benefit from his relationship with an urban king. This way of reading Abram's refusal could fit either understanding of his statement to the king. Genesis is not consistent on this point with regard to Abram/Abraham, who gladly took material wealth from the king of Egypt in exchange for Sarai in Genesis 12. The sojourn in Egypt text comes from the J source, as do the story of Lot living in a tent near Sodom in Genesis 13 and the destruction of Sodom story in Genesis 19, which has Lot living in a house in Sodom. The story in which Abram refuses the wealth of the city in Genesis 14 comes from a source nearly all interpreters identify as something other than the standard three that make up Genesis.[10] The previous story, from the J source, had allowed Abram and Sarai to escape Egypt with some of its wealth. The combination of sources in Genesis creates an ambivalent attitude toward cities and the ways the ancestors were related to them. In both traditions the ancestors stand apart from urban life, but in one it is the source of some of their wealth, while being both a refuge from starvation and a threat of captivity (J). In the other they are fully independent from urban resources and powerful in their own right. The anti-city tone of the J source in Genesis 1–11 fits well with the story of the destruction of Sodom, but the relationship to a text like Genesis 12:10–20 is more complex. Abram and Sarai need the city to survive the famine, but they are able to stand apart from it in the end and take advantage of it through a combination of wit, deception, and divine assistance.

One of the most remarkable texts in all the Bible is Genesis 18:16–33, in which YHWH and Abraham have an extended moral conversation about destroying an entire city for its wickedness. The complexity of the dialogue and the stories surrounding it enable a wide variety of theological interpretations. YHWH tells Abraham that there is a great "outcry" against Sodom and Gomorrah (18:20) because of their sin, but does not identify the source of the outcry. In the full book of Genesis it seems impossible to avoid reading this text in light of the sixth-century destruction of Jerusalem. If this is the case, then there are two central questions generated by the dialogue. First, would the presence of a limited number of righteous people be enough to prevent the divine punishment of a city?[11] The dialogue offers an affirmative answer to that question, but the required number is ambiguous. The challenge Abraham offers to the divine plan requires the examination of the population of the city, an examination that reveals an insufficient number of righteous persons reside there to make it worth saving. The dialogue does not arrive at its logical conclusion, though. Abraham talks YHWH down from fifty righteous persons to forty-five to forty to thirty to twenty and, finally, to ten, but the story does not inform the reader of the final tally of righteous persons. The destruction of Sodom in the next chapter leads to the inference that there were fewer than ten. Readers are also left to wonder whether a smaller number of righteous persons might be rescued from the destruction, even if there were not enough to save the whole city. The second question is whether the rescue of Lot has any relation to Abraham's negotiation with YHWH. Almost all of this tradition comes from the J source. The single P verse in 19:29 acknowledges the rescue of Lot from the "overthrow" of the cities, but presents it as a favor God does for Abraham. The rescue story from the J source (19:12–23) is more ambiguous. Lot had behaved in a righteous manner by offering hospitality to the angelic visitors. Modern readers cannot help but be appalled by Lot's offer to let the mob gang-rape his daughters (vv. 7–8), but the text offers no judgment on this behavior. When Lot hesitates in the midst of the disaster, the text attributes his rescue to the mercy of YHWH (v. 16). Finally, the actions of Lot's daughters in verses 30–38 and the identification of Lot as the progenitor of the Moabites and Ammonites make it difficult to view him as a model of righteousness. Lot's close relationship to Sodom endangers his life and the lives of his family members, and complicates the portrait of his character in Genesis. Ed Noort has demonstrated the connections between the sparing of Lot and the sparing of Noah in the J version of the flood story. The parallel texts in 6:9 and 19:19 attribute the rescue to divine favor rather than the virtue of Noah or Lot.[12]

One more element of the story further magnifies its ambiguity. In Lot's own brief negotiation with the angels, in 19:20–22, he is able to accomplish something Abraham had failed to do. Lot convinces the angels to spare the city of Zoar from destruction. Lot does not plead for the salvation of Zoar based on the righteousness of any of its inhabitants, however, but on the basis of its size. Lot fears for his life outside the city and argues that Zoar is "a little one." What is it about the size of the city that makes it salvageable? Perhaps its wickedness is not great enough to require destruction. One particular word introduced in the negotiation arouses curiosity. The angel promises Lot that they will not "overthrow" (hpk) Zoar, using a word that has not yet appeared in either YHWH's conversation with Abraham nor the angels' instructions to Lot in 19:12–14. The word appears a second time in 19:25 in the summary of YHWH's actions against the cities of the plain. The third appearance of the word in this context is the most surprising, because it is in the one verse that comes from the P source, 19:29. The word itself is not rare, appearing about ninety times in various forms in the Hebrew Bible, but the use in reference to an action against a city is relatively unusual.[13] At first glance, this might seem a challenge to the common source division of the text. Why would P make use of this same rare expression that J uses? A solution appears in three other texts: Deuteronomy 29:22, Lamentations 4:6, and Jeremiah 20:16. The first two of these texts explicitly refer to Sodom and use this verb to describe the divine action against it, and the Jeremiah text uses the verb to describe divine actions against unnamed cities that are like Sodom and Gomorrah. Deuteronomy 29:23 not only lists Sodom and Gomorrah but also two other cities, Admah and Zeboiim, overturned along with them. So, the tradition connecting *hpk* to the fate of Sodom and Gomorrah seems to have been widespread and could have ended up in two different sources independently. In the end, Zoar does not suffer the fate commonly associated with Sodom, and the only available reason is its comparative size. The sparing of Zoar raises a final question about why Lot and his daughters do not remain there, rather than flee to the isolated cave. Genesis 19:30 reports that Lot was afraid to remain in Zoar but does not supply the reason for that fear. Does he fear the people who live there, or is he afraid that the divine stay of execution for the small city is only temporary?

The discussion above has already acknowledged the sojourn of Abraham and Sarah in Gerar, but this text, along with the similar visit of Isaac and Rebekah to the Philistine city, requires additional attention. The stories come from the E and J sources, and the latter, concerning Isaac, seems more concerned about possible entanglement with the people of Gerar and their king. Both father and son enter into negotiations with King Abimelech after he discovers their deceptions concerning their wives. In 20:14–17 Abimelech provides material wealth to Abraham and Sarah, and exonerates them for their behavior, after criticizing Abraham repeatedly. In return, Abraham asks YHWH to heal the infertility of the women of Gerar. The negotiations with Isaac in 26:12–33 are more extensive and complex. According to 26:12 Isaac settled and farmed in Gerar, but this eventually brought him into conflict with the Philistines over water rights. When Abimelech asks Isaac to leave because "you have become too powerful for us," Isaac moves, but apparently not far enough. Genesis 26:17 finds him settled in "the valley of Gerar," and the conflict with the Philistines over wells arises again. The successive conflicts drive Isaac farther and farther from Gerar, until he ends up in Beersheba, and this move finally creates adequate distance from the Philistine city. YHWH appears to Isaac in Beersheba, his servants dig yet another successful well, and even Abimelech comes to him to make a peace offering. Isaac seems to find the proper balance in relation to foreign cities, far enough away to prevent conflict, but close enough that the comparative success of his way of life is visible, a concern consistent with the ideology of the J source. With this balance achieved, the story is prepared to move on to Jacob.

The differing perspectives on the ancestors and their ways of living do not always fall out neatly along the dividing lines of the traditional sources of the Pentateuch, because even the sources are composite in nature. Multiple traditions hold the ancient ancestors at a distance from urban life. The opening chapter of this book gave some attention to methods of reading the text, but many aspects of such methodological issues do not become clear until they become grounded in the discussions of actual texts, so it has been helpful already at certain points to turn again to these methodological matters. The debate that most roils the field of Pentateuchal studies is often cast in terms of "sources vs. supplements." The issues that animate debates about the composition of the Pentateuch are too complex for simple labels, but it most often comes down to whether the material that makes up the current form of the Pentateuch existed in large linear collections in written form that were combined by a redactor. The alternative is that the Pentateuch grew as material accrued around independent blocks of tradition.[14] This need not be the kind of either-or question that many portray. If the claims in the "Neo-Documentary Hypothesis" concerning the thorough preservation of sources are correct, then the process of formation of those sources should still be visible. This allows for the possibility that the accrual process the "supplementarians" see is the process by which the sources were formed. This kind of solution is particularly appealing in a debate such as this one, in which both sides are able to produce such thoroughly convincing cases for their positions. One of the great difficulties for this kind of process becomes apparent in the ancestral material. It requires that three sources—J, E, and P—possessed different traditions about Abraham, Isaac, and Jacob, and that at least two of them—J and P—connected those traditions together into the famous three-generation sequence of patriarchs.[15] If, as the discussion here contends, the final product of the composition process of the Pentateuch, and much of the rest of the Tanakh, is a combination of Judahite and Israelite sources, then the sources may have produced their own combinations independently. If Jacob was an Israelite ancestor and Abraham a Judahite ancestor, and the two regional collections of traditions began to come together after the Assyrian defeat and dispersal of Israel, then the origin of both sources postdate this event.[16] The argument matters here because the continuous sources are able to develop a more complete sense of the ways of life they presume for the ancestors, which may inform us about the ways of life of the audiences. This will become more apparent and important in the texts about the formation of Israel in the next chapter.

If the stories of Abraham and Isaac, located in the south and associated with the traditions of Judah, and the Israelite traditions about Jacob were brought together by multiple sources of the Pentateuch and the book of Genesis, then it would not be surprising to find some unevenness in the attitudes toward urban life even among texts from the same source. Table 3.1 demonstrates the pattern of locations where Genesis places Abraham and Jacob.

Table 3.1
Geographical Locations Linked to Abraham and Jacob in Genesis

Abraham	Jacob
Ur (11:28)	Beersheba (28:10)
Haran (11:31; 12:4)	**Bethel/Luz** (28:19; 35:1)
Shechem (12:6)	Haran/Paddanaram (28:10; 29:4; 31:18)
Bethel (12:8; 13:3)	**Mahanaim** (32:1)
Egypt (12:10)	**Mizpah** (31:39)
The Negeb (13:1; 20:1)	**Peniel/Penuel** (32:30–31)
Sodom (14:17–24)	**Shechem** (33:18)
Mamre/Hebron (23:19)	Mamre (35:27; 49:30)
Kadesh (20:1)	**Gilead** (31:23)
Shur (20:1)	
Gerar (20:2)	
Beersheba (21:31–33; 22:19)	
Moriah (22:2)	

The lists above highlight whether places in or near Israel are located in the *south* (italic) or **north** (bold) of Canaan. The distribution reveals Jacob's association primarily with northern locations and Abraham's with southern locations.[17] The exceptions are places in Canaan the two lists have in common and seem to represent editorial adjustments during the literary process of bringing the two figures together. In the most prominent cases, Abraham in Shechem and Bethel and Jacob in Beersheba and Mamre, the traditions are thin, making them more likely candidates for editorial addition. The list also includes places outside of Canaan visited by Abraham and Jacob.

Jacob's primary interaction with a city comes when he arrives at Shechem in 33:18. The great northern ancestor is a nomadic shepherd throughout most of his life. The story of his arrival at Shechem in 33:18–20 is an E text, and his interaction with Hamor is peaceful and cooperative. Jacob makes a financial arrangement to secure land on which to pitch his tents.[18] By contrast, the J text that begins at 34:1 presents the violent interaction between the clan of Jacob and the people of Shechem. Hamor is presented as a prince, and has a son with the same name as his central city, a feature that may connect him to Cain and the name issues that arise in the J materials of the Primeval Story. The narrative that proceeds after the sexual assault of Dinah presents a picture of life in the city and its governance. When Shechem wishes to marry

Dinah, Hamor meets with the sons of Jacob and proposes an arrangement between the two groups that would include economic interactions as well as intermarriage. When Jacob's sons respond with the condition that all the men of Shechem be circumcised in order to enable the arrangement, Hamor and Shechem return to their city, and 34:20 shows them meeting at the city gate with all of the men of the city to propose the arrangement. The agreement and resulting massacre create another negative portrait of the relationship between the ancestors and urban life. The city is a dangerous place for Israelite women, and the Israelite ancestors find themselves in conflict with urban dwellers, a conflict Simeon and Levi choose to resolve with brutal violence. Jacob's apparent objection, though weak, along with the harsh condemnation of these two brothers at the beginning of the poem in Genesis 49, reveal mixed perspectives about this conflict in the book of Genesis.

The reference to Israel as a place in Genesis 34:7, "because he had committed an outrage in Israel," is the first such use in Genesis and one of only two in the entire book. Such an obvious anachronism invites exploration into the context of the writing of the text. Of the forty-three occurrences of "Israel" in Genesis, twenty-eight use the term as the alternative name for Jacob as an individual character. The next most common use is the seven references to the "sons of Israel," either to name the twelve sons as specific characters or, in another obvious anachronistic construction, the group of people that are the Israelites. The first occurrence of this kind is in 32:32, when the story of Jacob's wrestling match ends with the etiological statement about the Israelites ("sons of Israel") not eating the thigh muscle of an animal. Twice the term "Israel" appears alone to name a group of people (47:27 and 48:20), and two more occurrences place it in the phrase "tribes of Israel" (49:16 and 49:28) to name a later, larger group. The other use of "in Israel" is at 49:7, also within the "Song of Jacob," a text filled with anachronistic references.[19] In addition to the strangeness of referring to Israel as a place here, one that would contain the city of Shechem, the specific phrase about perpetrating an outrage in Israel occurs at two other prominent places in the Hebrew Bible. In Judges 20:6, in the aftermath of the gang-rape and murder of the unnamed "concubine," the Levite to whom she belonged uses this phrase to denounce the people of Gibeah. This is the occasion of the first major act of aggression among the Israelite tribes, when the event leads the other tribes to attack Benjamin. In his famous "letter to the Exiles," Jeremiah uses the same phrase in 29:23 to condemn the behavior of two prophets in Babylon, Ahab and Zedekiah, who were reportedly burned to death by Nebuchadnezzar as an act of divine judgment against dishonest and adulterous behavior. The phrase is thus connected to Israel's earliest days in the land and its expulsion from the land.

Jacob's statement to his sons after the massacre is ambiguous. The sons have plundered the city of Shechem and taken its material wealth, after killing all of its male inhabitants, and Jacob's concern in 34:30 is with the attitude of the inhabitants of the larger region. He claims to be small in number and fears a declaration of war against him and his household. Positive relations between the ancestors and urban dwellers might have multiple motivations, and fear might be one of them. The idea that the existence of the ancestors in Canaan might be precarious because of the threat of attacks by other inhabitants is a new issue presented by this text. The abilities of Abraham and Isaac to fend for themselves through the use of military power or artful negotiation, and the many promises of divine protection, seem absent from Jacob's fearful reaction. The tone of Jacob's condemnation later, in the poem he recites immediately before his death, is entirely different. Jacob, or the poem placed in his mouth, seems morally offended by the behavior of Simeon and Levi, and he effectively disowns them, saying:

> Simeon and Levi are brothers;
> > weapons of violence are their swords
> May I never come into their council;
> > may I not be joined to their company—
> For in their anger they killed men
> > and at their whim they hamstrung oxen.
> Cursed be their anger, for it is fierce,
> > and their wrath, for it is cruel!
> I will divide them in Jacob,
> > and scatter them in Israel. (49:5–7)

The poem is typically considered older than its narrative context, and of independent origin. Jacob's condemnation of a violent act against a foreign, Canaanite city is surprising in light of later events. He presents being divided and scattered as an atypical condition, punishment for an act he considers cruel. The use of the word "scatter" is reminiscent of the Babel story, though any direct connection between the sources seems doubtful. It does indicate that whoever was responsible for the Song of Jacob considered an un-scattered Israel good and divinely blessed. The presentation of the interaction between the sons of Jacob and the people of Shechem seems quite different from J's presentation of the events in Genesis 34.

The combination of sources in Genesis 35–36 has Jacob unsettled and on the move. Various sources have him in Bethel, Ephrath/Bethlehem, and Migdal-Eder, with a trip back to Mamre to bury his father. One of the small but frequent features of the Torah is the naming of places. In some instances a character explicitly names a place, and at other times it is the voice of the narrator. Naming places may be most common in the wilderness traditions of Exodus and Numbers, but the ancestors in Genesis are involved in this activity too. Within the boundaries of the stories about Abraham, Isaac, and Jacob, there are about eighteen cases of naming. Some are the naming of objects, such as wells, trees, stones, or altars, but eleven involve the naming of places. In a few cases the word "city" appears in proximity to the name, while in others the name matches the name of what later appears as a city. Table 3.2 identifies these texts, the thing that is named, the name, the person whose experience the name reflects, and who names the place.

Table 3.2
Naming Cities and Places in Genesis

Text	Location	Name	Namer	Voice reporting the naming
19:22	city	Zoar	Lot	Narrator
21:31	place	Beer-sheba	Abraham	Narrator
22:14	place	YHWH-Yireh	Abraham	Abraham
26:33	city	Beer-sheba	Isaac	Narrator[20]
28:19	place/city	Bethel	Jacob	Jacob[21]
31:48	pillar/place	Mizpah	Jacob	Jacob
32:2	place	Mahanaim	Jacob	Jacob
32:30	place	Peniel	Jacob	Jacob
33:16	place	Succoth	Jacob	Narrator
35:7	place	El-bethel	Jacob	Jacob
35:15	place	Bethel	Jacob	Jacob

The three great ancestors most often look like wandering herders or occasional farmers in the book of Genesis, but they name a lot of places. None of the places they name look anything like cities at the time they do the naming, but for the writers and readers of the texts, for whom such urban settings became important, the stamp of the ancestors is upon them. By the end of Genesis, the ancestors will have departed Canaan, but they had left some things behind. There were five bodies in a cave-tomb at Machpelah, and there were some places that had received names connected to moments in the ancestors' lives. Later Israelites would associate the great ancestors with the cities they lived in and visited, without any indication that this posed a problem.

The model of development of the Pentateuch proposed by Thomas Römer and Israel Finkelstein suggested that placing Abraham and Jacob together, as grandfather and grandson, was part of the project of constructing a common past for northern and southern Israelites, with Judah in the dominant position.[22] In the current form of Genesis Abraham enacts Israel's arrival in Canaan, with connections back to Mesopotamia. The material typically assigned to the P source locates his family origins far to the southeast in Ur, while the J source places him initially in Haran. Abraham makes brief appearances at northern sites like Bethel and Shechem, but the bulk of the narratives about him take place in southern locations, as Table 3.1 demonstrates. Without the construction of a familial connection Jacob is left as one who is simply from that area, the "wandering Aramean" of Deuteronomy 26:4. One of the most remarkable features of the Ancestral Story is that the two most important figures are never portrayed together.[23] The independent origins of the Abraham and Jacob material place some limits on the consistency of their presentation, but they still bear significant resemblance, especially in the J material. As Theodore Hiebert concludes, "J pictured his ancestors engaged in the sedentary agriculture typical of biblical Israel in his day."[24] This comment should be joined with the observation that both of them also move around a lot. The lifestyles of Abraham and Jacob are similar, even if they tend to occupy different geographical locations. Chapter 8 will demonstrate that the writer of Jubilees, apparently unwilling to leave Abraham and Jacob unacquainted, included traditions in which the two great ancestors interacted.

The career of Joseph in Egypt is by far the largest body of material narrating interaction between any of the Israelite ancestors and a city/empire in Genesis. The first task in addressing this collection of material will be to identify the parts that specifically address urban life. For the first part of the narrative Joseph is a captive, a situation that only happens in relation to power like that an empire possesses, so there is potential for an anti-urban framework in this part of the story. The Ancestral Story has dealt with captivity on two previous occasions: Sarai in Genesis 12 and Lot in Genesis 14. The treatment Joseph receives in the house of Potiphar may reflect the dangers of urban life. Joseph's talent and the divine blessing that accompanies it bring Potiphar prosperity, and Joseph enjoys the rewards, but the incident with Potiphar's wife displays the accompanying temptations. Even in prison Joseph's abilities and divine favor allow him to rise above circumstance and bring him even greater power, but the actions of Joseph are difficult to interpret. Does the narrative voice in this part of Genesis understand his work within the Egyptian empire in entirely positive terms? The Potiphar story in Genesis 39 is from the J source and ends with the evaluation "the LORD was with him; and whatever he did the LORD made it prosper." The story of Joseph in prison and earning the notice of Pharaoh in Genesis 41–42 is almost entirely from the E source. It does not contain the same kind of narrative evaluation as the Potiphar story, but Joseph continually attributes dreams and his ability to interpret them to his God. The convoluted story that brings Jacob's family to Egypt in 42:1–46:5 is the result of a complex combination of J and E materials, with J providing more overt statements of divine blessing and control. Joseph's speech to his brothers in 45:4–9 stands out as the clearest expression of a divine plan to save the family of Jacob by bringing them to Egypt during the famine. The closest equivalent in the E material is the divine appearance to Jacob in a dream in 46:1–4, telling him, "I myself will go down with you to Egypt, and I will bring you up again." The P account of Jacob's family in Egypt picks up at 46:6 and becomes intertwined with the continuing J and E accounts. It is in a P text in 47:5–12 that Pharaoh himself meets with Jacob, having granted Jacob's family a good place to live in Goshen, and Pharaoh receives Jacob's blessing in return. It would be surprising to see the J source portray the Israelites gathered together into one place by their own choice. The use of Egyptian locations for the Israelites in Genesis and Exodus receives further attention below. The E account continues Joseph's plan to stockpile food at 47:13, and the severity of the famine enables him to trade the surplus and acquire all of the land in Egypt for Pharaoh (47:20), the behavior that raises the most difficult moral problems within the Joseph narrative. The bargain the people are forced to strike with Joseph in verses 23–26 seems the epitome of imperial oppression. Joseph looks like Pharaoh, even in his mummified death in the final verse of Genesis. Even a prominent Israelite, when allied with imperial power, can become an oppressor, but the victims in this case are all Egyptians. These were people against whom Israel's God would direct brutal plagues in the coming narrative.

The following chapter will need to deal more extensively with the character of Moses, but here it is important to recognize that he and Joseph are opposites in an important way. Joseph begins his life as a shepherd, like his father, and his herding ways help lead to his apparent demise. In the long story, however, Joseph transforms from a Hebrew shepherd into a pharaoh-like Egyptian administrator. By the time his father arrives in Egypt, Joseph has married an Egyptian woman, Aseneth, and fathered two sons with her. There is a significant later tradition addressing part of this problem in the work commonly known as "Joseph and Aseneth." The story seems primarily concerned with Aseneth's Egyptian identity and features her conversion to Judaism. It does not address this other aspect of Joseph's identity, his vocation, which also makes him look Egyptian.[25] Moses' character moves in the other direction. The daughters of the priest describe Moses to their father as "an Egyptian" in Exodus 2, but after he has fled Egypt for his life, encountered sisters by a well, been summoned by their father, married one of the daughters, and begun tending the father's flock, he resembles Jacob. Moses looks like an Egyptian when he arrives in Midian in Exodus 2:15–19, but the narrative takes great pains to transform his appearance, so that he matches the appearance of Jacob/Israel himself. Despite Moses' movement in the cultural direction of a Hebrew, his descendants find little if any place in Israelite tradition. Joseph's half-Egyptian sons, on the other hand, not only find a place among the Israelites but are also each elevated to full tribal status by the story in Genesis 48. These observations make Israel's relationship with Egypt complex and difficult to interpret. The absence of Egyptian characters in Canaan during the stories of the Israelite settlement in Joshua and Judges is a puzzling feature that will be treated in a later chapter.

The interaction of Israel's ancestors with cities and their inhabitants raised important questions for the writers of Genesis, the writers of its sources, and the readers of both. The great ancestors of Israel in Genesis are not urban people. They do not build cities. Their interaction with existing cities of their day is often negative and threatening. They do, however, provide the possibility of a favorable view of the cities familiar to the authors and audiences by erecting altars in cities of later significance, though the portrayal of those places are lacking any of the visible features of cities within the Genesis narrative. The ancestors are not fully nomadic, though all of them demonstrate that type of behavior at times. Persons engaged in herding, settled agriculture, or some combination of the two at the time when these texts were produced could have recognized themselves in the ancestors. The Primeval Story presented a sense of ambivalence about city dwelling. While it blunted the harsh anti-city elements of the J Primeval Story, the continuing presence of these elements may leave urban readers of the Bible uncertain about the Bible's understanding of their ways of life. The stories of the ancestors leave an equally ambiguous picture, but, given the strength of the anti-urban stance in its most powerful source, this is a positive movement toward a perspective more accepting of urban life.

Modern urban readers are likely not to find much that is familiar in the ways of life of the characters in Genesis. The frequent movement of these characters may be the most important exception, though. There may be a reason that the relation of the characters to the places where we see them is difficult to determine. The primary sources of Genesis, J and P, did not view this in the same way. The J source pictures the ancestors as inhabitants of the land of Canaan, closely connected to it, even though they sometimes move within it. The need to connect the ancestors to many places in the land may help create a sense of instability in the portrayal of their lives, but they are at home there. It is in the movement out of the land that they become aliens. The final move into Egypt is an exile from the land to which they will eventually return. The P source on the other hand, portrays them as sojourners or aliens in the land of Canaan. They receive the promise of this land, but they do not yet possess it as inhabitants.[26] The exodus is a necessity in order to place the Israelites at Mount Sinai, where they build the tabernacle and receive an abundance of instruction from Moses. The centrality of Jerusalem and the temple in P makes the description of decentered religious practices by the ancestors in the land problematic, a situation that other texts later in the story will have to continue to negotiate.

OBSERVING THE ANCESTORS FROM AN URBAN VANTAGE POINT

The ways in which we view our ancestors can have a lot to do with the ways we view ourselves, but the relationship is fragile. Some Americans, for example, understand their ancestors as dissenters, fleeing religious conformity and persecution, while others see explorers breaking free from the limitations of an old world. They did not apply these values consistently, though, as the development of rigid Puritanism in some parts of early America and the brutal practice of slavery in others indicates. The ways in which ancient Israelites viewed their ancestors varied as well, and because the Bible blends many traditions, readers receive a contested portrait. Most Protestant groups in the United States have a rural and small-town past. A small percentage of their congregations were in cities, but even these often found themselves a poor fit for their urban settings and eventually struggled with decisions to move into the suburbs. Their stained-glass windows showed Jesus, David, Moses, and Abraham tending sheep, and the backdrop of their baptisteries presented pastoral scenes around a peacefully flowing Jordan River. The traditions in their sacred texts were uncertain about urban living, and they strained to find a way of following those traditions that fit into the rhythms of a city. In his work on Christian traditions Dieter Georgi observed that "theology at large and Protestantism in particular as an institutionalized entity never made themselves at home in large cities." He found "a curious absence of urban concerns in institutional theology before and after the Reformation."[27] Georgi contended that the early Christian communities possessed a strong urban affinity, particularly embodied in Saint Paul, but that it began a movement away from this identity in the second century, a movement that found its most persuasive voice a few centuries later in Augustine.[28]

There are many readers of the Bible in many times, including the twenty-first century, whose encounters with an urban world resemble those of the Israelite ancestors in Genesis. Their movement is more likely to be from small town to metropolis than from a pastoral landscape to an ancient city that is closer in size to what we might call a town. Nevertheless, the degree of social and cultural transition is similar, and the attitudes expressed in the text about encounters with a new setting may be influential. The phenomenon Richard Florida has called "the Big Morph" involves the conflict between the Protestant work ethic and the "bohemian ethic." These two forces do not align perfectly with rural/small town and urban settings, respectively, but they have obvious affinities. There are ironies on both sides of the equation. The Protestant work ethic fed industrialization, making the building of cities that could concentrate labor a necessity, and all the while it was distrustful of the urban culture this created. The bohemian ethic prizes most the creativity that an urban setting makes possible by bringing a diverse population together, but the amassing of population threatens the individuality that lies at the core of this creative movement.[29] The story of the ancestors in Genesis flows out of empire and passes back into it. The most prominent cities in this story are Babel (Babylon), Sodom and Gomorrah, and the unnamed capital of Egypt. All of these places have enormous symbolic value, but the symbolism is difficult to characterize. Erin Runions has explained a similar phenomenon in the modern world: "Babylon is an uncertain symbol, alternately fetishized and demonized. Sometimes it is an object of desire. Frequently it signals dangerous incursions into national sovereignty and hierarchical authority."[30]

The urban and anti-urban traditions in Genesis 12–50 may collide more subtly than they did in Genesis 1–11. Almost everything about the literature in the second portion of the book is more subtle. The anti-urban voice is greater in quantity, because there is more material, but the shift that will become more prominent further into the Bible, from a claim that cities are evil to a claim that a particular kind of city is evil, is already beginning. Modern readers may find a variety of views they hold toward urban life confirmed in different texts, so there is no "biblical" answer to the social and moral dilemmas that cities pose, but there is a critical, contested conversation that may inform our own. The preceding discussion has made significant use of approaches that highlight the multiple sources of tradition within Genesis 12–50. My view is that this is the most effective way to approach these texts and to take seriously the seams, fractures, and incoherencies that are so common within it; but there is a payoff for readers not often observed in evaluations of such an approach, one that is not dependent on getting all of the source division of the text exactly right. Observing these competing traditions reveals that Israelite culture engaged in a contested conversation about many issues, including the nature and value of cities. The books of the Bible host this conversation and make it visible to careful readers. Rather than providing a single biblical answer to the challenges of urban life, biblical texts invite readers into a conversation about their own urban contexts, not to find an answer but to engage creatively in a life-giving dialogue. The gravity of the discussion will grow as the story of Israel moves toward the establishment of its own urban center and the hierarchy of power it generated.

4

Building Cities for Pharaoh

The Exodus Story and Engagement with Empire

The book of Exodus opens by describing the presence of seventy descendants of Jacob in Egypt. There is little in these few verses about the kinds of living conditions readers are to assume for this group, but soon the Israelites become so great in number that the Egyptians fear their size. The statement in 1:7 that "the land was filled with them" is figurative, rather than any kind of literal claim within the world of the story, and again there is no sense of how readers are to imagine the Hebrews living in Egypt. Numerous texts in Genesis 45–50 had identified the location of their settlement as "Goshen," which Pharaoh specifically described as "the best part of the land" in 47:6, and their prosperity in that place, described in 47:27, mirrors the growth and expansion in Exodus 1:7. The common conclusion that this area was located within the Nile Delta region of northeastern Egypt matches the notion of fertility in Genesis and Exodus, but the connection between the name and any particular location is imprecise. Goshen disappears from the biblical text, until two final references in the plague narrative at Exodus 8:18 (English 8:22) and 9:26. Even if readers are to perceive it as a pleasant, fertile place where the descendants of Jacob could live healthy and prosperous lives, this is not a permanent condition in the story. Their servitude ultimately has them crying out for divine help in Exodus 2:23.

The story of the ancestors in Canaan and the exodus story began as two independent traditions of origin. The stories were combined by the sources of the Pentateuch and, subsequently, by the Pentateuch itself. The intertwining of the traditions is accomplished primarily by the Joseph narrative, but is supplemented by the frequent statements by YHWH and Moses that the land to which the Israelites were traveling was promised to Abraham, Isaac, and Jacob. The ancestors' interactions with Egypt had been mixed. For the families of Abraham and Jacob the fertility of Egypt provided a rescue from famine, but the danger of the place had revealed itself in the captivity of Sarah and Joseph, and the entrapment of Jacob's other sons.

SLAVERY AND ESCAPE

In the description of the enslaving of the Hebrews in Exodus 1–2, the location seems different. The story does not portray the Hebrews as household slaves throughout the land, but living in particular places working for Pharaoh, building "cities of storehouses." The P source had used the place name "Rameses" in Genesis 47:11, along with its reference to Goshen in 47:6, but the absence of "Goshen" in the Greek text of Genesis 47:6 makes it possible that the P source never mentions such a place.[1] Exodus 12:37 and Numbers 33:3–5 describe the Israelites beginning their journey out of Egypt in Rameses. Regardless of the nature of the place called Goshen, the text portrays enslaved Hebrews living as a concentrated population in an urban setting. The city from which they depart has the name of more than one famous pharaoh, whether or not readers assume, as *The Ten Commandments* and *The Prince of Egypt* encourage them to, that this is the name of the pharaoh in the story. The character alternately identified as Pharaoh and the "king of Egypt" is surely to be understood as an urban person, and he represents the kind of imperial power with which Israel would be engaged throughout its national story. Furthermore, they are building the cities as an act of forced labor, so they are compelled to engage in an activity that Genesis has presented in negative terms. Egypt appears far back in the biblical story in Genesis 10:6 as one of the descendants of Ham, and a relative of the cursed Canaan. The familial relations in Genesis 10:6–14 are not clear, of course, but the category is plain enough. Egypt goes with Canaan and Cush, and thus with Nimrod, the originator of all empires.

The exodus story is enormously problematic from a historical perspective. The lack of any direct evidence leaves historians talking about the plausibility of the traditions.[2] It seems much more productive to look at the exodus story as a vehicle for addressing other issues and experiences in ancient Israel. If the exodus story was not attached to the experience of anyone outside of the biblical text, or if it reflects the experience of only a small group within early Israel, then why did it become the national story? It is written so that it could be the experience of several million people, a population that might have been achieved in Israel only during the height of the monarchies.[3] The story would have enabled all of Israel to understand its ancestors as those who escaped the oppression of an imperial city into a land of abundance and freedom. The exodus tradition was likely one of two primary origin stories in Israel, before it was subsumed under Judah. The other was the Jacob story, in which a "wandering Aramean" moved into Canaan from the north. The Pentateuch, and even the sources behind it, found ways to link these two origin stories, one of which claimed independence from urban, imperial power, while the other claimed that Israel's God and greatest leader had faced down such power and won.

Israel's interaction with Egypt was long and complex. The following chapter explores the occupation of Canaan more explicitly, but it is necessary to preview the observation there that Israel's engagement with Egypt in Canaan is more certain than the enslaving of a group of people who understood themselves to be Israelites in Egypt. The presence and projected power of Egypt in the Levant during the Bronze Age varied, but it was always present, and Egyptian influence in the area continued into the Israelite monarchy. The documents from the fourteenth century known as the Amarna Letters include correspondence between leaders of political entities in Canaan and their Egyptian sponsors. The letters come from an archive discovered in Egypt, so almost all of the correspondence comes from Canaan to Egypt. The six Amarna letters from Abdi-Heba of Jerusalem to Pharaoh demonstrate that this Canaanite king relied on and made use of Egyptian power against opposing groups in his territory.[4] Numerous other letters among the Amarna correspondence also either appeal to Egypt for assistance or communicate arrangements for anticipated intervention. Dozens of letters, for example, refer to the military campaign into Canaan by Thutmose III in the fifteenth century.[5] It seems reasonable that persons living in Canaan who were in conflict with the city-states would have perceived their conflict to be with Egypt as well. Given this information, it is puzzling that Egyptians are entirely absent from the stories of early Israel in Canaan. The ancestors in Genesis encounter Egyptians only in Egypt, and the incursion of Israel into Canaan in the book of Joshua describes no Egyptian presence or influence there. The conflict in Canaan is with Canaanites and immediately surrounding groups, like the Philistines, Moabites, and Ammonites.[6] These are the enemies of Israel from the period of the monarchy, apparently projected back into the story of their entry into Canaan after the exodus.

Even in Egypt the treatment of the Israelites varies. They begin as welcome guests and Pharaoh grants them good land. Theodore Hiebert has argued that Joseph uses some deception in his interaction with the pharaoh in Genesis 46. His suggestion to the brothers in 46:34 that they characterize themselves and their ancestors exclusively as herders indicates that the J tradition did not understand them that way. The deception allows them to enter Egyptian agricultural society without the Egyptians perceiving them as competitors.[7] This argument is not entirely convincing, but inside the story, the Egyptian people do not look like enemies of the Israelites, regardless of whether it is because Joseph and his brothers tricked them concerning their vocational identity. The multiple failed attempts by Pharaoh to control the population of the Israelites in Exodus 1 are due in part to the failure of his people to help him. There is little sense of conflict between the Israelites and ordinary Egyptians, and one particular tradition hints at favorable relationships.

The strange "despoiling" tradition offers a mixed picture of the interaction between the Israelites and ordinary Egyptians. It appears early, during YHWH's initial instructions to Moses in Exodus 3:21–22. The introduction to the subject of the Israelites taking the wealth of Egypt with them is based on the "favor" of the Egyptians toward them. In verse 22 the Israelite women are to "ask" their Egyptian neighbors for jewelry and clothing, but by the end of the verse, the act of the Israelites has transformed into one characterized by the word the King James Version translated as "despoil" and the NRSV rendered as "plunder." The tradition appears again as a bracket around the Passover event in Exodus 11–12. When YHWH describes the plan to Moses again in 11:1–3, the Israelites are to ask for silver and gold objects. The response of the Egyptians is again based on favor, and there is no sense of looting or plundering. After the death of the firstborn sons, the tradition is mixed in 12:33–35. The Israelites ask for jewelry and clothing, and YHWH grants the Israelites favor in the eyes of the Egyptians, but the passage ends with the same act of "plunder" described in 3:22.[8] If the story of Abram and Sarai in Egypt in Genesis 12 is a reflection of the exodus story, then the departure of the ancestors with all of the servants and livestock for which Abram had initially traded Sarai to Pharaoh is the matching element to the despoiling tradition, and it is also one that leaves the reader with a sense of ambiguity. Abram acts deceptively and benefits from the transaction that puts his wife in danger, while protecting himself. Pharaoh allows Abram to keep the servants and livestock, but this may be more out of fear than favor. The despoiling in Exodus follows plagues sent by YHWH as in Genesis 12. Another parallel to both of these events in Genesis and Exodus is the return from exile in Babylon in Ezra–Nehemiah. When the Israelites in Babylon are preparing to return, "All their neighbors aided them with silver vessels, with gold, with goods, with animals, and with valuable gifts, besides all that was freely offered" (Ezra 1:6). In the next verse Cyrus himself gives back the objects Nebuchadnezzar had taken from the temple decades earlier during the invasion of Jerusalem. The release of slaves in Israelite legal tradition eventually required supplying them with resources that might aid their independent survival for some time—livestock, grain, and wine (Deut. 12:13–14). It is difficult to say how stories about the release of Israelites from slavery or captivity are related to such legal requirements within their community, but the similarity of these situations should be kept in view.

A lot is at stake in the interpretation of the "despoiling tradition" beyond the basic moral question of stealing from people who have just suffered a tragedy. To what extent should the Israelites benefit from and make use of the wealth of cities, particularly those associated with empires? Is this the initial supply of resources due to released slaves, or is it a dangerous connection to imperial power? The three passages in Exodus are notoriously difficult to assign to the standard sources. Exodus 3:21–22, 11:1–3, and 12:35–36 are all in contexts predominately assigned to the E source, yet many interpreters have proposed that they are insertions from J.[9] The despoiling tradition seems intimately connected to the golden calf story, though, which creates a connection with the E source.[10] Another important connection is the end of the golden calf episode when the Israelites "plunder" themselves of the jewelry in 33:6. English translations are typically unable to render this Hebrew word, the same one in all three expressions of the despoiling tradition, with the same English word in this final case, because "despoil" or "plunder" does not sound like something people would do to themselves. The favor of the Egyptians, and the precious metals that go with it, turn out to be a snare for the Israelites in the wilderness, one of which they must rid themselves. The addition of the P material that describes the construction of the tabernacle in Exodus 35–40 provides a different solution for the final form of the Pentateuch, since this is the only logical source in the narrative for the materials necessary for making the implements of worship for the tent-sanctuary. The result of the combination of these traditions is a tension-filled text concerning questions about whether Israel can or should enrich itself with the wealth of an imperial city. Perhaps they are not tempted to take it at all, but it is freely given to them. Perhaps they take it and it ends up bringing them trouble, but maybe it can be put to proper use with careful divine instruction. A similar problem will appear concerning the wealth of the cities in Canaan in Joshua. Even the most severe form of the Holy War traditions, the ban, cannot dispose of the metal objects, which must be carefully safeguarded into the treasury of YHWH (Josh. 6:19). Once the battle of Jericho and its aftermath have passed, however, this issue looks forgotten in Joshua.

The story of the monarchy presents a complicated picture of relations with Egypt. First Kings 3–11 reports extensive connections between Solomon and Egypt, but 1 Kings 14:25–26 reports conflict between Solomon's son Rehoboam and Shishak, the king of Egypt. At about the same time, Egypt appears to have provided refuge or asylum for Jeroboam, son of Nebat, when he was in conflict with Solomon and Rehoboam. Near the end of the monarchy, King Josiah of Judah dies in battle with the Egyptian pharaoh Neco (2 Kgs. 23:28–30), and Neco installs Josiah's son, Eliakim, as his own puppet king in Judah (23:34). While the story of the monarchy may include elements of a positive relationship between Israel and Egypt, the story ends in conflict. Nevertheless, during the many Babylonian incursions and invasions, Egypt offers a place of refuge to some Judahites who flee Jerusalem (25:26), and from the sixth century on there seem to have been significant Jewish communities living in Egypt in places like Elephantine and Alexandria. The full historical veracity of all of these accounts is not the important issue, but rather that they combine to produce a picture of Egypt that varies in perspective. Egypt can be enemy or ally, place of refuge or captivity. This variegated view during a period when the materials in the Torah were developing is projected back onto the story of Israel living in and escaping from Egypt. Theodore Hiebert has argued that the view of Egypt in the J material is particularly complicated, consisting of negative and positive perspectives. Further, he has demonstrated that the portrayal of Egypt during the sojourn of the Israelites there in Genesis and Exodus sometimes reflects agricultural traditions in the hill country of Canaan.[11] Traditions in the Pentateuch address political tensions over multiple centuries. The issues at play include agriculture and its relation to royal power. The ancestors display a way of life that includes both cultivation and herding, and they must maneuver among the powers centered in cities and empires in order to succeed in this way of life. The view of the finished text seems to be that neither a rigid antagonism nor a naive dependence is adequate to the situation. The ancestors, like Israel in later times, could benefit from the favor of empires, but the relationship was always risky.

A series of texts that reflects a desire to return to Egypt receives more attention below, because they appear within the wilderness narratives. At this point, one question about these passages deserves some consideration. They are currently embedded in contexts that use them to exemplify Israelite disobedience or lack of faith in the wilderness. The persons giving voice to such sentiments appear as foils for Moses. Given the mixed sentiments about Egypt that persist for so long in the story of Israel, is it possible they originated in a genuine tradition that urged better relations with Egypt, including the possibility of Israelites relocating there, like some of the great ancestors did in times of difficulty? If so, the current text has reformulated the sayings as part of an argument against looking to Egypt for safety or protection, one that may have been useful at later times both to dissuade persons considering flight to Egypt and to express opposition to communities already established there.

In light of this complex mixture of traditions about Egypt and their particular uses at various places in the text, Israel Finkelstein has offered a plausible model for the development of the exodus tradition based on "long-term cultural memory." These memories could have begun with the conflicts between Canaan and Egypt in the second millennium, and spread among northern Israelites, where the exodus tradition became one of the two founding narratives, along with the collection of stories about Jacob, the eponymous ancestor. Later events, particularly the reassertion of Egyptian power in the Levant in the seventh century, as Assyria declined, further shaped the exodus tradition. Priestly scribes with little knowledge of the desert regions of the wandering tradition performed the final redaction of the Torah during the Persian period. This long, convoluted process is part of what served to obscure locations and create such an unwieldy plot.[12] This model fits with the general idea that the exodus story addresses social and political issues of later periods.

The previous chapter discussed the problem of Joseph's Egyptian identity, and pointed toward similar issues for Moses. Moses is a disputed figure, one for whom, like the exodus story, there is no evidence outside the biblical text. The Egyptian identity of Moses makes the later development of such a character unconnected to any ancient traditions seem unlikely, because this identity presents a serious inconvenience for the writer. Joseph had begun his life like all great Israelites, as a shepherd, but circumstances turned him into an influential Egyptian official, one with power over many lives, including his own family members fleeing the famine in Canaan. The lack of concern over this transformation in Genesis is curious, but the book of Exodus is not so complacent about the identity of Moses. Exodus 2 does not hide Moses' Egyptian identity, but encloses it within a Hebrew identity at the beginning and end of the chapter. The story of Moses' birth appears to have been developed from the similar story of the birth of Sargon.[13] The most important thing it provides for Moses in terms of identity is a Hebrew explanation for his apparently Egyptian name. When the fugitive Moses arrives in Midian and helps the daughters of the priest, they identify him to their father as "an Egyptian," but to readers of Genesis he is already beginning to look familiar. Moses flees Egypt because a family member seeks to kill him, and he arrives at a well and helps a group of young women water their sheep. The resemblance to Jacob continues to build when the father of the women invites Moses to eat, he marries the oldest daughter, and he begins tending the father-in-law's sheep. In a few short verses at the end of Exodus 2 Moses is converted from an Egyptian into a Hebrew, and not just any Hebrew, but the ultimate Israelite and the father of Joseph, whose identity had moved in the other direction. The effectiveness of this transformation may be questionable, though. Joseph's half-Egyptian children can be prominent in Israelite tradition, but Moses' children are nearly erased from memory. The two named sons, Gershom and Eliezer, disappear from the Torah after Exodus 18, and Moses seems to adopt Joshua in Numbers 16:13 in the process of making Joshua his successor. There are only fleeting references to Gershom and Eliezer in Judges 18 and 1 Chronicles 23, and these names appear elsewhere as sons of Levi and Aaron, respectively. The vanishing lineage of Moses may be further indication that the tradition was uncertain what to do with the Moses character. While a divine commission assures his place among the Israelites, his two wives were a Midianite and a Cushite.

Long ago in Genesis, the plot of the exodus had appeared in miniature in the story of Abram and Sarai in Egypt. Plagues saved Abram from death and Sarai from captivity, and the ancestral couple departed Egypt with material wealth. In closer proximity the story of Moses looks similar. Fleeing Pharaoh he finds his way to a prosperous life and eventually to Horeb/Sinai and an encounter with YHWH. Escaping the clutches of imperial, urban power becomes a recurring theme. This recurrence came up in the discussion of the despoiling tradition above, but merits some further attention on its own. It is easy and common to say that the return of the Israelites from exile looks like a second exodus, and there are biblical texts that seem to look at it that way. Psalm 106 contains a large quantity of references to the exodus and wilderness stories. The conclusion of the poem in 106:47 and its position in the book of Psalms, however, make it look like far more than a recollection of YHWH's saving acts in the distant past.

> Save us, O LORD our God,
>   and gather us from among the nations,
> that we may give thanks to your holy name
>   and glory in your praise.

Being swallowed up by the nations is a perennial threat for Israel, and perhaps some things may be clearer if we look at the exodus story as a retelling of the exile in the past. Postcolonial interpretations of history may include the identification of "metanarratives," the stories empires tell about themselves and attempt to force their subjects to embody. A successful imperial metanarrative causes subjugated people to accept the superiority of the empire.[14] As Leo Perdue observed, "The [Babylonian] metanarrative includes the religious contention that Babylonia is the center of the world and is protected by the high pantheon of gods, especially Marduk, whose temple, the Esagila, was located in the capital city of Babylon. Marduk, as the head of the Babylonian pantheon, chooses the ruling monarchs and oversees their rule."[15] Successful resistance to the empire requires a more powerful narrative. When

Deuteronomy is added onto the Pentateuch, it creates a plot in which the Israelites are escaping to another city, "the place where I shall cause my name to dwell," one that rivals Babylon in its claim to centrality. Does this claim overwhelm the promise of land and a way of life like the great ancestors had? The discussion of the wilderness narratives later in this chapter will reveal that they are a mixture of competing traditions. In the Priestly wilderness story the Israelites move through the wilderness in ordered fashion, gathered around a central sanctuary like a city moving through the desert. Even in such a desolate place their way of existence imitates their eventual life in and around Jerusalem. Another tradition, the J source, shows a beleaguered group, struggling to survive in harsh conditions and to find its way into the fertile land of the central hill country, where they may emulate the lives of the great ancestors. This tradition presents a potential metanarrative that does not involve a replacement city. There is an alternative to the centralization of empire, according to the J source.

It is difficult to say to what extent the ancient Egyptian understanding of cities influenced the Israelite understandings presented in the biblical tradition. Carolyn Routledge has presented evidence of two different patterns of urban development in ancient Egypt. Amarna represented a distinct pattern, and the collection of letters found there from the middle of the second millennium establishes that there was significant contact between this city and Late Bronze Age Canaan. Amarna was not the norm, however, because it was a deliberate city built all at once, where none had previously existed. The design feature that made Amarna distinct was a single temple at its center. This fit the religious reforms of its designer and builder, Akhenaten.[16] The more common type of city, exemplified by Per-Ramesses, was square with four quadrants, each with a temple at its center. This still means that temples were at the core of urban planning, with processional pathways between palace and temple(s). The relationship between king, deity, and temple was built into the idea and structure of a city.[17] The Israelite traditions in the Bible reflect a diversity of views on this matter. Kings, priests, and prophets are often in conflict about control of resources and institutions. The ancient Israelites maintained many traditions about their origins and wove a wide variety of them together into their national stories, a couple of versions of which ended up in the Bible. The connections to Egypt likely helped to form some of these traditions, in which they sometimes imitated and sometimes resisted the ancient empire. The story of Solomon's building projects and his establishment of urban institutions in 1 Kings 4–10 contains extensive recollections of foreign interaction, influence, and assistance, a matter that will receive more attention in the next chapter.

The exodus story in the Bible was eventually combined with a massive collection of legal material, which provides further insight into how the Israelites viewed and addressed the urbanization of their society. Though these legal texts arose over a long period of time, their placement links them to the experience of escape from slavery in Egypt. The society these laws attempt to define is juxtaposed to the Egyptian one from which the audience inside the text has just escaped. The cognitive dissonance can be overwhelming for modern readers. Perhaps the most jarring conflict is the presence of laws regulating slavery woven into a story of a group escaping from slavery. Less obvious are the assumptions about urban life present in a story about a group fleeing an oppressive urban existence.

CITIES AND THE LEGAL MATERIAL

The legal material in the Torah enters the discussion in this book at several points. Legal texts are a part of the survey of references to cities in chapter 1 that seeks a definition of "city." The discussion of war traditions in relation to conquered cities in the next chapter will require some attention to legal texts in the Torah. This chapter provides a place to look at the legal material more comprehensively, within its wilderness narrative contexts, and to ask what its assumptions about urban life seem to be. In many cases the legal texts seem so completely out of place that the wilderness cannot be their presumed setting. How the laws understand and reveal, or conceal, their contexts is a vital issue in this section, and the following section on the wilderness narrative develops it further. The Priestly wilderness story in particular constructs an artificial environment in the wilderness that resembles a city and makes the practice of the law possible there.

While there are some earlier texts that qualify as legal material, such as the Passover legislation in Exodus 12–13 and the Sabbath regulations for collecting manna in Exodus 16, the first sustained section of laws in the Torah is the Ten Commandments in Exodus 20 and the text often called the Covenant Code in the three following chapters. The Decalogue is almost entirely free from any assumptions about particular ways of life or social organization. It assumes that people live within reasonable proximity to each other so that the kinds of acts it forbids in 20:13–17 might be a problem, but this applies to many kinds of settings. The Covenant Code material in 21:10–23:19 has a decidedly rural tone. Many of the laws deal with the keeping of livestock and the cultivation of crops, including grain and grapes. The combination of settled agriculture and animal herding fit what appear to be the origins of the Israelites in the land of Canaan. Only occasionally does a greater level of societal organization come into view.

The placement of Exodus 20:22–26 is a matter of some dispute. It is a legal text concerning the building of altars that follows immediately after the closing narrative framework of the Ten Commandments, but the introductory formula in 21:1 separates it from the Covenant Code. The text is important here because it envisions religious shrines. YHWH instructs Moses concerning "every place where I cause my name to be remembered." The sequence of instructions about constructing shrines looks like an expansion or explication of the command against worshiping idols at the beginning of the Decalogue. One of its concerns is about the possibility that stone altars might take on a shape that would allow them to function as idols: therefore, it permits no chiseling of the stones used to build altars. Another concern is the building of structures around altars that might serve as settings for sexual activity related to fertility rites.[18] The details of how such worship activity might have functioned are not of great significance here, but the recognition that Israel will have religious shrines points toward the eventual concentration of population at such places. Though 20:22–26 may appear to be a fragment of independent origin, the need for such a text becomes apparent near the end of the Covenant Code, when a festival calendar appears at 23:14–19. The calendar delineates three festivals each year and requires all males to "appear before the Lord GoD." The instructions in verses 18–19 require both an altar on which to offer sacrifices and a structure called "the house of the LORD your God" in which grain offerings could be stored. Unlike Deuteronomy, this part of Exodus does not insist that there be only one place where Israelites travel for these kinds of worship activities; but it does envision a limited number of such sanctuaries, and sanctuaries both require and create societal organization. Recall that the ancestors in Genesis visited many of the places that would later become Israelite shrines and built altars there. The previous chapter observed that in these simple stories no human settlements were visible around these sites. This is not a situation that could exist at an actual cultic site outside the text. Readers or hearers of the Torah familiar with these places would have had an idea of them as populated settlements.

The Covenant Code stipulates one other type of special place, one to which a person accused of murder might flee for protection while the case is adjudicated (21:13). Later developments in Numbers 35 and Deuteronomy 19 use the term "cities of refuge" for such places and attempt to delineate their number and relative locations, but the version in Exodus 21 is much simpler and does not define the place explicitly as a city. It is easier to imagine a judicial procedure in a more urbanized setting, as is the case in the instructions of Deuteronomy 19, but Exodus 21 provides no such detail. The practice of protecting a person under these circumstances would have required some resources. A walled city that could provide protection from anyone seeking revenge would make a more logical setting for the process.

One other place where a higher level of social organization appears in the Covenant Code is in the judicial instructions in 23:6–8, but the wording is ambiguous. The initial instructions in verses 6–7 might fit within an informal system of justice, but the statement against bribes in verse 8 may assume a more formal one. The NRSV rendering of "officials" is unwarranted, though. The statement is literally "a bribe blinds those who see clearly." The second-person address in verse 8 is odd. While it follows the pattern present throughout the Covenant Code, second-person-masculine-singular address, the instructions around it make sense addressed to everyone. The narrative presumption of the Torah is that YHWH is always speaking to or through Moses. If the assumed context in verse 8 is a more developed legal system, then those instructed not to take bribes would not be the general population of Israel, and this is where the NRSV seems to be going with "officials." If, on the other hand, those rendering judgment could be members of the general population, such as the elders that Boaz gathers at the gate in Ruth 4, then this command could still fit an informal system.

Based on the evaluation above, the Covenant Code fits best within a nonurban setting, though the presumed development of sanctuary sites would produce a momentum toward urbanization, as would prove to be the case later in the story of Israel. The Covenant Code is commonly associated with the E source, though it is possible that it existed independently before its use in E.[19] The close connections between it and the Code of Hammurabi have been well documented, but two differences may be worth noting.[20] First, the Code of Hammurabi describes its own urban setting. In the epilogue the king declares that he has inscribed his laws on a stela and placed it in the city of Babylon. The setting could hardly be more different than in Exodus where the law is delivered to a shepherd leading a group of people wandering in the wilderness. Second, some of the laws in the Code of Hammurabi, for example most of 200–240, address a society that is significantly organized, specialized, and stratified, and these are not among the close parallels in Exodus 21–23. If the process that produced the Covenant Code used the Code of Hammurabi selectively, then it looks as if laws that would have fit a more highly organized urban culture did not make it through the process. At the same time, though, if the Code of Hammurabi was developed for a more urbanized culture, the removal of just the texts that betray such a setting overtly would not remove that setting's influence on the whole collection.

A set of laws typically assigned to the J source appears in Exodus 34:14–26. It is this collection, not the one traditionally labelled "the Ten Commandments," that is accompanied by a count of ten and a command to write them on tablets

(34:27–28). The first law in this list is an expanded form of the command not to worship other gods and the command against making idols follows it. After that, however, the list departs from expectations that may be created by the traditional Ten Commandments in Exodus 20. The only other law from Exodus 20 also present in Exodus 34 is the one concerning Sabbath, and it seems almost hidden among lengthier descriptions of the festivals of Unleavened Bread, Weeks, and Gathering. The festival descriptions highlight the presumed setting of this legal code, one that is agricultural, defined by the cycle of planting and harvest. The command concerning offerings in verses 19–20 presumes that the audience also keeps livestock. Even the brief Sabbath command in verse 21, which makes no reference to the order of creation, stresses that this is a pause in agricultural work that Israelites should observe even during the most intense periods of that cycle—plowing and harvest. As Hiebert has concluded about this set of laws, "In the details of these regulations can be seen the mixed agricultural economy reflected elsewhere in J's southern narratives and indeed in the epic as a whole."[21] The structure of the Torah, however, places these laws immediately before the building of the tabernacle, perhaps obscuring the setting 34:14–26 presumes.

One of the features that most clearly characterizes cities is designed public space. Daniel Sperber's *The City in Roman Palestine* addresses urban space in a period later than the focus of this work, but is still helpful. Sperber begins his analysis with a discussion of the market area, the center of urban experience. The movement of his book is then from center to periphery, dealing with walls at the end. The idea of a center in an ancient Israelite city would not have been a market but a shrine or sanctuary, though there could have been overlap between the two. The idea of designed public space comes into clear view in the Torah with the construction of the tabernacle in Exodus.[22] The nature of this tradition is unique because the book of Exodus treats it twice. The divine instructions to Moses in Exodus 25–30 are repeated as a narration of construction in Exodus 36–40. Within the book of Exodus the duplicate texts may be intended to surround the golden calf episode in Exodus 32–34. The ultimate experience of improper worship is contained by presentations of proper worship. Another effect of the repetition, though, is to emphasize the sense of planning. The most important component in terms of designed public space is the courtyard, described by YHWH in 27:9–19, and constructed under Moses' supervision in 38:9–20. The court is a one-hundred-cubit-by-fifty-cubit rectangle, defined by pillars with linen hangings attached. The tent with the altar in front of it sits within the court. The last thing Moses does in 40:33 is put up the screen that covers the entrance to the court. This is the act that finishes the tabernacle work. The tabernacle is a reflection of the temple, of course, and it is important to look at several characteristics it possesses. It requires a community both to build and maintain the tabernacle, so there is a permanent population presumed around it. Even if the tabernacle was an entirely imagined space, the community around it would have been part of that imaginative act and a vital component of what the authors of these texts claimed a space for worship should be. As Mark George explains,

> The tabernacle narratives are primarily mental space. They must be, because they are written accounts of the tabernacle, not the physical structure itself. But the mental space of the tabernacle narratives is not sealed off or separate from its physical space. It is related to physical space because it effects itself in, and on, physical, material space. The ideas a society has about space shape the ways in which it will interact with and alter the natural world.[23]

The text also assumes a population that needs access to the tabernacle for performing acts of worship, but that access requires some sense of control. There is something from which the court must be separated, hence the curtain. The building of the tabernacle in Exodus presents a designed space like a city that has an inside and an outside. The following section demonstrates that the enactment of laws in the P wilderness narrative requires a delineated space "outside the camp," so the tabernacle lies at the center of a sequence of layered spaces.

The idea of a center and a periphery is present in the portrayal of God in biblical texts, and is something ancient Israel seems to have taken from its larger cultural context.[24] When YHWH comes down off of Mount Sinai at the end of Exodus and inhabits the tabernacle, it becomes central for the remainder of the Sinai pericope. As the Israelites move through the wilderness beginning at Numbers 10, the tabernacle reasserts itself as the center of the community every time they stop. In the biblical narrative, the tabernacle is the precursor of stationary shrines or sanctuaries in Israel, beginning with Shiloh and ending with Jerusalem, so it is a precursor to Israelite cities. Historically, it is more likely that the tabernacle is a projection of the Jerusalem temple back into the distant past and Israel's wilderness experience. Perhaps the most important ideological point is that the enslaved Israelites who had been building cities for Pharaoh in Egypt have become free Israelites building a dwelling for YHWH, even if the setting for the structure and the structure itself are odd and temporary. The next section of this chapter explores the wilderness narratives, including the Priestly portrayal of the tabernacle as a city moving through the wilderness.

It is difficult to gain a precise perspective of setting from the description of the use of the sanctuary in Leviticus 1–7 for at least two reasons. First, when any reference to setting appears it is still connected to the wilderness environment, which is an unnatural place for such a sanctuary. When the community disposes of the parts of a bull not used in a sin offering (skin, head, legs, entrails, and dung), they are to take them to a place "outside the camp" and burn them (4:12). The instructions for sacrifices end with a reminder in 7:38 that this is "in the wilderness of Sinai." The depiction of the Day of Atonement ritual in Leviticus 16 is similar. The observers are in "the camp," and just outside is the wilderness. What little delineation of space is present is difficult to apply to a city and a sanctuary within it, but the presence of an inside and an outside is essential to the story. Second, the abstract distinction of holiness is another reason for the paucity of references to space. Samuel Balentine has demonstrated that the Torah, including Leviticus, is concerned with distinguishing the boundaries between the common and the holy, and the sanctuary allows the divine presence to exist in safe separation from impurity.[25] Leviticus 1–7 addresses this issue, however, with a remarkable absence of the physical aspects of such boundaries. Finally, the purpose of these texts seems to be something other than providing instructions to be followed by the persons conducting the rituals. James Watts has argued that the primary purpose is rhetorical. The texts show signs of being shaped for oral recitation, the purpose of which was to convince the hearers of the centrality of the rituals. Such a purpose might have made a precise sense of space less important. The placement of the rituals in the Israelite camp, under the supervision of Moses and Aaron at the foot of Mount Sinai, would have added to the persuasive authority of the texts.[26] Another step further might be the conclusion that such texts are not meant to be instructional at all, but to replace the sacrificial ritual. In contexts where readers would have had no access to sacrificial ritual, in the diaspora or in Jerusalem without a temple for performance, reading and hearing the texts could have functioned as a replacement. The compilation of texts about worship makes little sense without the image of a temple. The structure that later sat in the center of Jerusalem is projected back into the wilderness. In similar fashion, it is projected forward into diaspora settings through the use of texts in places where the physical performance of sacred rituals was impossible.

The vague sense of place present in much of the legal material comes into greater focus in Deuteronomy. The Deuteronomic Code in 12–26 reminds readers multiple times that YHWH has chosen a particular place as a "dwelling for his name." In 12:1–10 and 14:22–23 the Israelites are to bring all of their offerings to this place, which assumes a considerable system prepared for receiving them. The latter text is followed by additional instructions for those who live so far from the central sanctuary that transporting their produce and livestock is impractical. They are to sell their produce for money before traveling, then use the money to purchase similar products for the ritual meal after they arrive, making sure to provide a suitable portion for the Levites. Here is a place where the overlap between temple and marketplace mentioned above seems like a necessity. Deuteronomy 16:1–8 adapts Passover into a pilgrimage festival that requires Israelites to travel to the central sanctuary for the seven-day observance. These kinds of adjustments to the law assume a highly developed urban society around the central sanctuary. The tension between the urban settings presumed by much of the legal material and the wilderness setting in which the traditions are received in the narrative of the Pentateuch requires a closer examination of the wilderness setting and how the various traditions about the wilderness are connected to the settings to which the Israelites are traveling.

LIVING IN THE WILDERNESS

The organization of the Israelite camp in the book of Numbers absorbs a great deal of attention. The level of detail in Numbers 1–2 can be overwhelming. Even if a group of escaped slaves from Egypt originated the tradition that led to this part of the Torah, the organization of the tribes in the wilderness seems to have more to do with the lives of the audience than with how those wanderers would have organized themselves. The texts about the camp and the tent of meeting come from the Priestly source, so the ordering of the worship space at the center makes sense. Theodore Hiebert has proposed a very different view of the wilderness environment in the J materials in Numbers. In J texts, the Israelites are not at home in wilderness settings, as nomadic herders would be, but the wilderness is a place of divine punishment, where their lives are constantly in danger. The Israelites are on the move from one place of settled agriculture, the Nile delta in Egypt, to another, the central hill country of Canaan. The J story of the spies in 13:17–24 is particularly concerned with the suitability of the land for growing grapes. For the J tradition the conditions in the desert are the starkest contrast to the kind of land where they are headed and where their way of life fits.[27] The tensions between the views of life expressed in the wilderness settings merit close attention.

There are many reasons why the wilderness narrative in Numbers 10–21 is difficult to follow.[28] First, as noted above, Finkelstein has suggested that the final redactors of the Torah were likely unfamiliar with the geographical settings of the southern desert.[29] Second, the bulk of this part of the text consists of wilderness stories somewhat different in form that have had imposed upon them a repeated pattern of human complaint, divine anger, Moses' intervention, and divine response. A final reason is that the book of

Numbers is a combination of sources, each looking at the wilderness, and the Israelites within it, from a different perspective and presenting their narratives for different purposes. In quantity, P dominates the section, providing just over half of the material, but without the long legal sections in chapters 15, 18, and 19 it is close to the length of the other two collections. Recent work by Joel Baden in particular has convincingly moved more of the non-priestly material into the E source, giving it about 30 percent of the section compared to J's 20 percent. The discussion of the three different wilderness narratives below relies upon a fairly precise identification of the texts from each source, which is provided in the table in appendix 4.

Reading Numbers from the beginning also provides P with additional influence. About 90 percent of the first ten chapters come from P. The materials related to the census and the arrangement of the encampment stamp P's sense of order onto the book at the beginning. Two of the more important efforts to describe the literary structure of Numbers help to illustrate the tension present in the framework of the text. Jacob Milgrom has outlined Numbers as alternating sections of law and narrative, with six of the former, including the first and last sections, and five of the latter. Milgrom's scheme places long legal sections, 1:1–10:10 and 33:50–36:13, at the beginning and end of the book and places the narratives within the resulting legal framework.[30] In this scheme the presentation of law is the primary enterprise. Mary Douglas produced a very different scheme, with seven "story" sections, including the opening and closing of the book, and six sections of law placed within the story framework. One of the major differences between these two ideas is Douglas's identification of most of the P material in the first ten chapters, Numbers 1–4 and 7–9, as story.[31] This way of thinking about the book lends itself more readily to seeing the P material that appears in Numbers 10–21 as a continuation of that story. P is telling a story about the wilderness from the beginning of the book of Numbers to the end, and about half of the material in Numbers 10–21 participates in this story. This provides a different way of viewing the book of Numbers and the Priestly material within it.

The journey in the wilderness, as told by P, is an ordered story that continues the initial establishment of that order at the foot of Mount Sinai. The legal texts within Numbers 10–21 presume this order, as those in Numbers 1–10 did, though some adjustments are necessary. The section that begins in 5:2, for example, opens with "Command the Israelites to put out of the camp everyone who is leprous, or has a discharge, and everyone who is unclean through contact with a corpse. . . ." The fulfillment of such a command presumes a clear delineation of boundaries between the inside and outside of the camp, and the law itself is worded for life in the camp. The collection of laws in Numbers 15 refers to a different setting. The introductions in verse

2 and verse 15 say, "When you come into the land . . . ," but the story in 15:32–36 about the man gathering wood on the Sabbath demonstrates the enforcement of 15:22–31 while the Israelites are still in the wilderness. The conclusion of the story in verse 36 describes the site of the man's execution as "outside the camp." The regulations about gifts and offerings and the rights and responsibilities of priests in 18:8–32 sometimes presume a setting in which the Israelites are already settled in the land. The offerings in verses 27–30, for example, come from the threshing floor and the winepress. The introductory story of the testing of the staffs in Numbers 17, however, which establishes the rights of Aaron's tribe and descendants as priests, is set in the wilderness, with the tent of meeting as the sight of the action. The tent of meeting also makes appearances within the legal text at verse 23 and verse 31. The instructions for killing the red heifer to produce ashes for purification in 19:1–13 are specifically written for a wilderness setting, with references to the outside of the camp at verse 3 and verse 9, and the tent of meeting at verse 4. The law has a perpetual nature, as verse 10 and verse 21 state, but its origins are placed in the wilderness, and there is no distinction between the ability to practice the ceremony and the acts of purification it makes possible in the wilderness or in the land. There is no difference between the ability to live according to the law in the wilderness, around the tabernacle, and in Jerusalem, around the temple. Mark George has demonstrated the relationship between a description of space inside a text and the understanding of space and "spatial practice" outside the text:

> Spatial practice involves manipulating and altering physical reality and physical space in order to effect and implement a society's ideas about space. As such, spatial practice is performed space, in the sense of actions that must be taken to create it. Human action is required as part of spatial practice, both initially and (repeatedly) thereafter, in order for a society's ideas about space to be realized.[32]

Regardless of the degree to which such descriptions of space match particular spaces outside the text, they express the way the writers and audience thought spaces should be. It would make sense that they would have sought to make real spaces match their understanding, but there are always constraints in the construction of real spaces, whether they involve lack of resources or opposing understandings.

Baruch Levine has proposed that the legislation in Numbers 19 was generated by concerns about the establishment of cults of the dead during the Josianic reform.[33] Even if this proposal or some other like it is correct, the projection of such a concern back into the wilderness period, by placing the texts within Numbers 1–21, supports the sense that P builds a space in the wilderness that corresponds to Jerusalem and the temple. The combination of legal and narrative texts serves that goal, and the P wilderness story speaks to a very specific way of life in the Israel of its future, one situated in the urban center of Jerusalem with the temple at its center. If it is easy for readers to find all of the P material in Numbers to be an impractical, even impossible, way for a band of fugitive slaves to move through the wilderness, that is because its intent is something quite different. The order that comes from YHWH on Mount Sinai is enacted in the wilderness for forty years and, in the process, carried to Zion. Both the legislation and the structure are continuous from mountain to mountain.[34] The story of Sinai and Zion moves in both directions. The Torah looks forward to the establishment of Jerusalem, and its writers look backward to support a vision of Jerusalem in their own time.

The Yahwist's portrait of the wilderness is harsh and forbidding. In Numbers 10:29–32 Moses must bargain hard to convince Hobab to stay with the Israelites to guide them through the alien landscape. Hardship arises immediately upon the departure from Sinai in Numbers 11. The description of the manna, which differs starkly from P's description in Exodus 16, is also in contrast with their fond memories of the agricultural production in the Nile delta they left behind in Egypt. Though the J fragment in Exodus 16:4–5 describes "bread from heaven," YHWH gives it there as a test of the Israelites' willingness to observe the Sabbath. In Numbers 11 the manna sounds like a food source available in the wilderness that requires extensive labor to make it edible, and which produces a monotonous diet. The quails provide a more attractive food source, but they are not natural to this environment. God must send them there with a strong wind, and a plague accompanies eating them. These depictions fit a general pattern in which Numbers texts are more negative than similar ones in Exodus. One element adding to the negativity in both books is the desire to return to Egypt. Thomas Römer has argued that these "Egypt nostalgia" texts (see Exod. 14:11–12; 16:3; and 17:3; and Num. 11:18–20; 14:2–4; 16:12–14; and 20:2–5) are more at home in the book of Numbers, while the examples in Exodus look more like later interpolations. Some of the negativity that goes with the Numbers traditions has seeped into those in Exodus.[35] Egypt seems to serve, at once, as both a temptation and a model of a place that provides what the Israelites need to survive. The duality of these two aspects of Egypt resembles the duality of Egypt in the lives of the ancestors as demonstrated in the previous chapter. An earlier section proposed the possibility that the Egypt texts represent a real tradition, from a time in Israel's history when migration to Egypt was an option that some were taking. These statements could have existed as a positive proposal, before they were co-opted by the exodus narrative as foils for Moses. This move allows Moses to condemn any future thoughts of a return to Egypt, including those in the time of the writers.

The quail story in J is followed by the account of the spies. The spies go into the hill country in Numbers 13 and report back on the excellent fertility of the land there, but most of them are overwhelmed by the size of the people in Canaan and the fortifications of its cities. Agriculture is the positive aspect of the spy report and cities are the negative. The latter impedes the free practice of the former. When YHWH threatens but forgives them after the dispute among the spies, they travel into the hill country to take possession of it, but the Canaanites and Amalekites defeat them. In response to their setbacks the Israelites make a vow in 21:2 that in return for YHWH's help defeating these people in the future they will "utterly destroy their cities." The Israelites recognize, based on the spy report, that they will need divine assistance to defeat a more powerful foe. The cost of the divine help will be the loss of resources that results from the total destruction of the cities, but they are willing to pay it. They will trade cities for fertile land. The place to which the Israelites are headed in J is the hill country of Canaan, where they will destroy the cities and live the agrarian lifestyle promoted throughout the J narrative.

The differing geographical perspectives of the three sources are revealed in part by the places to which each of them refer. A complete list for each source is in appendix 5. The wilderness is the opposite of the agrarian setting the J source presumes, and the Israelites travel through it as a punishment for the lack of faith demonstrated in the spy story. Hiebert has carefully connected J's portrayal of the wilderness with that source's depiction of the promised land in other J texts. The practice of mixed agriculture by the ancestors in Canaan, the Israelites while in captivity in Goshen, and in their projected future in the central hill country form a line of development for which the wilderness is an interruption. The J spy story in Numbers 13:17–33 even contains an etiological story explaining the naming of the Wadi Eshcol that is agricultural in nature.[36] The Israelites in this source want to settle in fertile land and grow crops, a desire reflected in the names they give to places and stories they tell about them. The J material in Numbers 10–21 portrays the wilderness as a dangerous setting, which is the opposite of the place where this group of people naturally fits. In Hiebert's words Israel's behavior "does not give evidence of a people whose attitudes and values are shaped by the contours of the wilderness environment. The picture is just the opposite: J's narratives depict the desert as an alien and frightful place. Throughout, these stories reflect details and attitudes deriving from the sedentary agricultural society that typified biblical Israel and of which the Yahwist was a member."[37] J makes no attempt, like P does, to reconstruct an environment in the wilderness that corresponds in important ways to the environment of its audience. The "forty years in the wilderness" motif is absent from J. It appears eight times in the

Pentateuch, four in Deuteronomy and four in Priestly texts (one in Exodus and three in Numbers). The J wilderness story could easily take place within a few weeks or months. The city the Israelites construct in the wilderness in P is permanently sustainable. There is no hurry to reach the promised land. To the contrary, they must slow down, because humans can live a normal life span in this environment and it will take forty years for the old generation to die off completely. The city does not need fertile land to support itself, but can survive on the divine provision of food. If the wilderness camp, with the tabernacle at its center, is Jerusalem projected back into the exodus story, what can this analog to the divine provision of food be? The only possibility is the collection of resources that flowed into Jerusalem because of its identity as the nation's central worship site.

The E narrative does not present as negative a picture of the wilderness as J does. YHWH sends an angel to guide the Israelites through the area, and the overwhelming issue in the E collection is the series of disputes about human leadership. There is a tent of meeting in E, but it sits outside the camp. The orderly pattern presented in Exodus 33, where all the Israelites stand by their tents to observe Moses as he goes out to the tent of meeting, is challenged during the wilderness adventures. The task of leadership overwhelms Moses immediately in Numbers 11 and he asks for help. The story is very specific at 11:25 that the elders who receive some of Moses' spirit and assist him in leadership are limited in their practice of prophesying, a task unique to Moses. The E wilderness narrative is dealing with different issues, ones that involve the relation between the center and the periphery. The primary Israelite geography in this source is the trans-Jordan territory, a place that would end up on the periphery of Israel, so these spatial arrangements and the issues they raise about centralized and shared leadership fit the source. The relation between peripheral and centralized power is complex and requires continuous acts of negotiation.

Most of the material in Numbers after the Balaam narratives in 22–24 is from P. The primary remaining exception is the negotiation between Moses and the Reubenites and Gadites concerning the trans-Jordan territory, which is mixed with P material in Numbers 32. The story describes the trans-Jordan tribes as cattle-herders, attracted by the quality of the grazing land east of the river, an allotment they receive upon promising to cross with the other tribes to fight for the land on the west side first. It seems to assume the conquest of the trans-Jordan area described in the E portions of 21:21–33.[38] The text of Numbers 32 in its current form, however, has several areas of incoherence, which invite the possibility of identifying more than one story. The task has been taken up most rigorously by Liane Marquis, who has reconstructed two stories of the trans-Jordan tribes in Numbers 32 and assigned them to the E and P sources.[39] As usual, two general sets of criteria should apply to any such solution. First, does the division produce separate stories that are each internally coherent, or at least substantially more coherent than the present text that combines them? Second, do the reconstructed stories fit the material typically assigned to that source that comes before and after them? Marquis's proposal satisfies these criteria well, with the exception of 32:7–15. These verses present a notorious difficulty because they combine elements peculiar everywhere else to one particular source. For example, other than in Numbers 32:8, only Deuteronomy refers to the setting of the spy story as "Kadesh-barnea," and only the J source contains the tradition of the spies visiting the Wadi Eshcol. Further, the sudden, explosive anger of Moses in this passage disrupts the story and does not fit the careful deliberation with which he leads in the rest of the chapter. The decision by Marquis to remove these verses from the subsequent source division, and treat them as a later insertion for a writer only aware of the Pentateuch in its combined form, is prudent and effective. The result is that the remaining text falls into two distinctive stories.[40]

The story that comes from the E source continues the trans-Jordan conquest of Numbers 21. The territory, including cities and towns, that the Israelites take from kings Sihon and Og become the inheritance of the tribes of Reuben and Gad. In return, the members of these two tribes promise to lead the Israelite tribes across the Jordan and secure the possessions of all the other tribes before returning to the east side. The tribe of Manasseh extends the trans-Jordan conquest into Gilead in 32:29, and Moses gives them this land as their inheritance. In this story the trans-Jordan tribes fit naturally into the place, as the Amorites had before them. They are able to herd their cattle and live in the same cities and towns as the people from whom they had taken the land. There is no sense of anything on the west side of the river being essential to their existence or identity as Israelites. This story would appear to mark the end of the E narrative, with greater emphasis on the settlement of the land on the east side of the Jordan River and the role of Moses in installing the tribes of Reuben, Gad, and Manasseh there. In the P story, the Gadites and Reubenites negotiate not just with Moses, but also with Eleazer the High Priest and leaders from the other tribes. Crossing the Jordan with the other tribes is not part of their original offer, but a concession Moses extracts from them. Their agreement to fight along with the Israelites is consistent with the marching formation from the P source in Numbers 2–4, and this story thus presumes the tribes to be moving into the promised land organized around the tabernacle.[41] The presence of Eleazer in this text is a reminder of the centrality of Israel's official religious institutions at every point in its movement from Sinai forward. The P account of the trans-Jordan tribes follows the story of the war with Midian from the same source that fills Numbers 31. This highlights one of the major differences from the E story and its presumption of cultural continuity. Numbers 32:16–24 asserts that the trans-Jordan tribes will need to build their own cities, which is consistent with the picture of destruction in the war stories of Numbers 31.[42] The idea of Israel as a new entity, built according to a distinct divine plan handed down at Sinai and replicated at every moment throughout the wilderness journey, is a very different understanding, requiring a different view of Israel's relationship to the places it settles and what those places had been before they arrived. It also requires a different way of telling the story about how the Israelites moved through the wilderness and came into that place. The combination of these traditions into the present book of Numbers created a confusing and disjointed story, but the reconstruction of the sources here demonstrates how the different visions were combined into a single narrative. Even though both sources possessed a tradition of the settlement of the trans-Jordan by Rueben and Gad, and agreed that this settlement had a significant urban component, their visions of Israel are different and, when placed together, produced a narrative filled with tension. Most significant is the disagreement about the cultural continuity of ancient Israel's urban settings. The P source assumes existing cities must be destroyed by the Israelites before they build new ones, but the E source can have the Israelites take control of the existing cities and live in them. The holy war tradition in places like Deuteronomy 2:30–35 and 7:2–6 and Joshua 6 fit the idea that destruction is necessary and will break any strand of cultural continuity with the Canaanite inhabitants of the land that might lead to impurity or disobedience.

PAST EXPERIENCE AND THE SHAPING OF NEW PLACES

Among the observations that became clear in the preceding pages of this chapter is that the ancient Israelites did not all understand their pathway to, and arrival in, the promised land in the same way. It is likely that influence flows both ways in this relationship. The environment in which people live can shape the way they think about their past and how they arrived in their current place, and the pathway toward a place can influence how a community shapes itself and its environment. The story of the exodus takes the Israelites from slavery in an empire to residence in the land of Canaan. Three different stories look at this process in different ways, and those perspectives seem tied to certain locations and ways of life in what would become Israel. The result is a mixed, and sometimes tense, presentation of cities and urban life in this part of the biblical tradition. Is the city a place of captivity or freedom? Does a city hold a set of cultural assumptions that cannot be adapted to a new people, but must be destroyed? Migrating people in the modern world may look on cities in different ways. There may be economic opportunities there that do not exist elsewhere, because cities draw resources into themselves. Those taken to a new place against their will, or forced out of the place they used to live, may look at the new place as one of captivity or temporary dislocation. Existing urban environments may accept them, but only if they are willing to conform to the culture in some ways. Contemporary religious communities that draw upon the biblical tradition are likely to be able to find their own perspective of cities, or a perspective similar to theirs, in the Bible because of the variety of perspectives from which to choose.

The question of cultural continuity for migrating people is unlikely to involve deciding whether to use captured cities or destroy and rebuild them. Some of the same issues are involved, however, in questions about cultural assimilation. In modern cities questions about assimilation and ethnic segregation are made more complex by the interaction of what sociologists call choice and constraint. The existence of ethnic ghettos is likely never driven purely by one of these factors, but one of the two is often dominant. Some ethnic enclaves exist primarily because of the desire of residents to maintain more of a culture they brought with them from the places where they used to live. A prime example would be the Hasidic Jewish neighborhoods in certain parts of New York City, which offer economic and social advantages to new arrivals and long-time residents. The polar opposite is the housing projects in a city like Chicago, where African American citizens were forced into engineered spaces by attempts to separate them from other parts of the population.[43] The development of culture is driven by the desire for human identity. Cultural identity always involves acts of negation and the identification of others who are not part of the group. Views on the subject in ancient Israel were apparently multiple and contested, and these were projected back onto the lives of the ancestors and the story of their movement into the "promised land." In urban settings this is always more complex because of the wider variety of people and the differing ways they understand the path they and their ancestors took to arrive in their current place. The desire to create a single national story in the Bible meant it was a tangled one. The ability of modern urban communities to tell a unifying story of themselves is an even greater challenge.

Laws are always a mixture of attempts to determine behavior and to describe it, and these prescriptive and descriptive functions may be difficult to separate. As ways of living evolve, rules adjust along with them, and the new expressions can be transposed onto the people of the past as cultural memory forms. The next chapter deals with the development of Israel and Judah as nations, and the rise of cities and centralized power within them. The experiences described in this chapter and the previous ones are illuminated in new ways by examining the ways traditions were formed in the midst of this transition toward a national identity.

5

Give Us a King

The Monarchy and the Urbanization of Israel

Biblical scholarship has struggled for a couple of centuries to make sense of the origins of ancient Israel in Canaan. The "conquest" story readers are able to extract from the book of Joshua has an appeal that is difficult to overcome. Its captivating effect on modern readers may be a reflection of what it would have done for ancient ones. The book of Judges, and even Joshua itself in 13:1, recognize how far from any sense of reality this story travels. The emergence of Israel, which can be marked by its appearance on the Merneptah Stele at the beginning of the twelfth century, coincides with the most intriguing decades in the history of the ancient Mediterranean world. This time marks the end of the Bronze Age and beginning of the Iron Age and a disruption in the patterns of civilization in the area so great that Eric Cline has now famously called it a "collapse." In his wide-ranging study, *1177 B.C.: The Year Civilization Collapsed*, Cline demonstrated that the late Bronze Age in the area including Greece, North Africa, Asia Minor, Mesopotamia, and the Levant was shaped by a complex international economy that had produced many "flourishing" civilizations. The twelfth century, however, witnessed a catastrophic decline across the entire region that is easy enough to observe three millennia hence, but notoriously difficult to explain. Cline and others have proposed the idea of "systems collapse," a cascading effect with multiple causes including earthquakes, drought, social upheaval, influx of new people groups, and disruption of international trade.[1] Part of the appeal of such an explanation is that none of these previously offered explanations by itself, nor a combination of a few of them, seems to offer adequate force for the scale of the catastrophe. By modern standards, the process happened in slow motion, of course. The transformation of the modern world by personal computers, the internet, and smartphones took place mostly within just two decades, and the collapse of the world economy in 2008 happened in a matter of months. Cline picked 1177, a documented date of an important encounter between Egypt and the "Sea Peoples," for dramatic effect in the title, but the "collapse" was a series of events lasting a century or more.

More important than understanding a precise combination of causes is the recognition that the vacuum formed by this collapse left space for new expressions of human civilization to emerge. The development of Israel (north) fits into this window well. Israel Finkelstein has demonstrated relatively rapid growth of the population in the central hill country of Canaan in the first part of the Iron Age. Initially, these were not cities of any size, with the exception of the small group of sites Finkelstein calls Gibeon-Bethel, which by the tenth century were characterized by significant fortification walls. During a period that could be identified with the appearance of Saul as Israel's first king, the area exhibits signs of urban development. This development was not the result of any significant military invasion and conquest, because the area was sparsely populated in the Bronze Age.[2] It looks more like the emergence of a new kind of societal organization among people moving into the area.

One of the central questions any new society formed during this period would have confronted was how it related to the previous social organization in the area. There are obvious material advantages to some kinds of continuity. Making use of the resources that survived the collapse would have been a necessity for survival. Nevertheless, if the experience of prior social structures ended in failure, then some differentiation would have been desirable, if not necessary, and the biblical story of Israel is a masterpiece of differentiation. So, the balance between continuity and differentiation would have been crucial in two senses: materially and ideologically. The differentiation presented in the text is most often theological and ideological in tone. This makes historical analysis very difficult because the theological agenda sometimes opposes a straightforward report, specifically with regard to the process of urban settlement.

The relationship between Israel's god, YHWH, and particular locations is difficult to describe. This is almost certainly because both the biblical literature and archaeological evidence from outside the Bible express multiple positions, sometimes even in competition with one another. Mark Smith has examined the depiction of Baal as an important part of the context for understanding this development. Most significant here are his observations about Baal of Sapan and Baal of Ugarit. The former links Baal to a mountain and the latter to a city. The dominance of Baal of Sapan and the presence of this mountain deity even within the urban temple at Ugarit have led Smith to the conclusion that "it is the mountain outside the city that empowers the city itself. The ritual perception of the city and its patron god derives from the mountain outside the city and less from the city."[3] In literary texts "Mount Sapan serves as the literary mirror for the city and its patron god."[4] Though Baal appears with both of these names, they are not independent deities. The association with a mountain is the older way of identifying the deity, whose power can be transferred to the city while maintaining a connection to the more ancient site. These observations invite comparisons to biblical and other Israelite texts that associate YHWH with mountains (Teman, Paran, Seir, Nebo, Tabor, Herman, Horeb, and Sinai) and with cities (Hebron, Samaria, and Jerusalem). The movement of local associations of YHWH, like that of Baal, seems to be from mountains to cities. Problems created by a multiplicity of sites associated with YHWH were addressed by the centralizing force in Deuteronomy and the Priestly literature of the Hebrew Bible.[5] The more difficult element of Smith's argument is that Jerusalem functions as both city and mountain. "Where Sapan offers a mirror image for Ugarit, these twin realities form a single set of images for Jerusalem's identity."[6] In the narrative of the Hebrew Bible, however, Sinai possesses the twin images first. The Priestly narrative in the Pentateuch meticulously develops the idea of a temple (tabernacle) constructed by divine design at Sinai and a stage-by-stage, forty-year transfer of this temple to the land of Canaan, where it eventually appears again on Mount Zion. Even during the desert sojourn the tabernacle has a city constructed around it, with the tribe of Levi camped at its center attending the temple and three of the tribes camped on each side forming a wall around it.[7] The wilderness may have been uninhabitable and life-threatening for the Yahwistic source, but the P source shapes the composite narrative more than the others, forcing a fit with Smith's conclusion that "human spaces make divinity possible for human communities."[8] Matching a consistent theological picture with the rough-and-tumble formation of a state is likely an impossible task. The smooth, easy story of the formation of Israel in the biblical book of Chronicles is perhaps the greatest compromise to this tension. One of the costs is the almost complete removal of the northern state from the story. Further, the story of Judah is even more concentrated on the development of centralized institutions in Jerusalem than in the Samuel–Kings account.

The story of Israel becomes an urban story with the development of the monarchy. The archaeological evidence that is available demonstrates an inexorable movement toward urbanism, but it may be difficult to determine the pace of the transformation. This is another place where the connections between the story inside the text and the events outside the text are imprecise, but they were moving along similar pathways. Still, the text contains older traditions that retain earlier attitudes about cities and urban life, so there is significant tension about these issues within the text, a tension that may reflect social conflicts outside the text. Like earlier chapters, this chapter follows that story and pays attention to how the text presents urban settings and people, while also paying attention to the contexts in which the texts were produced and how the needs of those contexts are addressed in the story.

THE EMERGENCE OF ISRAEL IN CANAAN

When the Israelites begin to move into the promised land in the biblical story, cities are often obstacles and enemies, things to be attacked and defeated. In Numbers 32:1, two of the tribes, Reuben and Gad, had noticed that the land on the east side of the Jordan River might be a better place for herding. Moses agreed to let them take the trans-Jordan land, as long as they agreed to cross into Canaan and help the other tribes secure the territory there. The previous chapter demonstrated that two different sources preserved this trans-Jordan tradition and used it to present very different understandings of the origin and shape of early Israel. The problem with Canaan on the west side of the Jordan becomes apparent as soon as Joshua leads the Israelites across the river. It is full of cities, ruled by kings, and Jericho stands right in front of them. This situation lends itself to a narrative of conquest. An invading group of people like the Israelites could move around in the parts of the land between the cities and attack them one at a time. It is easy to see how the narrative can become circular in its reasoning, presenting a political situation that makes the plot possible. At times the design of the narrative exposes itself, as in Joshua 5:10–12, when the Israelites, having just crossed the Jordan, celebrate Passover in Gilgal. Joshua 1–5 is at pains to present the character named Joshua as a reflection of Moses. Earlier material about Joshua in Exodus and Numbers, and the reports to come in Joshua 6–12, may create a sense of a one-dimensional leader, focused almost entirely on military operations, so a sequence of stories that reflect the broader leadership of Moses expands the portrait of Joshua. If Moses had presided over the original Passover event in Egypt and the one-year anniversary of Passover while the Israelites were at Mount Sinai, then placing the first celebration of Passover in Canaan within the Joshua story is fitting. The brief report does not contain Joshua's name, however. No character appears leading the celebration. It appears to be a report that has been inserted here in order to associate it with Joshua, who is all around it. The text reports that the manna ceased on this occasion and the Israelites "ate the produce of the land," even though they had not yet engaged any of its inhabitants and had not lived through an agricultural season in which to grow crops. This is one example of how the story of the conquest, as constructed in Joshua, serves literary and theological interests more than historical ones.

The story of the battle of Jericho receives much attention because of its central place in the plot of the book of Joshua and the remarkable image of walls, the feature that most defines cities, falling. Is the bringing down of walls more than just a military tactic? Is it also a declaration that walls are not to be part of Israel's identity? The archaeological evidence concerning Jericho during the Bronze-to-Iron transition has been rigorously debated for more than a century, but a consensus has formed among archaeologists that there are no signs of significant destruction at Jericho in any time period that can be associated with the emergence of ancient Israel in Canaan.[9] The ideological defeat of the city takes on greater prominence. The triumph of the Israelites over a powerful walled city, with the help of their God, opens the process of conquest presented in Joshua 6–12. That this is the one city "utterly destroyed" highlights the ideological defeat and denounces the centralization of political and economic power in walled cities ruled by kings.[10] Jericho appears again at the head of the list of defeated kings in Joshua 12.

The curse Joshua pronounces after the battle in 6:26 is a puzzling anomaly. The nature of Jericho as an oasis in the midst of the desert assured that it would always be a place where humans gathered, and Jericho continues to appear as a significant city throughout the remainder of the biblical story. Joshua's curse has no apparent effect and seems forgotten in the biblical tradition. Perhaps it is only to be understood within its immediate confines, warning any of the Israelites accompanying Joshua against remaining there and rebuilding the city. The line that follows the curse is curious because of its claim that Joshua became well known in the land for destroying cities, while it has been the building of cities that more often brings renown in the biblical story. Joshua is the ideological opposite of Cain and Nimrod. This is the kind of story in which the hero can gain fame for destroying cities even while the momentum of the story is toward greater urbanization. The tentative attempt in chapter 1 to define cities in the ancient world raised questions about whether a wall was the defining feature. While this question is impossible to answer with certainty, the wall is the only physical feature of Jericho visible in Joshua 6. The spies had entered the city earlier in Joshua 2, and even there the wall around it is the dominant feature. Rahab and her family live inside the wall, which is what allows the spies to escape after the gate has been closed. Readers have long noticed the poor fit of the Rahab stories in Joshua 2 and Joshua 6. In 6:22 Joshua sends men into Rahab's house, after the wall has collapsed, to rescue her and her family. It may be that the wall and its destruction are so vital to the understanding of Joshua's defeat of the city that such incoherence is tolerable in the book of Joshua, and a lot of material is placed between these two stories that may help reduce the sense of conflict between them. There is a layer of the story in which condemnation of cities is prominent, but the book of Joshua presents a mixed view. Some of the cities in the list in Joshua 12 are important Israelite cities later in the biblical story. The list does not claim Joshua destroyed the cities, but only that he defeated the thirty-one kings. Whether the Israelites under Joshua's leadership in the story occupied the cities or destroyed them and rebuilt them is not a concern of this particular text.

Interpreters have long noticed the variation in rules for warfare in the Hebrew Bible. The primary issue raised by such variation concerns cultural continuity. The previous chapter shows the variation in texts like Numbers 32, where materials from different sources view the need for destruction of Canaanite culture differently. To what extent can the vision of Israel as a new kind of society in the land of Canaan make use of the elements of the former culture? The primary texts that command total destruction of all that comes before Israel in Canaan are in Deuteronomy, but they are preceded canonically by texts that offer a more nuanced picture. Numbers 21:21–31 contains a tradition in which the Israelites defeat the Amorite king Sihon and take possession of his cities on the east side of the Jordan.[11] Some translations of this text, especially in 21:25, can be deceptive: One possible reading is that Israel took all these cities and Israel dwelled in the cities of the Amorites, in Heshbon, and in all its daughter(-cities). Many translations render one or more of the places the Israelites occupy here as "villages." It may be that some of the settlements called "daughters" of Heshbon would better fit our concept of a town or a village, but the text seems primarily interested in placing them within Heshbon's control or political orbit, rather than describing their size. The occupation of foreign cities by the Israelites is inconsistent with the ideology of the conquest of the promised land elsewhere. The account of the defeat of Sihon and the Amorites in Deuteronomy 2:26–37 is quite different. According to verse 34 the Israelites left no survivors as they captured each of the towns. The account comes closer to the idea of the ban, exemplified by Jericho, but the Israelites keep the livestock, and the disposition of the structural components of the cities is unclear. Deuteronomy does not speak of the Israelites moving in and occupying defeated cities. Deuteronomy 7:1–6 is also a text that has many elements of the ban, as God specifically commands the Israelites to "utterly destroy" enemies. They are not to intermarry with them, specifically because this would lead to the worship of foreign gods. This specifically religious concern continues in the commands to destroy all religious objects and structures in verse 5. Once again the possibility of occupying cities that these foreigners had built is not explicitly addressed, but a lot of destruction is inherent in the command.

The city of Hazor offers a fascinating case. Of all the ancient cities excavated in Canaan, Hazor is the one that most experts agree experienced significant destruction around the beginning of the twelfth century. The evidence indicates that a large, walled Bronze Age city on the site was burned and abandoned at about that time. The archaeological portrait fits the story of Joshua's destruction of the city in 11:1–15, and the possible timeframe, well enough for some to claim it confirms the biblical tradition.[12] Archaeological evidence, however, cannot precisely identify who destroyed the city, which is why it is a matter of such dispute. Calling those who did it "Israelites" does not resolve the problem, because such an identity in the thirteenth century is too ambiguous. The important questions the story and the various attempts to interpret the archaeological evidence raise have to do with cultural continuity. The wilderness narrative presented different perspectives concerning the way in which the Israelites occupied the trans-Jordan territory. The traditions associated with the E source in the Pentateuch generally portray the Israelites taking over the territories of the Amorites and other people in that territory and moving into the cities and towns they had built. The ways of life which the Israelites brought to the place were a natural continuation of the ways people had lived there before. Another strand, associated with the P material, also included the story of the occupation of the trans-Jordan territories, but presented it primarily in terms of destruction and rebuilding. The other primary narrative source, J, does not contain the trans-Jordan settlement tradition, because its focus is entirely on the occupation of the central hill country on the west side of the Jordan River. This source is concerned with the agricultural fertility of the land, and the presence of Canaanite cities is portrayed as a barrier to the way of life it envisions for the Israelites, a mixed agricultural lifestyle that has little use for cities one way or the other. There have been important proposals about this transition that present various types of revolts against the urban elites of Canaanite society. These revolts were part of the collapse of the city-state system that made the way for new social patterns. Baruch Halpern argues that the archaeological remains at Megiddo, an important city in the central hill country, do not support a simple commoners-versus-elite conflict. Political alliances and tensions would have been much more complex than this.[13] The work of Eric Cline and others, mentioned earlier, describes this collapse but avoids the idea of a single cause or even a small set of causes. Israelite traditions likely contain various degrees of genuine memory of these events. The observation of a mixed set of memories can fit within the historical conclusion that the transition had many causes. The most important point to recognize about the biblical story is that it seeks to bring multiple traditions about the formation of Israel together, which is why the story may seem conflicted and even incoherent in places and why there is no single view of urban life and Israel's relation to it.

Jerusalem is the ultimate biblical city, of course, but the biblical presentation of Jerusalem is far from clear. There are two occasions in the life of Abraham that have some connection to Jerusalem in Israelite tradition. First, the story of Abram's encounter with a mysterious priest called Melchizedek of Salem appears in Genesis 14:17–24, a story that received some attention in chapter 3 because of the accompanying interaction between Abram and the king of Sodom. The only other reference to Salem in the Old Testament is in Psalm 76:2, where it is in poetic parallel to Zion, clearly referring to Jerusalem. The Aramaic translation of Genesis known as Targum Onqelos calls Melchizedek "king of Jerusalem," and Josephus credits Melchizedek with naming Jerusalem (*Jewish Wars* 6:438). Other Second Temple Jewish literature makes similar connections, but the story in Genesis is so sparse that little is certain about Jerusalem's possible appearance there.[14]

The connection between Jerusalem and the Akedah story is more intriguing because of the story's centrality to the Abraham narrative, but there is nothing in the Old Testament narrative linking the place the story calls Mount Moriah to Jerusalem. The connection is present in Judaism and Islam today, which makes the Dome of the Rock such an important and contested place. The linkage between the places is ancient, though, found as far back as the writings of Josephus (*Antiquities* 13:226), and an even older reference in Jubilees 18:13. Muslim tradition understands this as the site where Abraham bound and nearly sacrificed Ishmael. Surah 37:102–108 tells the story without naming the son, but the tradition's power within Islam only makes sense if it is Ishmael. Such stories place claims on the city and help to provide it with a divine aura. The elusiveness of the biblical story allows flexibility for such traditions to develop, and it is now impossible for Judaism or Islam to separate Jerusalem from this story. Samaritan tradition presents the Akedah story of Genesis 22 on Mount Gerizim, in the north, in its Pentateuch, but the tradition has faded away with the practitioners of Samaritan religion. In Christian tradition the practice of reading Isaac as a type of Jesus, or the entire story as an allegory of the crucifixion, though dubious, has connected the story inextricably to Jerusalem.

The initial ideological appearance of the city of Jerusalem spreads throughout the book of Deuteronomy, where the city and its temple are the unnamed "place where I [YHWH] will cause my name to dwell." Deuteronomy needs to promote centralized worship in the temple without violating the narrative conceit of the speeches delivered by Moses to the Israelites in Moab while they were on the verge of entering Canaan. The first explicit reference to Jerusalem by that name in the Old Testament is in Joshua 10 when the city's king constructs an alliance to fight against the Israelites and the Gibeonites. Joshua wins a famous victory against the five kings, but the disposition of the city of Jerusalem after the battle is unclear. The next reference to Jerusalem is in Joshua 12, where it appears in the list of thirty-one Canaanite cities and kings Joshua conquered. So, the great city of Israel's future is just one among many at this point. Later in the book of Joshua, however, during the land allotment, 15:63 claims that the tribe of Judah did not take Jerusalem, so two of the major parts of the book of Joshua, the battle stories of 6–12 and the land allotment of 13–22, are not in agreement on this point. A reference to Jerusalem in 18:28 clouds the issue further by reporting that Jerusalem was part of the territory the tribe of Benjamin occupied. Part of the confusion about Jerusalem in the book of Joshua fits within the tension that characterizes the entire book. The primary contradiction is between 11:23, which claims Joshua took the whole land and apportioned it to the Israelites, and 13:1, which asserts that Joshua died having left much of the land not yet under Israelite control. The dispute about whether Jerusalem was within the inheritance of Judah or Benjamin is somewhat different, and the relationship between the two tribes is confusing in other places as well, such as 1 Kings 12:21–23. The tribal assignment of Jerusalem and the point in the national narrative when it came under Israelite control are both questions about which various traditions disagree. Part of the conflict between Joshua and Judges is that the traditions each book reports have been placed in a superficial chronology. Judges opens with the framing statement that recalls the death of Joshua, an event reported at the end of the book of Joshua too. So, these two books that open the Deuteronomistic History are presented end to end in the biblical plot, but there is no reason to assume that the traditions in Joshua are older than those in Judges, or that they are set in an earlier period. Judges 3:9 identifies the first named judge, Othniel, as the nephew of Caleb, so there is no great chronological separation between the collections. The previous chapter observed that Joshua is a character completely unknown to at least one significant collection of biblical tradition (J), so it must have been possible to tell the story of the settlement without him. Joshua receives no mention in any of the stories in Judges 3–16, which are predominately Israelite in origin, and are frequently dominated by Joshua's own tribe of Ephraim.

The opening chapter of the book of Judges continues the confusion about Jerusalem. Judges 1:8 reports that the tribe of Judah took Jerusalem, apparently agreeing with Joshua 12, but Judges 1:21 claims that Benjamin did not drive the Jebusites out of Jerusalem, a statement in conflict in different ways with two different traditions in Joshua. The dispute over Jerusalem and the tribes of Judah and Benjamin that arose in Joshua persists, so it is likely that at least two different tribes preserved traditions about the city.[15] The appearance of Jerusalem in Judges 19 is indirect and odd. In the horrific story, the Levite and his concubine choose not to spend the night in Jebus, because it is not an Israelite city, an irony that develops as the narrative progresses. In 19:10, the narrator reminds readers that Jebus and Jerusalem are the same city. The travelers continue to Gibeah for the night instead, where they are attacked and the woman suffers a brutal sexual assault. The story may serve many purposes, but one of them is a polemic concerning the city of Saul (Gibeah) and the city of David (Jerusalem). This is a good indication that a city like Jerusalem can sometimes play the role of a character in an ancient story that has little to do with the city's own history. The identification of Jerusalem as the city of the Jebusites in Judges 19 fits with the preceding account in Judges 1:21, and the next appearance of Jerusalem in 2 Samuel 5, when David and his army attack the Jebusites and take Jerusalem from them.

Another pair of competing traditions about the founding of Jerusalem exists in the two stories of David taking the city, in 2 Samuel 5 and 1 Chronicles 11. Traditions about David taking Jerusalem from the Jebusites after he becomes king are also complicated by the report at the end of the story of David's battle with Goliath, where 1 Samuel 17:54 reports that David took the head of Goliath with him to Jerusalem, long before David takes Jerusalem from the Jebusites. The two reports of the conquest of Jebus present different portraits of David. In 1 Samuel 5:6–10, David is the hero of the story. He leads his army against the Jebusites and takes the city: "David occupied the stronghold and named it the city of David" (5:9a). The naming of cities has appeared many times in this study so far, beginning with the naming of "Enoch" in Genesis 4:17. Most often a place receives a name etymologically connected to an event that happens there, like Bethel or Gilgal. There is no report of the naming of Shechem, but it has the name of the son of the king in Genesis 34. The city called Rameses in Exodus 1 has the name of some famous pharaohs whom we know of from other sources, but the book of Exodus never names any of its pharaoh characters. Second Samuel 5:9 is the one example in the Bible of a person naming a city after themselves. "The city of David" has an ambiguous quality about it, though, because it is used relatively rarely compared to the other two names, Jerusalem and Zion. For the most part, it is restricted to Samuel–Kings and parallel passages in Chronicles. The two times the label "city of David" appears in the New Testament it refers to Bethlehem, David's traditional birthplace. Visitors to the present-day Jerusalem can become confused by the use of the phrase to refer to the area on the southeast corner of the city, outside the current walls, which appears to be the ruins of the city during the time when David is most often presumed to have reigned there. The story of Jebus/Jerusalem includes a strange element in 2 Samuel 5:6b when the Jebusites taunt David with the line "You will not come in here, even the blind and lame will turn you back." David's challenge to his troops in 5:8 includes the taunt "Whoever would strike down the Jebusites, let him get up the water shaft to attack the lame and the blind, those whom David hates." The remainder of the verse links this saying of David to the practice, apparently reflected in Leviticus 21:16–23, that the blind and the lame are not to enter the temple. It is not difficult to see why 1 Chronicles 11:4–9 would remove all of the references to the blind and the lame. The taunt from the Jebusites in 11:5 is merely, "You will not come in here." The expansive effort to sanitize David's image would benefit from the removal of a saying that would make David look weak or cruel, or that would not match current temple practice. The more surprising difference is that an alternate hero of the story emerges. Rather than David, Joab is the decisive figure in the battle, and 11:8 credits David with the repairs of the city after the victory. David himself does not name the city in the Chronicles version of the story, but a passive construction reports that "it was called the city of David." The total effect of the changes presents a less spectacular, but humbler, David, one who fits the general trends of the book of Chronicles that cleans up the reputation of the great king. The David character in 2 Samuel 5 looks too much the opposite of Joshua, who had refused to benefit materially from his conquering of cities. The origins of Jerusalem as an Israelite city, and its names, are enigmatic. That the name contains no divine element is surprising. Having read the biblical story to this point, one would expect David to give the city a name commemorating God's help in his victory. It appears that the name of Jerusalem was ancient and fixed. Even the name David gives it does not continue to be the primary name by which it was called. The changes in the story made by the writer of Chronicles also allow for a complex answer to the question about the continuity of the city.

The existence of Jerusalem (Urusalim) as a Bronze Age Canaanite city received definitive confirmation more than a century ago from the Amarna Letters, a collection of cuneiform tablets from a fourteenth-century Egyptian archive. Six of the letters are from a person identifying himself as the king of Jerusalem. This Abdi-Heba declares his unwavering allegiance to Pharaoh and complains of harassment from various people living on the border of his territory. Jerusalem seems to have been a city-state kingdom of moderate power and influence in the Judean hills. This would have been several centuries before the city was part of the kingdom of Judah, and linked to the biblical character named David and his subsequent dynasty.[16] It is precisely in this period that the varied, and sometimes contradicting, claims about Jerusalem in the biblical stories of Joshua, the judges, and David fit. Among the forces generating conflicting traditions is the differential level of comfort various writers seem to have had with continuity between Canaanite culture and Israelite society. A story in which Jerusalem is a new city built by David and his heirs would seem impossible, but they could rebuild its central institutional structures, palace and temple, in accounts that sound as if little remained from what was there before.

One of the ongoing debates in biblical archaeology is the date of the emergence of Israel as a territorial state. The basic data on this matter are not a subject of dispute. There was almost certainly a period of time in which several large cities were built that exhibit strong similarities in construction and in cultural artifacts. William Dever lists Hazor, Megiddo, Gezer, and possibly Lachish as prime examples of this kind of city construction. The common patterns indicate a centralized concept of urban planning and city building.[17] The dispute lies in whether this phenomenon should be dated to the tenth or ninth centuries. For the main purpose of this study, that one-hundred-year difference may mean fairly little. The general movement toward urbanization is still present. What is at stake is whether this development fits into the time period commonly associated with the biblical Solomon character, conforming to the idea that the Davidic dynasty ruled over a unified Israel. The impact on our reading may be the extent to which we see attitudes about urbanization reflecting the time when the story took place or the time when the texts were produced. My argument will always lean toward the latter. The portrayal of a unified Israel during the time of Saul, David, and Solomon is an ideological claim supporting a unified Israel in the seventh through fifth centuries, the period of recovery from destruction and defeat. The discussion below addresses this subject more.[18]

The rise of the Israelite state happened regardless of the degree to which it matches the various stories present in the biblical tradition. The manner in which this political and economic shift took place is a matter of significant dispute. State control of territory required a number of factors, and there is no obvious order of development of these factors or set of causal relationships among them. In *The Sacred Economy of Ancient Israel*, Roland Boer begins his discussion of the formation of the state with the formation of "estates," which were the earlier form of an extractive economic institution. Estates in the Levant formed around temples and contained persons who were "nonproducers" in agricultural terms. The support of nonproducers required a means of extraction from surrounding subsistence farmers. Such arrangements are visible in biblical texts that designate portions of offerings for groups of priests, such as Deuteronomy 18:1–8. Temple estates eventually combined with palaces in the movement from estate to state.[19] Relations between palace and temple are present in texts about monarchic succession, such as 1 Kings 5:15–22 (English 5:1–8). Following the long list of provisions for Solomon's house, extracted as tribute from the surrounding lands, he reports his plan to build the temple:

> Now Hiram king of Tyre sent his servants to Solomon, when he heard that they had anointed him king in place of his father, for

Hiram had always been a friend of David. Then Solomon sent word to Hiram, saying, "You know that David my father was unable to build a house for the name of the LORD his God because of the wars which surrounded him, until the LORD put them under the soles of his feet. But now the LORD my God has given me rest on every side; there is neither adversary or misfortune. Behold, I intend to build a house for the name of the LORD my God, as the LORD spoke to David my father, saying, 'Your son, whom I will set on your throne in your place, he will build the house for My name.'" (1 Kgs. 5:1–6)

Along with the absence of distraction from war, a period of peace would also make room for the prosperity that could generate the economic resources for a building project like the temple.

The operation of estates and states leads to class differentiation within a society, but Boer is careful to draw a distinction between the rise of the state and the rise of a ruling class. The common assumption is that the two entities arise together, and are organically related, but Boer contended that the state, instead, is a tool seized by the ruling class. The ruling class must then make itself appear to be indispensable to the formation and operation of the state.[20] This view opens the possibility that a state might operate in a more egalitarian fashion, but examples of such a state in the ancient world are hard to come by. Because states controlled the means of production, including the production of texts, the textual portrayal of states should always be suspect.

The first chapter of this book addressed some important questions about literacy in the ancient world, and in the Levant specifically. The conclusion of the previous paragraph points toward a need for a more precise discussion of some issues at this point. Arguments about literacy in ancient Israel tend to fall along ideological lines in two ways. Proponents of the arguments for more widespread and earlier literacy typically want to push the dates of composition of biblical books further back into periods closer to the settings of the stories within the books. The other impetus, besides dating of texts, is the desire to broaden the extent of the population by whom and for whom texts were written.[21] The case for earlier and broader literacy typically depends on a small collection of texts, including Lachish Letter 3, Yavneh Yam Ostracon 1, the Kuntillet 'Ajrud Inscription, and the Gibeon Inscribed Jar Handles. Disputes about such writings revolve around whether persons other than official, professional scribes could have produced them. Christopher Rollston has taken each of these items in turn and evaluated the possibility that they are evidence of what he called "non-elite literacy." In every case he found the argument for such literacy unconvincing.[22] For the purposes of this study, two related questions about literacy are most important. First, was it primarily, or almost entirely, produced by the official institutions of the state? Second, were writing and reading primarily urban activities? While Rollston's "non-elite literacy" would not have to be nonurban, widespread literacy outside of cities would have to be nonelite. One factor that typically does not come up in arguments about the extent of literacy is what nonelite persons would use this skill to do. The ability to read and write in any system is a skill requiring significant time and effort, and probably significant expense, to acquire and maintain. The practice of reading and writing would require expensive materials. Why would a nonelite person commit such resources, even if they had them, which is unlikely, to such an activity that would not aid in their survival? The evidence supports the conclusion that literacy was concentrated among elite persons who had some official attachment to the state and who would have lived in cities where their scribal activity could be supported and was needed. Of course, the extension of state power would have required literate representatives of the state outside of the central city for the purposes of record-keeping and correspondence, but this is a lower level of literacy than that associated with writing and reading literary texts like those found in the Bible. The urban concentration of scribal activity would have been even more the case with the kind of high-level literacy involved in writing and reading the kinds of literary texts in the Bible. The persons responsible for producing the Bible would have been elite urban dwellers who had some connection to official institutions, and it is reasonable to expect that the biblical literature would reflect this perspective, even if some of the traditions embedded within it had an anti-urban, or even antistate, perspective.

Part of the seizure of the state in ancient Israel, as in many other places, meant taking control of the official narrative as well. A great deal of evidence has accumulated over recent decades that this kind of move to control the national narrative is exactly what happened in ancient Israel, though the motivations for doing so may not have been purely economic. First Samuel presents a complicated portrait of the development of the Israelite state. Careful reading of 1 Samuel 8–17 reveals a complex relationship among the three figures the story connects most closely to these origins: Samuel, Saul, and David. These characters lurk in prior texts as well, such as the horrific story in Judges 19. The story of the Levite and his concubine sits among a collection of chaotic stories that participate in an argument for Israelite statehood. The framing claim, "In those days there was no king in Israel, all the people did what was right in their own eyes," helps open the section in Judges 17:6 and brings the entire book of Judges to a close in 21:25. The story features four locations, three of which might be understood as urban. The Levite man lives in a nonurban place, "the remote parts of the hill country of Ephraim." The unnamed concubine is from a village, Bethlehem of Judah, and the story begins when she runs away to return to the home of her father. On the return journey to Ephraim the travelers have two options for spending the night, the cities of Jebus and Gibeah. The narrator takes extra steps to identify Jebus as the future site of Jerusalem, which was still inhabited by Jebusites at the time of the story, and to remind readers that the residents of Gibeah were Benjaminites. Thus, the two cities are associated with David and Saul, respectively. Bethlehem is also associated with David, of course, and the hill country of Ephraim was the home of Samuel's family, according to 1 Samuel 1:1. The rape and murder of the woman take place in Gibeah, and result in a declaration of war against the tribe of Benjamin by the other tribes. The ambivalent behavior of the Levite, the character with whom readers might associate Samuel, fits the ambivalence of Samuel himself later in the story of the origins of the Israelite monarchy. The Levite condemns the behavior of the Benjaminites in the story but shows no concern for his concubine and may even be the one who ultimately ends her life when he dismembers her. On the other hand, the dismemberment story resembles the act of Saul in 1 Samuel 11:1–11, when he dismembers a yoke of oxen and sends out the pieces as a call to war. Samuel condemns the behavior of Saul at several points and anoints David to replace him in 1 Samuel 16, but then leaves the story and does nothing to help David attain power. The story in Judges 19 manages to cast doubt upon Saul and the city associated with him without taking an obvious pro-David tone. Jebus/Jerusalem remains a blank slate that is included in a general suspicion of cities and their danger, but has no opportunity to confirm or resist such suspicions. The furtive views of these places and the characters within them point toward other texts, without providing easy, overt conclusions.

Evidence has mounted over recent decades that the story of Israel's origins differs from the narrative framework offered in the Hebrew Bible, so readers must be attuned to two different stories and ask questions about what the differences between them reveal. The idea of a "united monarchy" during the tenth and ninth centuries appears increasingly unlikely. Rather, Israel and Judah seem to have had separate origins during the early Iron Age. The destruction of Israel and its capital in Samaria in the late eighth century sent many refugees southward into and around Judah. The early stages of the production of the Hebrew Bible itself were an effort to create a common story that could incorporate members of the northern tribes into Judah. Among those who would have settled in urban environments, particularly in Jerusalem, would have been a professional class of scribal elites.[23] Finkelstein has argued that evidence indicates a rapid growth in the population of Judah in the final decades of the eighth century that natural growth cannot explain. At the same time, the area between Shechem and Ramallah, which would have been the southern part of the kingdom of Israel, demonstrates a significant decline. Migration southward into Judah, as a result of the Assyrian military campaign into Israel, would explain both of these observations.[24] One of the mysteries of the account in Samuel–Kings is that while it favors the kingdom of Judah, it also contains northern texts, some of which reflect negatively on David. If the finished product of the story of David's rise to power in 1 Samuel 16–2 Samuel 5 was a product of Judah, why would it contain such texts? The most likely solution seems to be that the influence of the northern scribes was significant enough to merit the inclusion of these traditions in the narrative, even if the Judahite perspective maintained primary control of the story.[25] Daniel Fleming offers a slightly different, but not incompatible, description of the process. Fleming's assertions that in the accounts of David and Solomon in Samuel–Kings that "Israel" is the "principal category" and that "Judah takes center stage only with the division into two kingdoms" might seem to deny the control of a Judahite perspective, but Fleming is describing the way of presenting the story in the text. The text presents Judah's founding leaders, David and Solomon, as kings of all Israel.[26] Ideologically, this is a Judahite move, one that allowed Judah at the time the text was produced to claim a sense of priority in the distant past, and to maintain that Israelites in its own present could reflect that distant past by being part of a nation under Judahite leadership.[27]

Michael Satlow pointed to a fascinating combination of features of the Siloam Tunnel Inscription that may help illuminate this situation. The tunnel often referred to today as "Hezekiah's Tunnel" appears to have been constructed in the late eighth century, at a time from which similar water projects in Judah have not been found, while they were common in northern Israelite cities. The inscription itself is odd because it was produced inside the tunnel, far underground, where only those responsible for digging the tunnel were likely to have seen it. It was not intended as a public monument, or one inscribed for the king. Further, the content of the inscription describes and praises the work of the diggers, but makes no mention of the royal sponsorship of the project.[28] Satlow concluded that northern engineers may have produced the tunnel for the king of Judah, but expressed a sense of independence through the content and placement of the inscription. If this was the behavior of subversive engineers from the north, then it might point to a similar situation among professional scribes, who came from the north and sold their skills to the Judahite monarchy, but retained some sense of independence in their work.[29] They were able to embed their own traditions into a text that presented a pan-Israel story from a Judahite perspective.

The relationship of Chronicles to the Deuteronomistic History has long been a mystery. So many texts in the latter follow the former so closely that literary dependence is apparent, but this does not mean that the writer of Chronicles used a version of the Deuteronomistic History identical to that found in the Masoretic Text. The Greek version of Samuel–Kings was almost certainly produced from a Hebrew version different from the Masoretic one. This, along with internal evidence from the Masoretic version, indicates the Deuteronomistic History went through many stages. The most startling feature of Chronicles is the nature of the omissions. Not only does it leave out all of the material like that found in Joshua and Judges, but large sections of the story of the monarchy are missing, including all of the accounts of the northern kings and prophetic figures like Elijah and Elisha. It is not possible to enter the mind of the writers of Chronicles and declare their motives with certainty, and the motives seem to be many, but if later writers wished to erase the embedded northern traditions and limit their impact on the story of Israel as a nation, their moves in this part of the story would look much like what is present in the book of Chronicles.

The incorporation of Israelite material into Judahite literature, some of which added tension to the narrative, may provide a helpful analogy for thinking about how anti-urban traditions sit within books produced by elite urban scribes, and which present an overall positive portrayal of cities and urban life. The model of development of the Israelite and Judahite states presented here contains at least two locations where anti-urban traditions might have been popular. One is the hill country in the central portion of Israel, the area chapters 3 and 4 associated with the J source in the Pentateuch and its vision of a mixed agrarian economy. In the J portions of Genesis 1–11 cities appeared to be an opposing way of life for the characters who formed Israel's distant past. For the ancestors of Israel who lived this lifestyle in Canaan, cities were places of danger and conflict. The J wilderness narrative presented Canaanite cities as a potential barrier to establishing this way of life in the hill country. The combination of these traditions points to the hill country as a possible center for anti-urban sentiments. The other place where anti-urban traditions might have resonated was an early stage of the development of Judah, when northern Israel was much wealthier and more developed. The traditions that portray David as a wilderness warlord may display some anti-urban, or at least anti-elite, sentiment. This latter collection, however, would have been overridden by the effort to use these texts to present a kingdom of Judah that could absorb Israelites moving from the north in the wake of the Assyrian invasion of the late eighth century. Jacob Wright has demonstrated that the earliest David material presents its hero as such a warlord figure. The introduction of David in 1 Samuel 17:12–14 describes him as the youngest of eight sons, and a passage near the beginning of his wilderness years reports that "Everyone who was in distress, and everyone who was in debt, and everyone who was discontented gathered to him; and he became captain over them," and "those who were with him numbered about four hundred" (1 Sam. 22:2). The stories of David as a desert chieftain later became part of his "fugitive" period when his story was combined with Saul's.[30] This material may not have been directly anti-urban, but the group it portrays is one made up of outcasts from society. David could not remain such a figure, of course, if he was to become the literary means of uniting the scattered Israelites with the kingdom of Judah. In order to serve as the model king in such a story, David had to become the builder of Jerusalem. No matter the extent to which David was an urban person, he had to become one in the hands of urban scribes who used him to unite an increasingly urban people. Nevertheless, traces of another portrait of David are present, particularly in 1 Samuel. Like northern traditions identified above, these are not present in the later book of Chronicles.[31]

The ambiguity of David's relationships to Saul, Jerusalem, and Solomon is visible in the conflicts among the Masoretic version of Samuel–Kings, Chronicles, and the version of Samuel–Kings reflected in the Greek text. Raymond Person has labeled these three versions of the story of Israel's monarch "competing contemporary historiographies." Regardless of the precision of Person's use of "contemporary" in reference to their production, it is difficult to escape the conclusion that these three versions would have been available as options for readers during the Persian and Hellenistic periods.[32] One sign of this competition may be the strange beginning of the book of Chronicles. Interpreters have long been puzzled by the bare genealogies in 1 Chronicles 1–9, leading up to the story of David that begins in 11:1. What, for example, did the writer of Chronicles expect when members of the reading audience saw Noah's name and the names of his three sons in 1 Chronicles 1:4? The old idea of Chronicles being a "supplement" as reflected in the title of the Greek version, Paralipomenon, does not fit this observation. This part of the text does not supplement but, rather, needs a supplement. Surely the writer expected readers to know something of Noah, to fill in the gap with some version of the flood story, but which one? On this point there are many options. Not only are there the separate Yahwist and Priestly flood accounts and the particular combination of them in the book of Genesis, but also books like Jubilees and 1 Enoch treat Noah and the flood story extensively. The latter makes more of it than a story of divine judgment or punishment in the distant past but also weaves it into its vision of an apocalyptic future. Is it possible that the writers of Chronicles wanted to accomplish other tasks in the book and did not wish to limit their audience to those who preferred any one particular story of the flood, the ancestors, or the exodus? If presenting an alternative portrait of the monarchy was what mattered most to these writers, then other portions of the Israelite tradition that might have been a barrier to acceptance of their revision could be removed. This also had the effect of removing many, or even all, of the traditions that were anti-urban in perspective. The focus of Chronicles became almost entirely centered on Jerusalem.

The location of David's kingdom and his connection to the Jerusalem temple present additional points of tension. In Samuel–Kings David becomes king of only Judah first, and the geographical center of his power is Hebron. Hebron appears early in the biblical tradition, most closely associated with Abraham and Sarah. Genesis 23:19 identifies Hebron with the place where Israel's ancestors were buried, in the "cave of Machpelah," that Abraham purchased to use as a tomb for Sarah. Hebron also appears among the cities the Israelites defeated when they entered Canaan in Joshua 10–12, but traditions about Hebron become a matter of confusion and conflict after this. According to Joshua 14:13–14 Joshua gave Hebron, formerly known as Kiriath-arba, to Caleb and his descendants as a reward for Caleb's faithfulness during the spying episode recorded in Numbers 13–14, which had identified Caleb as a member of the tribe of Judah. According to Joshua 15:13–19, Joshua gave Hebron/Kiriath-arba to Caleb, because of Caleb's exploits to win the city from the Anakites who held it previously. A third version of this tradition appears in Judges 1:20, and fits more closely with the Joshua 15 tradition that connects the land grant to Caleb's defeat of the Anakites. So, the first city of David was one at the very center of the territory of Judah, but one which had a disputed past. Along with the account of David's anointment as king, 2 Samuel 5:3 also reports that David made a covenant with YHWH at Hebron. This note, along with the story in 2 Samuel 15:7–12 of Absalom going to Hebron to worship YHWH, may indicate that it was the site of an early YHWH sanctuary before Jerusalem.[33] Wright has argued that the Caleb traditions may point to resistance from clans and tribes to the nation-state efforts of the Judahite royalty.[34] In the face of totalizing claims of Jerusalem as the only city that mattered, how might other communities, including other cities, maintain a sense of status or identity other than as satellites in orbit of the great city? The Caleb traditions attempted this by taking its claims to land and loyalty all the way back to Moses and Joshua, before a monarchy even existed in Israel.

Hezekiah's Passover, portrayed in 2 Chronicles 30, demonstrates the power of cultic centralization, and how that force and the force of urbanization can feed each other. This account represents the kind of material Chronicles adds to the Deuteronomistic History, lest the omissions get all the attention. Passover traditions in the Hebrew Bible are extensive, beginning in Exodus 12–13, where the narrative of the founding event blends with instructions for a perpetual commemoration. Appendix 6 shows the distribution of Festival Calendars in the Pentateuch and the festivals each contains, along with the location of additional Passover materials. The assumption that Passover is a pilgrimage festival, to be observed in Jerusalem, is essential to this story, and Hezekiah raises the accompanying claims to a higher register. According to 2 Chronicles 30:3, keeping the Passover in the proper place was more important than doing it at the correct time. The royal proclamation in verses 6–9 threatens the people throughout Israel and Judah with divine judgment if they do not come to Jerusalem for the observance. The throng of people celebrating Passover in one place seems to create confusion in verses 17–20, requiring Hezekiah's intervention. Finally, in verses 23–26, Hezekiah bribes the people with massive numbers of sacrificial animals to get them to stay in Jerusalem and extend the length of the festival. The people are required to celebrate the Passover in the city and depend on its resources to stay there. Second Chronicles 35 also adds a massive Passover event to the reign of Josiah a century later. This event also gathers a large crowd of Israelites into the central city. While Hezekiah's Passover is evaluated as the greatest since the days of King Solomon (30:26), Josiah's is the greatest since the days of the prophet Samuel (35:18). With the quality of a religious observance measured by the size of the spectacle, urban religion becomes the norm.

READING THE MONARCHY IN THE MODERN WORLD

Modern readers may be bewildered by the combination of traditions in the multiple versions of the story of the Israelite monarchy. Further, trying to find a coherent position concerning urban life during that period can be difficult, if not impossible, but it may be this tension that provides the best resource. The first United States census in 1790 showed a population that was 5 percent urban and 95 percent rural, a situation that changed gradually over the next fifty years, but then began to shift drastically. From 1840 to 1940 the urban share of the population grew from 11 percent to 57 percent. The remainder of the twentieth century witnessed continued change in this ratio until the urban population reached 81 percent by the year 2000. The United States had become an urban nation, like much of the rest of the world, but this is an identity with which much of the country is uneasy. The idea of Americans as frontier settlers and claims about small-town values still hold significant ideological power. Religious images of the world are typically about forests, mountains, and ocean sunsets. The city is a place from which one must periodically escape, particularly for any kind of religious renewal. Those who find themselves attracted to urban life may experience an ambivalent tension about this way of life that matches the ambivalence of biblical traditions. The city provides economic opportunity for those without land, like those ancient ones who may have gathered themselves around David. Urban life also consolidates power, though, and makes enormous levels of economic inequality possible. The diversity of backgrounds, cultures, and experience that many drawn to an urban setting find appealing can also be the cause of conflict. There are reasons to be wary of urban life.

The introductory chapter of this book gave some attention to Richard Florida's *The Rise of the Creative Class*, a powerful and distinctive examination of American urbanization in the third millennium. Florida's "creative class" makes up the primary component of the influx to the centers of cities that had been abandoned when they were still centers of industrial production in the 1970s and 1980s.[35] Not only does this group bring new patterns of work and living to cities, but also new ways of thinking about a place. It turns out that technology did not replace the need for people to be in close proximity to one another. Many of the resources required to generate and feed creativity require centralized space for face-to-face encounters and experiences. At a time when many economists and urban theorists were talking about a world flattened by the connective potential of technology, Florida insisted that "the world is both flat and spiky at the same time."[36] At the time when the biblical materials arose, Israel probably shared some aspects of this dual identity. Using available data, Christopher Rollston has concluded that a scribal culture had begun in Jerusalem in the tenth century. He has also emphasized the presence of a scribal culture in the southern Levant in the Late Bronze Age, based on the Amarna correspondence.[37] His conclusions point to two important ideas for this study. The development of scribal culture is a long process, and it requires the resources of a city and official institutions to create and sustain it. The writing samples from the fourteenth and the tenth centuries to which Rollston points to make his case are relatively short and simple. They are single-purpose communications, records, or declarations that could hardly be called literature. Still, a scribal culture would have been necessary to produce such writing. It would likely be another few centuries before the kind of literature that forms biblical books might have arisen, but this would also be part of a long, continuous process of scribal development. The remains from the place known as Kuntillet 'Ajrud have entered the discussion here. The place was a small fortress in the Sinai desert near a significant water source that seems a natural, even necessary, place for travelers through the area to stop. A number of the inscriptions found there appear to be the practice work of a novice scribe. The materials are usually dated to the late ninth century. William Schniedewind has placed these inscriptions together in a plausible order to reconstruct a process of scribal learning. Because the inscriptions are few and fragmentary he has used a template of scribal education derived from much more substantial evidence in Mesopotamia and Ugarit.[38] Kuntillet 'Ajrud was not likely a scribal school of any size because too few persons would have been in residence there, and the primary purpose of the site appears to have been military in nature. There could have been need of a scribe at such an outpost, in order to send communications to officials in a supporting city, and Schniedewind has developed evidence that this was likely Samaria.[39] Even scribes in remote places were connected to those at the center, where there would have been many.

To what extent the idea of a creative class might apply to communities of scribes that growing cities in the ancient world would have accumulated is hard to say for certain. The rarity of manuscripts and training would almost certainly have meant that such persons lived in high concentrations in a limited number of places. The examples of writing from Iron Age Israel come primarily from cities, but it is possible that the tells formed by cities preserved such writings better or that these tells have received a disproportionate amount of archaeological attention. Still it is difficult to imagine nonurban sites could have been settings for intense scribal activity and growth. The discussion of Kuntillet 'Ajrud above demonstrates the need for centralized support for a working scribe in a remote place, and this remote scribal activity appears to be merely functional and administrative. Some might point to Qumran as an obvious exception to this claim, even though it is outside the timeframe of this discussion, but there are many problems with using Qumran as an example, most of which relate to the singular nature of the phenomenon. It is uncertain whether a large number of texts were produced there, and even if they were, then it was over a relatively short period of time. Qumran was not a sustained scribal culture, if it was a scribal culture at all. If there were working scribes there, then it would seem that they came from Jerusalem, with their skills already developed, to escape Roman pressure. The wilderness did not generate a scribal culture. At most it gave temporary haven to a group that had fled there.

The Israelite monarchy, with its expanding cities and religious institutions in the ninth and first half of the eighth centuries, would have provided a potential setting for the development of a scribal culture. The cities and supporting administrative centers would have provided the necessary resources and the reasons for producing a growing quantity and complexity of written materials. If the scattered scribes from Israel, in the aftermath of the Assyrian invasion, found a new home and place of work in Judah and helped form a productive, hybrid scribal culture throughout the late eighth and seventh centuries, then this culture was in for a harsh repetition of history as the late seventh and early sixth centuries approached. The urban scribal way of life and the literature it produced intertwined and fed each other. How would this culture respond to the destruction of its city by the ultimate city, Babylon?

Looking across two and a half millennia, we might find the Bible to appear provincial. A counterclaim to this assumption has two important aspects. First, the Bible, as a limited canonical collection, is the product of a much later time. Literary production in ancient Israel was far broader and more varied than this confined set of texts indicates. Second, in their culture, texts like those in the Bible represented the highest level of artistic and intellectual expression. Contemporary urban dwellers who keep these ideas in mind might find ancient counterparts in this literature, creating new ways of thinking and engaging the challenges of their world.

6

Plowed Like a Field

*The Destruction of Israel and
the Differentiation of City and Empire*

When the Bible tells the story of the destruction of Israel, the focus is almost entirely on its major cities. Second Kings 17 reports the invasion of Israel by King Shalmaneser of Assyria during the reign of King Hoshea, an event that occurred in the latter part of the eighth century. The focus of the invasion report is the impact on King Hoshea and his capital city of Samaria, which the Assyrians besieged for three years before capturing it. Even the theological explanation of this disaster emphasizes the disobedience of cities, as 17:9 reports: "The people of Israel secretly did things that were not right against the LORD their God. They built themselves high places at all their towns, from watchtower to fortified city. . . ." The analogous event a century and a half later, the destruction of Jerusalem by King Nebuchadnezzar and his Babylonian army, is similarly reported and explained. In this case, four reports in 2 Kings 25, 2 Chronicles 36, and Jeremiah 39 and 52 describe the invasion of the city and the destruction of its palaces and temples. The references to nonurban places and persons are brief and have to do with what was not destroyed. Second Kings 25:12 reports that "the captain of the guard left some of the poorest people of the land to be vinedressers and tillers of the soil," and Jeremiah 52 repeats the report. Jeremiah 39:10 provides a similar description: "Nebuzaradan the captain of the guard left in the land of Judah some of the poor people who owned nothing, and gave them vineyards and fields at the same time." Persons in rural settings and occupations are the ones who remain, and the next chapter demonstrates the ways in which the biblical tradition, and the most common ways of reading it, have seen such a situation as an "empty land."

Preceding chapters of this book show the long and complex development of Israelite traditions concerning cities and urban life. Chapter 5 demonstrates that the stories in the biblical literature about the development of Israel as a nation have ideological purposes and must be read carefully alongside each other and alongside the archaeological evidence. The need to define a "pan-Israel" in the distant past helped to place the primary focus on temple and palace, and the urban orientation of Israel gained something of a grudging acceptance through the story of the monarchy. The increasing urban orientation of Israel outside the text is often reflected within it, whether deliberately or not. The remarkable text in Isaiah 7:1–9 receives attention for a lot of reasons, but one feature seldom recognized is the way it speaks of Israel's capital cities. In a text where Damascus is synonymous with Aram, Samaria is also synonymous with Israel, and Jerusalem is synonymous with Judah. In this story of a threat of war and possible military and diplomatic alliances, the Israelites, their kings, and their cities are at play on the world stage with the other nations in the region. The unnamed enemy throughout this story of the interaction between Isaiah and King Ahaz, which appears nowhere else in the biblical tradition, is the deadly, ominous threat of Assyria. The event Isaiah 7 describes is often called the "Syro-Ephraimitec War." The book of Isaiah does not directly report the outcome of the war, only that Isaiah, based on the word of YHWH, advised Ahaz against joining an alliance with Syria (Aram) and Israel to fight the Assyrians. The outcome of the war is reported in 2 Kings 16:5–9 and 2 Chronicles 28:5–7 in remarkably different ways. In the 2 Kings account, Israel and Aram besiege Jerusalem, but Ahaz appeals to the Assyrian king Tiglath-pileser and pays him a tribute using precious metals from the temple. Tiglath-pileser responds by attacking Damascus and rescuing Ahaz and Jerusalem. In the 2 Chronicles version of events, Aram ultimately attacks Judah and kills 120,000 of its soldiers. There is not adequate information outside the Bible to adjudicate among these varying accounts. The numerical figure on the latter report seems exaggerated, and the former account is too useful as a negative evaluation of a king of whom the book of Kings already takes a dim view. Regardless of which account reflects realities outside the text most closely, all of them show a complex web of relations among kings and nations, as cities struggle for survival in a highly militarized context. In the aftermath of the conflict, 2 Kings 16:10 even describes King Ahaz of Judah traveling to Damascus to meet with Tiglath-pileser after the rescue.

The number of soldiers from Judah mentioned above, who were killed by the Assyrian army, provides an occasion to discuss the population of Israel, Judah, and their cities. The counting of people in biblical texts seems wildly exaggerated at times. This begins with the enumeration of persons involved in the departure from Egypt in Exodus 12:37. The count there is "about six hundred thousand men on foot, besides children." If that number is the adult men, then the traditional number of two million total persons is conservative.[1] A similar count appears at the end of the first census in Numbers 2:32. These numbers seem impossibly large for a group of foreigners living in Egypt, a band of fugitive slaves traveling through the wilderness, or even a society settling into the land of Canaan at the beginning of the Iron Age. The Davidic census in 2 Samuel 24:9 counts 1.3 million soldiers between Israel and Judah, which would point toward a population of four million or more in the tenth century, and the number in the Chronicles version of the story is even larger. First Chronicles 21:5 claims 1.57 million soldiers. These counts appear to be far beyond any reasonable estimates. The numbers in biblical texts provide no reliable information about how many people lived in Israel and Judah at the time they were destroyed. A combination of archaeological evidence and anthropological method may offer more useful estimates. William Dever has produced estimated populations for Israel and Judah during the eighth century. Based on the excavation of cities and towns and the carrying capacity of the land, the total population of the two kingdoms would have been approximately 350,000. Dever delineated these numbers further to estimate a population of 218,000 for Israel and 137,000 for Judah.[2] These totals are roughly 10 percent of the biblical figures, which prove to be ideological. The scaling down of our understanding of the size of the Israelite population should also include a parallel reduction in what it means to talk about urban settings. Cities in ancient Israel did not amass great populations, because there were no great populations to amass. More important is the observation that there were walled cities that were becoming political, administrative, and religious centers toward which the lives of people were becoming increasingly oriented, even if they did not live in them. The discussion below will demonstrate that the presentation of the condemnation and destruction of Israel and Judah was also oriented toward these urban settings.

Israel's great enemies of the eighth through sixth centuries are also embodied in cities. Nineveh and Babylon both made mythic appearances in the primeval texts of Genesis 1–11, and both cities are connected to the greatest city-builder of all time, Nimrod. Israel's experience of failure as an urban entity at the hands of urban empires would require a careful differentiation between some urban settings and ways of life and others. The story develops along multiple parallel lines. The books of Kings and Chronicles each tell the story of the continuing development and eventual end of Israel and Judah as nations. At the same time, the prophetic literature and the book of Psalms respond to the same story from a different perspective, using different kinds of literary forms. Their concerns have more to do with shaping a future beyond the destruction. The book of Lamentations offers another point of view, one from inside the city that provides more vivid descriptions of the suffering of the people. Because Lamentations speaks from a postdestruction perspective, it will function as a useful transition to the next chapter as well. In the discussion within this chapter it will help to highlight the threat posed to cities by siege warfare, and the importance, both real and symbolic, of the capture of capital cities in warfare. The view of cities in the prophetic literature is nuanced and often ambiguous, in part because of the nature of the literature itself. Marti Nissinen has demonstrated that the Israelite prophets were not alone in the symbolic and ideological use of cities, a phenomenon that also appears in Assyrian prophecy from a similar period.[3] Cities represented religious and royal power, and prophets spoke to these representations. Nissinen may have overstated the case that cities were more ideological than spatial in the language of prophets, but it is vital to keep both of these aspects in clear view as the discussion proceeds.[4] Cities and their influence are sometime at the forefront, but they often lurk in the background. They embody power that destroys but also the resources to assist in recovery. Cities are the natural environment of the prophetic characters and the objects of their condemnation. Before looking more closely at these texts, it will be helpful to examine how their production relates to the ideas about scribal practice and culture that previous chapters have explored.

THE PRODUCTION OF PROPHETIC SCROLLS

It has become increasingly clear that the work of oral proclamation by prophetic figures and the fully formed prophetic scrolls with which modern readers are familiar are two ends of a long and complex process. The impact of that process on the shape and content of the scrolls will be addressed below, but at this point it will be helpful to look at the nature of the composition process and its connection to urban contexts. The work of turning prophetic work into literature often obscures elements of the settings in which the oracles and sermons of the prophets would have been delivered, because the scrolls configure their readers as the audiences. The nature and purpose of prophecy as oral delivery would have required a substantial audience to make sense, though. The locations that remain in the prophetic literature are consistently urban. The prophets address cities and their inhabitants and often include leaders, such as kings and priests, in their addresses. Isaiah son of Amoz does not appear frequently in the book that carries his name. The three most famous narrative scenes take place in the temple (Isa. 6), at a carefully described location just outside the city (Isa. 7), and in the palace (Isa. 38–39).

More subtle are the references to additional prophetic figures with whom Isaiah interacts in 8:2 and 8:16. In the former texts Isaiah is also able to summon a priest to be a witness to his act of writing. The production of a scroll would have been a communal task in many ways, and the setting for such a community, with the resources available for such literary production, was almost certainly urban, specifically Jerusalem.

It is not possible to delineate every stage in the development of prophetic scrolls, but it is possible to identify some elements of the process. Karel van der Toorn has developed a collection of evidence pointing toward the existence of written prophecy in Israel in the period before the invasion of Jerusalem by the Babylonian army, but these units would not yet have resembled the massive scrolls that ended up in the Bible. The writing of individual prophetic statements provided the raw material for a later process of composing large collections, most likely produced by persons who understood themselves as followers of the prophets.[5] The current shape of the scrolls is a product of the Persian period, with continuing editorial work extending into the Hellenistic era. Van der Toorn uses the story in Jeremiah 36 as a model for how the composition of larger collections of prophetic material might have worked. The portrayal of writing in the Bible should be viewed with adequate caution. Richard Horsley observes that scribal activity was often retrojected into stories and characters of the distant past, such as Solomon and David. However, Horsley contends that by the time of Jeremiah such portrayals were likely more reliable.[6] Still, the story need not reflect precisely an event outside the text, involving Jeremiah and Baruch, to be a useful reflection of how the composers of the book of Jeremiah understood their own work. While the divine command in 36:2 instructs Jeremiah to write all the words the Lord has spoken to him on a scroll, in 36:4 a scribe named Baruch appears to do the writing while Jeremiah dictates. The scroll is a scribal production. After Baruch writes the scroll it has an interesting life. First, Baruch reads it in the temple, as Jeremiah commands him, and the son of a royal official hears him read it and reports it to a group of royal officials. These officials summon Baruch to come and read the entire scroll to them, after which they warn Baruch to hide himself and Jeremiah while they go to report the contents of the scroll to King Jehoiakim. When the king hears about the contents of the scroll, he sends his own reader, a person named Jehudi, to retrieve it from the secretary's chamber where the officials had left it and has this person read it to him. As the reading proceeds, Jehoiakim cuts pieces of the scroll off and burns them in a fire. When Jeremiah and Baruch learn of the destruction they produce a new scroll. Only two people in the story demonstrate the ability to read: Baruch and Jehudi. Everybody else has the scroll read to them.[7] Even the royal officials who reported the scroll's contents to the king did so based on memory form Baruch's reading, having left the scroll behind in the chamber to go make their report. The story of the second scroll in 36:32 includes the revealing note that more words like those in the original scroll were added.[8] Thus, the scroll that exists when the entire story is complete is one produced by a professional scribe. It is not the first one written and it has grown in content since the first one was produced. These characteristics demonstrate the way the scribes who produced books like Jeremiah may have understood the process of their work and its relationship to the earlier work of the prophetic figure. These realities were separated by multiple layers of development. Even the second scroll which Baruch writes in this story is not presented as the equivalent of the book of Jeremiah, which tells the story of that scroll.[9] It seems reasonable to assume that the narratives like this one were added during the latest stages, when the book of Jeremiah was taking on a full sense of being a literary work.[10] So, the prophetic books with which modern readers are familiar stand at the end of a long scribal process, and were formed under the influence of a scribal culture, almost certainly in an urban environment. The writing and reading of such scrolls are strictly the work of professional scribes. The point of view of the book, from within Jerusalem, was the point of view of the scribes. The appearance of several additional books written using the persona of Baruch, likely from the second century BCE to the second century CE, indicates that scribes throughout these centuries continued to see Jeremiah's scribe as a reflection of themselves, their work, and their social position.[11]

PROPHETIC VIEWS OF CITIES
AND THE IMPERIAL ENEMY

The most challenging aspect of the common prophetic position is its need for the enemy empire. Isaiah and Jeremiah assert this position most clearly, but the prophetic scrolls also recognize the conundrum it generates. Isaiah 10:5–6 demonstrates the tension when YHWH declares,

> Ah, Assyria, the rod of my anger—
> the club in their hands is my fury!
> Against a godless nation I send him,
> and against the people of my wrath I command him. . . .

Jeremiah is even more thorough and direct in its portrayal of Babylon as the military ally of Israel's God. Multiple positions appear in Jeremiah. Some advocate opposition to Babylon as a faithful response to the threat of destruction, and others insist that God will continue to protect Judah and

Jerusalem, no matter the surrounding circumstances. These perspectives appear in places like 7:4, where Jeremiah identifies the "deceptive words" of his opponents; in 23:17, where he repeats the sayings of those he characterizes as untrue prophets; and in 28:1–16 when Jeremiah comes into conflict with the prophet named Hananiah. Jeremiah argues for the acceptance of divine judgment and cooperation with Babylon, and his conflict with those who take other positions sometimes places him in physical danger. The task of promoting compliance with an invading enemy when resistance, or escape to the relative safety of Egypt, were more popular options would have been difficult for Jeremiah and anyone connected to him.[12] Jeremiah 25 is one of many places where this prophet forecasts the coming destruction at the hands of Babylon. The threat in 25:18 focuses specifically on Jerusalem and the cities of Judah and Judah's kings and its officials. The pronouncement of judgment near the beginning of Jeremiah had threatened that foreign kingdoms would come and "set up their thrones by the entrances of the gates of Jerusalem, against all its walls encircling, and against all the cities of Judah" (Jer. 1:15). This latter image effectively makes the ruler of Babylon the ruler of Jerusalem. It portrays giving away the city and its surrounding land to a foreign power.

Perhaps the most important development in scholarship of the prophetic literature in the twenty-first century has been the recognition that the prophetic traditions generated before the two great catastrophes had to adjust to a new reality after the destructions of Israel and Judah. The switch is usually named in one of two ways. One important way of thinking about the divide is the identification of "predisaster" and "postdisaster" literature. Much of the material in the first half of each of the four great prophetic scrolls focuses on the impending destruction of Israel and Judah. Judgment oracles, many likely delivered orally at first, in which the prophet announces "the word of YHWH" against the people of Israel and Judah are the dominant literary form. The scrolls themselves, however, are the product of a later time, one in which Judah sought to rebuild itself during the Persian period. How would such audience hear the accusations that led to their national demise? In the words of Louis Stuhlman and Hyun Chul Paul Kim, "Prophecy as written communication attends to survivors. It takes shape during and after the frightful events; all the while it engages in artful reinterpretation and reenactment."[13] The writing of the scrolls thus becomes a renegotiation of the proclamations of death and destruction, in order to produce literature that might help bring new life to a community recovering from catastrophe. Another view of this shift uses the language of trauma and deals more directly with the impact on human experience. David Carr has described a process of addressing trauma in the development of the book of Hosea: "It was there, in Judah, that these prophecies of Hosea became the seeds of later Old Testament theology. It was there that Hosea's vision of faithfulness was eventually accepted as a way to engage Judah's communal trauma. With time his prophecy and his broader monotheistic vision transcended its original context and helped later generations deal with their trauma."[14] My own work on the prophetic literature has sought to add the work of the prophets as literary characters in the finished scrolls. As the Servant in Isaiah 40–55, Jeremiah, and Ezekiel experience the suffering their words proclaim, they begin to embody the shift in thinking about suffering as divine punishment to suffering as part of obedience to YHWH. This pivot emerges as the interpretive center for the prophetic literature, and the city of Jerusalem becomes the primary collective character, the victim of destruction, and the place that seeks survival in its reconstruction. The prophets who also take on the mantle of suffering do so as city dwellers. Ezekiel, for example, performs elaborate symbolic actions in which he builds a model city and enacts its siege, then becomes a captive himself, tied up and lying on his side for hundreds of days. The opening section of this chapter observed that the audiences of prophetic proclamations are usually not present in the written texts, a situation that is also typical of the literary portrayal of symbolic behavior by prophets. If they performed these acts at all, they have now been transformed into literary vehicles in which the immediate surroundings of the performances are no longer visible in the text. They are now surrounded by the scroll and its reading audience. The response of the prophet's audience is no longer important in comparison to the response of the reading audience.

There are exceptions to this general trend of removing the audience, particularly when an audience inside the text is necessary for the prophetic drama to work. Ezekiel 24:15–17 offers an important example. When YHWH kills Ezekiel's wife and commands him not to mourn her death, members of his community observe his unexpected behavior. In response to their question about his failure to mourn, Ezekiel pronounces the oracle about a coming destruction so fast and fierce that the audience will not have time to mourn. The audience in the text is necessary to form the narrative connection between the symbolic act and the saying. This is a different kind of symbolic prophetic act because it is, more accurately, a nonaction, and this may have been more difficult to portray in the ways that Ezekiel's other symbolic actions are portrayed.[15] A similar text appears in Haggai 2:10–14, but in this case it is an oracle by the prophet that does not involve symbolic action. The oracle consists of questions YHWH commands Haggai to ask of the priests, and the narrative can only move to its conclusion if the priests' responses are included.[16] Another text that lies in between these that have an audience in the text and the more common oracles and symbolic acts that have no audience is the combination of Jeremiah 7 and 26. Jeremiah 7 is the famous "temple sermon" of Jeremiah. YHWH commands Jeremiah to stand at the temple gate and deliver the oracle, but there is no audience or response in the text. The public response appears in the trial of Jeremiah in chapter 26, after he is arrested for preaching the temple sermon. All three of these texts in which prophetic speech and action have an audience in the text take place in urban settings.

The visions of Ezekiel require attention here because of their urban context and the powerful manner in which they portray destruction and restoration. There are four visions in Ezekiel, and the first, second, and fourth are closely related. When Ezekiel views the "glory of God" in these visions, what tradition has construed as the divine chariot, thus the *merkabah* vision, it is in one of two places. Babylon is the setting of the first vision and Jerusalem of the second and fourth. Along with the locations, the movement of the divine glory in each vision is also central to its meaning. In the first vision, the *kabod* is in Babylon and moves in no particular direction. The divine presence is with the exiles in Babylon and is stationary in that place. The second and fourth visions are essentially reversals of one another. In Ezekiel 8–10 the divine glory rises up out of Jerusalem and departs eastward, while the entire new temple vision in 40–48 revolves around a divine return from the east and descent back into Jerusalem. The glory of YHWH cannot be present for the destruction of the city that takes place between these two moments. Whether it intends to or not, the sequence of visions in Ezekiel makes the divine presence entirely urban. One possible response to that is the notion of *kabod*, the word Ezekiel uses for "glory" in these visions: Because it comes from the Hebrew root that has to do with heaviness or density, the idea developed that the divine presence in the Jerusalem temple was its densest, but not only, manifestation. It is possible to assume that the less dense divine presence, representing other places, accompanies the *kabod*, but there is no explicit mention of this in the text. If cities are the dwelling place of YHWH, or at least of YHWH's densest presence, then they cannot be entirely negative entities. They can be punished for disobedience, and they can embody the punishing force; but these roles are distinct from their essential existence.

There is at least some dispute concerning if and how the prophetic message of judgment and destruction was aimed toward cities. Joseph Blenkinsopp has contended that the first half of the book of Isaiah contains a "back to nature" emphasis that is anti-urban in its intent. He found this theme in texts that portray urban settings reverting back to their wilder origins. Cities portrayed as pastureland appear in 5:17, 27:11, and 32:14, and the famous theophany of Isaiah ben Amoz in chapter 6 includes a striking image of depopulation:

> "Until cities lie waste
>   without inhabitant,
> and houses without people,
>   and the land is utterly desolate. (6:11)

The destruction and depopulation theme is Isaiah's proclamation in 32:13–14:

> For the soil of my people
>   growing up in thorns and briers;
> yes, for all the joyous houses
>   in the jubilant city.
> For the palace will be forsaken,
>   the populous city deserted;
> the hill and the watchtower
>   will become dens forever,
> the joy of wild asses,
>   a pasture for flocks.

Blenkinsopp argued that this divine action against cities is a response to the abuse and injustice of elite, urban populations against peasants who lived a more traditional, rural way of life.[17] There is no denying that the coming disaster projected in these texts will affect cities through destruction and depopulation, but it is difficult to see that the impact is only against cities if the land itself is "utterly desolate" and the fertility of the soil is also affected. The following text in Isaiah 32:15–20 presents a more complicated picture, however, as it seems uncertain that the city will benefit from the great restoration in the same way that rural settings will:

> My people will abide in a peaceful habitation,
>   in secure dwellings, and in quiet resting places.
> The forest will disappear completely,
>   and the city will be utterly laid low.
> Happy will you be who sow beside every stream,
>   who let the ox and the donkey range freely. (32:18–20)

Blenkinsopp's interpretation of this restoration as a reversal of urbanization resulting in a "rural utopia" is possible, but it relies on a reading of verses 18–19 that seems out of place in the text.[18] If this is a pro-rural, anti-urban text, then why does the forest suffer like the city? J. Roberts has proposed that "the city" here does not refer to urban locations in Israel or Judah, but perhaps to the cities that have attacked and destroyed them, such as Nineveh or Babylon.[19] This would make verses 15–20 a more internally coherent text but would mean that the referent of "the city" has changed drastically since verse 13, without any clear signal. The LXX reading of these verses does not mention a city at all, and could indicate either a textual corruption that placed it here, or a text that the translator(s) found so confusing they emended it. Before leaving the issue behind, it seems necessary to ask what a city and a forest have in common, if the Hebrew text placing them in parallel is the appropriate one for our interpretation. The most obvious similarity, in contrast to the other kinds of settings in the immediate surroundings, is that these two take a long time to develop. Forests and cities that had been destroyed would not be back to their ideal state for a long time. Nevertheless, the oracle still promises prosperity and happiness, even at the beginning of a long national recovery.

The other side of this issue has emerged in the claims of Lester Grabbe that the Israelite prophets were not particularly focused on urban settings or elite members of society in their words of condemnation and predictions of destruction. Instead, the focus of their critique was on shrines. Grabbe contended that shrines may or may not have been in urban locations, but he had difficulty identifying a shrine in a rural location. The shrine that Samuel attends in 1 Samuel 9 is not in the center of the town but appears to be attached to the town. Samuel and the people making use of it live in the town. Grabbe's conclusion that the association of shrines with high places or trees in 1 Kings 11:7 or 2 Kings 11:10 places them "out in the country" is without any evidence and defies logic.[20] He is correct that there is likely not as clear a distinction between urban and rural in the ancient world as in modern times. Cities would have been dependent on agricultural production without means to transport food long distances, and he assumed from this that prophetic critique could not focus just on cities. His assertions that agricultural land was the "traditional wealth of the elite" seems particularly problematic, though, in light of the massive labor requirement necessary to make land valuable.[21] In his conclusions, Grabbe seemed to be looking for, and not finding, a critique of the abuse of urban power and influence coming from a rural perspective.[22] As the discussion above concluded, the prophets were urban persons, working in urban environments, and their words of judgment were aimed at these places, primarily Jerusalem. This does not mean that the behavior they condemned could not have also taken place elsewhere or that persons from rural areas were not also participants. Likewise, at least some of the impact of the coming destruction would affect rural areas and their occupants, even if cities took the direct blows. To say of the prophets that "there is no favoritism: they hate everybody," is too blunt an assessment.[23]

A careful assessment of the prophetic message must navigate between the extremities of these issues. The behaviors that the prophets denounced were political, economic, and religious, and these spheres of life overlapped to a much greater degree in the ancient world. By the time the prophets came along, the centralized institutions of palace and temple were the focus of these activities, so these were their primary targets. Participation in these institutions was not limited to people who lived in cities where they were located, so urban occupants were not the exclusive offenders against whom they spoke. The prophetic scrolls are not inherently opposed to urban institutions, though. They assume these institutions can operate in a righteous manner. They all seek the restoration of Jerusalem and the temple, even if their visions of that task differ. The examination of these visions of restoration in the next chapter must wait until after a closer examination of the destruction and what it meant particularly for urban environments.

Through the intense period of threat, invasion, and destruction the roles that foreign cities play shifts. At least four important foreign political entities participate in Israel's understanding of its fate: Nineveh, Tyre, Babylon, and Edom. The first two of these are specific cities, while the third is both city and imperial nation, and the last is a territorial kingdom. There is some ambiguity in the presentation of each of these foreign entities, but the degree of ambiguity concerning Nineveh is striking. The extremes are present in the books of Jonah and Nahum, which in the Greek order of the Book of the Twelve are next to each other. The order in the Hebrew Bible, followed by most modern Bibles, places Micah between them, and it is tempting to think that the tension about Nineveh could have been the reason for this movement, if the Greek order is older.[24] The Greek sequence of Jonah-Nahum-Obadiah could even be a sequence that looks outward toward foreign nations, before the closing sequence of the Twelve comes back to an emphasis on Jerusalem.[25] In this case, it would be what Jonah and Nahum have in common, a fixation on Nineveh, which brings them together. Steven Holloway has highlighted the two very different roles of Nineveh in biblical memory. It demonstrated that no empire was too powerful for Israel's God to bring to justice, and that even the sins of this wicked city were not too great for this God's mercy. Thus, Nineveh "functioned as a wildcard for theological meditation."[26]

The function of Babylon also demonstrates a high degree of ambiguity. The earlier discussion demonstrated the view that YHWH used both Nineveh and Babylon as weapons to punish the disobedience of Israel and Judah, and would ultimately punish them for playing that role. The image of Babylon is one of the most powerful and ubiquitous in the Bible and in various traditions of reading it. Ulrike Sals has argued that the Bible raises the image of Babylon to a level so far greater than the material presence of the city and empire itself that it "divinizes" it, rendering its condemnation and destruction that much more powerful. This status allows Babylon to rise and be defeated over and over again. The Hebrew Bible constructs a "three-way relationship" among YHWH, Babylon, and Jerusalem, and the relationship to this ultimate other city, which repulses and attracts, is essential to Jerusalem's identity.[27]

The city of Tyre appears in the Hebrew Bible with surprising frequency, and its portrayals are diverse in scope. Aside from the texts that use Tyre as an important northeastern boundary point along the Mediterranean coast, the early appearances of Tyre in the biblical story involve the relationship of its kings, Hiram and Huram, with David and Solomon. Second Samuel 5 and 1 Chronicles 14 report Hiram sending building materials to David for his palace. In 1 Kings 5 and 2 Chronicles 2, Hiram (or Huram) supplies Solomon with material and workers for the construction of the temple in Jerusalem. Philippe Guillaume has emphasized the ways in which Tyre became a "template for Jerusalem." Tyre had become an enemy of Jerusalem in some prophetic texts, like Jeremiah 25 and Ezekiel 26, but the similar fates of the two cities, at the hands of the same enemies, and the memory of the relationship with David and Solomon presented different possibilities. The connection of the Second Temple to Solomon's temple created a connection to the latter's origins in Tyre, and the patronage of Cyrus mirrored that of Hiram and Huram. Guillaume argued further that in biblical memory Tyre functioned as an ideal of material luxury and isolated grandeur that Jerusalem emulated, and which its occupants imagined when it fell short.[28]

In 1 Samuel 8 the Israelites say, "Give us a king like other nations." Though they never say this line about having a great city outright, they behave as if it is an equal desire. The scribes who wrote the biblical books did not portray cities as inherently evil, even if some of the traditions they inherited tended in this direction. Nevertheless, the workings of cities as seats of empire and targets for destruction often meant that they were the primary actors in terrible stories, and those looking for negative depictions can find plenty of examples. The full picture around such texts, however, presents a more nuanced perspective. Nineveh, Babylon, and Tyre are all multifaceted characters in biblical traditions, and prophetic texts use their relationships to Israelite cities in malleable and complex ways.

THE CITY AS REFUGE AND PLACE OF DEATH

The destruction of a city was a brutal act in the ancient world, in part because of the way cities were designed. They were built on hills with walls to make them impenetrable, which led to the development of siege warfare. Once a city was conquered, there were practical and ideological reasons to extend the destruction to an extreme level, which the discussion below will explore. Despite the preoccupation with cities in the various accounts of destruction, there is a remarkable lack of detail about the lived reality of the people residing in those places. The stunning exception to the rule is the book of Lamentations, often hidden because of its size and its inability to find an easy place within the biblical canons. The personification of the city of Jerusalem, particularly as an abused woman, presents serious challenges and potent possibilities for the view of cities it helps to form. The grammatical challenges presented by the most common word for city in Biblical Hebrew, ʿir, have arisen in earlier discussions. The word is grammatically feminine, so whenever it is the subject of a verb, represented by a pronoun, or modified by an adjective, those other parts of speech are required to be feminine for grammatical reasons. The one strange variation to this feminine grammatical identity is that when ʿir is made plural it takes the plural ending most often used on masculine nouns. Still, even in this seemingly masculine form, the other words associated with it will always be feminine. These grammatical necessities raise interesting questions about personification. Is the personification of Jerusalem in the book of Lamentations necessarily feminine because of the grammar of the word? This might be the case, but the poet(s) of this book take extra measures to highlight the feminine identity of the city. The most prominent device is the use of the word "daughter" along with the name Zion. Lamentations is not the only place this construction appears, but nearly half of the occurrences of "daughter Zion" in the entire Hebrew Bible appear in this tiny book.[29] It was once a popular claim that the designation of cities in the ancient Near East as female figures derived from the understanding of cities as goddesses, married to their corresponding male gods. More recent work has called this assumption into question and revealed a more diverse use of female personification that cannot be traced back to one primary origin.[30] The primary emphasis of the female imagery in Lamentations, which most often uses the daughter terminology, is the sense of endearment. The use of language referring to a young woman may also have been intended to portray the vulnerability of Jerusalem in this context.[31]

The problematic feminine portrayal of cities appears in many places in the prophetic literature. In many parts of Jeremiah, Jerusalem is portrayed as an unfaithful wife, who will be punished in the upcoming invasion. The threat becomes most poignant in 13:26–27:

> I myself will lift up your skirts over your face,
>   and your shame will be seen.
> I have seen your abominations,
>   your adulteries and neighings, your shameless prostitutions
>   on the hills of the countryside.
> Woe to you, O Jerusalem!
>   How long will it be before you are made clean.

The threat of exposure comes in divine language through the prophet and stands in full contrast to the safety ordinarily provided by a city and its walls, and it is cast in the most extreme terms of sexual violence.[32] The feminine grammar of cities may have made them more useful as a component of the marriage metaphor than grammatically masculine nations would have been, but the discussion above established that nations and their capital cities could be interchangeable in prophetic speech. The use of cities and the feminine identity they carried could have been avoided in these texts.

Hosea 1–3 is perhaps the earliest and most concrete portrayal of the marriage metaphor between Israel and YHWH. The narrative(s) that sound like a literal marriage of Hosea to a woman characterized as unfaithful or impure functions as a parallel to YHWH's marriage to Israel, and it helps call attention to the problems of the metaphor. In the metaphorical marriage between God and Israel, like Hosea's marriage in the text, the husband is always presumed to be the innocent party, while all of the fault for the disrupted relationship is placed on the female participant in the relationship. The woman's unfaithfulness has offended the man, and his anger and violence in response are always justified, regardless of whether the accusation is true. This assumption appears most dramatically in the horrific legal text prescribing the trial by bitter water in Numbers 5. When a metaphor is repeated regularly, the comparison begins to move in both directions. If the metaphor states that God is "like a husband," over and over again, eventually it starts to imply that a husband is like God.[33] The reversal of the metaphor both strengthens and legitimates the hierarchal nature of marriage already present in most cultures. When these problems are combined, the accusations of infidelity that justify a violent divine response to Israel's infidelity serve to justify spousal abuse in human marriages, both within the text and in social contexts in which these texts are used, including modern contexts. The violent response of the male speaker in Jeremiah above, and of Hosea in 2:3–4 illustrate the point:

> I will strip her naked
>   and expose her as in the day she was born,
> and make her like a wilderness,
>   and turn her into a parched land,
>   and kill her with thirst.

The woman in this text is entirely in the man's control. She has no voice with which to object to the accusations or his treatment of her. Julia O'Brien gives attention to the function of this metaphor as one part of a collection of divine images, including God as "authoritarian father" and "angry warrior." These images and the tendency of readers to accept them uncritically demand a response that identifies the problematic assumptions and destructive results of such reading practices.[34] The operation of this metaphor will come into play again below in the discussion of the destruction of cities, which often take on a feminine identity.

The ways in which foreign invading armies attacked Israel may also support the power of the marriage metaphor. Beyond simple individual weapons like swords, spears, and sling-stones, most of what archaeology can recover and reconstruct about ancient warfare has to do with attacking cities. The artifact known as the Lachish Relief was found in Nineveh in the nineteenth century and depicts the Assyrian attack on the Judahite city of Lachish, probably the second most important city after Jerusalem. The scenes depicted on the stone reliefs are accompanied by an inscription that identifies Lachish, and appears to match the events described in the biblical version of Sennacherib's invasion of Judah at the end of the eighth century, which mentions Lachish specifically in 2 Kings 18:13–18. The scenes depict siege warfare against a city. Sennacherib's own annals also provide an account of the invasion of Judah, including forty-six walled cities. The focus of Sennacherib's record is on cities and towns, including Jerusalem, the one he was not able to enter, but kept surrounded so that King Hezekiah could not escape.[35] Regardless of the extent to which ancient armies may have marauded in the countryside, the focus of the effort and the accounts left behind was the conquering of cities.

Jacob Wright describes a motivation for the destruction of cities as the central element of warfare using the concept of "urbicide," which he defined as "the premeditated and deliberate destruction of cities, their iconic architecture, and their identity."[36] The prophetic literature participates in this practice most clearly in the portions of the scrolls commonly called the "oracles against the nations." These pronouncements of judgment against foreign powers can be found in many places, but each of the scrolls also has a specific concentration of this material, such as in Isaiah 13–23, Jeremiah 46–51, and Ezekiel 25–32. The Book of the Twelve also concentrates this type of oracle in Nahum, Obadiah, and parts of Amos. In these cases the warfare is imagined, as vengeance for the role these enemies played in the destruction of Israel and Judah or as the culmination of long-term regional conflicts, but they also reflect the descriptions of warfare in the royal records of some of the nations against whom they are pronounced.[37] When the Israelite prophets threatened divine visitation on their enemies, the destruction of their major cities was the focus of attention. Amos 1:9–10 and Isaiah 15:2–3 may serve as examples:

> For three transgressions of Tyre,
>   and for four, I will not revoke the punishment;
> because they delivered entire communities over to Edom,
>   and did not remember the covenant of kinship.

So I will send a fire on the wall of Tyre,
  fire that shall devour its strongholds.
                                        Amos 1:9–10

Dibon has gone up to the temple,
  to the high places to weep;
over Nebo and over Medeba
  Moab wails.
On every head is baldness,
  every beard is shorn;
in the streets they bind on sackcloth;
  on the housetops and in the squares
everyone wails and melts in tears.
                                        Isaiah 15:2–3

As Wright observes, "Cities were to be the crowning cultural achievements of
their populations, sources of pride, symbols of royal power, places of habitation
offering a secure haven from the natural world. . . . The authors of these
texts evidently had trouble imagining a more insufferable form of political
humiliation than the demolition of cherished cities."[38] Earlier descriptions of
cities have given attention to the organization of villages around the major
city, which would have participated in its political and economic life. A threat
to the city would have been a threat to these satellite communities as well.

The desire of prophetic texts to portray Jerusalem, Samaria, and other cities
as deserving of divine punishment and potentially redeemable at the same
time posed a significant literary and theological challenge. This challenge
was magnified by the need to use the great enemy empires as the tools of
YHWH's cause. The extremes of such an effort, and the distortions it can
render, are on full display in one of the most vivid and horrifying texts in all of
the biblical tradition. In Ezekiel 23 the two conquered capitals receive female
names and are portrayed as sisters:

> The word of the LORD came to me: Mortal, there were two women,
> the daughters of one mother; they played the whore in Egypt; they
> played the whore in their youth; their breasts were caressed there,
> and their virgin bosoms were fondled. Oholah was the name of the
> elder and Oholibah the name of her sister. They became mine, and
> they bore sons and daughters. As for their names, Oholah is Samaria,
> and Oholibah is Jerusalem. Oholah played the whore while she was
> mine; she lusted after her lovers the Assyrians, warriors clothed in
> blue, governors and commanders, all of them handsome young men,
> mounted horsemen. (23:1–6)

After the attack of Assyria on Samaria/Ohola, the text portrays an equally
brutal attack on Jerusalem/Oholibah by the Babylonians. The shocking nature

of the text presents profound difficulties for interpreters. The subjection of female characters to shaming, rape, and murder by male characters, including YHWH, threatens to make any kind of reading complicit in such acts. The most apparent interpretations join in on the abuse of these women. YHWH states that these two sisters became his wives and "bore sons and daughters" for him. The linking of the two women to the central cities of the two nations, rather than the nations as a whole, is a difficult feature. As the text above noted, the use of capital cities as equivalent terms for the whole nation is present in other texts. The primary accusations have to do with making foreign alliances and idolatry. Because of the location of the palaces and temples in these cities, they would have been the central location for these sins, but they would not necessarily have defined the limits.

The sons and daughters of the two women, who would seem most likely to be the inhabitants of the cities, also suffer in the ensuing violence:

> I will direct my indignation against you, in order that they may deal with you in fury. They shall cut off your nose and your ears, and your survivors shall fall by the sword. They shall seize your sons and your daughters, and your survivors shall be devoured by fire. They shall also strip you of your clothes and take away your fine jewels. (23:25–26)

The identity of the children is not entirely clear, and the parabolic or allegorical nature of the texts may make this ambiguity unavoidable. To what extent are these children to blame for their part of the suffering? Can their fate be separated from the fate of their mothers? The allegorical portrayal of the sisters may allow for some sense of separation here, but it is a slippery matter:

> But righteous judges shall declare them guilty of adultery and of bloodshed; because they are adulteresses and blood is on their hands. For thus says the Lord GOD: Bring up an assembly against them, and make them an object of terror and of plunder. The assembly shall stone them and with their swords they shall cut them down; they shall kill their sons and their daughters, and burn up their houses. Thus will I put an end to lewdness in the land, so that all women may take warning and not commit lewdness as you have done. (23:45–48)

There is an audience for this text that lies outside the harsh punishment, and that may even participate in it. These two women take on the sins of Israel/Samaria and Judah/Jerusalem. Is there space in the text for innocent bystanders?

A text with similar characteristics appears in Ezekiel 16. The cover names and some of the allegorical flavor are missing in this tirade against Jerusalem. Still, the city is portrayed as a woman and a child-bride of YHWH, and her sins, mostly dalliances with foreign powers like Egypt, Assyria, and Babylon, are portrayed as the actions of a whore. Once again, Samaria enters the portrait of disobedience, but this time paired with Sodom and used to compare the sins of Jerusalem, which are worse than either of these other cities. The story takes a surprising turn, particularly for a text so early in a prophetic scroll, and speaks of restoration, but these words of recovery are tempered in two ways. First, in verses 53–55, the restoration of Samaria and Sodom come first. The state of these cities at the time of Ezekiel would not have provided a promising sense of hope. Second, the restoration of Jerusalem would not be based on its righteousness or the greatness of its past but on its shame for its disobedient behavior.[39] The text specifically mentions the pride and arrogance of Sodom, and Jerusalem is painted as a follower of the ways of the "sister city." The assumption of this claim, though, is that cities do not have to behave this way. Jerusalem's shame about its past offers the possibility for a new covenant between YHWH and its people and a future not characterized by the attitudes of Sodom.

The beginning of this chapter observed that all of the descriptions of the destruction of Judah (2 Kgs. 25 / Jer. 52; 2 Chr. 36; and Jer. 39) not only focused the force of the destruction onto the city of Jerusalem but also described the defeat as a reduction of the nation to a rural scene. Nothing but vineyards and fields and the vinedressers and tillers who worked in them would remain. In the dramatic trial of Jeremiah, Jeremiah 26:9 portrays the people questioning the prophet: "'Why have you prophesied in the name of the LORD, saying, "This house shall be like Shiloh, and this city shall be desolate, without inhabitant?"' And all the people gathered around Jeremiah in the house of the LORD." Jeremiah 26:16–18 reports that others rose in defense of Jeremiah: "'This man does not deserve the sentence of death, for he has spoken to us in the name of the LORD our God.' And some of the elders of the land arose and said to all the assembled people, 'Micah of Moresheth, who prophesied during the days of King Hezekiah of Judah, said to all the people of Judah: Thus says the LORD of hosts,

> Zion shall be plowed as a field;
> Jerusalem shall become a heap of ruins,
> and the mountain of the house a wooded height.

The quotation from the prophet Micah also appears in the book of Micah at 3:12. Again the end of a nation and its freedom is portrayed as the destruction of its urban center and the reduction of its identity to a rural or agricultural setting. To be a nation, which the Israel projected in the biblical text apparently wanted and expected to be, it needed urban centers. The destruction of those was the destruction of the national identity.

For the people writing the texts, urban scribes, this meant the destruction of their homes and the end of their way of life. The previous chapter observed the evidence that scribes from the northern nation of Israel were among the refugees who fled to Judah when the Assyrian Empire invaded and destroyed the northern nation, including its major cities. The analogous situation a century and a half later, when the Babylonians conquered Judah, would have been the deportation of scribes to Babylon. If the characterization of the "exile" that contemporary scholarship has reached is roughly correct, and a relatively small group of elite citizens of Judah went to Babylon, then it seems likely that some members of the scribal class would have been among them. The next chapter will examine some of this evidence more closely and evaluate the common perception that during most of the sixth century the land of Judah was empty. For those producing the traditions that would find their way into biblical books, the land may have been empty of them and those like them, and an understanding of the disastrous events would develop that required growth of this idea, even if it bore little or no resemblance to the situation outside the text.

THE DESTRUCTION OF CITIES
IN THE MODERN WORLD

Military invasions of cities in the modern world do not typically look like those in the ancient world, because of the development of artillery and air power. Surrounding a city and bombarding it with artillery may still be described as a "siege," but this is different from an ancient siege. Modern cities do not have walls to penetrate. The most notable exception is the famous siege of Leningrad that lasted more than two years during the middle of World War II. The size of the city, compared to the walled portions of ancient cities, meant that there was still some land for food production in Leningrad and there were limited ways in and out. Still, the death toll in Leningrad may have been as many as one million. The organization of political and military power in larger nations has also reduced the military advantage of completely destroying individual cities. Targets are more likely to be the facilities that produce weapons.

The pattern that many cities in the United States have gone through in the last fifty years presents an interesting comparison to an ancient siege. The core of many American cities became hollowed out in the mid to late twentieth century. A long list of American cities, including Baltimore, Boston, Chicago, Cleveland, Detroit, Minneapolis, Philadelphia, and St. Louis reached their peak populations in the 1950s and 1960s. These numbers are sometimes masked by the counting of populations of "metropolitan areas." Within many of these cities, African American neighborhoods and areas were often effectively walled off by the building of housing projects and the placement of interstate highways, bridges, railroad lines, and overpasses.[40] Economics kept people from leaving, rather than military threat, and the difficulties of moving in and out of these areas effectively reduced commerce. The advent of "food deserts" in many cities also resembles the impact of ancient sieges.

During this period some cities went through consolidation with the county government, so that the two are no longer separate. The primary migration was not away from the metropolitan area but to the suburbs. There are several important causes for this development, but race was a driving force. The integration of public schools after the 1954 *Brown v. Board of Education* decision and the effects of the Civil Rights Act of 1964 began to erode the barriers between white and black communities, resulting in "white flight" to the suburbs. The growth of automobile manufacturing and the development of road systems made travel into the city for work easier, and "bedroom communities" sprouted. The development of the suburban shopping mall made downtown retail areas unnecessary, and they dwindled. This trend has reversed over the past two or three decades, but the new businesses that come into these growing urban areas often do so at the expense of those that had continued to operate.[41] The forces of gentrification treat the return to cities as if they were empty while the gentrifiers were not there. The cities were damaged by internal forces rather than external invasion, but the evaluation of the restoration in the next chapter can lead to some observations about what the two have in common.

7

Let Them Go Up

*Rebuilding Jerusalem and Reasserting
the Divine Claim on Urban Life*

The story of Israel during the two centuries after the exile, the time often called the Persian period, is not well attested in the biblical literature. The narrative in Ezra–Nehemiah is entirely focused on rebuilding Jerusalem, and that will be a significant theme throughout this chapter. The canonical story of Israel in the Persian period is thoroughly urban. Obviously, the surrounding land had to be farmed to provide food for the cities and a foundation for the kind of economy the Persian Empire would have demanded in order to produce maximum tribute, but references to agriculture appear only obliquely in Ezra–Nehemiah and Haggai. The extent to which agricultural activity would have survived throughout the sixth century, and thus been continuous, will require further treatment below. The Ezra–Nehemiah story also limits its attention to the persons who had returned from exile in Babylon and came to Jerusalem. This theologically and ideologically driven focus of attention has helped generate rigorous debates about the history of Israel in the Persian period.

The group of people taken captive to Babylon in the late seventh and early sixth centuries, and their family members who eventually returned to Judah several decades later, became known as the "golah" group. The name seems to have derived from a verb that means "expose." The various ways these people might have understood themselves to have been exposed cannot be listed with any certainty, but the abundance of possibilities yields a sense that it is a fitting name. On the other hand, were they any more exposed than other groups who were affected differently by the conquest? That they saw this as a way of differentiating themselves may be an initial indication of a self-centered view that lacked awareness of the experiences of other people. Only fragments of information are available about the lives of these people while they were in Babylon, but it appears that their experience there was primarily urban. One reflection of this in the biblical text is the letter Jeremiah sends to the exiles in Jeremiah 29:1–23. A number of assumptions seem to be at play when Jeremiah urges them to "Seek the welfare of the city where I have sent you into exile, and pray to the Lord on its behalf, for in its welfare you will find your welfare." The letter need not have been sent by a historical Jeremiah to a group in Babylon that existed outside the text in order to reflect the situation there. More significantly, the letter need not represent the situation of the exiles in Babylon precisely in order to reveal how the writers of Jeremiah and their audience perceived that situation. The exiled community the letter posits is living in an urban environment and they are persons capable of functioning productively in that environment. Further, living productive urban lives will best prepare these persons or their descendants for a return to the land of Judah after the exile. So, the return that is most visible in the text is a return to Jerusalem. The need for such preparation is further defined in the prior admonition from Jeremiah: "Build houses and live in them; plant gardens and eat what they produce. Take wives and have sons and daughters; take wives for your sons, and give your daughters in marriage, that they may bear sons and daughters; multiply there, and do not decrease" (29:5–6).

Rainer Albetz uses the "golah" term more broadly, describing both those scattered earlier by the Assyrian Empire and those who relocated to Egypt in the Babylonian period as the "Assyrian golah" and the "Egyptian golah."[1] This usage properly points to the problem of allowing one group to own that terminology. The problem created by naming groups has received significant attention from Jill Middlemas, who recognized that naming groups and naming the time period risks making one particular kind of experience normative. With this realization she proposes replacing the term "Exile" with "The Templeless Age," asserting that it was the loss of the geographical and architectural center of its religious identity that most defined this time for Judah.[2] At the same time, such terminology emphasizes urban experience and identity by placing its focus on that particular urban center. There is some evidence outside the Bible about the lives of exiled citizens of Judah living in Babylon during the sixth century.[3] Albertz points to evidence that those exiled from Judah lived in lands that the Babylonian Empire was attempting to resettle, and that they had relative autonomy to develop their communities and engage in agriculture. One cuneiform tablet from the early fifth century indicates the presence of a settlement called "the city of Judah."[4] Whoever named the place seemed to have seen it as a reflection of this group's past experience, and perhaps a projection of its future. This discussion of naming helps bring into view a broader range of Judahite society and experience, but it should not hide the recognition that the story of exile to Babylon and return to Jerusalem did win the ideological battle within canonical texts and has had an outsized effect in shaping the way readers of the Bible think about that period of time.

Another likely reason the narrative of return was focused on Judah's capital city is that most or all of the returning people descended from persons who had lived there before. The extent of the actual deportation and of the population left behind in Judah has been a matter of dispute. The disagreement itself reveals the paucity of data on which to base useful conclusions. The old assumption that the majority of the Judahite population was taken into captivity by the Babylonians, while only a small number remained in Judah, was based in large part on a literal reading of 2 Kings 25:12 and 2 Chronicles 36:21. The exclusive attention to the community of returned exiles in Ezra–Nehemiah also feeds this assumption. These texts, however, are ideologically and theologically motivated. Not only have the narratives in Kings and Chronicles long presented the story of Israel as the story of its central institutions and little else, they also wish to portray the Babylonian invasion as an act of divine retribution unequalled in Israel's past. Only something near total destruction will fit the needs of the story. It was in the interests of Ezra–Nehemiah to present a desolate and deserted landscape in and around Jerusalem, an interest explained in greater detail below. For contemporary historians and archaeologists, the idea that the vast majority of the population of Judah—at least tens of thousands, if not hundreds of thousands, of people—was deported to Babylon is untenable.[5] Neither the logistics of such a massive movement, nor the motive to carry it out seem reasonable in any way. The previous chapter concludes that the total population of both kingdoms during the eighth century was moving toward four hundred thousand before the Assyrian invasion, with more than half of those in Israel. Assuming significant movement into Judah from Israel as a result of that invasion, the population of Judah by the end of the seventh century could have been as high as three hundred thousand, perhaps ten thousand of whom may have lived in Jerusalem.[6] The alternative view, that a relatively small group of people was exiled, while the vast majority stayed in Judah, has been most clearly expressed in Hans Barstad's work *The Myth of the Empty Land*. The presentation by Oded Lipschits in his monumental work, *The Rise and Fall of Jerusalem*, is somewhat different, but leads to similar conclusions. The Babylonian invasion brought severe disruption to life in Jerusalem, but life in the remainder of Judah appears to have been largely unaffected.[7]

The story of exile and return became the dominant narrative for the literature in the Tanakh, which explains a portrayal that leaves the impression of a huge deportation. This reading of the text can coexist with historical conclusions that the deportation was much smaller. If the deportation was limited and small, then its primary focus was almost certainly the urban elites of Jerusalem. The idea that the walled portion of Jerusalem was emptied as a result of the Babylonian invasion might be closer to the reality outside the text. Even if relatively few people were taken captive, a significant level of destruction could have rendered the city uninhabitable. The destruction of a walled city and its major structures, such as temples and palaces, seems like a lot of effort for a conquering army, so it is appropriate to wonder what the payoff would be. The previous chapter explores the concept of "urbicide." Destroying a city beyond what was necessary to invade and conquer it may have expressed symbolic and psychological power for an empire. This kind of destruction fits the presentation of some texts in the Bible and accounts of city destructions from that period in other sources.[8] Once again, however, there were theological and ideological reasons for the writers of 2 Kings, 2 Chronicles, and Ezra–Nehemiah to portray the destruction in more complete form than what might have taken place in events outside the text. The rationale of Ezra 3–6 will not work unless the temple and its altar need to be rebuilt from the ground up. A clear discontinuity in worship allowed for the destruction of Jerusalem to be understood as a punishment, even an atonement, for the sins of Jerusalem, cleansing the city and its temple for a new beginning. The heroic portrait of Nehemiah is dependent upon the necessity of rebuilding the walls of Jerusalem. Sara Japhet has documented the ways in which the story of the exodus and the story of the restoration resemble one another. For Japhet the story in Ezra–Nehemiah is deliberately shaped to follow the exodus story. It is possible that it works the other way around, but it seems most likely that both stories fit what Japhet calls "an overarching historical cycle, of enslavement and deliverance, as a fulfillment of the word of God," without one necessarily functioning as a model for the other.[9]

Regardless of the reasons—historical, ideological, or theological—the portrayal of the restoration in the biblical literature ends up looking like the rebuilding of a city. The events that dominate the two parts of Ezra–Nehemiah are the rebuilding and dedication of the new temple at the center and the wall around the perimeter.[10] The shortage of resources in Jerusalem during the early part of the Persian period is a subject that arises in two different sources, Nehemiah and Haggai. In both cases the purity of the city and the function of the sanctuary within it are directly linked to the productivity of the land. Perhaps even more than in other parts of the biblical story, agriculture is presumed but invisible. While in reality the success and livability of the city would be entirely dependent on productive agriculture around it, Haggai 2:15–19 reverses this idea, making the fertility of the ground dependent upon the proper operation of the temple at the center of a restored Jerusalem. This orientation of the story will continue after an examination of the kinds of people who would have been responsible for constructing it.

SCRIBALISM IN THE RESTORATION

The opening chapter of this book gave some attention to the development of scribal culture in ancient Israel, and the subject has surfaced at other points along the way. It is significant to this study for two reasons. Scribes are the ones who produced the texts, so their perspectives are present in it, even if they were making use of traditions they did not produce. In addition, scribes were necessarily urban persons. The activities of a city would have required the services of scribes, and the city provided the necessary milieu for a scribal culture to develop and flourish. The relative scarcity of written texts with which literary scribes worked would have required centralized collections. Scribes were not just those who wrote texts, but also the primary ones who could read and interpret them. The book of Ezra–Nehemiah elevates scribes to a new status within the story of Israel. The rebuilding of the city of Jerusalem in the book of Nehemiah functions as a stage for Ezra the scribe. Donna Laird has introduced the concept of cultural capital, originated by sociologists Pierre Bordieu and Jean-Claude Passeron, to the many aspects of the restoration project depicted in Ezra–Nehemiah, including the portrayal of scribes. Because the ability to read was scarce, and written documents possessed authority, scribes possessed this cultural capital which they could use to promote the rebuilding of the city and establish their power within it.[11] The grand scene in Nehemiah 8 brings Ezra before an assembled crowd at the Water Gate, eventually flanked by an array of lesser scribes, prepared to explain the words that Ezra reads. The scene will not work in a rural setting. It needs a city, but it needs much more.[12] While Ezra–Nehemiah portrays the rebuilding of Jerusalem as a faithful Israelite task, it is also one that depends on the sponsorship of the Persian Empire. The characters named Ezra and Nehemiah both come to Jerusalem with sponsorship from the empire, and the initial group that had come before them to rebuild the temple had similar imperial support. The Torah that Ezra reads has the authority of Moses (Neh. 8:1), but it also has the authority of Persia.[13] Thus the scribe and his book, which work in tandem in the scene, have enormous power, and it is centralized power to which others must travel. Jack Miles has observed that the scroll of the law in this scene has replaced, and even become, the divine presence in the story, to the extent that the people bow down before the scroll in Nehemiah 8:6. They are not in the temple in this scene, where the divine presence traditionally resided, but standing before the platform where the great scribe stands with the scroll.[14]

The extent to which such scenes took place outside of the text is difficult to say. For a broader public to be aware of the contents of written scrolls, something like them would have been necessary, but did such performances become normative? The previous chapter examined the scene in Jeremiah 36, in which Baruch the scribe writes a scroll containing the proclamations of Jeremiah. Baruch takes the scroll and reads it publicly in the temple, after which he is summoned by royal officials, who also need a scribe to read a complex text to them. The scroll was eventually destroyed by the king, but Baruch re-created it with additional material. This story likely reflects some of the way the scribes who produced the prophetic scrolls understood themselves and their work. If the scene in Ezra is also a reflection of how scribes at the time of its composition viewed their work in relation to the law and the community, then persons living outside of Jerusalem would have become dependent upon pilgrimages to the city not just for sacred rituals, but for their understanding of the laws that governed various aspects of their lives. This would have been one more force that made such a city a center of gravity in an ancient culture. Like the Baruch story, which reveals some of the ways the scribes who produced the book of Jeremiah understood themselves and their work, the story of Ezra may demonstrate the relationship between scribes, the "law of Moses," and the populace of Judah in the Persian period and beyond.

John Kessler has noted some of the difficulties in locating a high degree of literary output at the beginning of the Persian period in Jerusalem. The population recovered slowly and resources would have been limited in the period around 520. While the completion of the temple at about this time would have accelerated the growth of the city, development was likely modest until the middle of the fifth century. Kessler outlines a number of factors that would have made possible literary production somewhat beyond what the level of resources might predict.[15] Ehud Ben Zvi has pointed to the later time period, often labeled Persian II (450–333), the beginning of which correlates approximately with the traditional date for the arrival of Nehemiah, as a more likely period for the acceleration of literary activity in Jerusalem. Ben Zvi identifies the resources necessary for "the presence of a group of literati, and of a number of literati that is proportionally higher than expected in relation to the total population of a small province." These included the training and continuous support of a group of scribes and the need for the work that these persons would perform.[16] Ben Zvi concludes that the material in the Bible is so pervasively focused on Jerusalem that finding a center for its production in any other place seems impossible. Thus, looking for the right time in this place for such literary production leads to the Persian II period. The presence of a Jerusalem-centric text and the work of scribes in that place are phenomena that would have fed each other. The more these "literati" could position Jerusalem as the center of the story, the more Jerusalem would have been able to control and draw in the resources of the province of Yehud.[17]

Nehemiah 8:1 identifies "the scribe Ezra," and 8:2 calls him "the priest Ezra," so the two roles are not exclusive here.[18] Ezra brings "the book of the law of Moses" with him to the public gathering and reads it. Twice the passage refers to the audience as those who could "understand," but does not say what might cause others not to be able to understand. Perhaps it is age or language. Interpretive difficulties arise at 8:4, because the initial scene, with just Ezra reading the "book of the law of Moses" directly to the crowd, seems to come to an end. A separate account that fills 8:4–8 places Ezra on a stage, surrounded by a large collection of persons who are named in the text. Ezra reads "in the book, in the law of God" with the help of these other persons who explain the reading (8:7) to the crowd. The audience needs the help of the Levites in order to understand the reading, which makes them seem different from the audience in 8:1–3 that could apparently understand the reading directly. In 8:8 the actions of Ezra and the Levites become combined in a way that is not clear. The verb "read (qrʾ)" appears in plural form. This could be understood as a description of the combined task of Ezra reading aloud from the book and the others interpreting, but it raises questions about when this verb, which can also mean "proclaim" or "encounter," corresponds closely to what modern persons understand as reading. The reading work of the scribe is separated from the audience by a group of interpreters, who explain the reading, though 8:8 presents all of this collectively as part of the process of reading the law.[19] An important point this scene reinforces is the distance between the person who can write texts and read them and a general audience that not only cannot read, but must have a public reading explained to them.[20] If there are two layers of development in the composition of the story, verses 1–3 followed by verses 4–8, then the concentric spheres of scribal hierarchy between a written text and a public audience may have been multiple in some times and places, but not at others. Nehemiah 8:1–3 may portray one kind of reader-audience relationship and 8:4–8 another. The two texts together could also represent a growing hierarchy within the scribal world. In the second layer of the text the scribal world is one to which the people who gather in Jerusalem do not have direct access, and one in which they cannot participate without assistance. Jacob Wright has emphasized the ways in which the writers of Ezra–Nehemiah were changing the perception of the Torah to elevate the status of their own role. "The book depicts a shift from the study of texts and Torah as a means of reestablishing the temple to the study of Torah as an end in itself."[21] The end product of this process is a many layered discourse, as Wright describes further:

> The authors of Ezra–Nehemiah are exegetes, and they imbue their activities with greater authority by creating a historical memory according to which the heroes of the restoration did long ago what they are doing now. In deciding how to proceed with the restoration without their own king, and later when the high priesthood is corrupt, the Judeans follow the examples of the Persian kings and submit themselves to the absolute authority of their written traditions.[22]

It was this practice by the Persian rulers, recalled from the disputes of Ezra 4–5, which assured the group returning from exile the exclusive right to rebuild the temple and reestablish the worship of YHWH in Jerusalem.

Elsie Stern argues that "the representation of Torah in [Ezra–Nehemiah] corresponds to an oral-literary economy rather than a scriptural one."[23] This situation requires a "text-broker," and Ezra plays this role in Nehemiah 8. The use of the scroll, which is a sacred object in this text functions as an "authorizing strategy" for the program promoted by the scribe and his elite audience.[24] Like Baruch, Ezra became a legendary scribal figure, and multiple books over the next several centuries became associated with his name, indicating that future scribes continued to understand their work in some relation to this giant figure of the past.[25] The power of Ezra in the text becomes their power as scribes in their own contexts. Seth Sanders has demonstrated another aspect in which the portrayal of scribal characters demonstrates "scribes' identification and self-presentation."[26] The figures with which Sanders works, the ancient Adapa of Mesopotamian culture and the corresponding Enoch in Judaism, are not connected to narrative figures like Baruch and Ezra, but to mythic figures of the ancient past. These characters transcend particular historical situations in order to play a more powerful role in the formation of scribal culture and identity. Scribes like Baruch and Ezra may have been more attached to historical events, but they took on a legendary scribal status that at least mimicked that of Enoch in Jewish tradition.

CONTINUING THE STORY OF JERUSALEM

With this background in mind, it will be helpful to look at the story of Jerusalem at two points, its destruction and its rebuilding. The previous chapter examined the destruction of the city primarily through prophetic literature, which attempts to explain the events and their causes leading up to the destruction. Here the view of destruction will be from the position of the city, as best expressed in Lamentations, and looking back through the experience of restoration and rebuilding. Information about the first siege of Jerusalem in 598–597 BCE is available outside the biblical text in the Babylonian Chronicles, which narrate events from a Babylonian perspective. The first siege appears to have lasted a few months, resulting in Nebuchadnezzar's successful invasion of the city, after which he took the current king of Judah, Jehoiachin, prisoner and replaced him with another. The text also reports that Nebuchadnezzar extracted a tribute from Judah, with which he returned to Babylon.[27] The biblical descriptions of this event in 2 Kings 24:10–12 and 2 Chronicles 36:9–10 are more detailed but do not provide any direct disagreement with the Babylonian text. Both accounts specifically identify some of the loot as coming from the temple. There may be some value to looking back at a clearer case of parallel texts, the accounts of Sennacherib invading the area a little more than a century earlier. In this case, though the Assyrian Chronicles and the biblical accounts from 2 Kings 18–19 and 2 Chronicles 32 are obviously looking at the same events, there is significant disagreement among them. Both sides claim victory.[28] In the biblical accounts, Jerusalem, led by Hezekiah, withstands the Assyrian invasion, and keeps Judah at least somewhat intact. Biblical accounts differ among themselves as to whether Hezekiah paid Sennacherib tribute. Second Kings 18:13–16 says that he did, but the parallel passage in Isaiah omits that detail, as does 2 Chronicles. All three texts describe the magical defeat of the Assyrian army that sent Sennacherib back to his own city. The framework issue, on which accounts from both sides agree, is that stories of invasion and conquest center upon the siege and capture of the central city. The warfare depicted is all urban. This example reveals more clearly that such accounts have nationalistic perspectives and ideological purposes. Perhaps all of this makes the biblical descriptions of the final siege of Jerusalem most surprising. The common adage that "history is written by the victors" may be turned on its head in this instance. The account of the losers not only found its way into writing, but persisted through time better than the account of the winners. The siege description is only in biblical texts, and it is portrayed as a complete defeat for Judah. Because the chronology of surrounding events that have parallels in the Mesopotamian literature is a reasonable match, it seems logical to assume that the biblical account of a three-year siege, in the years 588–586, is reliable. Jerusalem fell to Nebuchadnezzar in 586. Texts that reached their final forms during or after the restoration retained the tradition of a devastating loss.

The little book of Lamentations portrays Jerusalem during the days of the Babylonian siege from a perspective inside the city not present in any of the other books that give account of the destruction. Jerusalem is the main character of Lamentations, which opens with the mournful lines:

> How lonely sits the city
> That once was full of people!

The remainder of 1:1 personifies the city with female images like "widow" and "princess," and in the next verse she is crying. The female personification of Jerusalem in Lamentations has been the subject of significant discussion, which chapter 6 discusses at length. The most common grammatical expression is something like "daughter Zion," which is not without some difficulty. Nearly half of the uses of this phrase and similar ones are in Lamentations, with most of the remainder in Jeremiah. Adele Berlin has surveyed the options for reading the phrase, including the portrayal of a city goddess and a common genitival reading like "daughter of Zion," referring to a female inhabitant(s) of Jerusalem. Berlin reaffirmed what has been the most common reading of the phrase, the appositional genitive, which equates Jerusalem with the female figure it is describing.[29] This grammatical decision leads to the conclusion that the city itself is understood as the victim in this collection of poems. The exclusive focus on urban suffering in Lamentations reflects the description of urban warfare and the stories of the siege from outside the walls. Descriptions of the inside of the city appear at numerous places in Lamentations:

> Her gates have sunken into the ground;
>   he has ruined and broken her bars. (2:9a)
> because infants and babes faint
>   in the streets of the city. (2:11c)
> The sacred stones lie scattered
>   at the head of every street. (4:1b)
> The old men have left the city gate,
>   the young men their music. (5:14)

Restoring this setting physically and healing the wounded bodies and spirits of its inhabitants would be a monumental task.

Evidence has already been presented above that the "Restoration" was a slower and more difficult process than many interpreters have described, perhaps because the Bible offers a description that is less than realistic. Carla Sulzbach points to the importance of the production of texts in a process of recovery: "With a homeland that was radically reduced in size, a monarchy lost, a temple that had lost the grandeur of its predecessor, and a city that was badly in need of repair, the only places that allowed for limitless expansion and glory were the textualized memories. . . ."[30] As an example, Sulzbach points to Lamentations 2 and Psalm 24, texts that are mirrors of one another. The presentation of total destruction and "triumphant" restoration in these two texts are both mythic in scope, Lamentations 2 in the direction of dystopia and Psalm 24 in the direction of a utopia. The dystopic destruction of the past is more connected to an actual event at the time of the writing, since there was a significant destruction, while the utopic presentation is visionary, and based upon a grandiose memory of the past.[31] It is important to remember the complex relationships between the concrete realities of the past, present, and future and the textual presentations of each. Ehud Ben Zvi brought this idea of complex memory into sharper focus, contending that Jerusalem became the "central site of memory." This memory was a combination of material sites and a Jerusalem that existed "in the mind and in the shared imagination of the community."[32] Memory intertwines materiality and imagination.

The first mention of Jerusalem in Ezra–Nehemiah is in the "Decree of Cyrus" in Ezra 1:2–4. The purported royal document from the Persian king refers to Jerusalem as both the dwelling place of Israel's God and the future site on which that God has commanded him to build a temple. The building of this house for YHWH in Jerusalem is then the only task the text identifies in 1:5 for the group of Judahites about to return. When the next chapter begins to introduce the list of persons who returned, 2:1 states that they "returned to Jerusalem and Judah, all to their own towns ('ir), so the focus of return is not entirely on Jerusalem, but the central city receives priority and the other places of return are also towns or cities."[33] The list appears in Ezra 2 and Nehemiah 7. The conclusion of the list in Ezra 2:70 speaks similarly of everyone, even extra cultic personnel, returning to their cities. A textual difficulty in this verse may have some impact on the way readers perceive the situation in relation to the re-urbanization of Judah. The complexity is increased by the nature of the parallel passage in Nehemiah 7:73 and the ancient translation (interpretation) in 1 Esdras 5:46. The Hebrew text does not mention Jerusalem by name, either in Ezra 2:70 or Nehemiah 7:73. The text seems to assume its conclusion in "their cities." Some English translations add Jerusalem on the basis of its inclusion in 1 Esdras 5:46.[34] Ezra contains a double appearance of "their cities" in this verse, which appears only once in the Nehemiah parallel.[35] The existence of such a complex textual history in itself reveals possible conflict in understanding the nature of the settlement of Judah in the early Persian period. A document like the list, incorporated into the book, might not be as Jerusalem-centric as the book itself.

While Ezra 3:1 acknowledges the presence of Israelites "in cities," it quickly gathers them all to Jerusalem for the reestablishment of the altar and the first

efforts at sacrificial worship.[36] The assumption of the story in Ezra is that
the community begins its new story with the instigation of sacrificial worship
at a central site. Chapter 4 of this book already explored the implications
of Deuteronomy's centralization of worship for urbanization. Scholars
have offered a variety of understandings of the relationship between Ezra–
Nehemiah and Deuteronomy, but on this point it is clear that the narrator in
Ezra–Nehemiah envisions worship in no place other than Jerusalem, so the
two books are in agreement. The narrator of Ezra, along with the characters in
the text, go directly to the site of the temple, set up the altar, perform sacrificial
rituals, and begin the process of laying new foundations for the building. The
departure from Babylon in Ezra 1:5–11 had guaranteed this destination with
the sponsorship of Cyrus and his gift of the temple paraphernalia that had
been taken by Nebuchadnezzar. A story like this operates on multiple levels.
Assuming some chronological distance between the initial return it depicts
and the composition of Ezra–Nehemiah, the story depicts a community that
moves from one urban context to another, with the power and authority that
supports them in their departure transported to the site their ancestors had
built. The place sits entirely empty, awaiting their arrival. For the community
for which the book was written, the story asserts the centrality of Jerusalem
and its temple, removing all other aspects of life in Judah from view. This
approach to recording the story develops a view that supports the work of the
author by connecting it to both Persian sponsorship and the temple complex
with the city around it.[37] The story the book called Ezra–Nehemiah tells
interacts with the Persian imperial ambitions in multi-faceted ways. As Leo
Perdue has demonstrated, all empires attempt to establish a meta-narrative of
their own, and subject peoples must decide how to respond. Not all members
of the society in Persian Yehud would have agreed on the same response, but
the writers of Ezra–Nehemiah support full cooperation with Persia.

The development of this authority is necessary in the text because
opposition is about to arise from a group that the text of Ezra does not define
well. The dispute and its settlement carry the story back into the world of
scribes and centralized power. The language of the book of Ezra has been a
matter of mystery and dispute. Along with Daniel 2:4–7:28, Ezra 4:8–6:18 is
one of two extended texts in the Hebrew Bible written in Aramaic. The shift
in language coincides with a shift in worlds, and the world represented by
the Aramaic language, the world of Mesopotamian scribes, was one in which
the writer(s) of Ezra and his scribal community were likely comfortable.[38]
Demonstrating this linguistic and cultural fluency may have been one of the
purposes of changing languages. The Aramaic portion of the text begins by
quoting an official imperial document, which assumedly would have been
in Aramaic, but even when the document is complete, Aramaic remains the

language of the framing narrative. The arguments concerning this linguistic phenomenon are complex and disputed. The most helpful idea is that it signals cultural boundaries both in the text and in the social situations it reflects. Laird concludes, "The Aramaic acts as an interface and signals the boundary between the Jerusalem community and the rest of the world."[39] As the ones who could operate across these boundaries the scribes of Judah held power they gave to themselves in the texts they had produced. The relationship between the scribal ability to cross international, linguistic boundaries, and the mythic scribal ability to cross the threshold between heaven and earth will be a matter for further consideration in the final chapter of this study.

At least one alternative temple to the one in Jerusalem was present in the Egyptian city of Elephantine, where a significant Jewish community had developed by the sixth century.[40] The documents known as the Elephantine Papyri shed some light on the nature of this community and its worship. The documents in this archive are roughly contemporaneous with the setting of the stories in Ezra–Nehemiah. References to a Jewish community in Egypt are sparse in the Hebrew Bible. Jeremiah 43:7–44:30 refers to a group that went to Egypt during the trials of the Babylonian crisis, but the book of Jeremiah views this group negatively, and its presentation of them is part of its polemic in favor of the exiles in Babylon.[41] The evidence in the papyri reveals the attempts of this group to set up an urban community around a temple that, in some ways, mimicked Jerusalem. When their temple was destroyed by local opponents, they appealed for help to rebuild it, and understood it to be a project supported by the Persian Empire.[42] The work of Melody Knowles examines four aspects of religious practice in the Persian period, with careful attention to how they are mapped onto geography: Animal sacrifice, use of incense, offerings, and pilgrimage. The practice of animal sacrifice was a matter of dispute, as its existence at Elephantine indicates, and the presence of additional worship sites at Lachish and Gerizim indicate some plurality of practice, but the general sense of centralization in Jerusalem was present.[43] Knowles also finds some differences in the degree of centralization concerning the use of incense. The use of incense in other places was acceptable according to the writers of Malachi, but not to the writers of Chronicles.[44] The diversity of expressions about these matters may indicate that even though the centrality of worship in Jerusalem is clear in a literary work like Ezra–Nehemiah, this may have been more of a prescriptive polemic than a description of the historical situation. Knowles concluded as follows: "According to the extant textual and artifactual evidence, the practice of centrality was neither univocal nor consistent. In the course of tracing the various and varying practices of Jerusalem's centrality in the Persian period, the sacred geography of the city emerges as a negotiated social process, a social process that itself is constructed and made visible by practice."[45] That Ezra–Nehemiah is negotiating the status of the returnees and the city of Jerusalem is apparent. Unfortunately we do not have the words of those with whom it was negotiating.

The introductory section of this chapter already presented some of the difficulties involved in developing a clear portrait of Judah during the Persian period, and the conflicts between the kind of historical sketch that is possible and the narrative Ezra–Nehemiah presents. The most complete picture of Jerusalem from the late seventh through the fifth centuries is in the work of Oded Lipschits, *The Fall and Rise of Jerusalem* (2005). During the Babylonian period Judah lost half or more of its population, with the most significant decreases in and around Jerusalem. The loss was likely a combination of death, deportation, and departure to places like Egypt. During this time several sites in the territory of Benjamin became larger and more prominent, and the population remaining in Judah was predominately rural. Lipschits characterizes Judah in the sixth century as an area that experienced "a sharp decline in urban life."[46] Evidence indicates a shift back toward the prominence of Jerusalem during the Persian period, but not at the levels portrayed in Ezra–Nehemiah. The forty-two thousand returnees depicted in the lists in Ezra 2 and Nehemiah 7 appear to be too large by a factor of at least ten, if not more. The growth of Jerusalem and its immediate surroundings was gradual, even though it held the status of a provincial capital in the Persian Empire.[47]

While the focus of the narrative in Ezra–Nehemiah is on Jerusalem, there are elements of the story that acknowledge settlement elsewhere. The duplicate lists in Ezra 2 and Nehemiah 7 catalog the numbers of people living in other places. Within the narrative, these have all gathered in Jerusalem to begin the temple project. In Nehemiah 8 they come together for Ezra's reading of the law. The settlement lists in Nehemiah 11 have received somewhat less attention, perhaps because they contain no actual population numbers. The one numerical aspect of Nehemiah 11 may imply that Jerusalem was underpopulated. Nehemiah 11:1–2 implies that some volunteered, but others had to be selected by lot to repopulate the central city. Deirdre Fulton compares the two versions of the Nehemiah 11 list in the MT and LXX, which vary considerably, and compared these two lists with those found in Ezra 2 and Nehemiah 7. It becomes apparent that these lists have sociopolitical purposes and that they come from different stages in the restoration of Judah and the redaction of Ezra–Nehemiah.[48] Fulton has also observed that the larger, and later, list in Nehemiah 11 of the MT expands Judean settlement into what may have been disputed territory, in a way that would have suited the Hasmonean dynasty.[49] Regardless of whether the specifics of this proposal are correct, the broader idea that the lists are in conflict with one another, and that they betray political intentions and layers of development in Ezra–Nehemiah that extend beyond the early Persian period, is useful.

If the depiction of Judah and Jerusalem in Ezra-Nehemiah are nothing like a historically accurate portrayal, particularly with regard to the development of an urban society in the area during the fifth century, then what were those who produced this account doing? The Persian period was likely one in which a greatly diminished Jerusalem struggled for power and prestige. Cities to the north, particularly Mizpah, had become important administrative centers, and the temple at Gerizim had gained influence as a religious shrine. The previous chapter gave some attention to Ezekiel's portrayal of the new Jerusalem and its temple in Ezekiel 40–48. The nature of the vision and its presentation in Ezekiel make its Jerusalem obviously an act of the imagination.[50] Sanders has argued that the obsession with measurements in Ezekiel's vision is part of a new, emerging scribal identity in which language was their primary mode of influence, rather than political power.[51] It is too easy to assume that because the portrayal of Jerusalem and its temple in Ezra–Nehemiah is not presented as a vision and is unspectacular in its dimensions that it is less an act of imagination, if it is one at all. The realization that the number of returnees and their effect on the population of Jerusalem are greatly exaggerated, however, demonstrates that imagination is at work. Once again, a lack of political power may have been the motivator. Instead of measuring a city and its structures precisely, like Ezekiel, the scribes behind the Ezra–Nehemiah tradition count people, but these people are also only present inside the text. The diminished power and influence of Judah and Jerusalem that extended well into the Persian period, especially in comparison to Israelite sites north of it, presented difficulties for the community that understood itself as the "Golah" group that possessed the ancient traditions of Israel's religion and the authority that went with them. An intense re-urbanization was part of their imaginative response to this political reality, along with the exclusion of other participants in their project in Ezra 4 and the expulsion of foreign wives in Ezra 9–10 and Nehemiah.[52]

Chapter 5 of this book develops the idea that cities, as constructed human spaces, make human experience of the divine possible. The story of the building of the first temple in the Jerusalem of David and Solomon operates with the assumption that Israel's god needs a house in the city. The narrative of Ezra–Nehemiah continues to operate with that assumption. As Mark Smith put it, ". . . cities were temples writ large."[53] Interpreters have long been baffled by the order of the building projects in Ezra–Nehemiah. How and why can the building of a temple precede the building of walls? This was one of several factors involved in the proposal to reverse the historical chronology of Ezra and Nehemiah that gained some traction in the first half of the twentieth century. The historical aspect of this issue is not resolvable given the present evidence, but it is more important here to consider why the story in Ezra–Nehemiah is presented in this way. If the Jerusalem in this narrative is primarily a literary construct, in terms of its size and population, and the roles of various officials, including scribes, within it, then the architecture can be a literary construct as well.

Another important aspect of the city-building account in Ezra–Nehemiah is the way it interacts with the imperial project of the Persian Empire. Subject peoples adopt a variety of strategies for survival and advancement within an empire, and the biblical literature displays a diversity of such approaches. The deference to Persian sponsorship in Ezra–Nehemiah is not always matched in other literature, and even within this work that refers so thoroughly to the importance of the support its heroes receive from the empire, there are subtle signs of subversion. The metanarrative of the Persian Empire included the portrayal of Persian kings as divinely chosen rulers of the world. Though their policy of religious and cultural tolerance allowed a degree of freedom for the communities that were subject to the empire, the Persian king was understood as the choice of the local deities to rule the lands in which their people lived, and this view is visible in Ezra–Nehemiah.[54] Other texts, particularly the books of Haggai and Zechariah, appear to support reestablishment of the Judahite/Israelite monarchy, particularly in the person of Zerubbabel, whom they portray as the rightful Davidic heir.[55] The book of Ezra gives Zerubbabel a significant role in rebuilding the temple, but does not mention his royal connections or any intent to establish him as an Israelite monarch.

Two texts in the Hebrew Bible make oblique references to agricultural production in Judah during the Restoration. The statement of the prophet in Haggai 2:16–19 says,

> But now, consider what will come to pass from this day on. Before a stone was placed upon a stone in the LORD's temple, how did you fare? When one came to a heap of twenty measures, there were but ten; when one came to the wine vat to draw fifty measures, there were but twenty. I struck you and all the products of your toil with blight and mildew and hail; yet you did not return to me, says the LORD. Consider from this day on, from the twenty-fourth day of the ninth month. Since the day that the foundation of the LORD's temple was laid, consider: Is there any seed left in the barn? Do the vine, the fig tree, the pomegranate, and the olive tree still yield nothing? From this day on I will bless you.

The implication is that the failure to give appropriate energy and resources to the rebuilding of the temple in Jerusalem has resulted in reduced agricultural production in the area. Haggai promises the renewal of divine blessing that will bring prosperity in return for building YHWH's house. Nehemiah 5:1–3 also reports economic hardship due to poor agricultural production, but does not present the situation as divine punishment or lack of blessing:

> Now there was a great outcry of the people and of their wives against their Jewish kin. For there were those who said, "With our sons and our daughters, we are many; we must get grain, so that we may eat and stay alive." There were also those who said, "We are having to pledge our fields, our vineyards, and our houses in order to get grain during the famine."

No cause is given for the famine, but Nehemiah blames oppression by the wealthy members of the community for the failure to deal with it adequately. Both Nehemiah and Haggai centralize the concern for agricultural production around the city of Jerusalem and the temple. While both Ezra and Nehemiah emphasize Persian imperial support for the province of Yehud, the city of Jerusalem, and the rebuilding of the temple, Knowles has argued that texts throughout Chronicles, Ezra–Nehemiah, Haggai, Zechariah, and Malachi emphasizing the economic aspect of centralization indicate that support from the empire was minimal. Centralization of religious institutions required centralization of the economy, and this was fed by the practices of tithes and offerings and pilgrimage.[56] The growth and development of Jerusalem would depend on the prosperity of the land and people around it, which are largely invisible in biblical texts.

PSALMS IN THE CITY AND THE CITY IN PSALMS

The book of Psalms is famous for its pastoral imagery. It opens with a poem comparing a wise and righteous person to a tree planted beside a river. Its most famous line speaks of Israel's God as a shepherd and places the singer in pleasant pastures. Even when Psalm 23 travels into danger in verse 4, a lonely valley is the setting. Natural images are common in many parts of the collection from the majestic heavens of 8:3, to the rising sun of 19:6, to the multitudes of animals in their places of 104:14–23. The countryside, the forest, and the isolated brook are not the places where the book of Psalms is taking its readers, however, but are just places along the way of a journey. The book is telling a story, the same story the narrative portions of the Hebrew Bible are telling, and the center of that story is Jerusalem. Even the psalms with quiet, serene settings move toward more urban ones, whether it is toward the crowd of scoffers and the righteous congregation in Psalm 1, or the banquet hall to which Psalm 23 moves when it leaves behind the shepherd's lonely haunts.

A few psalms early in the collection are preoccupied with city life, even though Jerusalem does not appear by name until Psalm 51, and only appears one more time in book 2 (Psalm 68). Appearances of Zion are somewhat more common. Approximately forty occurrences are spread fairly evenly throughout the book. Of the seventeen occurrences of Jerusalem, eleven are in book 5. Psalm 48 presents a notably positive portrayal of the city it calls Zion:

> Walk about Zion, go all around it,
>   count its towers,
> consider well its ramparts;
>   go through its citadels,
> that you may tell the next generation
>   that this is our God,
> our God forever and ever.
>   he will be our guide forever.
>   (vv. 12–14)

Earlier lines in the psalm claim that foreign leaders who come to the city have been intimidated by the place and its God. A somewhat different picture appears several poems later in Psalm 55:9–11, in which a distressed singer proclaims in fear:

> Confuse, O LORD, confound their speech;
>   for I see violence and strife in the city.
> Day and night they go around it
>   on its walls,
> and iniquity and trouble are within it;
>   ruin is in its midst;
> oppression and fraud
>   do not depart from its marketplace.

Though Psalm 55 does not mention Jerusalem by name, verse 14 describes walking in "the house of God." Regardless of its identity, the city that is designed to provide protection from the dangers outside its walls can harbor deadly dangers inside of them.

The destruction of Jerusalem appears in the book of Psalms, most poignantly in Psalm 89, which ends book 3. When the poem, which is constructed in reverse fashion compared to all other lament poems, turns from the eternal covenant with David and its benefits in verses 1–37, the destruction of the defining aspects of the city stand just after the removal of the crown from the Davidic heir's heard in verses 40–41:

> You have broken through all his walls;
>   you have laid his strongholds in ruins.

All who pass by plunder him;
he has become the scorn of his neighbors.

The king has become city-less and exposed. The city was an essential part of his identity.

That lost identity is restored when the end of the book of Psalms becomes fully focused on Jerusalem and the temple, however. The sequence of poems in 120–134 all possess the phrase "a Song of Ascents" in their superscriptions. There are disputes, of course, about whether all of the superscriptions are original parts of the psalms which they now begin.[57] Loren Crow delineates a "nucleus group" among these Psalms 120–134 and separated the material of that group from what the redactor of the collection added. His conclusion was that the perspective of the nucleus group is grounded in the experiences of family life and small communities. The additions of the redactor, on the other hand, produce a more national perspective and bring the focus to Jerusalem, the national center. The result is a collection of psalms that is not filled with the idea of pilgrimage, but is shaped to serve that idea in its present form.[58] The presence of the same sequence of Psalms 121–132 in 11QPsa provides evidence for the influence of this grouping. The final shape of the book of Psalms was in flux for a long time, and until a late date.[59] Psalms 120–134, alone as a small collection and placed as they are now in the book of Psalms, become pilgrimage songs urging the reader up Mount Zion to a rebuilt temple. The final line of the last poem in the sequence places YHWH on Zion, and offers YHWH's blessings to Israel.[60] This explanation raises questions about how persons who did not have access to Jerusalem and the temple could participate in the blessings these psalms offer. The activity of YHWH in relation to Diaspora Jews may be a matter that the formation of the book of Psalms also addresses by making possible a reading or hearing experience that was portable.[61] Only at the latest stage were the Songs of Ascents installed in their present position, where they lead the Israelites in literary fashion up to the restored Jerusalem and set the stage for the crescendo of the Hallelujah psalms at the end of the book. Reading or hearing the book may have been an experience available to persons who could not travel to Jerusalem.

THE BUILDING OF ANCIENT
AND MODERN URBAN COMMUNITIES

What are the connections between the contemporary process of gentrification and the "restoration" of Jerusalem? The comparison of ancient and modern civilizations and their processes and motivations requires caution, but failure to look at them together neglects the possibilities comparison might hold. The most obvious similarity between the two is the process of displacement, which occurs in at least two ways. First, there is the basic activity of persons moving in and persons moving out, which can be accomplished based on a number of factors. In the modern world the primary force is economic. Older, less expensive housing is purchased and either destroyed or renovated. The persons who had lived in these communities are not able to afford the new housing and are forced to relocate. A second, less obviously destructive form of this activity is the driving up of housing costs by the influx of new residents, coupled with a housing market that cannot keep up with new demand. Again, existing residents are forced out by economics.

A more subtle force is the changing of the culture: the influx of primarily younger, urban residents and the businesses and development that follows them creates a climate in which existing residents, perhaps older or members of ethnic minorities, no longer feel comfortable or welcome in the community. These people may be able to resist the economic force of developers, but they sell their property because the place no longer feels like their neighborhood. This last factor, combined with the racial and ethnic lines along which these economic forces work, makes gentrification a highly charged subject in the modern world. Even experts in this field do not agree whether gentrification is more about the movement of people or a movement of capital, so it seems likely that some combination of the two are always involved.[62] Richard Florida's work has described, and is sometimes even blamed, for this phenomenon. Florida's most recent attempt to describe a "new urban crisis" addresses the issue of gentrification head on. While he has argued that gentrification is only extensive in six American cities, Florida acknowledges that the way many cities throughout the world are developing right now creates growing economic inequality and tension.[63] Despite the intended and unintended negative consequences that sometimes accompany contemporary urban development, Florida offers concrete solutions to help create "an urbanism for all" and insists that cities are still the best way to solve social and economic problems.[64]

It seems unlikely that such forces expressed themselves in the same way in Judah and Jerusalem in the Persian period, but texts like Ezra 3–5 demonstrate signs of exclusion and conflict based on cultural and ethnic identity. Nehemiah 11:1–2 presents a picture in which the leadership of the community lived in Jerusalem, but others had to be drawn there, selected by lot. The "urban renewal" project in this text presumes an underpopulated city and shows the reader no displacement. The inequality and tension identified as a result of modern gentrification is also present in Nehemiah 5, even if not for all the same reasons. Still other texts, like Ezra 4, demonstrate conflict between the returning group and those who have been living in the area in the meantime. In an urban environment, questions about who belongs and who does not belong are not easily addressed, but are a matter of shifting power dynamics and constant renegotiation.

8

Cities Reimagined

Jubilees and Its Alternative to Genesis's Portrayal of Cities

This study of cities and urban life in Israelite tradition began with Genesis 1–11 as its foundational text but gave careful attention to the J source as its predecessor, because J provided the texts that contribute most to the theme of city building in the Primeval Story of Genesis. On the other side of Genesis 1–11 from the J source that preceded it stands the remarkable book of Jubilees. Together these three texts form a trajectory of reflection on the Primeval Tradition. Jubilees is not the only additional treatment of the Primeval Tradition within Jewish literature of the Second Temple period. First Enoch, Aramaic Levi, and the Genesis Apocryphon are among the most prominent other examples. Some of these texts are only available in fragmentary manuscripts, and none give as full a presentation of the Primeval Tradition as Jubilees, which makes it the most fruitful to compare to Genesis. Jubilees follows a plot similar to that of the Torah until the crossing of the Red Sea, so the discussion of the texts from Genesis in the second and third chapters, and subsequent reading of the full Tanakh, calls for an examination of how Jubilees handles the traditions that form its foundations. The traditions related to cities seem to be ones that the writer(s) of this book handles in interesting ways. The questions raised throughout this book will continue to be at the center of the discussion of Jubilees. If the persons responsible for producing ancient Israelite literature like Jubilees were elite, urban scribes, how does that identity shape the way cities and urban life are portrayed in the book, particularly in light of some of Israel's ancient traditions that presented a negative view of such settings?

It is not easy to say exactly what Jubilees is. On the surface, it looks like a revision of the book of Genesis and the first half of the book of Exodus, composed in Greek. Most scholars who have worked with Jubilees date it to the second century BCE, a time when something like the finished version of Genesis we know would have existed and probably would have been widely known among members of the scribal class. The full Torah had almost certainly been translated into Greek when Jubilees was written. Questions about what to call Jubilees have no easy answer. It is probably the work most responsible for the coining of the phrase "rewritten Bible" by Geza Vermes. The term is problematic for a number of reasons, most significantly that the concept of "Bible" did not exist when the writer of Jubilees was working. Even if that writer thought he was "rewriting" Genesis and Exodus, these were not components of a fixed and final collection of sacred literature. Nevertheless, the connection between Jubilees and Genesis 1–Exodus 15 is so intimate that slipping into the language of rewriting or interpreting is difficult to avoid. Even an ardent critic of the term "rewritten Bible" like Eva Mroczek acknowledges that "[Jubilees's] interaction with Genesis sheds important light on the process by which older traditions were transformed and brought forward, and shows what this writer found compelling and troubling about the biblical texts."[1] Mroczek continues with an important warning that Jubilees is "a text with its own purposes and integrity," so that viewing it only as exegesis of biblical texts like Genesis and Exodus places inappropriate limits on how it functions as a literary work in its own right.[2] It is not just responding to or interpreting Genesis. It is promoting its own understanding of the world and Israel's ancient traditions.

The significance of Jubilees in Second Temple Judaism was a matter of dispute until the middle of the twentieth century when fragments of numerous copies were discovered among the Dead Sea Scrolls. Prior to this the only access to the book was the version preserved in the language of the Ethiopian Orthodox Church. With this new discovery, the place of Jubilees within Judaism was assured. Scholarship on Jubilees has accelerated over the past half century, and it is now possible and necessary to look at it alongside Genesis and its sources as an indicator of developing ideas in Second Temple Judaism.[3] Jubilees has often been overshadowed by the presence of the book called 1 Enoch, which comes from about the same time and also interacts with many of the traditions in Genesis. Gabriele Boccaccini has argued that Jubilees participates with 1 Enoch in expressing a form of Judaism that was in competition with the more dominant Zadokite view, but Boccaccini and other proponents have called this alternative "Enochic Judaism," which indicates which text they see as more central.[4] First Enoch is not constructed in a way, like Jubilees, that allows a comprehensive comparison to Genesis in how it treats various traditions, but it will arise occasionally as an additional point of comparison in the discussion below.

Scholarly work on Jubilees is still in its fairly early stages, but an increasing number of interpreters are turning their attention to this text, in large part because of what it might reveal about Second Temple Judaism. Jacques van Ruiten has produced a massive study called *Primaeval History Interpreted: The Rewriting of Genesis 1–11 in the Book of Jubilees*. As the title indicates, van Ruiten used the concept of rewriting as a framework, and his careful work with the text of Jubilees focused on the way the writer altered Genesis in order to harmonize the text, removing inconsistencies and tensions. Van Ruiten insists that "It was not my purpose to point out the influence of the era in which the author lived," but he observes that "at several points, one can see the Hellenistic world in the background."[5] Discerning the writer's motives was not at the center of his purposes, but Van Ruiten went on to provide a brief list of such influences, without considering the possibility that Jubilees came out of a world and a way of life that Genesis 1–11 presents negatively, an urban world. If the tension created by an increasingly urban Hellenistic world of the second century BCE presented difficulties for some readers of Genesis, then Jubilees looks like a way of looking at the Primeval Tradition that would have been more comfortable for readers living in that world.

James Kugel has identified a layer of later editorial work in Jubilees that he attributes to an "Interpolator." Source division of Jubilees does not have near the length of practice or sophistication as in the Pentateuch and other biblical texts, but Kugel makes a reasonable case that there is internal tension in the book which can be resolved by the separation of twenty-nine passages. These texts constitute slightly fewer than 150 verses, so the Interpolator passages make up a small percentage of the book. Most of them have to do with legal matters and have little bearing on the narrative material. A few cases that do have an impact will enter the discussion below. Perhaps the most significant point of disagreement between the original author and the Interpolator is the origin of certain legal traditions. Some texts in the earlier version of Jubilees may leave the impression that laws arose out of the practices of the ancestors, but the Interpolator insists that all laws have divine origin. To fix this problem the Interpolator reports that the practices of the ancestors were written on "heavenly tablets," so that they had already been inscribed by God. These kinds of insertions have a characteristic language that Kugel used to identify them.[6]

There is little chance that a writer at such a time could have thought of completely replacing the book of Genesis, so Jubilees may best be understood as an alternative account of ancient times that had two general goals.[7] The prominence of Genesis and Jubilees among the Dead Sea Scrolls, along with other alternatives like the "Genesis Apocryphon," reveals that reading communities could value and work with multiple, parallel sets of tradition.[8] One of the goals of Jubilees was to present traditions like those in Genesis that proved problematic in the author's own time in a way more compatible with the writers' own understanding. One particular problem led to a second goal. The relationship of Israel's great ancestors to the legal tradition presented significant difficulties. What did it mean for persons like Abraham, Sarah, Jacob, Rachel, and Joseph to live such exemplary lives without obedience to the Law? How could they build altars and give offerings to YHWH without regulations? The writer of Jubilees found a way to assert that the Law preceded the creation of the world so that even the heroes of Genesis could be obedient to it.[9] Jubilees opens with Moses on Mount Sinai, with the Angel of the Presence, so the law frames the entire story. The second goal of the writer was, therefore, to reinvigorate the Mosaic covenant in a period of apparent decline for the Jewish people, and the primary way of doing that was to place the entire story of Israel in a framework of the forty-nine-year cycle of the law of the Jubilee and connect this cycle to a contemporary Greek calendar.[10] For the purposes of this study the broader first of these goals is the most important, and the anti-city elements of Genesis look like one of the critical problems Jubilees confronts. The extent to which the writer of Jubilees recognized the anti-city-building elements of Genesis 1–11, even if the writer of Genesis muted the perspective of the J source in the redaction process, and eliminated it further, is a question to which this study will now turn.

The writer and audience of Jubilees would undoubtedly have been urban persons, and the practice of producing alternative presentations of ancient traditions already present in other sacred texts was acceptable to them; so if the writer detected an anti-urban bias in Genesis, then it is possible, even likely, that he would have worked to diminish or remove it. So, the treatment of the anti-city-building passages in Genesis by Jubilees may offer an important indicator of how readers in the third and second century BCE perceived the early parts of the Torah, and why they might have preferred a different version of Israel's ancient traditions.

Bernard Levinson has demonstrated that literature of this era not only updated the language of ancient texts, but also addressed points of incoherence and conflict with contemporary practice and understanding. The Temple Scroll, found among the Dead Sea manuscripts, reproduces the laws of Deuteronomy, many of which use conditional language. For example, Deuteronomy 23:21 says, "If you make a vow to the LORD your God, do not postpone fulfilling it." The Hebrew word translated as "if" (ky) has a wider variety of uses in Biblical Hebrew, and the opening of conditional sentences is not the most common one. More often Biblical Hebrew uses ʾm as a conditional particle, and there were even more than just these two ways of beginning a conditional sentence. By time the Temple Scroll was written, however, the use of ʾm had become much more standard, so the writers of the Temple Scroll updated the language of the conditional legal statements in order to fit the contemporary usage.[11] Levinson's examples are passages all written in Hebrew at both stages of development, so the demonstration of updated language is more precise and obvious than those that update perspective. Levinson also argued that Qoheleth and the Temple Scroll rewrote the law of vows from Deuteronomy 23:22–24 in order to align it with their own understanding of vows, which would be more analogous to the author of Jubilees rewriting Genesis to align it with a contemporary view of urban life.[12]

JUBILEES AND THE PRIMEVAL STORY

Two features dominate an attempt to look at the portion of Jubilees that corresponds to the Genesis 1–2 creation accounts. First, Jubilees begins with Moses on Mount Sinai, along with the Angel of the Presence, so that the law functions as the ordering framework of the book, rather than creation. This does not mean the ancestors in Genesis have the entire Torah, but extra pieces of Torah legislation are placed within the stories of the ancestors in Jubilees, and the entire book is framed by the Sinai covenant in literary terms. Second, Jubilees blends the creation accounts in Genesis 1 and 2 and harmonizes many of the tensions between the two. The harmonization process disrupts the overall form and rhythm of Genesis 1, a feature chapter 2 emphasized earlier. For example, Jubilees 2:7 inserts a lengthy description of the creation of Eden into the third day. Much of the account of the sixth day from Genesis 1 is intact in Jubilees 2:13–16, such as the language of "dominion" for human beings, but there is no mention of food, removing another point of conflict between the sources of Genesis. The omission of much of Genesis 2:4–7 merges the creation of humans in Genesis 1 with the forming of Adam, and the "image of God" language of Genesis 1 is absent.[13] The conflict between the two creation stories concerning how the humans received the divine image, whether by creative gift or by an act of disobedience, is not in Jubilees. Jubilees contains none of the declarations of goodness so prominent in Genesis 1. One effect of such omissions is a portrayal of a divine being not nearly so naïve as in Genesis 1.[14] Some readers of that era might have responded as many modern readers do, wondering how something so inherently and consistently good could go so bad so quickly. Others may have wondered how a divine being powerful and wise enough to create such a world could be so mistaken about the direction it would take. In Jubilees 1:7–14 the angel has already informed Moses of the bad end to which Israel will come, so readers are not left wondering how God's attitude about creation and humans can change so rapidly as it does in Genesis. The good and orderly creation of Genesis 1 does not fit easily with some parts of Genesis 1–11 that come from the J source. This was a type of narrative tension, or even incoherence, that the redactor of Genesis was apparently willing to tolerate, but which seemed to be too much for the writer of Jubilees.[15] Jubilees begins to remove this tension, created by the combination of the J and P sources in Genesis 1–11, from the beginning.

Jubilees revises the garden of Eden story in too many ways to describe fully here. One of its major goals appears to be retaining large portions of Genesis 1 and 2, while reducing the tension between them.[16] The confusion about the two named trees in the garden, so prominent in Genesis 2–3, is not present in the Jubilees account, in which only one special tree appears. Jubilees acknowledges the tree only in the scene in which the humans eat from it, after seven years of living in the garden. Genesis 3:6–7 shows the man and woman eating together, but Jubilees separates the portrayal of the woman eating the fruit and its effect on her from the man eating the fruit in Jubilees 3:17–22. There are no conflicting commands about eating, because the divine commands in Genesis 1:29 ("I have given you every plant . . . ; you shall have them for food") and Genesis 2:16–17 ("You may eat freely of every tree of the garden, but of the tree of knowledge of good and evil you shall not eat") are both missing. The woman quotes something like the second command in Jubilees 3:18.[17] The placement of the only reference to the tree is important because Jubilees inserts an entirely new section just before it in 3:15–16. The Angel of the Presence, who is always speaking to Moses in Jubilees, describes the work of the man in the garden in greater detail in this section. The angel refers to a group including himself ("we") in the garden teaching the man how to do the necessary work. Adam learns the skills necessary for farming from the angels before eating the fruit from the tree, so that knowledge of farming is explicitly separated from whatever knowledge he might have gained illicitly from the fruit. In the words of van Ruiten, "Adam is described as the ideal farmer" in Jubilees 3:15–16.[18] Jubilees takes the point one step further in 3:35, reporting specifically that Adam works the land outside the garden in the way the angels taught him inside the garden.[19] In Jubilees, knowledge of how to farm cannot be something humans were not supposed to have, but acquired illicitly. The additions in Jubilees also help fix a potential conflict in Genesis between Genesis 3:23 and 4:2, about whether Adam or Cain was the first farmer, a difficulty present even within the J source alone. While YHWH Elohim sends Adam from the garden to till the soil in Genesis 3:23, Cain is the first to appear doing it successfully in 4:2. Again, Jubilees explicitly describes Adam tilling the land outside the garden, in the same way he had been taught inside it, so there is no way to read the agricultural achievements of Cain as an advance.[20] Jubilees 3:27–28 also reports that all of the animals are expelled from the garden with Adam and Eve, providing another point of continuity between life inside the garden and outside. The animals are altered by the expulsion, however, as they all stop speaking after this occasion.

One of the more obvious differences between Genesis 1 and 2 is the use of time in the two narratives. The seven-day sequence is the primary frame for Genesis 1, while Genesis 2 pays no attention to the passage of time. In Jubilees God keeps Adam outside the garden for forty days after creating him and keeps Eve out for eighty days because of her impurity (3:12), and the humans are in the garden for seven years before eating the fruit, so Adam and Eve are brought into a world that marks the passage of time. Jubilees also resolves one of the most bizarre elements of Genesis 2: When YHWH Elohim recognizes that "it is not good for the man to be alone," he brings the animals to the man one at time to determine their suitability as a companion for him. In Jubilees God brings the animals to Adam for naming, and it is Adam who notices that all the others are male and female (3:3). While the divine character in Genesis 2 may appear to recognize a shortcoming in his work, Jubilees removes this possibility. Whether the writer of Jubilees was aware of the J and P sources and the way they create tension in Genesis is impossible to say, but the book seems more compatible with the P source. It is the traditions it shares with J that look the most different.

The story of the first family outside of the garden in Jubilees presents stark differences. The strange and puzzling statement of Eve at the birth of Cain is missing, eliminating the possibility that he is a unique or special child. Rather, the importance of Abel is elevated by a period of mourning his death by Adam and Eve for twenty-eight years.[21] Jubilees 4:1–6 tells the story of Cain and Abel without identifying their occupations or the content of their offerings. The conflict between the brothers is personal and does not represent a contest between ways of life. Jubilees does not link farming to Cain and his unfavorable sacrifice, and it does not refer to the separation of Cain from the ground when God curses Cain in 4:4–5. There is no way to prove the writer of Jubilees saw in Genesis the connections between the knowledge gained from the eating of the forbidden fruit in the garden and the ability to farm and build cities outside the garden, but such connections would likely have been troubling in a more settled, urban culture like the one the writer of Jubilees inhabited. In Jubilees's treatment of the traditions found in Genesis 1–4, it entirely removed the possibility of associating these ways of life with Cain, his lack of acceptance, his crime, or his punishment. One might wonder why Jubilees would include the story at all. Cain and Abel play no role in later biblical traditions. James Kugel argues that the whole of the Cain and Abel story might have been dispensable for Jubilees, but the reference to the blood of Abel fits with the emphasis on blood in Jubilees and may have led to the retention of the story, with the notable omissions.[22] Moreover, in the more expansive literary world in which Jubilees operated, the Cain and Abel tradition had much greater influence. The writer of Jubilees seems reluctant to eliminate significant traditions found in Genesis entirely but can present them in ways quite different from Genesis, including the removal of elements within them. This particular case provides an opportunity to think about why a writer in that period made such a choice. Within the Second Temple period, the Cain and Abel story appears to have become central in arguments about the source of good and evil in the world. These debates are present in the work of Philo and in the various Targumim. The Cain and Abel tradition in *Genesis Rabbah* also removes certain elements from the story, particularly those which problematize the divine role. It also adds a sequence of debates between the two brothers in order to distance the conflict between them from any divine action.[23] It presents Cain as an evil character from the beginning, so that the divine refusal to receive his offering no longer looks like an arbitrary choice. The discussions connected to the Cain and Abel story appear to have been lively and varied in the period when Jubilees was written. In such a context, the omission of the Cain and Abel story entirely would have taken a work like Jubilees out of such conversations.

The writer of Jubilees removes most of the challenging aspects of Cain's genealogy in Genesis 4:17–22. First, Jubilees resolves the long-standing problem of the identity of Cain's wife by reporting his marriage to Awan (Jub. 4:9), his sister, whose birth is reported in Jubilees 4:1 along with the births of Cain and Abel. Cain and Awan are the parents of Enoch, for whom Cain still names the first city, but Jubilees adds the building of houses to the city-building report, perhaps disassociating this report from the building of the public portions of cities alone. Instead, Cain is linked more closely with the building of permanent human dwellings.[24] Jubilees omits the remainder of the genealogy after Enoch and, with it, the sense of continuing conflict between settled life and nomadic life. In addition to removing the cultural founders like Jabal, Jubal, and Tubal-Cain, Jubilees 7:1 also adjusts the statement about Noah in Genesis 9:20 so that Noah is no longer the first winemaker. The resistance to human discovery is a tendency Jubilees seems to share with 1 Enoch. Both texts contain examples of angels teaching humans the elements of culture and civilization, in Jubilees 3:15 and 4:21 and 1 Enoch 8, but in Jubilees the instruction is positive, while in 1 Enoch it leads to warfare. In Jubilees these skills become heavenly gifts, rather than the innovations

of a problematic genealogical line, as they are in Genesis 4. It is possible
the writer of Jubilees had no use for Cain's genealogy. Van Ruiten has
taken such a position, emphatically arguing, "The author of Jubilees is quite
obviously not interested in the genealogical line of Cain. The genealogy that
matters is the line that started with Seth."[25] While uninterest alone might
explain the omissions, they also fit a pattern, including the omission of Cain's
farming occupation along with other texts that present negative associations
for city building. The lack of any reference in Genesis to the death of Cain
has presented a problem for interpreters for a long time. The primary effort
to fix this in ancient interpretations of Genesis was to claim that Lamech
killed Cain, and this act is the subject of his little song in Genesis 4:23–24.[26]
The Cain genealogy in Genesis reports no deaths at all, however, and this
provides even more indication that its primary concern is with ways of life and
technological and artistic developments that live on, beyond their inventors.
Jubilees adds a strange note at 4:31 about the death of Cain, whose house
made of stones falls and kills him.[27] The narrator of Jubilees reminds the
reader Cain used a stone to kill Abel, a tradition that developed in multiple
places outside of the Bible, and this account is presented so that it sounds
as if Cain's house avenges Abel. At the end of the story of Cain and Abel in
Jubilees, the shepherd and the settler are on the same side, having dismissed
Cain as just a murderer. In Jubilees 4:15 angels come from heaven to teach
the skills of human civilization to Jared, a descendant of Seth. The first city is
still named for Enoch, Cain's son, in Jubilees 4:9, so his name is perpetuated
beyond his own life. City building is not fully separate from this problematic
element of the story yet.

After truncating Cain's genealogy, Jubilees presents the genealogy of Adam
through Seth to Noah, a parallel to Genesis 5. Without the full counterpart
from Genesis 4:17–22, the Adam/Seth genealogy has no competition and
stands alone as the advancing path of human culture. Because Jubilees omits
the Lamech of Genesis 4:19–24, the genealogy of Cain provides no alternative version of the origin of Noah. The possibility of this move by Jubilees
makes it all the more surprising that Genesis retained the parallel characters
from J and P, like Enoch and Lamech. Whatever constrained the writer of
Genesis, allowing only the dilution of problematic aspects of the traditions in
his sources apparently did not constrain the writer of Jubilees.

The most striking addition to the story of Noah's family in Jubilees comes
when all three of Noah's sons build their own cities in Jubilees 7:13–17. They
do this because Noah commands them to build cities and plant trees. Even
Shem, the great ancestor of the Israelites, is a city builder. Each son names his
city for his wife, which is an occasion for more of the unnamed characters in
Genesis to receive names and a greater amount of attention in Jubilees. More

significantly, this may also redeem the act of naming cities, since there is no obvious negative connotation to characters like Shem and Japheth and their wives, nor to the naming itself. The attitude of the J source against "making a name" survived in diminished form in Genesis, but it disappears from the story in Jubilees. While Genesis appears to have taken Noah away from Cain in order to distance Noah from city building, Jubilees takes city building away from Cain and gives it to the sons of Noah. Its origins are now postdiluvian, and form no part of the evil or violence of humanity to which God responded with the flood.

With Noah's sons all playing the part of city builders, it makes sense that Nimrod himself is absent from Jubilees, except for the indirect genealogical reference in 8:7, if this "Nebrod" is even the same figure. Jubilees reduces the entire "Table of Nations" from Genesis 10 to a much briefer text in Jubilees 7:13–19 and is much more concerned with the division of lands among Noah's sons than with full genealogies.[28] In Jubilees 9, the sons of Noah more explicitly divide portions of the land they had received in the previous chapter for their sons. Ham has four sons—Cush, Egypt (Mizraim), Put, and Canaan—but the genealogy stops there and no further generations appear in the text. Aside from the same misplacement of the Canaanites as in Genesis, everything about Ham's descendants in Jubilees relates to Africa. The transition from Ham to Shem in Jubilees 9:2 is confusing, but by 9:3 Shem is dividing territory among his three sons—Asshur, Arpachshad, and Aram— three of the five named in Genesis 10:22. Most significantly, the territory he gives to Asshur includes Nineveh and Shinar, places that Genesis 10:8–12 associates with Nimrod. So, not only is Nimrod the city builder missing from Jubilees, the African and Mesopotamian identities which he held together in Genesis are divided in Jubilees. City building is evenly apportioned among all three sons of Noah, and the removal of Nimrod has disassociated the activity from imperial power and fame. Finally, the presence of Shem's descendant Terah in a Mesopotamian city like Ur is consistent with the division of territories in Jubilees. Without the appearance of Nimrod as the builder of Babel, there is no connection between these genealogies and the Babel story, which will receive further attention below.

Chapter 2 of this book offered a resolution to the isolated appearance of the "Sons of God" story in Genesis 6:1–4. By rearranging the order of the elements from Genesis in a reconstructed J source, it connected this story and the origins of the *gibborim* to Nimrod, the first *gibbor*. The place of this tradition in Jubilees needs separate attention here. Jubilees 5:1–19 seems dependent upon Genesis 6:1–4, but there are important additions and omissions. Along with material from Genesis, Jubilees used the Watchers tradition also found in 1 Enoch to develop this part of the narrative.[29]

Connecting the actions of the "angels of YHWH," which produced a race of giants, to the spread of corruption and injustice on the earth in 5:2 links them more closely to the flood story introduced in 5:3.[30] The judgment and destruction of the gigantic offspring in 5:7–11 further explains the absence of Nimrod the city builder in Jubilees. In the context of Jubilees, the sin of the angels is clearer. The separation between earth and heaven, allowing for the complete transcendence of God, is a primary theme throughout Jubilees. The angels "mingled the two spheres" when they procreated with human women, so God had to destroy the product of the mingling to set things right again.[31] God causes the mixed offspring to kill each other "by the sword" in 5:6–11, so they are removed from earth. At the same time, God commands the angels, the ones the Angel of the Presence refers to as "us," to bind the disobedient angels. The corruption these beings cause leads to the necessity of the flood in Jubilees. One of the problems with the Genesis account of the flood is that it accomplishes little or nothing. Jubilees provides the flood greater purpose because it wipes out the influence of these beings and their illicit offspring. Further, God produces a new nature for humanity and the rest of creation 5:12–19.[32] One more text after the Jubilees flood account looks back on the event in a speech of Noah, and blames the flood on the Watchers (7:21). A new collection of evil beings appears to corrupt humans at 10:1. These demons must be bound like the ones before the flood, but Mastema is among them and he convinces God to leave one-tenth of them unbound.

Jubilees removed almost any trace of Nimrod from its presentation of the Primeval Story, and it is easy to imagine that it might have done the same with the Babel story. If Babel is primarily an anti-city-building narrative, then it would ill-suit the purposes of Jubilees, but a version of it appears, even slightly expanded, in Jubilees 10:18–26. Van Ruiten claims that the divine interference in the building project is "incomprehensible," and it would have been so to the writer of Jubilees, so the Jubilees text makes a clear distinction between the building work and its purpose.[33] The first addition in Jubilees is the connection of Babel to Peleg, the descendant of Shem from Genesis 10:25. In Jubilees, Peleg and his son Reu are the ones who corrupt the settlement in Shinar with the plan to build a city with a tower in it, including a plan to use the tower to get to heaven (10:20). Reu also marries 'Ora, the daughter of 'Ur, who builds Ur of the Chaldees (11:1–6). This city, which will produce Terah and his family, is specifically condemned for idol worship, a theme the discussion of Abraham will take up below. The motive that so many readers mistakenly ascribe to the builders in Genesis is explicit in Jubilees. Jubilees makes it clear that the confusion and scattering of the people of Babel are not about halting city building, because God scatters the people into other cities (10:25). In the Jubilees account God finishes the task by overthrowing the tower. The goal of the tower builders would have been another example of what James Scott called the mingling of heaven and earth, which Jubilees resists so emphatically.[34] The text following the Babel story in Jubilees 10:27–34 reveals a further purpose for retaining the Babel story. After the flood Noah had established portions of land with proper boundaries for his sons, but in 10:29 Canaan, having been part of the dispersal from Shinar, desires and takes some of Shem's portion, specifically the land called Canaan.[35] So, Jubilees has used the Babel story as part of a narrative that initially assigns the land of Canaan to Shem and his descendants and explains how it came to be the illegitimate property of the descendants of Canaan. The confiscation of Canaan by the Israelites in later traditions is thus a return of the place to its rightful owners.

From time to time in this study, fame or "making a name" has accompanied the discussion of city building, and the Jubilees version of the Babel story provides occasion to pull the fragments of that theme together. In J and Genesis, the fame appears to some extent in all of the odd texts from Genesis 1–11 that chapter 2 examined. In Genesis 4:17 Cain named his city Enoch, after his son. In 6:4 the *gibborim* were "men of a name," or perhaps "famous men." The greatest *gibbor*, Nimrod became famous for hunting and building cities. Finally, the people of Babel built their city and tower in part to "make a name" for themselves. Of all these occasions of grasping for fame, omissions made by Jubilees leaves only the naming of Cain's city, an act surpassed when all three sons of Noah name cities for their wives. Cain and his city become a dead end in Jubilees, when part of his city, his own house, falls and kills him in Jubilees 4:31. The removal of the "making a name" theme from the Babel story in Jubilees is the final act that eliminates any negative connotation from fame and the naming of cities in its presentation of the Primeval Tradition.[36] The failure to retain some version of the Nimrod city-building tradition is the lingering mystery. Of course, this tradition is unnecessary in Genesis, but the composer of the Pentateuch seemed determined to keep all of the source material, including the passages from J that focus on city building and do not fit easily into the plot of Genesis. The writer(s) of Jubilees was apparently not constrained in the same way. Neither a personal commitment to retaining all traditions nor a need to satisfy any constituents of an audience that valued them was enough to keep problematic material in the book. Other Jewish sources from around the time of Jubilees did not make significant use of Nimrod, as they had Cain, so there may have been little conversation about this character in which Jubilees needed to engage.

The third account of the primeval world, found in the book called Jubilees, presents a sense of mystery equal to that found in J and Genesis. The author of Jubilees put in enough elements from Genesis for readers to recognize the story but seemed to have a free hand to make additions, subtractions, and modifications of many kinds. The first sign of literary freedom is the integration of the Genesis 1 and Genesis 2 creation accounts. In the process, Jubilees placed the origins of settled agriculture more clearly in the garden, in the work of Adam and Eve, making agricultural work a legitimate vocation, and removing mention of Cain's vocation helped maintain its legitimacy. Modern readers may not make the obvious connection between agriculture and city building because transportation has allowed them to grow apart spatially, but in the ancient world, city building required a close connection to agricultural production. The entire framework of competing ways of life was likely ill-suited to the purpose of the writer of Jubilees, so he removed any description of Cain and Abel's vocations or descriptions of their offerings, other than Abel being accepted and Cain not. The conflict between herder and farmer is absent. The ancestors of Israel can still be herders without their way of life being in a conflict with the lives of Jubilees' readers.

Having redeemed settled agriculture, the writer of Jubilees proceeded to diminish the reference to Cain's city building. Cain dies just one year after Abel when his stone house falls on him, so there is little time for him to influence human culture. After the flood, each of Noah's sons, including Shem, build cities and name them for their wives. Like farming, city building is a legitimate occupation in Jubilees. Jubilees has no need of Nimrod before or after the flood and leaves his city-building legend out, but retains a revised version of the Babel story in order to explain the disregard for boundaries leading to Canaan's possession of the land known by his name, which had legitimately belonged to Shem and his descendants.

In the J source YHWH sees settled life and city building as a threat and actively opposes it at every turn. Direct divine statements at what are now Genesis 3:22 and 11:6 express a sense of uneasiness about the abilities human beings have acquired, though it is unclear what God is protecting in the subsequent actions. Genesis mitigated the divine perspective on city building and managed to attach its worst excesses to genealogical lines and ethnic groups distant from and opposed to Israel's ancestors. Jubilees does not appear to have been bound by whatever constraints kept the J material relatively intact in Genesis 1–11, and it more fully freed the Primeval Narrative from its stance against urban life. To be sure, Jubilees had other purposes more important than this one, but it would be difficult to accept that all of the adjustments documented here were just an inadvertent result of all the other things the writer of Jubilees was doing.

If the trajectory of perspectives on city building in presentations of the Primeval Tradition that I have described to this point is correct, then it covered a period of several centuries of composing stories based on that tradition.

Modern readers another two thousand or so years later live in a world far more urban and technological than anyone in ancient times could have imagined. Nevertheless, the version of the Primeval Story to which we give the most attention is the middle one of the three. This is so because of canon-shaping forces within Rabbinic Judaism and early Christianity we understand only dimly. Contemporary reading practices often give more attention to issues like the purpose of whole books of the Bible or large sections of them. These can be helpful approaches, but we need to be careful not to assume there was a single purpose or that other effects less central to the book do not have profound impact. The world will continue to become more urban for the foreseeable future. For such a world to give authority to texts suspicious or even critical of urban life may be helpful if they warn us about the worst excesses of our way of life. Genesis points toward such a practice when it places Nimrod and the tower of Babel after the flood to associate city building more closely with the destructive empires of its own day.[37] At the same time, reading that fails to acknowledge a text's deep ambivalence about the way its own devotees live can be self-deceptive in dangerous ways. Ancient Israel attempted to address this by retaining or even crafting an identity for its heroic figures of the past that stayed connected to humble sheepherding ways even when the lives of those heroes later in life took on all the power and prestige of the palace. The verdict is still out on the apparent failure of Jubilees. Perhaps it was a brave attempt to jettison old traditions that no longer fit a new cultural identity. Though we do not yet understand the mechanism of rejection, Jubilees was abandoned by Judaism and most of Christian tradition. Still, its meager survival and recovery, along with the reconstruction of the J source of the Pentateuch, reveals that ancient Israel engaged in negotiation about many aspects of its tradition, including its relation to city life.

JUBILEES AND THE ANCESTRAL STORY

If Jubilees makes some of its choices in presenting its Primeval Story to produce a more positive view of urban life, then such a motive should also be present in the ancestral material that corresponds to Genesis 12–50, even though city building is not as central an issue in this part of Israelite tradition. Cities still play a role in the story, however, beginning with the larger story of Terah's family in Jubilees. Only the P source in Genesis places the family in Ur of the Chaldees, and the tradition included in Genesis is minimal, but Jubilees includes stories surrounding the birth of Terah in this place. Nahor and his father, Serug, participate in the evils of Ur, specifically divination and astrology (11:7), and Terah's birth is marked by an ominous attack on the agriculture of the region by Mastema (11:9–13). Abram distinguishes himself from the culture of the city and his family by refusing to worship idols and fighting of the crows sent by Mastema (11:18–21). The climax of Abram's resistance comes when he burns the house of the idols, resulting in the death of his brother, Haran, and the family's departure to the city of Haran, at the other end of the Tigris-Euphrates valley.[38] When Abram leaves Haran some time later, it is not over any conflict with the city. During a conversation in 12:28–32, Abram and his father part peacefully, and Terah raises the possibility that at some later point he will journey southward with Abram. Haran is not depicted as an idolatrous city like Ur.

The writer of Jubilees handled the traditions about the destruction of Sodom and Gomorrah in a much different manner than Genesis. Jubilees reduces the earlier story of conflict between Abram and Lot in Genesis 13 to a brief report of Lot's departure from Abraham to go live in Sodom. The ambiguity of Lot's dwelling place in Genesis is not present here. Jubilees had included Lot in the story of Abraham and Sarah travelling to Egypt, where Lot also received wealth, so uncle and nephew are connected more closely at the beginning of the story, and there is no conflict between them. Jubilees 13:22–29 tells the story of the abduction of Lot and Abram's battles to rescue him (Gen. 14) in abbreviated fashion. The refusal of Abram to take any spoils from the war, when offered by the king of Sodom (Gen. 14:22 and Jub. 13:29) retains all of the ambiguity present in the Genesis account.[39] A mere nine verses in Jubilees correspond to the sequence of events in Genesis 18–19. Because the Angel of the Presence continues to narrate Jubilees, the parts of the account involving angelic action are presented in first-person plural language. An abbreviated version of the visit of the angels to Abraham and Sarah makes up the first half of the account, and Abraham's negotiation with YHWH concerning Sodom is absent. The remainder of the Jubilees version (16:5–9) reports the judgment and destruction by fire of Sodom, Gomorrah, Zeboim, and the surrounding area in the Jordan valley. There is no angelic visit to Sodom and Lot's family before the disaster. The angels rescue Lot and his family because of God's regard for Abraham (16:7). Jubilees is more precise about the infractions that lead to the destruction. The Lord destroys the cities because of their impure behavior, specifically their sexual sins. No accusation that cities are inherently inhospitable is possible in this account. The destruction of the areas around the three named cities may serve to mitigate the assumption that the story of sin and punishment is centered on urban life. The final two verses of the Jubilees account reports the incestuous behavior of Lot and his daughters, removing the instigation of the daughters and the drunkenness of Lot in order to place primary blame on the father. The writer of Jubilees draws a parallel between Lot's illicit sexual behavior and the behavior of Sodom and renders judgment upon Lot's descendants, without naming Moab and Ammon specifically. Jacques van Ruiten has observed that Jubilees maximizes the differences between Abraham and Lot, the former becoming the perfect example of piety and the latter of sinfulness.[40]

The story of Abraham and Sarah traveling to Gerar and the resulting conflict with King Abimelech is not in Jubilees, but the story of Isaac in Gerar is. The discussion in chapter 3 addressed the Gerar traditions in Genesis, the first of which comes from the E source and the second from J. The J version of this story in Genesis 26, involving Isaac and Rebekah, makes use of the wife-sister motif also present in Genesis 12 and 20. The Jubilees version contains no direct mention of Rebekah, so no possibility of her being taken as a wife by a local man is present in the story. The only vague inclusion of this element is a version of the warning offered by Abimelech in 26:11, but in Jubilees Abimelech only includes anything belonging to Isaac in the warning, not specifically "his wife" as in Genesis. Jubilees 24:14–33 does contain a version of the conflict over wells that is as convoluted as the one in Genesis 26:12–33. Both stories begin with conflict that arises over Isaac's prosperity and his right to wells that had been dug by Abraham. As in Genesis, Isaac digs a series of successful wells as he moves away from the Philistines, but Jubilees adds names to Isaac's wells. In succession they are Harshness, Hostility, Breadth, and the Well of the Oath. The name of this final well signals a change in the story. The Jubilees version has an ending very different from the peaceful feast with Abimelech in Genesis. In Jubilees the final well Isaac's servants dig is dry, and Isaac credits this to an ill-advised oath he took to the Philistines, so he follows it with a curse in 24:28–32 which seems to embody the long conflict between the Israelites and Philistines that is expressed at length in the Hebrew Bible.[41] The conflict between Isaac and the Philistines is distant from their initial encounter in Gerar, so there need not be any negative reflection on the urban setting, but on the practice of swearing oaths specifically to the Philistines. The discussion in chapter 3 concluded that an important concern of the J source in Genesis 26 is finding the right location for Isaac and his family in relation to a city like Gerar. Future conflicts with the Philistines do not seem to be an important issue, and the story would function in much the same way no matter what city or group of foreigners it involved. The conclusion of the story in Jubilees has taken it in a different direction and made it specific to relations with the Philistines.

The tradition of the conflict between Jacob's sons and the city of Shechem finds expression in Jubilees 30, and the story is recognizable, but significantly shorter. Betsy Halpern-Amaru has demonstrated that the omissions and simplification of the story serve to bring the prohibition against intermarriage to the forefront.[42] Simeon and Levi are able to kill all of the men of Shechem through acts of treachery, but there is no mention of the circumcision ruse. It is understandable that Jubilees would not have wanted this sacred rite to be part of their deceit, even though 30:6 exonerates the brothers by placing a divine stamp of approval on their attack against Shechem. Jacob's fear of the people of Canaan after the event is also acknowledged in 30:25, but, unlike Genesis, Jubilees adds a note of divine protection, a fear of Jacob's family that prevents the people of the area from seeking revenge on them. While this story constitutes a negative interaction of Jacob's family with the people of a city, there is no general judgment against cities, and Jacob's sons are permitted to confiscate the spoils of their victory and bring them to Jacob. The negative view of Shechem stems from its foreign identity and the attitude of Jubilees to foreign marriage.

Jubilees 34 contains an additional story of conflict between Jacob and the people of Canaan. In this case a group of Amorite kings attacks Jacob's sons and steals their livestock. The origins of this story are difficult to determine. Nothing like it appears in Genesis, but similar traditions are in the Testament of Judah and at least one midrashic text.[43] The most curious element is the reference to Jacob building two cities, Robel and Tamnatares, at the end of the conflict in 34:8. Perhaps the latter can be connected to Timnah, which appears in the Hebrew Bible three times, twice in connection to the character (Gen. 38:14) or tribe (Josh. 15:10) called Judah. Curiously, in the Testament of Judah the book's namesake credits himself with the building of this city (Thamna) and Jacob with the other.[44] The placement of Jacob in the ranks of city-builders by Jubilees, along with the sons of Noah, including Shem, continues to elevate the status of this task. Jacob is a striking figure in Jubilees 34:6, commanding six thousand men, an image reminiscent of his grandfather Abraham in Genesis 14.[45] Not only does Jacob build cities, but he also has gathered around him enough people to populate them.

The Joseph of Jubilees may be even more brilliant than the character developed so fully in Genesis. In Jubilees 40:6–13 his rule over Egypt brings peace and prosperity to the whole land, earning him the admiration and love of all the Egyptians. He gathers an immense amount of surplus grain into the city in 40:13, and when the famine arrives in 42:1–3 he opens up the storehouses and gives the grain away to all the people. The use of the grain to acquire land for Pharaoh in exchange in Genesis 47:13–26 is a detailed and prominent story, one which Jubilees treats curiously. Almost as an appendix to the Joseph narrative, just before the death notices of Jacob and Joseph, Jubilees 45:8–12 summarizes Joseph's administrative success. The acknowledgment in 45:8 that he acquired livestock and land for Pharaoh in exchange for the food is in conflict with the claim that he gave the food away in the earlier story. Both Genesis and Jubilees end the account with Joseph

setting up a system of tribute to benefit Pharaoh, but Jubilees does not include
the pledge from the people to become Pharaoh's slaves. While Joseph looked
a great deal like an emperor in Genesis, that depiction is minimized, though
not absent, in Jubilees.

JUBILEES AND THE EXODUS STORY

While the story line in Jubilees continues until the account of the crossing of
the sea, corresponding to Exodus 14–15, there is a relatively small amount of
material in Jubilees related to the traditions found in Exodus. The following
list illustrates the portions of Jubilees that make up this part of the story of
Israel:

- Jubilees 47:1–12 tells of the early part of Moses' life and is roughly parallel to Exodus 2:1–15.
- Jubilees 48:1–4 mentions Moses' time in Midian and his return to Egypt.
- Jubilees 48:5–8 summarizes the plagues.
- Jubilees 48:9–19 reports the departure from Egypt and the Red Sea event.
- Jubilees 49:1–23 describes the origins of Passover, with regulations for its observance.

The final chapter of Jubilees (50) deals with Sabbath laws. Perhaps the
most striking addition to this material is the character called Mastema, who
had also appeared in some parts of Jubilees related to Genesis. The writer(s)
of Jubilees likely saw the infamous "bridegroom of blood" passage in Exodus
4:24–26 as a problem. Why would God attack and attempt to kill Moses after
going to so much effort to prepare him to deliver the Israelites? In a manner
reminiscent of the insertion of Mastema into the Akedah story, to be the
one who tempted Abraham to kill Isaac, Jubilees 48:2–3 makes him the one
who attacks Moses during the return journey to Egypt. Mastema also rallies
the Egyptians in Jubilees 48:12 to pursue the Israelites into the wilderness
after their departure from Egypt.[46] This move, along with the reduction of
the entire plague narrative to a few verses, removes all of the problematic
references to YHWH hardening the heart of Pharaoh.

The removal of these glaring theological problems from the exodus story
might serve to distract from a small insertion at Jubilees 47:9 that is important
for the development of this story. The Torah primarily presents Moses as a
character who receives the law from YHWH and speaks it to the Israelites,
but the scribes who produced the Torah had begun to make at least a minor
effort to make Moses look more like them. Moses writes twice in the book of
Exodus, at 24:4 and 34:28. The first occasion appears to indicate the writing

of what is commonly called the Covenant Code (Exod. 21–23), and the second what is often called the "Ritual Decalogue" (34:11–26). There are a few references to Moses writing in Deuteronomy, including writing the Ten Commandments on stone tablets (4:13 and 5:22) and the Song of Moses (31:22). Apparently, by the time Jubilees was written, some readers had begun raising questions about how Moses, whom Exodus says was raised in the palace of Pharaoh, was able to write Hebrew texts. Jubilees 47:9 continues Moses' contact with his biological parents after his mother had weaned him by bringing his father in to teach him to write. Unlike Exodus, Jubilees names the parents of Moses, Amram and Jochebed, at this early point of the story of his life. So the Moses of Jubilees receives a Levite education from his own father, while living with the daughter of Pharaoh. The Moses of Jubilees is a true Hebrew scribe.

The location of the Israelites in the land of Egypt at the end of the book of Genesis and beginning of Exodus is considerably vague. Chapter 3 addressed the ambiguous traditions concerning the place called Goshen and the city called Ramses. Jubilees 43:10 and 44:1–7 also associate the family of Jacob with these places and, like Genesis, Jubilees 43:10 remarks on Goshen as the best part of Egypt. These texts appear before the Israelites are enslaved in Genesis and Jubilees and indicate that the Israelites were an autonomous and prosperous people during the first part of their time in Egypt.

The enslaving of the Israelites in Egypt in Jubilees 44:9–16 is the location of one of the most remarkable differences from the biblical book of Exodus. The initial move of Pharaoh in Exodus 1:8–14 has always been somewhat puzzling. Forcing a group that he is afraid of into hard labor in order to keep them from revolting seems counterintuitive at best. Chapter 4 shows the surprising invisibility of Egyptians in Canaan during the story of the settlement of the Israelites in the books of Joshua and Judges, given the archaeological evidence that indicates significant Egyptian presence in the area during the late Bronze Age and early Iron Age. Jubilees, on the other hand, proves to be aware of the interaction between Egypt and Canaan. Jubilees 44:9–10 reports a remarkable military incursion into Canaan by the Egyptian king. In conjunction with this aggression many Israelites travel to Canaan to bury the bones of some of Jacob's children, and the Angel of the Presence tells Moses that some of the Israelites remained in Hebron, including Moses's father, Amram. The foe of the king of Egypt is a figure Jubilees calls "the king of Canaan," but it does not offer a more precise name or location. The story seems to be placed in a period when Canaan would have been ruled by many kings, each holding power over his own city-state and perhaps some of the region surrounding it. The character called the king of Canaan defeats Pharaoh and he is the one who suggests enslaving the Israelites, specifically because he thinks they intend to come to Canaan. While it still seems like a dubious strategy for keeping people under control, it is not this king of Canaan who would suffer the consequences of the failure of the plan. This story required Amram to return eventually from Canaan, which he does in 47:1, and this report is followed by the birth story of Moses. Jubilees omits the awkward story of the midwives and moves straight to Pharaoh's order to throw the boys in the Nile, leading to the placement of Moses in the basket by the river. Jubilees continues its propensity to add timing to stories that have little or none. Moses is in the basket seven days, and his mother comes to feed him during the night, while Miriam fends off the birds during the day. It is not clear what the additional details about Moses' family add to the story. None of them are named in Exodus 2, but Amram, Jochebed, and Miriam are all named here in Jubilees 47. The discussion in chapter 4 gave some attention to Moses' uncertain genealogy. The appearance of his parents in Exodus is ambiguous, and his sons never figure prominently in the story. The story of Amram travelling to Canaan for the burial of Jacob's children provides him a slightly greater connection to Israel's story. The encounter with the daughters of the priest of Midian is missing from Jubilees, so Jubilees does not present the concerted effort of Exodus to make Moses look like an Israelite. The report in Jubilees 47:9 about Amram teaching Moses Hebrew, which made Moses look more like the scribes who wrote the book, may also play this role of preventing him from looking too Egyptian.

Near the end of Jubilees a set of instructions for Passover appears. The corresponding place in Exodus 12–13 is complex and confusing. There are two sets of Passover instruction for the night of the event. In 12:1–20 God speaks to Aaron and Moses providing detailed instructions. In the text immediately following, Moses gives briefer instructions to the elders of the Israelites. After the departure from Egypt, Exodus 12:43–49 contains a set of general instructions for Passover that is not specifically connected to the initial event. The primary concern of this text is that participation requires circumcision for males, thus excluding foreigners, except for slaves who have been circumcised. Passover is specifically a household festival in this text. Exodus 13:3–10 contains instructions for the Festival of Unleavened Bread, as yet unconnected to Passover, though it is connected to the story of the departure from Egypt. Jubilees has consolidated the Passover traditions into a single text in 49:1–23. There is no mention of Passover in the surprisingly brief account of the plagues in 48:5–8. After the departure, however, 49:1–23 looks back on the death of the firstborn, attributed to Mastema, and connects that event to the Passover ritual. Jubilees 49:15 contains an element not present in any Passover text in the Hebrew Bible, a warning that Passover must be observed in order to prevent a plague of death in the future. This warning is followed in the next verse by a command to observe Passover only in "the sanctuary of the LORD." A previous verse (49:10) had indicated a vague need for travel, but it is obvious in this one that Passover is now a pilgrimage festival, requiring travel to Jerusalem, a requirement consistent with Deuteronomy 16:5–7, and the Passover celebrations sponsored by Hezekiah and Josiah in 2 Chronicles, and by the Golah community in Ezra 6. Jubilees 49:21 goes into even greater detail on the centralization of Passover, forbidding observance in any place other than the tabernacle or the temple.[47] There was no way to connect the religious observances of the ancestors to Jerusalem, and some of these occasions are connected to legal texts, such as the law of circumcision which accompanies the story of the covenant changing the names of Abram and Sarai in Jubilees 15:1–16. An important shift takes place in Jubilees 32, though. As noted earlier, the Jabbok wrestling match from Genesis 32 does not appear in Jubilees, but a tradition matching the other story of Jacob's name change in Genesis 35 appears in Jubilees 32:16–19. In both texts the event occurs at Bethel, and both Genesis and Jubilees record Jacob's earlier visit to Bethel, when he built an altar there. Bethel presents a number of problems for later Israelite tradition. How can there be a place called "House of God" when the house of YHWH is in Jerusalem? Later traditions would make Bethel the site of one of Jeroboam's golden bulls, magnifying the difficulty. Jubilees addresses this problem on the occasion of Jacob's second visit to Bethel, when Jacob has a vision in which an angel shows him the heavenly tablets and specifically commands him not to build a sanctuary there because it is not the right place (32:23). The centralization of Israel's worship in Jubilees begins with Jacob, and is written into the first set of Passover regulations.

COMPETING TRADITIONS IN ANCIENT ISRAEL

The discussion in chapter 5 posed a puzzling question about the book of Chronicles, particularly its opening chapters. The genealogies in the first nine chapters, beginning with Adam, correspond to the books of Genesis through Judges, and part of 1 Samuel. Why did the writers of Chronicles leave this part of the story mostly blank? There would have been various versions of the traditions about Israel in the distant past available at the time, and the primary goals of the writers of Chronicles were not dependent on the presentation of these traditions. Chronicles is concerned with the depiction of the monarchy and the temple and the relationship between the two, and it provides a different account of these than in Samuel–Kings. There would have been no need for these writers to discourage persons who preferred various versions of the earlier parts of Israel's story from encountering and accepting their version of the later parts. The skeletal version offered in the genealogies of 1 Chronicles 1–9 would have allowed readers to fill in the blanks with their own version of the traditions. After the examination of Jubilees in this chapter, it is possible to ask whether this idea works for it. Could a reader who preferred the Jubilees account of Genesis have filled in the beginning of Chronicles with those details without significant conflict? Chronicles makes no mention of Cain or Abel, so the differences in the portrayals of these characters in Genesis and Jubilees would not be an issue for a reader of Chronicles. The discussion above observed that Jubilees leaves Nimrod out of the Primeval Story, except for the possible genealogical reference to Nebrod in 8:7. First Chronicles keeps Nimrod in the genealogy of Ham, as in Genesis 10, and includes the statement about him being the first *gibbor*, but omits any reference to city building. So, Chronicles says a little bit more about Nimrod then Jubilees does but removes the part that would cause real difficulty for a reader of Jubilees. Recall also that Jubilees accused Canaan of transgressing the borders of the territory assigned to Noah's sons in 10:27–34, an idea not present in the discussion of the borders of the Canaanites in Genesis 10:18–21, where the traditional land of Canaan is presented as belonging to the Canaanites without dispute. First Chronicles removes any reference to borders from the presentation of Noah's sons.[48] First Chronicles 1 contains a large number of names that are not in Jubilees, mostly because Jubilees' is not interested in the genealogies of Ham and Japheth beyond the next generation. Jubilees contains expanded roles for characters like Arpachshad, Peleg, Reu, and Serug, compared to Genesis, but Jubilees presents no conflict for these, as it merely lists their names, as it did for Adam, Enoch, and Noah. The same pattern holds for the ancestors beginning with Abraham in Chronicles, because the appearance of only their names, with their lives left blank, allows readers to fill in whatever traditions about them they bring. Jubilees 19:12 lists the same six sons of Abraham by Keturah as in Genesis, though it stops there, while Genesis and 1 Chronicles continue one more generation for Midian. The inclusion of the genealogy of Ishmael from Genesis in 1 Chronicles presents no problems because Jubilees does not include it. Jubilees shows greater interest in the sons of Esau, because of their role in instigating the war between the families of Esau and Jacob in Jubilees 37, but the story names none of his sons, and the lack of a genealogy of Esau in Jubilees means that the inclusion of the Genesis version in 1 Chronicles presents no difficulty. All three books include the same list of eight kings of Edom, some of whose names resemble some of the descendants of Esau. Thus far, the conclusion would seem to be that the early chapters of Chronicles would present no difficulty for a reader of Jubilees, even though they have more in common with Genesis. The one problem that does arise is the character born in Jubilees 8:2 named Cainan, who is the son of Arpachshad and probably the father of Shelah, though the text of Jubilees is ambiguous at 8:5. This would appear to conflict with the genealogical line in Genesis 10 and 1 Chronicles 1, which moves from Arpachshad to Shelah to Eber. This is an important branch because they are the descendants of Shem leading directly to Abraham and, thus, the Israelites. The LXX version of Genesis 10:24 and 11:12–13 contain Cainan, however, so that version of Genesis does not differ from Jubilees on this point. The absence of the verses corresponding to 1 Chronicles 1:17–24 from the LXX and the disrupted state of what remains of the section make this case difficult to adjudicate. It seems likely that an ancient person whose understanding of the Primeval and Ancestral Traditions were like those of Jubilees who read Chronicles would have found Cainan's name there, eliminating even this one relatively minor conflict.

TELLING OUR URBAN STORIES

Interpreters of Jubilees agree that it presents a series of traditions that overlap with those in Genesis–Exodus 15 in a way that fits a different set of religious, political, and cultural assumptions. Some of those differences find easy agreement, such as the calendar-related concerns of Jubilees or its desire to extend the law back to the beginning of Israel's story. The primary concern of this study is less obvious in Jubilees, so the preceding discussion in this chapter leads to a more difficult question: Does the book of Jubilees have a significantly different view of cities and urban life than Genesis and Exodus, and, if so, how might we describe that view? The conclusions of chapters 2 and 3 complicate this question, because they revealed that there is no single perspective on this issue in the Torah. The differences between the J and P sources on many issues, including this one, are apparent, and the book of Genesis blends the views of these two sources and at least one more. Most significantly, this blending diminishes the anti-urban perspective of the J source. It is possible that this is a simple matter of dilution, but the discussions in chapters 2, 3, and 4 reveal that the P materials exhibit a positive view of urbanism, because of the centrality of Jerusalem to this source. The P source appears in important situations in the Pentateuch, such as Genesis 1–11 and the book of Numbers, to be more than just one source among two or three, but the one that frames and shapes the full text.

The discussion of Jubilees above and, on occasion, in some other texts that also present alternative ways of looking at Israel's distant past reveals a portrayal of urban life that avoids the negative elements present in Genesis. While it is possible for these differences to be coincidental, their quantity and consistency make such a claim seem unlikely. The ways that Israelites remembered their past was a matter of debate and negotiation, and it is possible that a text like Chronicles leaves that part of the story largely blank in order to accommodate multiple views on the part of its prospective readers. From time to time, this study has acknowledged the presence of anti-urban sentiments within modern religious traditions, particularly in Protestant Christianity. A review of the diverse alternatives for telling the story of the past within ancient Israelite literature demonstrated the power of telling stories that make the traditions of this people at home in urban settings. A renegotiation of the understanding of urban life in relation to ancient traditions may be analogous to what many contemporary religious communities need.

The first chapter of this book references the work of Dieter Georgi. Near the end of his work *The City in the Valley: Biblical Interpretation and Urban Theology*, which was his last, Georgi faulted the Christian religion and its "institutionalized scholarship" for many negative understandings of cities and their consequences: "Christian religion and theology have caused many of the catastrophic developments we face in the cities of today, although theology and religion hardly feel responsible. Responsibility was, rather, covered up or altogether avoided by noble retreat, an allegedly spiritual way out."[49] Spirituality and the city do not go together easily. Scholarly discussions of the temple and Jerusalem in ancient Israel often operate on a purely spiritual plane, but the scribes of ancient Israel wrote about a real city in which they lived, with buildings, streets, and a relatively large population of humans. Georgi developed a compelling case that the Christian Bible ends with a thoroughly urban vision of the world, one that may even be described as a redemption of Babylon.[50] This vision was a good fit for a church in the first century that was becoming an urban, communal religious experience.[51] This process was halted when the Roman Empire absorbed Christianity and made it a rural religion.[52] Georgi lamented that other influential literary works of the time, like 1 Enoch, 4 Ezra, 2 Baruch, and the sectarian Qumran writings did not emphasize the urban nature of Jerusalem or of the eschatological world to which their visions looked.[53] Such an emphasis may have been represented by Jubilees, which does not tell a story that fully arrives in Jerusalem, but reaches back into the distant past and renegotiates Israel's traditions in ways that might have made a more urban vision possible.

9

A Citified Text

The Transformation of City Building in the Biblical Tradition and Its Meaning for the Modern, Urban World

This book began with two simple observations. First, there is a layer of tradition in the Hebrew Bible that is anti-urban. This feature is most visible in the material attributed to the J source in Genesis 1–11, but it emerges on subsequent occasions as well. Second, the persons responsible for the final shape of the biblical literature were part of an elite class of urban scribes. This understanding may have been assumed frequently in the past, but careful analysis of the process has come to the forefront of scholarship over the past two decades.[1] The primary question this study follows through the Bible is how it navigates the inherent tension between those two observations. Chapters 2, 3, and 4 demonstrated that the combination of sources in the Pentateuch and other places often succeeds in diminishing the anti-urban tone of one or more of the sources alone. Chapters 5, 6, and 7 followed the stories of Israel as it became an urban story of a nation with urban centers, saw those centers destroyed, and began to rebuild them. Chapter 8 demonstrated that a distinctively different approach is present in another work of Second Temple Jewish literature, the book of Jubilees, which removes the tension in Israel's traditions of the distant past by eliminating many elements of the anti-city layer of tradition, altering some, and including different material that helps to cancel out the impact of others. The intensity of the presence of Jubilees among the Dead Sea Scrolls indicates that it held sustained significance among Jewish writings into the first century of the Common Era, but it ultimately did not make it into the more limited contents of most canonical collections. Along the way, the human process of urbanization has proven to be an interesting lens through which to look at many other biblical issues. The task of this final chapter will be to pull together many of the ideas that have emerged and use them to think about how we read the Bible in a world that is increasingly urban.

Before reaching a codified conclusion about these texts, it is necessary to achieve a clear way of thinking about the development of the literature this study has examined and a better understanding of it. The opening chapter presented a general framework relating the history of ancient Israel to the development of its literature. The central idea was that scribes in Judah, after both the Assyrian destruction of Israel and the Babylonian destruction of Judah, sought to develop a national story from diverse regional traditions. While much of the material had northern (Israelite) origins, the making of the biblical books was a southern (Judahite) production.[2] Other details about this process appeared in subsequent chapters as it fit the discussion of specific groups of texts. It is now possible to bring those observations together with some other recent proposals about textual development to imagine a more robust model and relate that model to the process of state development and urbanization in ancient Israel.

Brian Schmidt identifies a gap in the production of literature in the Levant through much of the ninth century, primarily as a result of a fifty-year period of military conflict. Evidence indicates that the pieces were in place for written literature to emerge prior to this period, as it had in nearby regions. The emergence of written literature in the late ninth century came when adequate stability returned to the region; and when such literature emerged, it emulated the practices of the Assyrian Empire.[3] Seth Sanders proposes a three-stage development of the Pentateuch, though he does not attempt to attach the kinds of precise dates that Schmidt does in his reconstruction. Sanders's model observes three different sets of literary values characterizing the three stages. The first stage valued coherence, as it integrated separate traditions into an extended narrative, a pattern resembling the Epic of Gilgamesh. The development of the sources used in the book of Genesis corresponds to this stage well. The joining of the Abraham traditions from Judah and the Jacob traditions from Israel into a single family story in Genesis is a dramatic example of this kind of literary work. The second stage valued comprehensiveness above all else and led to the development of the Pentateuch in the form we now have it. The dominance of comprehensiveness in the joining of the sources led to the narrative incoherence that makes the Pentateuch unique among all extant examples of ancient literature. The third stage was, at least in part, a response to the incoherence of the second. From Chronicles to Jubilees to the Temple Scroll, the literature of this stage attempted, through harmonization, omission, and creative interpretation, to fashion a more coherent story of Israel. At the same time, the coherence that had been of value in the first stage was joined in the third by a desire for perfection and relevance, as indications of the divine origin of the text.[4]

The possibility of fitting the models of Schmidt and Sanders together, along with the general framework used throughout this study and the observations about state development and urbanization in ancient Israel, is too tempting to resist. The most obvious fit is for the works like the sources of Genesis in their oral form to be part of Schmidt's "pre-gap" development. His notion of "oral literature" is helpful here. The common assumption that oral tradition is highly unstable, particularly when placed in harsh contrast to written forms, is an anachronism based on observations of modern gossip and the "telephone game," in which players whisper a message around the room from person to person and notice the changes that occur. If oral traditions were performative, not whispered ear-to-ear, then they would have been subject to stabilizing forces. The traditions behind the sources of the Pentateuch could be the oral literature that survived Schmidt's "Iron 1–Early Iron 2 gap," which would have been available for a fairly rapid development of written literature once the era of conflict in the ninth century was over. The writing of texts like these would then correspond to the urbanization and state formation that also took place once the political situation in the region stabilized.[5] Following this kind of procedure, the combined models may provide a progression something like this:

(1) In the era before the ninth century (Iron 1), oral forms, such as stories about Jacob, related to specific places, like Bethel, developed. Some of these elements may even have been combined to form larger narratives that would have had a more regional appeal.

(2) The first half of the ninth century, filled with military conflict in the Levant, delayed further development, especially the kind of writing that required significant resources, including the emergence of a highly skilled scribal class and suitable working conditions within which they could operate. This stage corresponded to the beginnings of a new urbanization process, but there had already been such a process in the Late Bronze Age, so anti-urban traditions could fit either time. This may have helped earlier anti-urban traditions survive into a new period.

(3) Through much of the eighth century, written sources continued to develop separately in Israel and in Judah, probably much more in the former, a situation that would allow for the dominance of coherence in Sanders's first stage to persist. Stable nations needed coherent stories of their origins to supplement the development of centralized institutions. The joining of the Jacob and Moses/exodus traditions could have happened in this era.

(4) The destruction of Israel and the southward migration of its scribes, along with other portions of the population, created a significant disruption

that could have led to the transition between Sanders's first and second stages. The need to combine northern and southern traditions is the kind of force that would have overridden the desire for coherence that dominated the earlier stage. Such narratives could have acted as unifying forces in nations composed of groups that understood themselves as somewhat autonomous tribes. The combination likely happened first in J or E. Putting Abraham and Jacob together, for example, necessitated some relatively minor incoherence, but it would have been more manageable at this stage because there were not stories in direct conflict with each other. One example would be Abraham's visit to Bethel in Genesis 12, a place that did not have that name until Jacob named it in Genesis 28. While this kind of incoherence is not glaring, like so many examples in the final form of the Pentateuch, it could have opened the door for a new set of values emphasizing comprehensiveness. Having both great ancestors visit this important place mattered more than a coherent understanding of the origins of its name.

(5) The relatively long period of history in which Judah was the only representation of Israel provided for the further development of the comprehensive stage. This would include the century or so between the destruction of Samaria and Jerusalem, the "exilic" period that filled much of the sixth century, and the Persian period in which the province of Yehud represented Israel. The experience of exile and return and the corresponding need to hold the idea of the nation together could have been the context allowing for an even greater degree of incoherence. The stories of multiple groups needed to be included, even if they did not all fit together ideally. Texts continued to build a national story.

(6) All of the texts reflecting Sanders's third stage comes from the late Persian or Hellenistic Period. The distinctive feature of this development is divergence.[6] The examples of literature that sought to reassert coherence did it in vastly different ways, so they appear to have been for different communities. The development of diaspora communities and sectarian groups within Judah during the Second Temple Period created potential homes for differing efforts to resolve the incoherence created by the comprehensive narrative. The moves made by the writer of Jubilees to remove anti-urban elements, documented in the preceding chapter, fit within this context.

The scheme above explains how anti-urban traditions could have developed, and were eventually isolated in particular strands or sources of tradition. Chapter 5 of this book proposed the central hill country and the frontier of Judah as contexts where such traditions would have fit. These traditions provide one specific example of the kind of texts that could find their way into larger collections with which they now look incompatible, during an era in which comprehensiveness was the dominant value in textual formation. A period of diverging communities would then have allowed some works to alter or remove these traditions in the interest of coherence. Jubilees is the most thorough example of this phenomenon. Later examples would have been the constructions of Israel's ancient past by Philo and Josephus. A different kind of incoherence could have emerged from this situation, though, if a single group read and revered both Genesis and Jubilees, which the Dead Sea sect apparently did. Evidence indicates a diversification of literary and theological perspectives within Judaism during the Hellenistic era. Pointing to the variety of complex traditions in texts like Jubilees, the Enochic literature, Aramaic Levi, and the Apocalypse of Adam, Richard Horsley proposes an "alternative" Torah developing alongside what we know as Genesis through Deuteronomy.[7] Sectarian division meant that no one tradition was dominant, a perspective difficult for modern readers looking back through the lens of a standardized biblical tradition to see. In Horsley's words,

> This cultural repertoire provided a rich reservoir from which creative scribes composed new texts. The evidence from the scrolls found at Qumran suggest that the escalating crisis of rival factions in the aristocracy and the Hellenizing reform became the occasion for creative scribal activity. The crisis of authority in Jerusalem may be what led some creative scribe(s) to compose books of alternative Torah, such as Jubilees or the Temple Scroll.[8]

The story of the world began with two accounts of divine creation that interpreters often compare and contrast, but emphasized a difference that receives little attention. In Genesis 1 the divine likeness, which includes the ability and authority to order the world around them, is an inherent part of the identity of human beings. The human capacity to do this ordering work is a reflection of the divine being whose work of creation put the world and all of its contents in proper order. This text comes from the Priestly source, which also provides one of the most stunning stories of the human ability to impose a divinely ordained order when a group of escaped slaves constructs a city in the midst of a forbidding wilderness, and moves it through that wilderness for forty years to its eventual home. The Priestly story of the Israelites in the wilderness in the book of Numbers shows them assembling a temporary temple every time they stop and aligning themselves in a concentric pattern around it that resembles a walled city with a sacred space at its center. If the wandering Israelites could do this in the middle of the desert for forty years, surely their descendants could and should follow the same plan by building and maintaining a holy city on Mount Zion. The P source of the Pentateuch consistently promotes this ordered, urban view of human life.

In the other creation account, which starts in Genesis 2:4, the divine likeness, the knowledge necessary to develop a human civilization, is not part of the original human identity. Instead, God puts this knowledge in a fruit that God forbids the humans to eat. When the humans eat the fruit and acquire this knowledge the initial garden environment in which they live is no longer a suitable setting. God expels the humans from the garden and adds some additional punishments that would limit the growth and advancement of human civilization, but, in an odd twist, allows them to retain the divine likeness they have acquired. So, Adam and Eve and their descendants have the capacity to build human civilization. In subsequent texts from the J source that provided this second creation story, God continues to limit the advancement of human civilization toward a more urban shape, by banishing Cain, scattering the people of Babel, and destroying Sodom and Gomorrah. In the wilderness story from this source the Israelites do not build a tabernacle, or organize a complex camp, and they do not seek a promised land in which to build a sacred city. Instead they are traveling to a suitable environment to practice the agricultural lifestyle prized by the Edenic story, and practiced by Israel's great ancestors, even as the threat of urbanity closed in on them.

The image of God has become an important theological concept within Christianity in particular. Reading Genesis 1–3 straight through as a single story yields incoherent results in relation to this idea. How can humans receive the divine image in 1:26–27, then acquire it again by eating the fruit of 3:7? A way of reading that attempts to resolve the incoherence of Genesis 1–3 by harmonization leads to strange conclusions about the divine image. The idea is present in the influential work of Martin Luther on Genesis. By making Adam and Eve the people created on the sixth day of the Genesis 1 story, Luther arrived at the conclusion that humans lost the image of God through an act of disobedience in 3:7.[9] He was right that a change occurred in this regard, but misread it as a loss rather than a gain. The conclusion he reached about the divine image may lead one to wonder what Luther did when he got to Genesis 3:22 when God said, "See, the man has become like one of us, knowing good and evil." There was no way for his reading to take this verse seriously, so he dismissed it with, "this is sarcasm and bitter derision."[10] Luther's harmonizing move reflects a common way of reading the early chapters of Genesis, collapsing it into a single story of perfection and "fall." By giving the image of God to Adam and Eve before they eat the fruit, Luther and readers like him are able to reshape the garden existence. The Adam and Eve whom Luther constructed had dominion over creation rather than the work of keeping and tilling it, and they had a full understanding of all the creatures that inhabited the garden, before they ate the fruit. Thus he declared that any knowledge human beings now have is, by comparison, "leprous."[11]

A misreading of Genesis like this one lies at the root of the assumption that the advancement of human civilization is evil and contrary to the divine intention.

This way of reading the text, exemplified by Luther's commentary on Genesis, may create difficulty for modern urban dwellers. Is the urban way of life in some way contrary to the biblical ideal? If the result of eating the fruit in the garden was both punishment and acquisition of the knowledge necessary to develop human civilization, then it is difficult for the negative aspect of the punishment not to taint the knowledge. Chapter 2 of this book offered the possibility of reordering the J material in Genesis 1–11 in order to reconstruct the initial J Primeval Story, placing the stories of Nimrod and the people of Babel before the flood. The result was a story of steadily increasing divine attempts to control human civilization that ended with complete destruction of an urbanized world by the flood. It would mean that the writer or redactor of Genesis changed the role of city building in the primeval plotline. At this point it is important to ask about the effect of the redactor's literary move, which included both weaving the J and P material together and choosing a particular order for the J material. Placing the ultimate anti-city story of Babel, and the closely related Nimrod narrative, after the flood diminishes the sense that city building led to the flood. Only Cain's city-building work remains as part of the story that leads up to God's choice to destroy the world. Instead of wiping out Nimrod's cities, including Babel, God scatters human beings and confuses their language in order to slow city building and limit its impact.

Modern readers exposed to readings of Genesis 1–3, like Luther's reading, might be left with the conclusion that the knowledge required to develop human civilization is the content of a "fallen" state of being, a way of life in opposition to the divine intent. Living in an urban environment is the only choice for the majority of human beings, however, so this reading creates an inescapable bind. Avoiding that bind requires a way of reading that acknowledges the challenges of urban environments and simultaneously sings their beauty with the verve of Carl Sandburg's "city of big shoulders." The phrase in Sandburg's poem about Chicago came to epitomize the strength of the city and its people and even became one of the many nicknames of the city. For the ancestors of Israel, cities were places of danger and captivity, but they were also havens from starvation in times of famine. The big shoulders of the city, despite the terrors that can happen beneath them, offered the possibility of support and protection. The reading of Genesis 1–11 that emerges as part of this study offers a different set of resources for modern urban readers. Deciding whether building cities, choosing to live in them, and affirming urban ways of life are against the divine intent is a life-taking or life-giving decision for people who find themselves in these settings. If readers of the

Hebrew Bible think they were intended to live in a quiet, peaceful garden, tending generous soil and abundant fruit trees, then living in the midst of brick and mortar, streets and sidewalks, and sirens and pedestrians may seem like an ungodly choice. On the other hand, if the entire plot of the Hebrew Bible is pointing toward the construction of a city, Jerusalem, then urban design is a divine plan.

The mythic garden is not the only setting that, taken in isolation, helps to perpetuate such a bias. From Abraham on Moriah to Moses on Sinai to Elijah at Horeb, definitive religious experiences take place on isolated mountaintops. Christian mystical traditions, particularly those associated with Celtic spirituality, like to point to "thin places," typically understood as locations where earth and heaven are closest together. Given the tendency toward quietism in these traditions, it is not surprising that such places are often isolated. But the Bible also presents the possibility of seeing such experiences in urban settings. Perhaps there are no more urban characters in the Hebrew Bible than the prophets. Whether they were of the establishment variety, advising kings and participating in the institutional religion of Israel, or antiestablishment firebrands railing against religious and royal power, there is no setting other than the city that fits their work. The visions and bizarre symbolic actions of Ezekiel require a Jerusalem setting, as do the interactions of Isaiah and Jeremiah with Israel's political and religious institutions.

At numerous points in this study the work of sociologist and urban theorist Richard Florida has been pertinent and useful. Florida's idea of a "creative class" explains much of the current impulse toward urbanism. Just when the dominance of a centralized, industrial economy began to wane at the end of the twentieth century, and a new information economy driven by technology seemed to make a centralized population unnecessary, a new wave of urban movement arose. Florida's work relates primarily to the United States, but the patterns are apparent in other developed nations as well. There is good reason to be cautious about comparing ancient cultures to modern ones. At the same time, there are perils involved in rejecting all the comparisons. In the field of orality/literacy studies, which has arisen a number of points in the preceding pages, this resistance has become known as "the great divide." Paul Evans has offered a useful critique of some recent developments in this direction, specifically addressing assumptions about orality and literacy. He warns of an "exoticization of ancient culture" that can arise when interpreters assume ancient cultures are discontinuous with modern cultures.[12] Assuming that ancient urban persons and their experiences are discontinuous from their modern counterparts may be problematic as well. The common experience of ancient scribes with modern urban "creatives," as Florida has labeled them, are worth considering.

The literature that is in the Hebrew Bible is the result of choices not to remove the traditions that present a negative view of city building, but to combine them with, and embed then within, traditions that offer other perspectives. The end of the biblical story was a city. Cities were the environment in which scribes worked and which made their products— written texts—possible. Jerusalem was also the center for the narrative. Jubilees demonstrates that treating anti-urban traditions this way was not the only choice, so it is necessary to consider its advantages. While the context of writing and the narrative center of the biblical tradition was urban, Israel, like all societies, also needed a rural periphery. At every stage of the observations made in this study, but particularly in chapters 3, 4, and 5, the idea of building a national story out of regional traditions is present. It is possible that the elimination, or severe alteration, of some traditions would have undermined such efforts. Could it be that Jubilees and 1 Enoch failed to sustain support and adherence because of this factor, among others? The conclusion of this study is not that there is a correct view of urban life to be found within the Bible, but that how to view this way of life is a critical question with which the full range of ancient Jewish literature, inside and outside of the Bible, grappled. It did so because survival in a world always in this kind of transition because of continued human population growth demands a rigorous examination of its effects. I have not tried to develop an urban spirituality, or even an urban theology, here because such a task is outside my expertise. Rather these pages are an attempt to demonstrate the way one influential set of ancient texts hosted a conversation that might provide resources for such an effort.

Appendix 1

Genesis 1 in Poetic Form

(author's translation)

When God began to create the heavens and the earth:
The earth was formless and empty,
darkness was over the face of the deep,
and the wind of God brooded over the face of the water.

God said, "Let it be light,"
and it was light.
God saw that the light was good,
and God separated between the light and the darkness.
God called the light Day,
and the darkness he called Night.
Evening was and morning was,
day one.

God said, "Let a hard surface be in the midst of the water,
and it shall separate between the waters."
God made the hard surface, and he divided
between the water that was below the surface
and the water that was above the surface,
and it was so.
God called the surface Sky.
Evening was and morning was,
a second day.

God said, "Let the water under the sky be gathered unto one place,
and let dry land appear."
And it was so.
God called the dry land Earth,
and the gathering of water he called Seas,
and God saw that it was good.
God said, "The earth shall sprout grass,
plants bearing seeds,
and fruit trees making fruits, according to their kind,
which their seed is in them upon the earth."
And it was so.
And the earth brought forth grass,
plants bearing seeds, according to their kind,
and fruit trees making fruit which their seed is in them,
according to their kind.
God saw that it was good.
Evening was and morning was,
a third day.

God said, "There shall be lights on the surface of the Sky
to divide between the day and the night.
They shall be for signs and for seasons,
and for days and for years.
They shall be for lights on the surface of the sky
to make light upon the earth."
And it was so.
God made the two great lights,
the larger light to rule the day,
and the smaller light to rule the night,
and the stars.
God put them on the surface of the sky
to make light upon the earth,
to rule over the day and over the night,
and to divide between the light and the dark.
God saw that it was good.
Evening was and morning was,
a fourth day.

God said, "The waters shall swarm with living creatures,
and flying creatures over the earth,
upon the face of the surface of the sky."

God created the great sea monsters,
and all the living creatures,
the creeping things that swarm the waters,
according to their kind,
and all the winged creatures, according to their kind.
God saw that it was good.
Then God blessed them saying,
"Be fruitful and multiply,
and fill the waters in the seas,
and birds shall multiply above the earth."
Evening was and morning was,
a fifth day.

God said, "The earth shall bring forth living creatures,
according to their kind,
livestock, creeping things, and wild animals of the earth,
according to their kind."
And it was so.
God made the living things of the earth
according to their kind,
and the livestock according to their kind,
and all the creeping things of the ground
according to their kind.
And God saw that it was good.
God said, "Let us make human beings,
in our image, as our likeness.
They shall have dominion over the fish of the sea,
the birds of the sky, and the livestock
and over all the earth,
over all the creeping things creeping upon the earth."
Then God created the human beings in his likeness.
In the likeness of God, he created them,
male and female he created them.
Then God blessed them,
and God said to them,
"Be fruitful and multiply,
and fill the earth and control it.
Have dominion over the fish of the sea,
the birds of the sky,
and all life creeping upon the earth."
God said, "Look, I give to you all plants bearing seed,

which are upon the face of the earth,
and all the trees, which the fruit of the tree is on them bearing seed.
They shall be food for you.
To all the animals of the earth,
to all the birds of the sky,
and to all the creeping things upon the earth,
which the breath of life is in them,
all green plants are for food."
And it was so.
God saw all that he had made,
and behold it was very good.
It was evening, and it was morning,
a sixth day.

The heavens and the earth and all their hosts were complete.
On the seventh day God finished all his work that he did.
God rested on the seventh day from all his work that he did.
God blessed the seventh day and made it holy,
for on it he rested from all his work that God created to do.
These are the generations of the heavens and the earth,
when they were created.

Appendix 2

The City-Building Texts
in Reconstructed J Order

(author's translation)

And Cain knew his wife and she conceived and bore Enoch. Then he built a city and called the name of the city the name of his son Enoch. And Irad was born to Enoch and Machuyael was born to Irad and Metushael was born to Machuyael and Lamech was born to Methushael. Lamech took for himself two wives. The name of the one was Adah and the name of the second was Tsilah. Adah bore Yabal, and he was the father of tent-dwellers who keep livestock. The name of his brother was Yubal, and he was the father of those playing the pipe and the lyre. Tsilah bore also Tubal-cain, the father of the fashioners of all tools of bronze and iron, and the sister of Tubal-cain was Naamah.

> Lamech said to his wives,
>> Adah and Tsilah hear my voice,
>> wives of Lamech give ear to what I say,
>> for I killed a man for wounding me,
>> a boy for striking me.
>> If Cain is avenged sevenfold, then Lamech seventy-seven.
> Then he began to call on the name of YHWH.[1] [The birth record of Noah, some of which is now found at Genesis 5:29, would likely fit here.]

And the humans began to multiply upon the surface of the ground, and daughters were born to them. The Sons of God saw the human daughters, that they were good, and they took for themselves wives from all which they chose. YHWH said, "My spirit shall not shield the humans forever, in going astray they are flesh, but the length of their lives shall be one hundred and twenty years. The Nephilim were on the earth in those days, and also after that, when the Sons of God came to human daughters and they bore children for them, the warriors from ancient time, men of a name.

Nimrod was the first to be a warrior on the earth. He was a mighty warrior before YHWH, therefore people said, "Like Nimrod, a mighty warrior before YHWH." Babel became his first kingdom, then Erekh and Akkad and Kalneh, in the land of Shinar. From that land he went out to Asshur and built Nineveh and Rechoboth-Ir and Kalach, and Resen between Nineveh and Kalach. It was the great city.

All the earth had one language and used the same words. When they migrated from the east they found a valley in the land of Shinar and they settled there. They each said to their companions, "Come, let us make bricks and bake them thoroughly," and they had bricks for stone and bitumen for mortar. And they said, "Come let us build a city for ourselves and a tower with its top in the sky, and we will make a name for ourselves, lest we be scattered upon the face of all the earth. And YHWH went down to see the city and the tower, which the humans had built. And YHWH said, "They are one people and have one language for all of them, and this is the beginning of what they will do. And now all which they propose to do will not be impossible for them. Come, let us go down and confuse their language there, and each will not be able to hear the language of their companion. YHWH scattered them from there upon the face of all the earth, and they ceased to build the city. Therefore, its name is called Babel, because there YHWH confused the language of all the earth, and from there YHWH scattered them upon the face of all the earth.

YHWH saw that the evil of the humans multiplied on the earth, and every inclination of the thoughts of their hearts was only evil every day. YHWH regretted that he made humans on the earth and it grieved his heart. YHWH said, "I will blot out from the face of the ground. . . ." [Continuation of the J flood narrative]

Appendix 3

The Sons of Noah and Their Genealogies in a Reconstructed J Source

(author's translation)

The sons of Noah, the ones going out of the ark were Shem, Ham, and Japheth, and Ham; he was the father of Canaan. These three were the sons of Noah; and from these the whole earth was dispersed.

Noah began to be a man of the soil and he planted a vineyard. He drank from the wine and became drunk, and he was uncovered in the midst of his tent. Ham, the father of Canaan, saw the nakedness of his father, and told his two brothers outside. Shem and Japheth took a garment, placed it on the shoulders of the two of them, and they walked backward and they covered the nakedness of their father. Their faces turned behind, and they did not see the nakedness of their father.

Noah awoke from his wine and he knew what his youngest son had done to him, and he said,

"Cursed is Canaan, a slave of slaves he shall be to his brothers.
Blessed by the LORD my God is Shem, and Canaan shall be his slave.
God will make space for Japheth, and he shall live in the tents of Shem,
  and Canaan shall be his slave."

Canaan became the father of Sidon his firstborn, and Heth, and the Jebusites, the Amorites, the Girgashites, the Hivites, the Arkites, the Sinites, the Arvadites, the Zemarites, and the Hamathites. Afterward the families of the Canaanites dispersed. And the territory of the Canaanites is from Sidon, toward Gerar unto Gaza, and toward Sodom, Gomorrah, Admah, and Zeboiim, unto Lasha.

Egypt became the father of Ludim, Anamim, Lehabim, Naphtuhim, Pathrusim, Casluhim. The Philistines came out from there, and the Caphtorim.[1]

To Shem, the father of all the children of Eber, the older brother of Japheth, children were also born. The descendants of Shem: Elam, Asshur, Arpachshad, Lud, and Aram. Arpachshad became the father of Shelah; and Shelah became the father of Eber. To Eber were born two sons: the name of the one was Peleg, for in his days the earth was divided, and the name of his brother was Joktan. Joktan became the father of Almodad, Sheleph, Hazarmaveth, Jerah, Hadoram, Uzal, Diklah, Obal, Abimael, Sheba, Ophir, Havilah, and Jobab. All these were the descendants of Joktan. Their dwelling place was from Mesha toward Sephar, the hills of the east.

And YHWH said to Abram, . . .

Appendix 4

Source Division of Numbers 10–21

Yahwist (J)	Elohist (E)	Priestly (P)
10:29–36		10:11–27
11:1–10	11:11–12	
11:13	11:14–17	
11:18–24	11:25–30	
11:31–35	12:1–16	
13:17–24		13:1–16
13:27–31		13:25–26
13:33		13:32
		14:1–10
14:11–25		
14:39–45		14:26–38
		15:1–41
	16:1b	16:1a
	16:12–15	16:2–11
	16:25–26	16:16–24
	16:28–34	16:27
		16:35–50
		17:1–19:22
	20:1a	20:1b–2
	20:3	20:4
	20:5	20:6–13
	20:14–22a	20:22b–29
21:1–3	21:4b	21:4a
21:16–20	21:5–15	
	21:21–35	

Appendix 5

Place Names in Numbers 10–21

J	E	P
Taberah (11:3)	Kibroth-hattaavah (11:34)	Canaan (13:2)
Canaan (13:17)	Hazeroth (11:35; 12:10)	Paran (13:3)
Negeb (13:17)	Paran (12:16)	Kadesh (13:26)
Wilderness of Zin (13:21)	Kadesh (20:1, 14)	Meribah (20:13)
Rehob (13:21)	Edom (20:14)	Mount Hor (20:25)
Lebo-hamath (13:21)	Wadi Zered (21:12)	
Hebron (13:22)	Arnon (21:13)	
Ahiman (13:22)	Sihon (21:21)	
Sheshai (13:22)	Jahaz (21:23)	
Talmai (13:22)	Jabbok (21:24)	
Wadi Eshcol (13:23)	Heshbon (21:25)	
Hormah (14:45)	Bashan (21:33)	
Atharim (21:1)		
Beer (21:16)		
Mattanah (21:18)		
Naheliel (21:19)		
Bamoth (21:19)		
Moab/Pisgah (21:20)		

Appendix 6

Festival Calendars in the Torah

Exodus 23:14–17

Unleavened Bread

First Fruits (*Shavuot*/Weeks)

Ingathering (*Sukkot*/Tabernacles)

Exodus 34:18–26

Unleavened Bread

Weeks/*Shavuot* (First Fruits)

Ingathering

Passover

Leviticus 23

Passover

Unleavened Bread

First Fruits

Weeks

Trumpets

Day of Atonement (*Yom Kippur*)
   Booths

Numbers 28–29

Beginning of Each Month

Passover/Unleavened Bread

First Fruits/Weeks

Trumpets

Day of Atonement

Fifteenth Day of Seventh Month
   (Booths)

Deuteronomy 16

Passover

Weeks

   Booths

In addition to these lists, the Pentateuch also contains instructions for Passover at Exodus 12:1–20, Exodus 12:21–28, and Exodus 13:1–16.

231

Notes

Chapter 1: Building the World

1. Edward O. Wilson, *Half Earth: Our Planet's Fight for Life* (New York: Liveright Publishing, 2016), 3. Wilson carefully catalogs the extinction of other species that has accompanied human expansion (35–44).

2. Ibid., 71–79. Wilson has estimated that human population will become fairly steady by 2100 between 9.6 and 12.3 billion. The mechanism for decline in growth is the switch from a reproductive strategy called r-selection to the one called K-selection. Put simply, the best strategy for the perpetuation of one's genetic material is a small number of better prepared offspring rather than a larger number of less prepared ones. Europe, for example, has already seen this shift, and the rate of reproduction has fallen to 2.1 children per woman who reaches maturity, a rate that will not produce continued population growth (190–91).

3. For an explanation of an approach to history similar to that which I will take here, see Angela Roskop Erisman, "New Historicism, Historical Criticism, and Reading the Pentateuch," *Religion Compass* 8 (2014): 71–80.

4. See Paul S. Evans, "Creating a New 'Great Divide': The Exoticization of Ancient Culture in Some Recent Applications of Orality," *Journal of Biblical Literature* 136 (2017): 749–53.

5. For a more thorough description of the development of urban theory, see Simon Parker, *Urban Theory and the Urban Experience: Encountering the City*, 2nd ed. (London: Routledge, 2015), 8–24.

6. Ibid., 39–48.

7. Richard Florida, *The Rise of the Creative Class, Revisited* (New York: Basic Books, 2012), 20–21. Florida has extended his discussion beyond just American cities, but the core of the data he uses and the arguments he constructs use American cities.

8. Ibid., 189.

9. The impact of this rapid social change is being documented. See, e.g., Peter Moskowitz, *How to Kill a City: Gentrification, Inequality, and the Fight for the Neighborhood* (New York: Nation Books, 2017).

10. Florida, *The Rise of the Creative Class*, 16.

11. Ibid., 65–98.

12. Jane Jacobs, *The Death and Life of Great American Cities* (New York: Vintage, 1992), 200–221.

13. For a thorough discussion of this word and its function and various proposals about its origin, see Frank S. Frick, *The City in Ancient Israel* (Missoula, MT: Scholars Press, 1977), 25–30.

14. For more on the characteristics of Nineveh and its place in the ancient world, see Robert R. Cargill, *The Cities That Built the Bible* (San Francisco: Harper-One, 2016), 53–64.

15. See Cargill's description in ibid., 221–22.

16. For a discussion of this word in the Hebrew Bible and parallel ancient Near Eastern literature, see Mark S. Smith, *Where the Gods Are: Spatial Dimensions of Anthropomorphism in the Biblical World* (New Haven, CT: Yale University Press, 2016), 103–6.

17. For more on this modern phenomenon, see Parker, *Urban Theory*, 79–83.

18. Jacob J. Baumgarten, "Urbanization in the Late Bronze Age," in *The Architecture of Ancient Israel: From the Prehistoric to the Persian Periods*, ed. Aharon Kempinski and Ronny Reich (Jerusalem: Israel Exploration Society, 1992), 143–50.

19. Ze'ev Herzog, "Settlement and Fortification Planning in the Iron Age," *The Architecture of Ancient Israel: From the Prehistoric to the Persian Periods*, ed. Aharon Kempinski and Ronny Reich (Jerusalem: Israel Exploration Society, 1992), 247–64.

20. William G. Dever, *Beyond the Texts: An Archaeological Portrait of Ancient Israel and Judah* (Atlanta: SBL Press, 2017), 391–99.

21. See J. W. Rogerson and John Vincent, *The City in Biblical Perspective* (London: Routledge, 2014), 5–7.

22. C. H. J. De Geus, *Towns in Ancient Israel and in the Southern Levant* (Leuven: Peeters, 2003), 168.

23. Ibid., 171.

24. Volkmar Fritz, *The City in Ancient Israel* (Sheffield: Sheffield Academic, 1995), 14.

25. Smith, *Where the Gods Are*, 103.

26. Ibid., 105.

27. See Dieter Georgi, *The City in the Valley: Biblical Interpretation and Urban Theology* (Atlanta: Society of Biblical Literature, 2005), xi–xxii.

28. Eva Mroczek, *The Literary Imagination in Jewish Antiquity* (Oxford: Oxford University Press, 2016), 118–22.

29. On the blending of the two, and the persistence of the influence of orality, see Evans, "The Exoticization of Ancient Culture . . . ," 755–61.

30. William M. Schniedwind, *How the Bible Became a Book* (Cambridge: Cambridge University Press, 2004), 48–57.

31. See Brian B. Schmidt, "Memorializing Conflict: Toward an Iron Age 'Shadow' History of Israel's Earliest Literature," in *Contextualizing Israel's Sacred Writings: Ancient Literacy, Orality, and Literary Production*, ed. Brian B. Schmidt (Atlanta: SBL Press, 2015), 105–11.

32. Roland Boer, *The Sacred Economy of Ancient Israel* (Louisville, KY: Westminster John Knox, 2015), 115–32.

33. Schniedewind, *How the Bible Became a Book*, 85.

34. See the full report on the find in Ron E. Tappey et al., "An Abecedary of the Mid-Tenth Century B.C.E. from the Judaean Shephelah," *Bulletin of the American Schools of Oriental Research* 344 (2006): 5–46.

35. Seth L. Sanders, *The Invention of Hebrew* (Urbana: University of Illinois Press, 2009), 131–33.
36. Richard Horsley has emphasized the significance of multiple levels of literacy and has cautioned that the presence of an artifact, like an abecedary, offers limited evidence concerning more advanced levels. See Richard A. Horsley, *Scribes, Visionaries, and the Politics of Second Temple Judea* (Louisville, KY: Westminster John Knox, 2007), 82–92.
37. Daniel E. Fleming, *The Legacy of Israel in Judah's Bible: History, Politics, and the Reinscribing of Tradition* (Cambridge: Cambridge University Press, 2012), 308–10.
38. For an example of this kind of argument, see Schniedewind, *How the Bible Became a Book*, 101–3.
39. Christopher A. Rollston, *Writing and Literacy in the World of Ancient Israel: Epigraphic Evidence from the Iron Age* (Atlanta: SBL Press, 2010), 129–30. See the discussion of Lachish Letter 3 in particular, and Rollston's judgment that "I would be disinclined to use this letter as definitive evidence of non-elite literacy."
40. Walter E. Aufrecht, "Urbanization and Northwest Semitic Inscriptions," in *Urbanism and Antiquity: From Mesopotamia to Crete*, ed. Walter E. Aufrecht et al. (Sheffield: Sheffield Academic, 1997), 123–25.
41. A logogram system of writing, like ancient Egyptian hieroglyphics, uses a separate symbol for each word. This means there are thousands of symbols, and many of them are complex. A syllabary system, like ancient Akkadian or modern Amharic, uses a different symbol for each consonant and vowel combination. With twenty to thirty consonants and six or seven vowel sounds, the number of symbols is about two hundred. An alphabetic system reduces the number of symbols to about twenty-five. Early alphabetic writing systems, like Ugaritic and Hebrew, did not include vowels, which added an additional degree of difficulty to the reading task. The development of the simpler systems could have allowed for an increase in literacy rates, but the limited availability of written materials, especially more sophisticated literature, likely meant that writing and reading remained restricted to a scribal class.
42. See Rollston, *Writing and Literacy in the World of Ancient Israel*, 127–35.
43. Ian M. Young, "Israelite Literacy: Interpreting the Evidence, Part II," *Vetus Testamentum* 48 (1998): 419.
44. Horsley, *Scribes, Visionaries*, 92.
45. Georgi, *The City in the Valley*, 217.
46. Ibid.
47. Ibid.
48. Jacques Ellul, *The Meaning of the City*, trans. Dennis Pardee (Grand Rapids: Eerdmans, 1970), 206–9.
49. Ibid., 5.
50. Harvey Cox, *The Secular City: Secularization and Urbanization in Theological Perspective*, 3rd ed. (Princeton: Princeton University Press, 2013), 28.
51. Ibid., 30–37.
52. Words: Catherine Cameron. © 1967 Hope Publishing Company, Carol Stream, IL 60188. All rights reserved. Used by permission.
53. For an account of Bates's experiences and how they relate to the poem, see Lynn Sherr, *America the Beautiful: The Stirring True Story behind Our Nation's Favorite Song* (Washington: Public Affairs, 2001).

Chapter 2: In the Shadow of Nimrod

1. Calling Genesis a "source" for Jubilees is problematic, if this designation leads to the assumption that the primary goal of Jubilees was to "rewrite" Genesis. This way of thinking about the relationship between the two works gives Genesis authoritative control of the traditions. It might be better to think of Genesis and Jubilees as alternative ways to construct Israel's traditions concerning the distant past, which share a lot of material.

2. I choose this term over the more common "Primeval Narrative(s)" because the "Primeval Narrative(s)" can describe a literary form and gives privilege to narrative portions of Genesis 1–11 over the non-narrative elements.

3. The term "final form" has some difficulties. No biblical text is truly finished, because the work of textual criticism and translation goes on. My use of the term refers to the Masoretic Text in Hebrew, which became stable and fixed in the Middle Ages.

4. The most prominent expression of the death of J has been in the work of Rolf Rendtorff. See "What Happened to the Yahwist? Reflections after Thirty Years: A Collegial Conversation between Rolf Rendtorff, David J. A. Clines, Allan Rosengren, and John Van Seters," in *Probing the Frontiers of Biblical Studies*, ed. J. Harold Ellens and John T. Greene (Eugene, OR: Pickwick, 2009), 39–66.

5. Ronald Hendel, "Is the 'J' Primeval Narrative an Independent Composition? A Critique of Crüsemann's 'Die Eigenständigkeit der Urgeschichte,'" in *The Pentateuch: International Perspectives on Current Research*, ed. Thomas B. Dozeman et al. (Tübingen: Mohr Siebeck, 2011), 204.

6. An understanding of the concept of "narrative worlds" can begin with the work of Erich Auerbach in *Mimesis: The Representation of Reality in Western Literature* (Princeton: Princeton University Press, 1953). In relation to the Bible, see especially his discussion of the Akedah story in Genesis 22 (7–23). It is further developed in Paul Ricoeur, *Time and Narrative*, vol. 1 (Chicago: University of Chicago Press, 1984), and Hans-Georg Gadamer, *Truth and Method* (London: Sheed & Ward, 1975), 269–78. Application to the Bible became more specific in the work of Amos N. Wilder. See, for example, *The Bible and the Literary Critic* (Minneapolis: Fortress Press, 1991).

7. For the identification and understanding of Cush and its relation to Africa, see David Tuesday Adamo, "The Images of Cush in the Old Testament: Reflections on African Hermeneutics," in *Interpreting the Old Testament in Africa: Papers from the International Symposium on Africa and the Old Testament in Nairobi*, October 1999, ed. Mary Getui et al. (New York: Peter Lang, 2001), 65–74, and *Africa and Africans in the Old Testament* (San Francisco: Christian Universities Press, 1998). Ephraim A. Speiser disputes this identification of Gihon and Cush. See E. A. Speiser, *Genesis: Introduction, Translation and Notes* (Garden City, NY: Doubleday, 1964), 19–20.

8. Speiser calls Shinar the biblical version of Sumer. See Speiser, *Genesis*, 67.

9. See the discussion of these elements and many responses to them in James L. Kugel, *The Bible as It Was* (Cambridge, MA: Harvard University Press, 1997), 100–107.

10. These numbers may differ somewhat, depending on what is identified as "genealogical material." I have not included characters like Lamech, Adah, Zillah, Seth, Enoch, or Nimrod, about whom there are poetic or narrative snippets embedded within genealogies.

11. The Greek text, and subsequent versions, contain the single sentence spoken by Cain to Abel. For a summary of issues surrounding this text, see Mark McEntire, "Being Seen and Not Heard: The Interpretation of Genesis 4:8," in *Of Scribes and Sages*, vol. 1, Ancient Versions and Traditions (New York: T&T Clark, 2004), 4–13.

12. On this change in Genesis, see W. Lee Humphreys, *The Character of God in the Book of Genesis: A Narrative Appraisal* (Louisville, KY: Westminster John Knox Press, 2001), 241. On the larger movement in the development of the divine character throughout the Hebrew canon, see Richard Elliot Friedman, *The Disappearance of God: A Divine Mystery* (New York: Little, Brown, and Company, 1995), 78–89.

13. For a description of this development, see Jack Miles, *God: A Biography* (New York: Vintage, 1996), 25–84. A more thorough treatment of how God's contact with humans changes throughout the entire Hebrew Bible can be found in Friedman, *The Disappearance of God*, 7–59.

14. The double descent of YHWH in the Tower of Babel story, at 11:5 and 11:7, has presented a puzzle for interpreters, and it receives more detailed attention in chapter 6 of this book.

15. Robert L. Cohn places more emphasis on the shift from Abraham to Jacob, using the word "numinous" to describe divine appearances to the latter. See Robert L. Cohn, "Narrative Structure and Canonical Perspective in Genesis," *Journal for the Study of the Old Testament* 25 (1983): 9.

16. For a more complete discussion of the way the divine character develops in Genesis 1–11 and beyond, see Mark McEntire, *Portraits of a Mature God: Choices in Old Testament Theology* (Minneapolis: Fortress Press, 2013), 29–37.

17. See, for example, Joel S. Baden, *The Composition of the Pentateuch: Renewing the Documentary Hypothesis* (New Haven: Yale University Press, 2012), 1–33; Jean-Louis Ska, "The Study of the Book of Genesis: The Beginning of Critical Reading," in *The Book of Genesis: Composition, Reception, and Interpretation*, ed. Craig A. Evans et al. (Leiden: Brill, 2012), 3–26; and Jan Christian Gertz, "The Formation of the Primeval History," in *The Book of Genesis: Composition, Reception, and Interpretation*, 107–37.

18. Baruch J. Schwartz, "Does Recent Scholarship's Critique of the Documentary Hypothesis Constitute Grounds for Its Rejection?," in *The Pentateuch: International Perspectives on Current Research*, ed. Thomas P. Dozeman et al. (Tübingen: Mohr Siebeck, 2011), 3–16.

19. Joel S. Baden, *J, E, and the Redaction of the Pentateuch* (Tübingen: Mohr Siebeck, 2009). Among Baden's helpful conclusions are that the Pentateuch is the result of four independent sources combined by a single redactor in the Persian period (306–12) and that the E source is absent in Genesis 1–11 (260).

20. Ibid., 260.

21. The former is the position of those who are typically labeled "documentarians," like Baden. See *The Composition of the Pentateuch*, 67–69. The latter position reflects the procedure of interpreters like Jan Christian Gertz. See "The Formation of the Primeval History," 107–14.

22. Baden, *The Composition of the Pentateuch*, 246.

23. Gertz, "The Formation of the Primeval History," 132–33.

24. E. Theodore Mullen, *Ethnic Myths and Pentateuchal Foundations: A New Approach to the Formation of the Pentateuch* (Atlanta: Scholars Press, 1997), 111.

25. The disappearance of this connection as the book of Genesis proceeds makes the wrestling match in 32:22–32 even more of a mystery. This text along with the account in Genesis 18 are the only two examples in the Bible of what Esther Hamori has labeled an *'ish* theophany. In each of these, God has to adopt a human form for the meeting. See *"When Gods Were Men": The Embodied God in Biblical and Near Eastern Literature* (Berlin: de Gruyter, 2008), 1–25.

26. Yigal Levine, "Nimrod the Mighty, King of Kish, King of Sumer and Akkad," *Vetus Testamentum* 52 (2002): 350–66.

27. See Modupẹ Oduyọye, *The Sons of God and the Daughters of Men: An Afro-Asiatic Interpretation of Genesis 1–11* (Maryknoll, NY: Orbis Books, 1984), 91–97.

28. See André LaCocque, *The Captivity of Innocence: Babel and the Yahwist* (Eugene, OR : Wipf & Stock, 2010), 7–9.

29. Seymour Chatman, *Story and Discourse: Narrative Structure in Fiction and Film* (Ithaca, NY: Cornell University Press, 1978), 53–56.

30. Some English translations have begun presenting parts of Genesis 1–3 as poetry, such as 1:27, 2:25, and 3:14–19. These verses do not look any more or less poetic to me than the whole of Genesis 1. Mark Smith argues that the parallelism of 1:27 "demarcates the human person from other parts of creation." He also observes that the threefold use of *br'* (create) in the verse is unique in the Bible and distinguishes human beings. See Mark S. Smith, *The Priestly Vision of Genesis 1* (Minneapolis: Fortress Press, 2010), 98–99. The parallel quality of 1:27 does not look significantly different to me than other paired lines in Genesis 1, but this leaves many other factors to distinguish the humans, including the use of *br'*, the blessing of the humans, and the command God gives to them.

31. Smith, *The Priestly Vision of Genesis 1*, 12–37.

32. For a more detailed discussion of this idea and the relation between Genesis 1 and Psalms 74 and 104, see Jon D. Levenson, *Creation and the Persistence of Evil: The Jewish Drama of Divine Omnipotence* (San Francisco: Harper & Row, 1988), 53–65.

33. Smith, *The Priestly Vision of Genesis 1*, 25–27.

34. Ibid., 29–32.

35. A number of interpreters have proposed that this creation narrative began as an eight- or nine-part account that has been forced into the current format of six days plus Sabbath. See, for example, the symmetrical pattern in Nahum Sarna, *JPS Torah Commentary: Genesis* (New York: Jewish Publication Society, 2001), 4.

36. See the discussion in David J. A. Clines, ed., *The Dictionary of Classical Hebrew*, vol. 7 (Sheffield: Sheffield Phoenix, 2010), 420; and in H. J. Zobel, "הדר," in the *Theological Dictionary of the Old Testament*, vol. 8, ed. G. Johannes Botterweck et al. (Grand Rapids: Eerdmans, 2004), 330–36.

37. For an example of this kind of reading, see Andrew Linzey, *Animal Theology* (Urbana: University of Illinois Press, 1994), 33–34.

38. Joseph Blenkinsopp, "The Structure of P," *Catholic Biblical Quarterly* 38 (1976): 275–76.

39. This is a common perception or explanation among nonacademic readers. For a more extensive attempt to raise the possibility, see Catherine L. McDowell, *The "Image of God" in the Garden of Eden: The Creation of Humankind in Genesis*

2:5–3:24 in Light of the mīs pî pīt pî and wpt-r Rituals of Mesopotamia and Ancient Egypt (Winona Lake, IN: Eisenbrauns, 2015), 178–202. McDowell's proposal requires the unusual dating of J after P, with a significant sense of literary dependence. Such dependence, with the striking lack of verbal correspondence, seems unlikely; thus the argument is dependent almost entirely on thematic parallels.

40. The description here is connected to the vague geography of the world of Genesis 1–11 outside of the garden. The four rivers that find their source in Eden include those which form the boundaries of world of the writer's knowledge as expressed in the Table of Nations in Genesis 10, the Blue Nile (Gihon) in the land of Cush as the southwest boundary, and the Tigris and Euphrates of Mesopotamia as the northeast boundary.

41. On the many inconsistencies in the supposed pattern, see André LaCocque, *Onslaught against Innocence: Cain, Abel, and the Yahwist* (Eugene, OR: Cascade, 2008), 123.

42. On the general idea of "backstories," see Gregory Mobley, *The Return of the Chaos Monsters* (Grand Rapids: Eerdmans, 2012), 1–15.

43. The poem about Tyre in Ezekiel 28:11–19 also places this ancient city/nation in Eden as part of its mythic origin, but there are no references to trees in the poem.

44. T. Stordalen, *Echoes of Eden: Genesis 2–3 and Symbolism of the Eden Garden in Biblical Hebrew Literature* (Leuven: Peeters, 2000), 347–48.

45. For a full rhetorical analysis of Genesis 4:1–16, see Mark McEntire, *The Blood of Abel: The Violent Plot in the Hebrew Bible* (Macon, GA: Mercer University Press, 1999), 17–30.

46. For a list of texts and some discussion of these meanings, see David J. A. Clines, ed., *The Dictionary of Classical Hebrew* 7:267–68.

47. Ibid., 268.

48. E. Lipiński, "הנק," in the *Theological Dictionary of the Old Testament*, vol. 8, ed. G. Johannes Botterweck et al. (Grand Rapids: Eerdmans, 2004), 58–65. Lipiński has related the use in Genesis 4:1 to the Greek concept of the *hieros gamos*, the reproductive activity of the gods that gives rise to the human race.

49. David E. Bokovoy, "Did Eve Acquire, Create, or Procreate with Yahweh? A Grammatical and Contextual Reassessment of הנק in Genesis 4:1," *Vetus Testamentum* 63 (2013): 33–35.

50. Ibid., 31–32. This would reflect the use of the Hebrew direct object marker to describe accompaniment rather than the standard sense of a direct object.

51. For more on the way these two characters are carefully introduced and the implications of the introductions for the entire story, see Mark McEntire, *The Blood of Abel*, 17–22.

52. If there is an assumption of a vegetarian diet at the beginning of Genesis 1–11, then it belongs exclusively to P, and J demonstrates no such understanding.

53. Jeffrey Szuchman, "Integrating Approaches to Nomads, Tribes, and the State in the Ancient Near East," in *Nomads, Tribes, and the State in the Ancient Near East: Cross Disciplinary Perspectives*, ed. Jeffrey Szuchman (Chicago: Oriental Institute of the University of Chicago, 2009), 1–14. On the movement back and forth between these two ways of life, see also Steven A. Rosen, "History Does Not Repeat Itself: Cyclicity and Particularism in Nomad-Sedentary Relations in the Negev in the Long Term," in *Nomads, Tribes, and the State in the Ancient Near East*, 64–65.

54. Thomas L. Thompson, *Biblical Narrative and Palestine's History* (Sheffield: Equinox, 2013), 93–104.

55. For more on this disappearance, see McEntire, *The Blood of Abel*, 28.

56. These efforts go back into antiquity. For some examples, see James L. Kugel, *The Bible as It Was*, 85–96.

57. Claus Westermann, *Genesis: A Practical Commentary* (Grand Rapids: Eerdmans, 1987), 32–33. See further discussion in McEntire, *The Blood of Abel*, 19–20.

58. This could include Cain's city-building activity discussed below.

59. Baden makes a statement of direct causation here, which seems too strong. "Cain's offering of the fruits of the soil in 4:3 is rejected in 4:5 because it consisted of produce from the ground that Yahweh had cursed in 3:17–19." See also Frank A. Spina, "The Ground for Cain's Rejection (Gen 4): 'adamah in the Context of Genesis 1–11," *Zeitschrift für die alttestamentliche Wissenschaft* 104 (1992): 319–32.

60. Regina M. Schwartz has called attention to these connections and the way they have been obscured in Christian interpretation by preoccupation with issues of human sexuality. See *The Curse of Cain: The Violent Legacy of Monotheism* (Chicago: University of Chicago Press, 1997), 48–50.

61. On the textual difficulties of this verse and possibilities for solving it, see Mark McEntire, "Being Seen and Not Heard: The Interpretation of Genesis 4.8," in *Of Scribes and Sages: Early Jewish Interpretation and Transmission of Scripture*, vol. 1, ed. Craig A. Evans (London: T&T Clark, 2004), 4–13.

62. On the relationship between agriculture and cities in ancient Mesopotamia, see Marc Van De Mieroop, *The Ancient Mesopotamian City* (Oxford: Oxford University Press, 1997), 142–75.

63. On this point, see René Girard, *Things Hidden since the Foundation of the World*, trans. Stephen Bann and Michael Metteer (Stanford, CA: Stanford University Press, 1987), 38–39.

64. Joel S. Baden, *The Composition of the Pentateuch*, 185–86. Baden understands each to be genealogies of Adam, from J and P, which "cover much of the same ground." He does not explain how he determined that there is variation with "no obvious significance" (189).

65. Ibid., 112. Daniel D. Lowery observed several more connections between the two genealogies in *Toward a Poetics of Genesis 1–11: Reading Genesis 4:17–22 in Its Near Eastern Context* (Winona Lake, IN: 2013), 75–77. Some of these observations seem valid, but others are forced, when enough evidence is already present to establish that they are related in some way.

66. Oduyọye, *The Sons of God and the Daughters of Men*, 67–70.

67. In the tradition reflected in 1 Enoch 8, one of the Watchers, Asael, teaches metalworking to humans. On the complications of this tradition and its likely insertion into an earlier version of 1 Enoch, see George W. E. Nickelsburg, *1 Enoch 1: A Commentary on the Book of 1 Enoch, Chapters 1–36; 81–108* (Minneapolis: Fortress, 2001), 190–96.

68. For more on the development of traditions about Enoch, see Kugel, *The Bible as It Was*, 100–107.

69. See Edmund Leach, "Anthropological Approaches to the Study of the Bible during the Twentieth Century," in *Structuralist Interpretations of Biblical Myth*, ed. Edmund Leach and D. Alan Aycock (Cambridge: Cambridge University

Press, 1983), 14. See also Paula McNutt's discussion of this issue, including her use of Leach's work in "In the Shadow of Cain," *Semeia* 87 (1999): 54–55.

70. McNutt, "In the Shadow of Cain," 45–56.

71. Oduyọye, *The Sons of God and the Daughters of Men*, 69–78. Meir Sternberg has demonstrated that the Hebrews of the Bible cannot be equated precisely with the Sons of Eber. See Meir Sternberg, *Hebrews between Cultures: Group Portraits and National Literature* (Bloomington: Indiana University Press, 1998), 7–9. Nevertheless, the Hebrews are certainly a subset of the Sons of Eber and possess their character.

72. On Lamech as the only speaker in both genealogies, see Lowery, *Toward a Poetics of Genesis 1–11*.

73. Richard Elliott Friedman, *The Bible with Sources Revealed: A New View into the Five Books of Moses* (San Francisco: HarperCollins, 2003), 41.

74. Christoph Levin, "The Yahwist: The Earliest Editor in the Pentateuch," *Journal of Biblical Literature* 126 (2007): 214.

75. It may seem too speculative to propose that the mysterious Naamah, daughter of Lamech in 4:22, replaces Noah in that genealogy. Their names look less alike in Hebrew than in the present English representations. Would the removal of Noah from that list have left a hole in the text, in the perception of the redactor, so gaping that it had to be filled with something? The reason such a possibility is worth mentioning, though, is that no other explanation, no matter how remote, has ever been offered for her presence.

76. The book of Jubilees may demonstrate some awareness of the problem and resolves it in 10:8–11 when Mastema negotiates the survival of one-tenth of the progeny of the Watchers as spirits after the flood. The changes in this part of the plot of Genesis in Jubilees are discussed more thoroughly at the end of this chapter.

77. For a more extensive development of both sides of the argument, see Helge Kvanvig, *Primeval History: Babylonian, Biblical, and Enochic: An Intertextual Reading* (Leiden: Brill, 2011), 362–70; and James C. VanderKam, *From Revelation to Canon: Studies in the Hebrew Bible and Second Temple Literature* (Leiden: Brill, 2002), 283–85.

78. Many of the observations about these connections were first made by Modupẹ Oduyọye in his book that has received far too little attention: see *The Sons of God and the Daughters of Men*, 23–34.

79. The source division in this section becomes somewhat fragmentary. See Friedman, *The Bible with Sources Revealed*, 47–49, and Speiser, *Genesis*, 64–73.

80. There is some dispute about the source of this genealogy. Friedman attributes it to an independent source (not J or P), as he does with Genesis 5. See *The Bible with Sources Revealed*, 40–49.

81. See the discussion in Speiser, *Genesis*, 67.

82. See the early recognition of this geographical problem by Philo in "Questions and Answers on Genesis," trans. Aram Topchyan and Gohar Muradyan, in *Outside the Bible: Ancient Jewish Writings related to Scripture*, vol. 1, ed. Louis H. Feldman et al. (Philadelphia: Jewish Publication Society, 2014), 811–12. Philo posits two potential solutions: the text is allegory, or an underground river comes out of Eden and connects to these four rivers unseen.

83. Oduyọye offered some helpful connections between the biblical material about Nimrod and parallel traditions from Africa, helping to confirm the African identity of the early Nimrod. See *The Sons of God and the Daughters of Men*,

25–28. Oduyọye's conclusion that the Israelites made Nimrod offensive to God because of his greatness is problematic. He did not deal adequately with the apparent approval by YHWH of Nimrod's hunter/warrior identity.

84. See, e.g., Nahum Sarna, *The JPS Torah Commentary: Genesis*, 73–74.

85. W. Gunther Plaut, *Genesis* (New York: Union of American Hebrew Congregations, 1974), 92.

86. Claus Westermann took the first step toward this conclusion with his declaration that "Nimrod is not to be pinned down to a historical figure." See *Genesis 1–11: A Commentary*, trans. John J. Scullion (Minneapolis: Augsburg, 1984), 515. Another step should be added, however, that he cannot be convincingly grafted onto any genealogy in Genesis.

87. See Friedman, *The Bible with Sources Revealed*, 40–41. It is certainly possible that P itself was already a composite document when the redactor received it, including the *Sefer Toledoth Adam* from Adam to Abram, even though such an element would not have fit perfectly with other genealogical material in P.

88. The failure of the text of Genesis to report the death of Cain has presented a problem for interpreters for a long time. The primary effort to fix this has been to claim that Lamech killed Cain, and this act is the subject of his little song in 4:23–24. This little genealogy reports no deaths at all, however, and this provides even more indication that its primary concern is with ways of life and technological and artistic developments that live on, beyond their inventors. The problem seems to have been apparent to the writer(s) of Jubilees, who omitted any genealogy of Cain and included an explicit story of his death. See the discussion of Gen. 4:23–24 in chapter 8.

89. Friedman assigns 10:22–23 to P, 10:21, 24–30 to J, and 11:10–26 to a separate source. See *The Bible with Sources Revealed*, 48–49. E. A. Speiser identifies 10:22–23 and 11:10–26 both with P; see *Genesis*, 65–79.

90. This figure cannot be precise because the text does not provide the age of Shem at the end of the flood or the age of Abram when he arrives in Canaan.

91. Speiser argues effectively that the "tower" is a cultic structure, even an idol whose head (שאר) in the sky should be read more literally, and that the brick-making process is sacral in nature. E. A. Speiser, *Genesis*, 75–76.

92. The three times Deuteronomy uses this root to describe YHWH's scattering of Israel as punishment (4:27; 28:64; and 30:3) are all also causative (*hiphil*).

93. For uses of this verb root followed by a location with no preposition, see Joshua 19:17 and 2 Kings 20:4. Speiser commented on the possibility of Asshur as a location here and Nimrod as the subject, but called the syntax "awkward" without explaining why it would be so. See *Genesis*, 67–68. The Greek text is somewhat ambiguous here as well, but "he went out to Asshur" is an acceptable rendering. See Susan Branford, *Genesis* (Leiden: Brill, 2007), 58–59, 283.

94. Lowery, *Toward of Poetics of Genesis 1–11*, 157–58.

95. On the parallel nature of the descendants of Cain and the descendants of Ham, see ibid., 77.

96. The absence of full genealogical continuity in Jubilees may help demonstrate such a concern was exclusive to the *Sefer Toledoth Adam*.

97. This is true whether the *Sefer Toledoth Adam* had been integrated into P before the redactor of Genesis received it or the redactor worked with it as a third independent source.

Chapter 3: Not in Ur Anymore

1. Theodore Hiebert, *The Yahwist's Landscape: Nature and Religion in Early Israel* (Minneapolis: Fortress, 2008), 83–91.
2. Ibid., 84–85.
3. See Daniel E. Fleming, *The Legacy of Israel in Judah's Bible: History, Politics, and the Reinscribing of Tradition* (Cambridge: Cambridge University Press, 2012), 22–27. Fleming has noted that the ways of representing the relationships between religious sites and kings and their capital cities differs in material from Israel compared to material from Judah. A more complete discussion of the differing polities between these two entities, particularly regarding centralization, takes place below.
4. Simon Schama, *Landscape and Memory* (New York: Vintage, 1995), 262–65. The ambivalent relationship between Israel and Egypt is a more significant subject in chapter 4.
5. On the role of deception in the ancestral material of Genesis, see John E. Anderson, *Jacob and the Divine Trickster: A Theology of Deception and YHWH's Fidelity to the Ancestral Promise in the Jacob Cycle* (Winona Lake, IN: Eisenbrauns, 2011), 1–46.
6. See a summary and discussion of the difficulties in J. A. Emerton, "The Riddle of Genesis XIV," *Vetus Testamentum* 21 (1971): 404–7. Emerton correctly identified the placement of Lot in Sodom as the strongest link between Genesis 14 and the J source.
7. See Volker Glissmann, "Genesis 14: A Diaspora Novella?," *Journal for the Study of the Old Testament* 34 (2009): 33–45.
8. See Benjamin Ziemer, *Abram–Abraham: Kompositionsgeschichtliche Untersuchungen zu Genesis 14, 15 und 17* (Berlin: de Gruyter, 2005), 157–62.
9. The identification of "Salem" here is probably a diversion. Its only function is the identification of "Melchizedek of Salem." The Bible mentions Salem only one other time, in Psalm 76:2, where it is in poetic parallel to Zion, clearly referring to Jerusalem. Later texts such as the Aramaic translation of Genesis known as Targum Onqelos and Josephus (*Jewish Wars* 6:438) make a connection to Jerusalem, but there is no observable city or shrine in the Genesis text. Other Jewish literature of the Second Temple period makes similar connections, but they appear to be later developments. See James Kugel, *The Bible as It Was* (Cambridge, MA: Belknap Press, 1997), 151–62.
10. For a statement of its distinctiveness, compared to the other sources, see Richard Elliott Friedman, *The Bible with Sources Revealed: A New View into the Five Books of Moses* (San Francisco: HarperCollins, 2003), 52. Joel Baden is more optimistic about connecting the majority of Genesis 14 to the J tradition; see *The Composition of the Pentateuch: Renewing the Documentary Hypothesis* (New Haven: Yale University Press, 2012), 274.
11. For a list of, and response to, many of these possibilities, see Ehud Ben Zvi, "The Dialogue between Abraham and YHWH in Gen. 18.23–32: A Historical-Critical Analysis," *Journal for the Study of the Old Testament* 53 (1992): 27–33.
12. See Ed Noort, "For the Sake of Righteousness—Abraham's Negotiations with YHWH as Prologue to the Sodom Narrative: Genesis 18:16–33," in *Sodom's Sin: Genesis 18–19 and Its Interpretation*, ed. Ed Noort and Eibert Tigchelaar (Leiden: Brill, 2004), 14–17.
13. The range of meaning of *hpk* is significant. Of about twenty occurrences in the Pentateuch, nine are in Leviticus 13, referring to the "turning" or "changing"

of the color of skin from diseases. Another three are in Exodus 7 describing the "turning" of the staff into a snake and the water of the Nile into blood. The description of "overturning" a city is not one of the more common uses.

14. This battle has been waged most recently in a massive volume of essays, edited by Jan C. Gertz, Bernard M. Levinson, Dalit Rom-Shiloni, and Konrad Schmid—*The Formation of the Pentateuch: Bridging the Academic Cultures of Europe, Israel, and North America* (Tübingen: Mohr Siebeck, 2016). For a statement on the current status of the issue, see the introductory article by the editors, "Convergence and Divergence in Pentateuchal Theory—The Genesis and Goals of This Volume" (1–10).

15. The most ardent proponent of the neo–documentary Hypothesis has presented a thorough argument for the independence of these sources and a demonstration of the purposes of each that is sufficient to explain why they would have made different choices about what to include from the ancestral traditions and how to combine the material. See Baden, *The Composition of the Pentateuch*, 221–26.

16. The most thorough argument for the combination of Israelite and Judahite sources, within a Judahite context and framework, is the work of Daniel E. Fleming in *The Legacy of Israel in Judah's Bible*. See especially the introduction to the argument (3–16).

17. The identification of the Jacob tradition with Israel enjoys near unanimous support among scholars who make such geographic assignments. The conclusion that the Abraham traditions were the product of Judah is a majority opinion, but Daniel Fleming's influential work has questioned this position. This seems to be the result of Fleming's desire to claim that Judah initially had no interest in Israelite origins apart from the rise of kings. Holding on to this assumption required a dismissal of Abraham as the great Judahite ancestor. Fleming claims Judah only became interested in such distant ancestors when it began to inherit Israelite traditions. Explaining the dominant southern orientation of the Abraham stories became problematic for Fleming, and the possibilities he offered for a non-Judahite origin of the Abraham tradition are strained to say the least. See *The Legacy of Israel in Judah's Bible*, 28–30.

18. It is common and easy to say that Jacob "purchased" or "bought" the land, and many English translations render the verb root *qnh* this way here. Philippe Guillaume has cautioned against making assumptions about ownership of private property in the ancient world. He prefers the use of the term "land tenure," which involves paying for permission to use certain land in a particular way. See *Land, Credit and Crisis: Agrarian Finance in the Hebrew Bible* (London: Routledge, 2012), 18–19.

19. The uses of "Israel" within the poem known as the "Song of Jacob" (49:2–27) are all unusual in different ways.

20. The naming of this place is entangled with the stories of Isaac naming several wells, which is reasonable because one interpretation of the city name is "seven wells." The other possible rendering is "well of oath," reflecting the accompanying story of the oath between Isaac and Abimelech. The competing traditions connecting the naming of Beer-sheba to Abraham or Isaac are for the E source and J source, respectively.

21. Bethel is the one clear case of a renaming. This J text and the E naming of Bethel in 35:7 acknowledge the prior name of the city as Luz. Curiously, when Jacob retells his life story in 48:3–7, in what appears to be a P text, he still

refers to the place as Luz. There is a P text concerning the naming of Bethel at 35:9–15, which does not even mention this prior name.

22. Israel Finkelstein and Thomas Römer, "Comments on the Historical Background of the Jacob Narrative in Genesis," *Zeitschrift für die alttestamentliche Wissenschaft* (2014): 317–18.

23. The combination of chronological elements, from J and P, produces a fifteen-year overlap in the lives of Abraham and Jacob. Jubilees creates scenes in which Abraham and Jacob are together. It is not surprising that some ancient readers might have found the lack of such scenes dissatisfying.

24. Hiebert, *The Yahwist's Landscape*, 91.

25. For a more extensive introduction to "Joseph and Aseneth," see George W. E. Nickelsburg, *Jewish Literature between the Bible and the Mishnah*, 2nd ed. (Minneapolis: Fortress, 2005), 332–38.

26. For more on these distinctions, see Hiebert, *The Yahwist's Landscape*, 88–89. Hiebert demonstrates the difference between the J and P perspectives by observing J's use of *yšb* (dwell or inhabit) and P's use of *gr* (alien or sojourner) for the ancestors in Canaan.

27. See Dieter Georgi, *The City in the Valley: Biblical Interpretation and Urban Theology* (Atlanta: Society of Biblical Literature, 2005), 196.

28. Ibid., 196–220.

29. Richard Florida, *The Rise of the Creative Class, Revisited* (New York: Basic Books, 2011), 157–66.

30. Erin Runions, *The Babylon Complex: Theopolitical Fantasies of War, Sex, and Sovereignty* (New York: Fordham University Press, 2014), 247.

Chapter 4: Building Cities for Pharaoh

1. While it is possible that the Greek text removed the reference to Goshen in 47:6 to avoid the conflict with Rameses in 47:11, the numerous other references to Goshen in this part of Genesis make such a move unlikely. Removing the one and only reference to Rameses in Genesis at 47:11 would have served this purpose much better.

2. For one of the more extensive efforts in this direction see James K. Hoffmeier, *Israel in Egypt: The Evidence for the Authenticity of the Exodus Tradition* (New York: Oxford University Press, 1999), 52–163.

3. Such a figure is doubtful. William Dever has estimated the populations for Israel and Judah during the eighth century at approximately 350,000. See *Beyond the Texts: An Archaeological Portrait of Ancient Israel and Judah* (Atlanta: Society of Biblical Literature, 2017), 449–53. The subject of populations during the monarchy receives more extensive treatment in chapters 5 and 6.

4. For more on these letters and their content, see Nadav Na'aman, *Canaan in the Second Millennium B.C.E.: Collected Essays, Volume 2* (Winona Lake, IN: Eisenbrauns, 2005), 173–91.

5. For more detail on this correspondence, see ibid., 99–107.

6. On the presence of Egypt in Canaan in the Late Bronze Age, and their absence from biblical stories of Canaan, see Paula McNutt, *Reconstructing the Society of Ancient Israel* (Louisville, KY: Westminster John Knox Press, 1999), 46–48.

7. Theodore Hiebert, *The Yahwist's Landscape: Nature and Religion in Early Israel* (Minneapolis: Fortress, 2008), 92–93.

8. For more on the literary features of this story, see Mark McEntire, *The Blood of Abel: The Violent Plot* (Macon, GA: Mercer University Press, 1999), 51–53.

9. See, for example, William H. C. Propp, *Exodus 1–18: A New Translation with Introduction and Commentary* (New York: Doubleday, 1999), 194. Propp uses the word "tentatively" in his assignment of the despoiling texts to the J source.

10. For a similar argument see Joel S. Baden, *The Composition of the Pentateuch: Renewing the Documentary Hypothesis* (New Haven: Yale University Press, 2012), 122–23. Baden also argued for 12:42–34 as a J text, confirming J's view that the Israelites leave Egypt with only their livestock.

11. Hiebert, *The Yahwist's Landscape*, 117–26.

12. Israel Finkelstein, "The Wilderness Narrative and Itineraries and the Evolution of the Exodus Tradition," in *Israel's Exodus in Transdisciplinary Perspective*, ed. Thomas E. Levy et al. (Switzerland: Springer, 2015), 39–50.

13. For a presentation of the similarities and differences between the two, see Christopher B. Hays, *Hidden Riches: A Sourcebook for the Comparative Study of the Hebrew Bible and the Ancient Near East* (Louisville, KY: Westminster John Knox Press, 2014), 113–18.

14. For further explanation of this concept, see Leo Perdue et al., *Israel and Empire: A Postcolonial History of Israel and Early Judaism* (London: Bloomsbury, 2015), 30–32.

15. Ibid., 73.

16. Carolyn Routledge, "Temple as the Center in Ancient Egyptian Urbanism," in *Urbanism and Antiquity: From Mesopotamia to Crete*, ed. Walter E. Aufrecht et al. (Sheffield: Sheffield Academic, 1997), 222–23.

17. Ibid., 228–32.

18. For a detailed discussion of issues in this text, see William H. C. Propp, *Exodus 19–40: A New Translation with Introduction and Commentary* (New York: Doubleday, 2006), 182–85. Propp proposed the altar law was a displaced portion of the E source.

19. For a detailed discussion of the Covenant Code and its relationship to narrative sources, see ibid., 141–54. On the relation of the Covenant Cod to its narrative surroundings, see also David P. Wright, *Inventing God's Law: How the Covenant Code of the Bible Used and Revised the Laws of Hammurabi* (Oxford: Oxford University Press, 2009), 332–44. Wright did not commit to the identification of an E source, but acknowledged that the narrative text he associates with the Covenant Code has frequently been assigned by others to E (493, n.49).

20. For a clear example, see Hayes, *Hidden Riches*, 121–45.

21. Hiebert, *The Yahwist's Landscape*, 126. It is difficult to say what he means by describing these narratives as "southern," or how he arrives at that conclusion. Such a location is not necessary to agree with his assessment that these laws reflect a mixed agricultural way of life.

22. On the tabernacle as "social space," see Mark K. George, *Israel's Tabernacle as Social Space* (Atlanta: Society of Biblical Literature, 2009), 41–44. George assumes the common position that the Priestly writing was produced during or after the exile, so that the tabernacle narratives within it are a response to the loss of sacred space. The stories were part of the process of renegotiating understandings of space in the wake of national disaster.

23. Ibid., 18.

24. Joel S. Burnett, *Where Is God?: Divine Absence in the Hebrew Bible* (Minneapolis: Fortress, 2010), 68–74.

25. Samuel E. Balentine, *The Torah's Vision of Worship* (Minneapolis: Fortress, 1999), 148–52.
26. James W. Watts, *Ritual and Rhetoric in Leviticus: From Sacrifice to Scripture* (Cambridge: Cambridge University Press, 2007), 55–62.
27. Hiebert, *The Yahwist's Landscape*, 121–24. On the other hand, I am not convinced by Hiebert's claims that J's Sinai theophany in Exodus 19:9, 16, and 18 consists of images of the kind of thunderstorm common in the hill country (124). This imagery still sounds more like a volcano to me.
28. Finding a convenient way to name this particular section of the texts is problematic. Many interpreters use "Numbers 11–21." The departure from Mount Sinai begins at 10:11, and the text follows the Israelites through their wilderness travels until the story breaks away to the Balaam episode in 22:1. So, the primary text I am addressing is Numbers 10:11–21:35, which I will typically call Numbers 10–21 for the sake of simplicity.
29. Finkelstein, "The Wilderness Narrative," 49–50.
30. Jacob Milgrom, *Numbers: JPS Torah Commentary* (New York: Jewish Publication Society, 1990), xv.
31. Mary Douglas, *In the Wilderness: The Doctrine of Defilement in the Book of Numbers* (Sheffield: JSOT Press, 1993), 103.
32. George, *Israel's Tabernacle as Social Space*, 86. George has drawn heavily from the work of Henri Lefebvre and his understanding of "social space." See *The Production of Space*, trans. Donald Nicholson Smith (Oxford: Blackwell, 1991). Especially important is the triad of concepts Lefebvre developed to understand social space (40–46). George combined these ideas about space with what he labeled the "New Historicism," to create a "spatial poetics" he could apply to the tabernacle. See George, *Israel's Tabernacle as Social Space*, 31–41. The most important result of this is the ability to understand the interaction between the tabernacle presented in the text and the web of social connections around the text's presentation.
33. Baruch A. Levine, *Numbers 1–20: A New Translation with Introduction and Commentary* (New York: Doubleday, 1993), 476–77.
34. For more on the theological development of this continuity, see Jon D. Levenson, *Sinai and Zion: An Entry into the Jewish Bible* (San Francisco: Harper & Row, 1985), 187–205.
35. See Thomas Römer, "Egypt Nostalgia in Exodus 14–Numbers 21," in *Torah and the Book of Numbers*, ed. Christian Frevel et al. (Tübingen: Mohr Siebeck, 2013), 70–84.
36. Hiebert, *The Yahwist's Landscape*, 122.
37. Ibid., 123.
38. There has been some disagreement about the assignment of the trans-Jordan traditions in both Numbers 21 and 32. Richard Elliott Friedman assigns both to the J source. See *The Bible with Sources Revealed*, 278–79, 300–303. Because Baden has argued convincingly that the material in Numbers 21 is E, and the two sets of texts fit logically together in the same source, the assignment to E makes more sense. See *The Composition of the Pentateuch*, 116–20.
39. Liane M. Marquis, "The Composition of Numbers 32: A New Proposal," *Vetus Testamentum* 63 (2013): 408–32.
40. See further discussion of the issues and problems in this text at ibid., 429–31.
41. For more on this detail, see ibid., 412–13.

42. Ibid., 410–11.
43. See the discussion of choice and constraint and the formation of ghettos in Simon Parker, *Urban Theory and the Urban Experience: Encountering the City*, 2nd ed. (London: Routledge, 2015), 88–93.

Chapter 5: Give Us a King

1. Eric H. Cline, *1177 B.C.: The Year Civilization Collapsed* (Princeton: Princeton University Press, 2014), 160–70.
2. Israel Finkelstein, *The Forgotten Kingdom: The Archaeology and History of Northern Israel* (Atlanta: Society of Biblical Literature, 2013), 37–41.
3. Mark S. Smith, *Where the Gods Are: Spatial Dimensions of Anthropomorphism in the Biblical World* (New Haven: Yale University Press, 2016), 83.
4. Ibid., 86.
5. Ibid., 95–96. The one problem with Smith's analysis is his speculation that the name of the singular place is famously unnamed in Deuteronomy in order to allow a changing of the site's location. It seems much more likely that the choice not to name Jerusalem has a narrative purpose. With the book of Deuteronomy self-consciously placed at the end of the exodus story on the precipice of the promised land, while Jerusalem is still a Jebusite city, use of the name would be disruptive to the plot.
6. Ibid., 107.
7. Ephraim and Manasseh must each have full tribal status in these texts to make the arithmetic work.
8. Ibid., 111.
9. For a summary of the issue and review of the massive literature on this question, see Thomas B. Dozeman, *Joshua 1–12: A New Translation with Introduction and Commentary* (New Haven: Yale University Press, 2015), 14–15.
10. See the discussion of this motif in a broader cultural context in Herbert N. Schneidau, *Sacred Discontent: The Bible and Western Tradition* (Berkeley: University of California Press, 1977), 5–6.
11. It is not entirely clear why Susan Niditch classifies Numbers 21:23–24 as an example of "the ban." There is no "annihilation" present, in fact quite the opposite. See *War in the Hebrew Bible: A Study in the Ethics of Violence* (Oxford: Oxford University Press, 1993), 28.
12. See, for example, Amnon Ben-Tor, "The Fall of Canaanite Hazor—The 'Who' and 'When' Questions," in *Mediterranean Peoples in Transition: Thirteenth to Early Tenth Centuries BCE*, ed. Seymour Gitin et al. (Jerusalem: Israel Exploration Society, 1998), 456–68.
13. Baruch Halpern, "The Dawn of an Age: Megiddo in the Iron Age I," in *Exploring the Longue Durée: Essays in Honor of Lawrence E. Stager*, ed. J. David Schloen (Winona Lake, IN: Eisenbrauns, 2009), 158–60.
14. On the development of the Melchizedek tradition in later Jewish texts, see James Kugel, *The Bible as It Was* (Cambridge, MA: Belknap Press, 1997), 151–62.
15. On the many tensions in these passages concerning Jerusalem, see Robert R. Cargill, *The Cities That Built the Bible* (San Francisco: HarperOne, 2016), 175–77.
16. For more on the character, geographical extent, and power of Jerusalem during the Bronze Age, see Nadav Na'aman, *Canaan in the Second Millennium*

B.C.E.: Collected Essays, Volume 2 (Winona Lake, IN: Eisenbrauns, 2005), 173–91.

17. William G. Dever, "Archaeology, Urbanism, and the Rise of the Israelite State," in *Urbanism and Antiquity: From Mesopotamia to Crete*, ed. Walter E. Aufrecht et al. (Sheffield: Sheffield Academic, 1997), 184–85.

18. See the discussion of this development in Daniel E. Fleming, *The Legacy of Israel in Judah's Bible: History, Politics, and the Reinscribing of Tradition* (Cambridge: Cambridge University Press, 2012), 179–85.

19. Roland Boer, *The Sacred Economy of Ancient Israel* (Louisville, KY: Westminster John Knox Press, 2015), 110–32.

20. Ibid., 132–39.

21. On the motives of scholars with particular faith commitments to promote early widespread literacy in ancient Israel, see Stephen L. Young, "Maximizing Literacy as a Protective Strategy: Redescribing Evangelical Inerrantist Scholarship on Israelite Literacy," *Biblical Interpretation* 25 (2015): 145–73.

22. Christopher A. Rollston, *Writing and Literacy in the World of Ancient Israel: Epigraphic Evidence from the Iron Age* (Atlanta: Society of Biblical Literature, 2010): 128–32. One general principle pointing toward more widespread literacy is the development of alphabetic writing during the Iron Age in the Levant, as opposed to syllabic systems like Akkadian. Some proponents of nonelite literacy have used this factor to support their claims, but Rollston has demonstrated that the development of alphabetic systems and the growth of literacy into nonelite circles do not necessarily correlate (128).

23. Michael L. Satlow, *How the Bible Became Holy* (New Haven: Yale University Press, 2014), 19–30.

24. Finkelstein, *The Forgotten Kingdom*, 154–55.

25. Ibid., 156–57.

26. Daniel E. Fleming, *The Legacy of Israel in Judah's Bible*, 4–7.

27. There have been attempts to delineate two different dialects of the Hebrew language in this period, one characteristic of Israel and one of Judah. Na'amah Pat-el has demonstrated that this linguistic distinction cannot be adequately demonstrated within the biblical literature. Differentiation of Israelite materials and Judahite materials in the text must be carried out based on other criteria. See "Israelian Hebrew: A Re-Evaluation," *Vetus Testamentum* 67 (2017): 1–37.

28. The inscription was rediscovered during the period of Ottoman control over Jerusalem and was taken to Istanbul, where it still resides in Turkey's archaeological museum.

29. Satlow, *How the Bible Became Holy*, 32–34.

30. Jacob L. Wright, *David, King of Israel, and Caleb in Biblical Memory* (Cambridge: Cambridge University Press, 2014), 37–50.

31. On the presence of older material about David embedded within narratives that serve the purposes of later times, see Konrad Schmid, *The Old Testament: A Literary History*, trans. Linda M. Maloney (Minneapolis: Fortress, 2012), 60–63.

32. For a more detailed discussion of this view of the relationship between the three literary traditions, see Raymond F. Person Jr., *The Deuteronomistic History and the Book of Chronicles: Scribal Works in an Oral World* (Atlanta: Society of Biblical Literature, 2010), 16–19.

33. For a discussion of these and other issues concerning Caleb and Hebron, see Wright, *David, King of Israel*, 183–86.

34. Ibid., 209–12.

35. See Florida's description of this group in *The Rise of the Creative Class, Revisited* (New York: Basic Books, 2012), 35–63.

36. Ibid., 188.

37. Christopher A. Rollston, "Epigraphic Evidence from Jerusalem and Its Environs at the Dawn of Biblical History: Methodologies and a Long Durèe Perspective," in *New Studies in the Archaeology of Jerusalem and Its Region: Collected Papers Volume XI*, ed. Yuval Gadot et al. (Jerusalem: Israeli Antiquities Authority, 2017), 10–16.

38. William M. Schniedewind, "Understanding Scribal Education in Ancient Israel: A View from Kuntillet 'Ajrud," *MAARAV, A Journal for the Study of Northwest Semitic Languages and Literatures* 21 (2014): 275–77. A scribal training program in such a remote place, methodologically connected to such large-scale foreign models as Nippur and Ugarit, would have needed a Hebrew exemplar, one based in a city with a significant population of scribes, like Samaria or Jerusalem.

39. Ibid., 284–87. See Schniedewind's rejection of various proposals that Kuntillet 'Ajrud may have been a religious site (272–75).

Chapter 6: Plowed Like a Field

1. It is possible to translate the words in these texts in a different way, based only on the changing of vowels, and produce a number 10 percent this size, but even that number sounds too large.

2. See William G. Dever, *Beyond the Texts: An Archaeological Portrait of Ancient Israel and Judah* (Atlanta: Society of Biblical Literature, 2017), 449–53. See also Israel Finkelstein and Magen Broshi, "The Population of Palestine in Iron Age II," *Bulletin of the American Schools of Oriental Research* 287 (1992): 47–60. Dever produced numbers a little lower than Finkelstein and Broshi, but they are close enough for the purposes of this study.

3. See Marti Nissinen, "City as Lofty as Heaven: Arbela and Other Cities in Neo-Assyrian Prophecy," in *"Every City Shall Be Forsaken": Urbanism and Prophecy in Ancient Israel and the Near East*, ed. Lester L. Grabbe and Robert D. Haak (Sheffield: Sheffield Academic, 2001), 175–76.

4. Ibid., 208.

5. Karel van der Toorn, *Scribal Culture and the Making of the Hebrew Bible* (Cambridge, MA: Harvard University Press, 2007), 173–84.

6. Richard A. Horsley, *Scribes, Visionaries, and the Politics of Second Temple Judea* (Louisville, KY: Westminster John Knox Press, 2007), 77.

7. On the continuing importance of oral performance of prophecy, even after it began to take on written forms, see Friedhelm Hartenstein, "Prophets, Princes, and Kings: Prophecy and Prophetic Books according to Jeremiah 36," in *Jeremiah's Scriptures: Production, Reception, Interaction, and Transformation*, ed. Hindy Najman and Konrad Schmid (Leiden: Brill, 2017), 76–79.

8. On the importance of this verse and what it reveals about scribal identity, see ibid., 90–91; and Konrad Schmid, "Nebukadnezar's Antritt der Weltherrschaft und der Abbruch der Davidynastie: Innerbiblische Schriftauslegung und universalgeschichtliche Konstruktion im Jeremiabuch," in *Schriftgelehrte*

Traditionsliteratur: Fallstudien innerbiblischen Schriftauslegung im Alten Testament (Tübingen: Mohr Siebeck, 2011), 226.

9. Ibid., 184–94.

10. For a more detailed account of the developing views of the production of the prophetic scrolls, particularly Jeremiah, see Robert R. Wilson, "Exegesis, Expansion, and Tradition-Making in the Book of Jeremiah," in *Jeremiah's Scriptures: Production, Reception, Interaction, and Transformation*, ed. Hindy Najman and Konrad Schmid (Leiden: Brill, 2017), 3–21.

11. For more background on the development of the Baruch character and the tradition of writing in his name, see Michael E. Stone and Matthias Henze, *4 Ezra and 2 Baruch: Translations, Introductions, and Notes* (Minneapolis: Fortress Press, 2013), 9–13. On the changing depiction of the relationship between Jeremiah and Baruch in the development of these successive writings, see Matthias Henze and Liv Ingeborg Lied, "Jeremiah, Baruch, and Their Books: Three Phases in a Changing Relationship," in *Jeremiah's Scriptures: Production, Reception, Interaction, and Transformation*, ed. Hindy Najman and Konrad Schmid (Leiden: Brill, 2017), 330–53.

12. On this point, see Barbara Green, *Jeremiah and God's Plan of Well-Being* (Columbia: University of South Carolina Press, 2013), 144–54.

13. Louis Stuhlman and Hyun Chul Paul Kim, *You Are My People: An Introduction to Prophetic Literature* (Nashville: Abingdon, 2010), 10.

14. David M. Carr, *Holy Resilience: The Bible's Traumatic Origins* (New Haven: Yale University Press, 2014), 39.

15. For a more extensive discussion of this text and its purpose in the book of Ezekiel, see Mark McEntire, "From Bound and Gagged to Swimming in the Water of Life: How God Breaks and Heals Ezekiel," *Review and Expositor* 111 (2014): 329–36.

16. For a more complete discussion of this text and the way it operates within the sequence of oracles in Haggai, see Mark McEntire, "Haggai—Bringing God into the Picture," *Review and Expositor* 97 (2000): 69–78.

17. See Joseph Blenkinsopp, "City to Landscape: The 'Back to Nature' Theme in Isaiah 1–35," in Grabbe and Haak, eds., *"Every City Shall Be Forsaken,"* 35–39.

18. Ibid., 44.

19. See J. J. M. Roberts, *First Isaiah: A Commentary* (Minneapolis: Fortress Press, 2015), 417.

20. See Lester L. Grabbe, "Sup-urbs or Hyp-urbs: Prophets and Populations in Ancient Israel and Socio-Historical Method," in Grabbe and Haak, eds., *"Every City Shall Be Forsaken,"* 112–16.

21. Ibid., 108.

22. Ibid., 116–21.

23. Ibid., 121.

24. Arguments about the two sequences have not focused on the tension between these two books but on chronological factors, the similarity of superscriptions, and the difficulties presented by the enigmatic book of Joel. For a presentation of these issues and arguments that the Hebrew order came first, see James Nogalski, *The Book of the Twelve: Hosea–Jonah* (Macon, GA: Smyth & Helwys, 2011), 3–4.

25. For a presentation of this position, see Marvin A. Sweeney, *The Twelve Prophets*, vol. 1 (Collegeville, MN: Liturgical Press, 2000), 28–31.

26. Steven W. Holloway, "Nineveh as Meme in Persian-Period Yehud," in *Memory and the City in Ancient Israel*, ed. Diana V. Edelman and Ehud Ben Zvi (Winona Lake, IN: Eisenbrauns, 2014), 279–80.

27. See Ulrike Sals, "'Babylon' Forever, or How to Divinize What You Want to Damn," in Edelman and Zvi, eds., *Memory and the City in Ancient Israel*, 304–8. On the simultaneous attraction and repulsion of Babylon, see also Erin Runions, *The Babylon Complex: Theo-Political Fantasies of War, Sex, and Sovereignty* (New York: Fordham University Press, 2014), 2–3.

28. See Philippe Guillaume, "Dislocating Jerusalem's Memories with Tyre," in Edelman and Zvi, eds., *Memory and the City in Ancient Israel*, 259–66. Guillaume also pointed to the later efforts of Herod the Great to build his palace after the pattern of Tyre.

29. Adele Berlin, *Lamentations: A Commentary* (Louisville, KY: Westminster John Knox Press, 2002), 10–11.

30. Peggy Day, "The Personification of Cities as Female in the Hebrew Bible: The Thesis of Aloysius Fitzgerald, F. S. C.," in *Reading from This Place*, vol. 2, *Social Location and Biblical Interpretation in Global Perspective*, ed. Fernando F. Segovia and Mary Ann Tolbert (Minneapolis: Fortress, 1995), 301–2.

31. Berlin, *Lamentations*, 12. On the general background of portraying cities as women and daughters in the Bible and ancient Near East, see Julia O'Brien, *Challenging Prophetic Metaphor: Theology and Ideology in the Prophets* (Louisville, KY: Westminster John Knox Press, 2008), 125–28.

32. For a more thorough description of this aspect, see Gerlinde Baumann, *Love and Violence: Marriage as Metaphor for the Relationship between YHWH and Israel in the Prophetic Books* (Collegeville, MN: Liturgical Press, 2003), 118–23.

33. This "reverse action" of metaphors has been given significant attention by Baumann, building on the general work on metaphors by Paul Ricoeur. See *Love and Violence*, 27–37. See further discussion of this issue in relation to prophetic literature in Yvonne Sherwood, *The Prostitute and the Prophet: Hosea's Marriage in Literary Perspective* (Sheffield: Sheffield Academic, 2009); and Sharon Moughtin-Mumby, *Sexual and Marital Metaphors in Hosea, Jeremiah, Isaiah, and Ezekiel* (Oxford: Oxford University Press, 2008).

34. O'Brien, *Challenging Prophetic Metaphor*, 49–61.

35. See further detail on these written accounts and artifacts in Philip J. King and Lawrence E. Stager, *Life in Biblical Israel* (Louisville, KY: Westminster John Knox Press, 2001), 246–51.

36. Jacob L. Wright, "Urbicide: The Ritualized Killing of Cities in the Ancient Near East," in *Ritual Violence in the Hebrew Bible: New Perspectives*, ed. Saul M. Olyan (Oxford: Oxford University Press, 2015), 147.

37. The records of both Assyria and Babylon demonstrate this practice. Ibid., 149–50.

38. Ibid., 157.

39. On this point, see Margaret S. Odell, *Ezekiel* (Macon, GA: Smyth & Helwys, 2005), 193–98.

40. Emily Badger and Darla Cameron, "How Railroads, Highways, and Other Man-Made Lines Racially Divide America's Cities," *Washington Post*, June 16, 2015.

41. See Richard Florida, *The Rise of the Creative Class, Revisited* (New York: Basic Books, 2012).

Chapter 7: Let Them Go Up

1. Rainer Albertz, *Israel in Exile: The History and Literature of the Sixth Century B.C.E.* (Atlanta: Society of Biblical Literature, 2003), 96–111.

2. Jill Middlemas, *The Templeless Age: An Introduction to the History, Literature, and Theology of the "Exile"* (Louisville, KY: Westminster John Knox Press, 2007), 1–6.

3. Albert summarizes the available evidence in *Israel in Exile*, 72–74.

4. Ibid., 100–101. The term appears in a tablet published in Francis Joannès and André Lemaire, "Trois tablettes cunéiformes à l'onomastique ouest sémitique" *Transeuphratène* 17 (1999): 17–34. On the implications of this site and its name, see Jeremiah W. Cataldo, *A Theocratic Yehud?: Issues of Governance in Persian Yehud* (London: T&T Clark, 2009), 72–73.

5. Hard numbers are difficult to come by. On the demographics of Judah just before, during, and after the exile, see Paula McNutt, *Reconstructing the Society of Ancient Israel* (Louisville, KY: Westminster John Knox Press, 1999), 151–54, 193–95. The numbers appear to have been smaller than many, including the biblical story, assume. The total number of over forty-two thousand for the returned community alone, in the lists presented by Ezra 2 and Nehemiah 7, seems much too large even for the entire population of Judah during the early Persian period. On these numbers, see Charles E. Carter, "The Province of Yehud in the Post-Exilic Period: Soundings in Site Distribution and Demography," in *Currents in Research: Biblical Studies 2*, ed. Tamara Cohn Eskenazi and Kent H. Richards (Sheffield: Sheffield Academic, 1994), 131–35.

6. See William G. Dever, *Beyond the Texts: An Archaeological Portrait of Ancient Israel and Judah* (Atlanta: Society of Biblical Literature, 2017), 449–53. See also Israel Finkelstein and Magen Broshi, "The Population of Palestine in Iron Age II," *Bulletin of the American Schools of Oriental Research* 287 (1992): 47–60. Dever produced numbers a little lower than Finkelstein and Broshi, but they are close enough for the purposes of this study.

7. Oded Lipschits, *The Fall and Rise of Jerusalem* (Winona Lake, IN: Eisenbrauns 2005), 190.

8. Jacob L. Wright, "Urbicide: The Ritualized Killing of Cities in the Ancient Near East," in *Ritual Violence in the Hebrew Bible: New Perspectives*, ed. Saul M. Olyan (Oxford: Oxford University Press, 2015), 148–55.

9. See Sarah Japhet, "Periodization between History and Ideology II: Chronology and Ideology in Ezra–Nehemiah," in *Judah and Judeans in the Persian Period*, ed. Oded Lipschits and Manfred Oeming (Winona Lake, IN: Eisenbrauns, 2006), 503–4.

10. Many interpreters have noted that the order of the two projects is illogical. This and other aspects of the Ezra–Nehemiah story have led to the proposal that the two primary characters returned to Jerusalem in the opposite order. The most important proponent of this view was probably A. van Hoonaker. Based on a possible confusion of Artaxerxes I and Artaxerxes II, van Hoonacker moved Ezra's arrival in Jerusalem by nearly fifty years, but this created different chronological problems. See "La succession chronologique Néhémie–Esdras," *Revue Biblique* 32 (1923): 33–64. For a more recent review of the issues and argument for the biblical chronology, see H. G. M. Williamson, *Ezra–Nehemiah* (Waco, TX: Word, 1985), xl–xliv.

11. Donna Laird, *Negotiating Power in Ezra–Nehemiah* (Atlanta: Society of Biblical Literature, 2016), 180–88.

12. On the performative aspects of the act of reading and its subsequent authority, see Elsie Stern, "Royal Letters and Torah Scrolls: The Place of Ezra–Nehemiah in Scholarly Narratives of Scripturalization," in *Contextualizing Israel's Sacred Writings: Ancient Literacy, Orality, and Literary Production*, ed. Brian B. Schmidt (Atlanta: Society of Biblical Literature, 2015), 240–43.

13. On the mixture of imperial power and local control based on sacred texts and ancient traditions, see Gary N. Knoppers, "An Achaemenid Imperial Authorization of Torah in Yehud?," in *Persia and Torah: The Theory of Imperial Authorization of the Pentateuch*, ed. James W. Watts (Atlanta: Society of Biblical Literature, 2001), 115–34.

14. Jack Miles, *God: A Biography* (New York: Vintage, 1995), 388–89. On the people bowing to the scrolls, see also Lisbeth S. Fried, "The Torah of God as God: The Exaltation of the Written Law Code in Ezra–Nehemiah," in *Divine Presence and Absence in Exilic and Post-Exilic Judah*, ed. Nathan MacDonald and Izaak J. de Hulster (Tübingen: Mohr Siebeck, 2013), 294–98. Fried's claim that Ezra carried the scroll with him in the processional in Nehemiah 12 and placed it in the temple is difficult to evaluate. No explicit mention of this idea is in the text, and the tradition of Ezra's scroll being in the temple only appears in writing much later in the writings of Josephus (*Contra Apion*, 1:29).

15. John Kessler, "Reconstructing Haggai's Jerusalem: Demographic and Sociological Considerations and the Search for an Adequate Point of Departure," in *"Every City Shall Be Forsaken": Urbanism and Prophecy in Ancient Israel and the Near East*, ed. Lester L. Grabbe and Robert D. Haak (Sheffield: Sheffield Academic, 2001), 151–58.

16. See Ehud Ben Zvi, "The Urban Center of Jerusalem and the Development of the Literature of the Hebrew Bible," in *Urbanism in Antiquity: From Mesopotamia to Crete*, ed. Walter E. Aufrecht et al. (Sheffield: Sheffield Academic, 1997), 196–97.

17. Ibid., 198–206.

18. On the combination of priestly and scribal roles, see Richard A. Horsley, *Scribes, Visionaries, and the Politics of Second Temple Judea* (Louisville, KY: Westminster John Knox Press, 2007), 79–80.

19. For more detail on the textual difficulties in this passage and the many efforts to explain them, see Juha Pakkala, *Ezra the Scribe: The Development of Ezra 7–10 and Nehemiah 8* (Berlin: Walter deGruyter, 2004), 146–50. Pakkala has proposed that Nehemiah 8:1–12a was part of the Ezra Memoir and initially sat between Ezra 8 and 9. The proposed editorial move by the composer of Ezra–Nehemiah highlighted the significance of the Golah group and the liturgical elements of the text. Pakkala's reconstruction produces an account of the story more like the one in Josephus.

20. Stern emphasizes that the actions of reading, interpreting, and sense-making in 8:8 are not sequential, but are all part of the Levites' "performance" of the text, which the people can understand. She is not able to explain, because the text provides inadequate information, precisely how this performance relates to what Ezra is doing with the "book." See "Royal Letters and Torah Scrolls," 250–51.

21. Jacob L. Wright, "Seeking, Finding, and Writing in Ezra–Nehemiah," in *Unity and Disunity in Ezra–Nehemiah: Redaction, Rhetoric, and Reader*, ed. Mark J. Boda and Paul L. Redditt (Sheffield: Sheffield Phoenix, 2008), 303.

22. Ibid.

23. Stern, "Royal Letters and Torah Scrolls," 242.

24. Ibid., 248–61.

25. For more detail on the character of Ezra and his role in the development of Second Temple, see Shaye J. D. Cohen, *From the Maccabees to the Mishnah*, 3rd ed. (Louisville, KY: Westminster John Knox, 2014), 136–39. It is possible that Ezra is an entirely constructed figure. His absence from the list of Israelite heroes in Sirach 44–50 has always been conspicuous. The use of the Ezra story here, as an indicator of how the scribes who produced texts about him viewed themselves, is not dependent on the degree to which we can locate a historical Ezra.

26. Seth L. Sanders, *From Adapa to Enoch: Scribal Culture and Religious Vision in Judea and Babylon* (Tübingen: Mohr Siebeck, 2017), 2.

27. The text of this chronicle is available in Jean-Jacques Glassner, *Mesopotamian Chronicles* (Atlanta: Society of Biblical Literature, 2004), 226–32. It may be useful to look at some of the more thorough descriptions surrounding this one, particularly the campaigns against Hatti. On the problems of classifying the various texts classified as Assyrian and Babylonian chronicles, see Caroline Waerzeggers, "The Babylonian Chronicles: Classification and Provenance," *Journal of Near Eastern Studies* 71 (2012): 285–98. The chronicle concerning Nebuchadnezzar's campaign in the Levant from which this material comes is one that does not have a clear provenance.

28. Christopher B. Hays, *Hidden Riches: A Sourcebook for the Comparative Study of the Hebrew Bible and the Ancient Near East* (Louisville, KY: Westminster John Knox Press, 2014), 221–30.

29. Adele Berlin, *Lamentations: A Commentary* (Louisville, KY: Westminster John Knox Press, 2002), 10–12.

30. Carla Sulzbach, "Building Castles on Shifting Sands of Memory: From Dystopian to Utopian Views of Jerusalem in the Persian Period," in *Memory and the City in Ancient Israel*, ed. Diana V. Edelman and Ehud Ben Zvi (Winona Lake, IN: Eisenbrauns, 2014), 320.

31. Ibid., 309–16.

32. Ehud Ben Zvi, "Exploring Jerusalem as a Site of Memory in the Late Persian and Early Hellenistic Periods," in Edelman and Zvi, eds., *Memory and the City in Ancient Israel*, 199–201.

33. The NRSV translates *'ir* as "towns" here, but many other English translation use "cities."

34. The identity of 1 Esdras as a literary work is a matter of dispute. It contains the final two chapters of 2 Chronicles, almost all of Ezra, and the first nine chapters of Nehemiah. Some see this Greek work as a reconfiguration of parts of those other books, while others see it as the major source of the current book of Ezra–Nehemiah. Still others regard it as an accidental fragment. The various positions appear in detail in a large collection of essays in Lisbeth S. Fried, *Was 1 Esdras First? An Investigation into the Priority and Nature of 1 Esdras* (Atlanta: Society of Biblical Literature, 2011).

35. For a thorough discussion of the textual issue, the various witnesses, and a plausible reconstruction of the development of the situation, see Williamson, *Ezra–Nehemiah*, 271–73.

36. Again, a textual issue arises because of the similarity between Ezra 3:1 and Nehemiah 7:73, which specifically designates "their cities." The correction here, to match Nehemiah 7:73, supported by Williamson, seems unnecessary.

On what basis the people may have been assigned to cities is unknown, and the text quickly removes them from those contexts. See ibid., 41.

37. On the development of this perspective, which she calls "doxic," see Laird, *Negotiating Power in Ezra–Nehemiah*, 74–76, 167–69.

38. On the significance of Aramaic and Babylonian scribal culture for Jewish scholars in the Second Temple period, see Sanders, *From Adapa to Enoch*, 151–56.

39. Laird, *Negotiating Power in Ezra–Nehemiah*, 156. See Laird's survey of the argument leading to this conclusion (152–56).

40. On the history of this other temple and the sources for evaluating it, see Gard Granerød, "The Former and Future Temple of YHW in Elephantine: A Tradition-Historical Study of Ancient Near Eastern Antiquarianism," *Zeitschrift für die alttestamentliche Wissenshaft* 127 (2015): 65–67.

41. For a fuller portrait of this the Jewish community in Egypt, see Albertz, *Israel in Exile*, 96–98.

42. For the texts of these letters, see Bezalel Porten, et al., *The Elephantine Papyri in English: Three Millennia of Cross-Cultural Continuity and Change*, 2nd ed. (Atlanta: Society of Biblical Literature, 2011), 126–53.

43. Melody D. Knowles, *Centrality Practiced: Jerusalem and the Religious Practice of Yehud in the Diaspora in the Persian Period* (Atlanta: Society of Biblical Literature, 2006), 8–15.

44. Ibid., 75.

45. Ibid., 128.

46. Oded Lipschits, *The Fall and Rise of Jerusalem*, 180.

47. For a helpful synthesis of a variety of perspectives on Jerusalem during this period, see Donna Laird, *Negotiating Power in Ezra–Nehemiah*, 15–21.

48. Deirdre N. Fulton, *Reconsidering Nehemiah's Judah: The Case of MT and LXX Nehemiah 11–12* (Tübingen: Mohr Siebeck, 2015), 116–17.

49. Ibid., 187–88.

50. On the ways that the vision of Ezekiel 40–48 fits into the symbolic world of the book of Ezekiel, see Dale F. Launderville, *Spirit and Reason: The Embodied Character of Ezekiel's Symbolic Thinking* (Waco, TX: Baylor University Press, 2007), 382–84. On the allotment of land and its arrangement in this imagined city, see Steven Shawn Tuell, *The Law of the Temple in Ezekiel 40–48* (Atlanta: Scholars Press, 1992), 62–63.

51. Sanders, *From Adapa to Enoch*, 122–27.

52. For more on this situation, see Laird, *Negotiation Power in Ezra–Nehemiah*, 21–26.

53 Mark S. Smith, *Where the Gods Are: Spatial Dimensions of Anthropomorphism in the Biblical World* (New Haven: Yale University Press, 2016), 103.

54. For a more detailed discussion of the Persian metanarrative and the ways a variety of Jewish communities arranged themselves in relation to it, see Leo G. Perdue et al. *Israel and Empire: A Postcolonial History of Israel and Early Judaism* (London: Bloomsbury, 2015), 109–28.

55. I am less certain about Leo Perdue's contention that the writers of Chronicles favored a restored Davidic monarchy in postexilic Judah. This argument is based on the idealization of David and Solomon in Chronicles, in comparison to their presentation in Samuel–Kings. There are other reasons for Chronicles to have charted this course. The desire to link the temple and

its administration to David, and particularly to an idealized David, is a more likely motivation. This is also the primary basis upon which Perdue classifies Chronicles as "resistance literature," which seems an unlikely designation. Ibid., 123–26.
56. Knowles, *Centrality Practiced*, 115–20.
57. For a review of the ways that the superscription has been interpreted throughout the history of Jewish and Christian interpretation, see Loren D. Crow, *The Songs of Ascents (Psalms 120–134): Their Place in Israelite History and Religion* (Atlanta: Scholars Press, 1996), 1–27.
58. Ibid., 145–58.
59. On the relatively late and uncertain development of the book of Psalms as modern readers know it, see Eva Mroczek, *The Literary Imagination in Jewish Antiquity* (Oxford: Oxford University Press, 2016), 25–44.
60. On the series of poems and the way Psalm 134 expresses its purpose, see Konrad Schaefer, OSB, *Psalms* (Collegeville, MN: Liturgical Press, 2001), 316–17.
61. Evidence from the Dead Sea Scrolls indicates that the psalms were copied intensely, and in different formats serving multiple purposes. See the discussion of this evidence in William L. Holladay, *The Psalms through Three Thousand Years* (Minneapolis: Fortress, 1993), 98–108.
62. See the discussion of this issue in Rowland Atkinson, introduction in *Gentrification in a Global Context: The New Urban Colonialism*, ed. Rowland Atkinson and Gary Bridge (London: Routledge, 2015), 5–7.
63. Richard Florida, *The New Urban Crisis: How Our Cities Are Increasing Inequality, Deepening Segregation, and Failing the Middle Class—and What We Can Do about It* (New York: Basic Books, 2017), 35–42.
64. Ibid., 185–216.

Chapter 8: Cities Reimagined

1. Eva Mroczek, *The Literary Imagination in Jewish Antiquity* (Oxford: Oxford University Press, 2016), 140.
2. Ibid.
3. For a more thorough discussion of the textual evidence related to Jubilees and its history, see James VanderKam, "The Manuscript Tradition of Jubilees," *Enoch and the Mosaic Torah: The Evidence of Jubilees*, ed. Gabriele Boccaccini and Giovanni Ibba (Grand Rapids: Eerdmans, 2009), 3–21.
4. Gabriele Boccaccini, *Roots of Rabbinic Judaism: An Intellectual History, from Ezekiel to Daniel* (Grand Rapids: Eerdmans, 2002), 89–103.
5. J. T. A. G. M. van Ruiten, *Primaeval History Interpreted: The Rewriting of Genesis 1–11 in the Book of Jubilees* (Leiden: Brill, 2000), 374.
6. See the discussion in James L. Kugel, "Jubilees," in *Outside the Bible: Ancient Jewish Writings Related to Scripture, vol. 1*, ed. Louis H. Feldman et al. (Philadelphia: Jewish Publication Society, 2013), 278–81.
7. John H. Choi has taken a somewhat different position on this issue, arguing that at the time Jubilees was written Genesis "did not represent a standard account of history" and "did not present any form of necessary restraint" for the writer of Jubilees. See *Traditions at Odds: The Reception of the Pentateuch in Biblical and Second Temple Period Literature* (New York: T&T Clark, 2010), 180–81. Michael Segal has taken a very different position from Choi, contending Jubilees is a unified composition of one author and its internal tensions are evidence of the constraints or preexisting sources. See *The Book of*

Jubilees: Rewritten Bible, Redaction, Ideology and Theology (Leiden: Brill, 2007), 14. Debate on the composition of Jubilees is in its early stages. For a view that includes two distinct layers of composition, see James L. Kugel, *A Walk through Jubilees: Studies in the Book of Jubilees and the World of Its Creation* (Leiden: Brill, 2012), 213–20.

8. On the importance of Jubilees among the Dead Sea collection, see Michael E. Stone, *Ancient Judaism: New Visions and Views* (Grand Rapids: Eerdmans, 2011), 131–36. The Genesis Apocryphon is too fragmentary to enter the discussion significantly here. On its connections to Jubilees, Joseph A. Fitzmyer has highlighted the connections between Jubilees and the Genesis Apocryphon; see Fitzmyer's *The Genesis Apocryphon of Qumran Cave 1 (1Q20): A Commentary* (Rome: Biblical Institute, 2004), 20–21.

9. For more on this point, see James C. VanderKam, *The Book of Jubilees* (Sheffield: Sheffield Academic, 2001), 12–13.

10. See the more detailed explanation of this in James L. Kugel, *A Walk through Jubilees*, 5–12.

11. Bernard M. Levinson, *A More Perfect Torah: At the Intersection of Philology and Hermeneutics in Deuteronomy and the Temple Scroll* (Winona Lake, IN: Eisenbrauns, 2013), 8–14.

12. Ibid., 50–61.

13. James Kugel argued the "image of God" would have been too anthropomorphic for the transcendent view of God that characterizes Jubilees. See *A Walk through Jubilees*, 32.

14. See the discussion of this problem with the divine character of Genesis in Mark McEntire, *Portraits of a Mature God: Choices in Old Testament Theology* (Minneapolis: Fortress, 2013), 29–37.

15. For a more thorough discussion of the "compiler's" approach and intent, see Joel S. Baden, *The Composition of the Pentateuch: Renewing the Documentary Hypothesis* (New Haven, CT: Yale University Press, 2012), 221–29.

16. For a more detailed account of this, see Jacques van Ruiten, "The Garden of Eden and Jubilees 3:1–31," *Bijdragen: Tijdschrift voor filosofie en theologie* 57 (1996): 306–7.

17. For more on the differences in the portrayal of Adam and Eve, the trees in the garden, and the divine interaction with the humans, see Betsy Halpern-Amaru, *The Empowerment of Women in the Book of Jubilees* (Leiden: Brill, 1999), 10–15.

18. Ibid., 313.

19. The translations of O. S. Wintermute, James VanderKam, and James Kugel all use "till" in 3:15–16 and 3:35. Nothing in the context of 3:15–16 makes the specific idea of plowing the ground necessary, but 3:35 specifically has "land" as the direct object of the verb and connects the work there to what Adam learned in the garden. See O. S. Wintermute, "Jubilees: A New Translation and Introduction," in *The Old Testament Pseudepigrapha*, vol. 2, ed. James H. Charlesworth (Garden City, NY: Doubleday, 1985), 59–61; and James C. VanderKam, *The Book of Jubilees, II* (Leuven: Peeters, 1989), 53; and Kugel, "Jubilees," in *Outside the Bible*, vol. 1, 297–300.

20. James M. Scott in *On Earth as in Heaven: The Restoration of Sacred Time and Sacred Space in the Book of Jubilees* (Leiden: Brill, 2004), 52–53.

21. See more on this point in Halpern-Amaru, *The Empowerment of Women*, 15–16.

22. Kugel, *A Walk through Jubilees*, 51.
23. On the development and use of the Cain and Abel story in the *Targumim*, Philo, *Genesis Rabbah*, and other Jewish literature of the Second Temple period, see Mark McEntire, "Being Seen and Not Heard: The Interpretation of Genesis 4.8," in *Of Scribes and Sages: Early Jewish Transmission of Scripture*, vol. 1, ed. Craig A. Evans (London: T&T Clark, 2004), 6–10.
24. Kugel, *A Walk through Jubilees*, 46.
25. Van Ruiten, *Primaeval History Interpreted*, 150.
26. On the many attempts to make this argument in the early centuries of the Common Era, see Emmanouela Grypeou and Helen Spurling, *The Book of Genesis in Late Antiquity: Encounters between Jewish and Christian Exegesis* (Leiden: Brill, 2013), 128–32.
27. Few interpreters have developed extensive arguments concerning the composition history of Jubilees. Kugel has taken a firm position on two stages of authorship: the original writer of the book and a later "Interpolator" who primarily inserted additional passages. The death of Cain in 4:31–32 is a text he attributes to the Interpolator. See *A Walk through Jubilees*, 51.
28. For more on this adjustment in Jubilees, see van Ruiten, *Primaeval History Interpreted*, 290–92.
29. On Jubilees' use of 1 Enoch here, see Segal, *The Book of Jubilees*, 108–9.
30. Ibid. On the connection between the angels of YHWH and the flood, see also Kugel, *A Walk through Jubilees*, 52.
31. This is the language of Scott in *On Earth as in Heaven*, 6–7.
32. On the new nature, see Kugel, *A Walk through Jubilees*, 54–55.
33. Van Ruiten, *Primaeval History Interpreted*, 345–50.
34. Scott, *On Earth as in Heaven*, 6–7.
35. The land seizure by Canaan also explains why his descendants are not African with the rest of the descendants of Ham. See Kugel, *A Walk through Jubilees*, 85–86.
36. Van Ruiten, *Primaeval History Interpreted*, 351.
37. See the reading of Genesis 11:1–9 in the light of colonial practices in South America by José Míguez-Bonino in "Genesis 11:1–9: A Latin American Perspective," in *Return to Babel: Global Perspectives on the Bible*, ed. John R. Levison and Priscilla Pope-Levison (Louisville, KY: Westminster John Knox Press, 1999), 13–16.
38. For more detail on the events of Abram's life in Ur and his departure to Haran, see J. T. A. G. M. van Ruiten, *Abraham in the Book of Jubilees: The Rewriting of Genesis 11:26–25:10 in the Book of Jubilees 11:14–23:8* (Leiden: Brill, 2012), 23–40.
39. For a detailed account of the similarities and differences of these accounts in Genesis and Jubilees, see ibid., 84–93.
40. See Jacques van Ruiten, "Lot versus Abraham. The Interpretation of Genesis 18:1–19:38 in Jubilees 16:1–9," in *Sodom's Sin: Genesis 18–19 and Its Interpretation*, ed. Ed Noort and Eibert Tigchelaar (Leiden: Brill, 2004), 42–46.
41. Kugel has noted that the LXX version of Genesis makes the final well unsuccessful in 26:32. See "Jubilees," 380–81.
42. Halpern-Amaru, *The Empowerment of Women*, 127–32.
43. See the discussion in Kugel, *A Walk through Jubilees*, 165–66.

44. See the discussion of this tradition in Esther Marie Menn, Judah and Tamar (Genesis 38) in *Ancient Jewish Exegesis: Studies in Literary Form and Hermeneutics* (Leiden: Brill, 1997), 133–34.

45. On the image of Jacob as a commander of an army and the similarity to Abraham, see Atar Livneh, "With My Sword and Bow: Jacob as Warrior in Jubilees," in *Rewriting and Interpreting the Hebrew Bible: The Biblical Patriarchs in the Light of the Dead Sea Scrolls*, ed. Devorah Dimant and Reinhard G. Kratz (Berlin: De Gruyter, 2013), 201–5.

46. For a detailed account of the replacement of God by Mastema in Jubilees 48–49, see Segal, *The Book of Jubilees*, 203–12.

47. In Kugel's source division of Jubilees, 49:2–17 comes from the Interpolator, who mentions only the sanctuary. It is the initial form of the work that mentions the tabernacle in 49:21. See Kugel, "Jubilees," 448.

48. On the differences between the genealogical material in Genesis and 1 Chronicles 1, see Ralph W. Klein, *1 Chronicles: A Commentary* (Minneapolis: Fortress, 2006), 56–73.

49. Dieter Georgi, *The City in the Valley: Biblical Interpretation and Urban Theology* (Atlanta: Society of Biblical Literature, 2005), 353.

50. Ibid., 46–51.

51. Ibid., 53–68.

52. Ibid., 51.

53. Ibid., 50.

Chapter 9: A Citified Text

1. One important illustration of this more deliberate focus is the appearance of the recent volume edited by Brian B. Schmidt, *Contextualizing Israel's Sacred Writings: Ancient Literacy, Orality, and Literary Production* (Atlanta: Society of Biblical Literature, 2015).

2. A process like this is described in detail in Michael L. Satlow, *How the Bible Became Holy* (New Haven: Yale University Press, 2014), 13–68.

3. See Brian B. Schmidt, "Memorializing Conflict: Toward an Iron Age 'Shadow' History of Israel's Earliest Literature," in *Contextualizing Israel's Sacred Writings: Ancient Literacy, Orality, and Literary Production*, ed. Brian B. Schmidt (Atlanta: Society of Biblical Literature, 2015), 105–11.

4. See Seth L. Sanders, "What If There Aren't Any Empirical Models for Pentateuchal Criticism?," in Schmidt, ed., *Contextualizing Israel's Sacred Writings*, 299–302. On the desire for perfection and efforts to develop it in this late stage, see Bernard M. Levinson, *A More Perfect Torah: At the Intersection of Philology and Hermeneutics in Deuteronomy and the Temple Scroll* (Winona Lake, IN: Eisenbrauns, 2013), 90–93.

5. Schmidt, "Memorializing Conflict," 108–9. The notion of "oral literature" may seem a self-contradiction to some, but this is the result of anachronistic thinking that presumes that writing is fixed and stable, while ancient oral performance was always impromptu or improvisational.

6. Sanders, "What If There Aren't Any Empirical Models," 300.

7. See Richard A. Horsley, *Scribes, Visionaries, and the Politics of Second Temple Judea* (Louisville, KY: Westminster John Knox Press, 2007), 117–18.

8. Ibid., 128.

9. See Martin Luther, *Luther's Works, vol. 1: Lectures on Genesis 1–5*, ed. Jaroslav Pelikan (St. Louis: Concordia, 1955), 62.

10. Ibid., 222.
11. Ibid., 66.
12. Paul S. Evans, "Creating a New 'Great Divide': The Exoticization of Ancient Culture in Some Recent Applications of Orality Studies to the Bible," *Journal of Biblical Literature* 4 (2017): 749–53.

Notes to Appendix 2

1. The source identification of 4:25–26a is a matter of dispute. E. A. Speiser assigned them to J, which would mean that J knew of two surviving sons of Adam and Eve, Cain and Seth, but did not connect either of them specifically to Noah. The deciding factor was the appearance of the divine name in 26b. See *Genesis: Introduction, Translation and Notes* (Garden City, NY: Doubleday, 1964), 34–38. Speiser seemed unwilling to split verse 26 in order to solve the problem. Richard Friedman made exactly that split, separating 4:26b, as the translation above does. Like Speiser, however, Friedman produced an awkward passive translation of 26b with no real subject. See *The Bible with Sources Revealed: A New View into the Five Books of Moses* (San Francisco: HarperCollins, 2003), 40. The verb לחוה, apparently a hophal form of ללח, is difficult. In the final form of Genesis, the masculine singular subject would seem to be Enosh, and this holds true whether the verb is translated in English as active or passive. Assigning 26b to J makes Lamech the most obvious subject, and I have translated for that effect. "He was cased to begin to call . . ." would be more correct technically but too awkward.

Notes to Appendix 3

1. In Genesis the genealogy of Egypt precedes Canaan. I have put Canaan first because it seems to follow more naturally from the cursing of Canaan. The order of the two is not a matter of great significance.

Bibliography

Adamo, David Tuesday. *Africa and Africans in the Old Testament*. San Francisco: Christian Universities Press, 1998.

———. "The Images of Cush in the Old Testament: Reflections on African Hermeneutics." In *Interpreting the Old Testament in Africa: Papers from the International Symposium on Africa and the Old Testament in Nairobi, October 1999*, edited by Mary Getui et al., 65–74. New York: Peter Lang, 2001.

Albertz, Rainer. *Israel in Exile: The History and Literature of the Sixth Century B.C.E.* Atlanta: Society of Biblical Literature, 2003.

Anderson, John E. *Jacob and the Divine Trickster: A Theology of Deception and YHWH's Fidelity to the Ancestral Promise in the Jacob Cycle*. Winona Lake, IN: Eisenbrauns, 2011.

Atkinson, Rowland. "Introduction." In *Gentrification in a Global Context: The New Urban Colonialism*, edited by Rowland Atkinson and Gary Bridge, 1–10. London: Routledge, 2015.

Auerbach, Erich. *Mimesis: The Representation of Reality in Western Literature*. Princeton: Princeton University Press, 1953.

Aufrecht, Walter E. "Urbanization and Northwest Semitic Inscriptions." In *Urbanism and Antiquity: From Mesopotamia to Crete*, edited by Walter E. Aufrecht et al., 116–29. Sheffield: Sheffield Academic, 1997.

Baden, Joel S. *The Composition of the Pentateuch: Renewing the Documentary Hypothesis*. New Haven: Yale University Press, 2012.

Balentine, Samuel E. *The Torah's Vision of Worship*. Minneapolis: Fortress, 1999.

Baumann, Gerlinde. *Love and Violence: Marriage as Metaphor for the Relationship between YHWH and Israel in the Prophetic Books*. Collegeville, MN: Liturgical Press, 2003.

Baumgartenn, Jacob J. "Urbanization in the Late Bronze Age." In *The Architecture of Ancient Israel: From the Prehistoric to the Persian Periods*, edited by Aharon Kempinski and Ronny Reich, 143–50. Jerusalem: Israel Exploration Society, 1992.

Ben-Tor, Amnon. "The Fall of Canaanite Hazor—The 'Who' and 'When' Questions." In *Mediterranean Peoples in Transition: Thirteenth to Early Tenth Centuries BCE*, edited by Seymour Gitin et al., 456–68. Jerusalem: Israel Exploration Society, 1998.

Ben Zvi, Ehud. "The Dialogue between Abraham and YHWH in Gen. 18.23–32: A Historical-Critical Analysis." *Journal for the Study of the Old Testament* 53 (1992): 27–46.

———. "Exploring Jerusalem as a Site of Memory in the Late Persian and Early Hellenistic Periods." In *Memory and the City in Ancient Israel*, edited by Diana V. Edelman and Ehud Ben Zvi, 197–217. Winona Lake, IN: Eisenbrauns, 2014.

────. "The Urban Center of Jerusalem and the Development of the Literature of the Hebrew Bible." In *Urbanism in Antiquity: From Mesopotamia to Crete*, edited by Walter E. Aufrecht et al., 194–209. Sheffield: Sheffield Academic, 1997.

Berlin, Adele. *Lamentations: A Commentary*. Louisville, KY: Westminster John Knox, 2002.

Blenkinsopp, Joseph. "City to Landscape: The 'Back to Nature' Theme in Isaiah 1–35." In *"Every City Shall Be Forsaken": Urbanism and Prophecy in Ancient Israel and the Near East*, edited by Lester L. Grabbe and Robert D. Haak, 35–44. Sheffield: Sheffield Academic, 2001.

────. "The Structure of P." *Catholic Biblical Quarterly* 38 (1976): 275–92.

Boccaccini, Gabriele. *Roots of Rabbinic Judaism: An Intellectual History from Ezekiel to Daniel*. Grand Rapids: Eerdmans, 2002.

Boer, Roland. *The Sacred Economy of Ancient Israel*. Louisville, KY: Westminster John Knox, 2015.

Bokovoy, David E. "Did Eve Acquire, Create, or Procreate with Yahweh? A Grammatical and Contextual Reassessment of הנק in Genesis 4:1." *Vetus Testamentum* 63 (2013): 19–35.

Burnett, Joel S. *Where Is God?: Divine Absence in the Hebrew Bible*. Minneapolis: Fortress, 2010.

Cargill, Robert R. *The Cities That Built the Bible*. San Francisco: HarperOne, 2016.

Carr, David M. *Holy Resilience: The Bible's Traumatic Origins*. New Haven: Yale University Press, 2014.

Carter, Charles E. "The Province of Yehud in the Post-Exilic Period: Soundings in Site Distribution and Demography." In *Currents in Research: Biblical Studies 2*, edited by Tamara Cohn Eskenazi and Kent H. Richards, 107–45. Sheffield: Sheffield Academic, 1994.

Cataldo, Jeremiah W. *A Theocratic Yehud?: Issues of Governance in Persian Yehud*. London: T&T Clark, 2009.

Chatman, Seymour. *Story and Discourse: Narrative Structure in Fiction and Film*. Ithaca, NY: Cornell University Press, 1978.

Choi, John H. *Traditions at Odds: The Reception of the Pentateuch in Biblical and Second Temple Period Literature*. New York: T&T Clark, 2010.

Cline, Eric H. *1177 B.C.: The Year Civilization Collapsed*. Princeton: Princeton University Press, 2014.

Clines, David J. A., ed. *The Dictionary of Classical Hebrew*, vol. 7. Sheffield: Sheffield Phoenix, 2010.

Cohn, Robert L. "Narrative Structure and Canonical Perspective in Genesis." *Journal for the Study of the Old Testament* 25 (1983): 3–16.

Cox, Harvey. *The Secular City: Secularization and Urbanization in Theological Perspective*, 3rd ed. Princeton: Princeton University Press, 2013.

Crow, Loren D. *The Songs of Ascents (Psalms 120–134): Their Place in Israelite History and Religion*. Atlanta: Scholars Press, 1996.

Day, Peggy. "The Personification of Cities as Female in the Hebrew Bible: The Thesis of Aloysius Fitzgerald, F. S. C." In *Reading from This Place*, vol. 2, *Social Location and Biblical Interpretation in Global Perspective*, edited by Fernando F. Segovia and Mary Ann Tolbert, 283–302. Minneapolis: Fortress, 1995.

De Geus, C. H. J. *Towns in Ancient Israel and in the Southern Levant*. Leuven: Peeters, 2003.

Dever, William G. "Archaeology, Urbanism, and the Rise of the Israelite State." In *Urbanism and Antiquity: From Mesopotamia to Crete*, edited by Walter E. Aufrecht et al., 172–93. Sheffield: Sheffield Academic, 1997.

———. *Beyond the Texts: An Archaeological Portrait of Ancient Israel and Judah*. Atlanta: Society of Biblical Literature, 2017.

Douglas, Mary. *In the Wilderness: The Doctrine of Defilement in the Book of Numbers*. Sheffield: JSOT Press, 1993.

Dozeman, Thomas B. *Joshua 1–12: A New Translation with Introduction and Commentary*. New Haven: Yale University Press, 2015.

Ellul, Jacques. *The Meaning of the City*. Translated by Dennis Pardee. Grand Rapids: Eerdmans, 1970.

Emerton, J. A. "The Riddle of Genesis XIV." *Vetus Testamentum* 21 (1971): 403–39.

Erisman, Angela Roskop. "New Historicism, Historical Criticism, and Reading the Pentateuch." *Religion Compass* 8 (2014): 71–80.

Evans, Paul S. "Creating a New 'Great Divide': The Exoticization of Ancient Culture in Some Recent Applications of Orality." *Journal of Biblical Literature* 136 (2017): 749–64.

Finkelstein, Israel. *The Forgotten Kingdom: The Archaeology and History of Northern Israel*. Atlanta: Society of Biblical Literature, 2013.

———. "The Wilderness Narrative and Itineraries and the Evolution of the Exodus Tradition." In *Israel's Exodus in Transdisciplinary Perspective*, edited by Thomas E. Levy et al., 39–50. Switzerland: Springer, 2015.

Finkelstein, Israel, and Magen Broshi. "The Population of Palestine in Iron Age II." *Bulletin of the American Schools of Oriental Research* 287 (1992): 47–60.

Finkelstein, Israel, and Thomas Römer. "Comments on the Historical Background of the Jacob Narrative in Genesis." *Zeitschrift für die alttestamentliche Wissenschaft* (2014): 317–38.

Fitzmyer, Joseph A. *The Genesis Apocryphon of Qumran Cave 1 (1Q20): A Commentary*. Rome: Biblical Institute Press, 2004.

Fleming, Daniel E. *The Legacy of Israel in Judah's Bible: History, Politics, and the Reinscribing of Tradition*. Cambridge: Cambridge University Press, 2012.

Florida, Richard. *The New Urban Crisis: How Our Cities Are Increasing Inequality, Deepening Segregation, and Failing the Middle Class—and What We Can Do about It*. New York: Basic Books, 2017.

———. *The Rise of the Creative Class, Revisited*. New York: Basic Books, 2012.

Frick, Frank S. *The City in Ancient Israel*. Missoula, MO: Scholars Press, 1977.

Fried, Lisbeth S. "The Torah of God as God: The Exaltation of the Written Law Code in Ezra–Nehemiah." In *Divine Presence and Absence in Exilic and Post-Exilic Judah*, edited by Nathan MacDonald and Izaak J. de Hulster, 283–300. Tübingen: Mohr Siebeck, 2013.

———. *Was 1 Esdras First? An Investigation into the Priority and Nature of 1 Esdras*. Atlanta: Society of Biblical Literature, 2011.

Friedman, Richard Elliott. *The Bible with Sources Revealed: A New View into the Five Books of Moses*. San Francisco: HarperCollins, 2003.

———. *The Disappearance of God: A Divine Mystery*. New York: Little, Brown, and Company, 1995.

Fritz, Volkmar. *The City in Ancient Israel*. Sheffield: Sheffield Academic, 1995.

Fulton, Deirdre N. *Reconsidering Nehemiah's Judah: The Case of MT and LXX Nehemiah 11–12*. Tübingen: Mohr Siebeck, 2015.

Gadamer, Hans George. *Truth and Method*. London: Sheed & Ward, 1975.

George, Mark K. *Israel's Tabernacle as Social Space*. Atlanta: Society of Biblical Literature, 2009.

Georgi, Dieter. *The City in the Valley: Biblical Interpretation and Urban Theology*. Atlanta: Society of Biblical Literature, 2005.

Gertz, Jan C. "The Formation of the Primeval History." In *The Book of Genesis: Composition, Reception, and Interpretation*, edited by Craig A. Evans et al., 107–36. Leiden: Brill, 2012.

Gertz, Jan C., et al., eds. *The Composition of the Pentateuch*. Tübingen: Mohr Siebeck, 2016.

Girard, René. *Things Hidden since the Foundation of the World*. Translated by Stephen Bann and Michael Metteer. Stanford, CA: Stanford University Press, 1987.

Glassner, Jean-Jacques. *Mesopotamian Chronicles*. Atlanta: Society of Biblical Literature, 2004.

Glissmann, Volker. "Genesis 14: A Diaspora Novella?" *Journal for the Study of the Old Testament* 34 (2009): 33–45.

Grabbe, Lester L. "Sup-urbs or Hyp-urbs: Prophets and Populations in Ancient Israel and Socio-Historical Method." In *"Every City Shall Be Forsaken": Urbanism and Prophecy in Ancient Israel and the Near East*, edited by Lester L. Grabbe and Robert D. Haak, 95–123. Sheffield: Sheffield Academic, 2001.

Granerød, Gard. "The Former and Future Temple of YHW in Elephantine: A Tradition-Historical Study of Ancient Near Eastern Antiquarianism." *Zeitschrift für die alttestamentliche Wissenschaft* 127 (2015): 63–77.

Green, Barbara. *Jeremiah and God's Plan of Well-Being*. Columbia: University of South Carolina Press, 2013.

Grypeou, Emmanouela, and Helen Spurling. *The Book of Genesis in Late Antiquity*. Leiden: Brill, 2013.

Guillaume, Philippe. "Dislocating Jerusalem's Memory with Tyre." In *Memory and the City in Ancient Israel*, edited by Diana V. Edelman and Ehud Ben Zvi, 257–66. Winona Lake, IN: Eisenbrauns, 2014.

———. *Land, Credit and Crisis: Agrarian Finance in the Hebrew Bible*. London: Routledge, 2012.

Halpern-Amaru, Betsy. *The Empowerment of Women in the Book of Jubilees*. Leiden: Brill, 1999.

Halpern, Baruch. "The Dawn of an Age: Megiddo in the Iron Age I." In *Exploring the Longue Durée: Essays in Honor of Lawrence E. Stager*, edited by J. David Schloen, 151–63. Winona Lake, IN: Eisenbrauns, 2009.

Hamori, Esther. *"When Gods Were Men": The Embodied God in Biblical and Near Eastern Literature*. Berlin: de Gruyter, 2008.

Hartenstein, Friedhelm. "Prophets, Princes, and Kings: Prophecy and Prophetic Books according to Jeremiah 36." In *Jeremiah's Scriptures: Production, Reception, Interaction, and Transformation*, edited by Hindy Najman and Konrad Schmid, 70–91. Leiden: Brill, 2017.

Hays, Christopher B. *Hidden Riches: A Sourcebook for the Comparative Study of the Hebrew Bible and the Ancient Near East*. Louisville, KY: Westminster John Knox, 2014.

Hendel, Ronald. "Is the 'J' Primeval Narrative an Independent Composition? A Critique of Crüsemann's 'Die Eigenständigkeit der Urgeschichte." In *The Pentateuch: International Perspectives on Current Research*, edited by Thomas B. Dozeman et al., 181–205. Tübingen: Mohr Siebeck, 2011.

Henze, Matthias, and Liv Ingeborg Lied. "Jeremiah, Baruch, and Their Books: Three Phases in a Changing Relationship." In *Jeremiah's Scriptures: Production, Recep-*

tion, Interaction, and Transformation, edited by Hindy Najman and Konrad Schmid, 330–53. Leiden: Brill, 2017.

Herzog, Zeev. "Settlement and Fortification Planning in the Iron Age." *The Architecture of Ancient Israel: From the Prehistoric to the Persian Periods*, edited by Aharon Kempinski and Ronny Reich, 231–74. Jerusalem: Israel Exploration Society, 1992.

Hoffmeier, James K. *Israel in Egypt: The Evidence for the Authenticity of the Exodus Tradition*. New York: Oxford University Press, 1999.

Holladay, William L. *The Psalms through Three Thousand Years*. Minneapolis: Fortress Press, 1993.

Holloway, Steven W. "Nineveh as Meme in Persian-Period Yehud." In *Memory and the City in Ancient Israel*, edited by Diana V. Edelman and Ehud Ben Zvi, 267–92. Winona Lake, IN: Eisenbrauns, 2014.

Horsley, Richard A. *Scribes, Visionaries, and the Politics of Second Temple Judea*. Louisville, KY: Westminster John Knox, 2007.

Humphreys, W. Lee. *The Character of God in the Book of Genesis: A Narrative Appraisal*. Louisville, KY: Westminster John Knox, 2001.

Jacobs, Jane. *The Death and Life of Great American Cities*. New York: Vintage, 1992.

Japhet, Sarah. "Periodization between History and Ideology II: Chronology and Ideology in Ezra–Nehemiah." In *Judah and Judeans in the Persian Period*, edited by Oded Lipschits and Manfred Oeming, 491–508. Winona Lake, IN: Eisenbrauns, 2006.

Johannès, Francis, and Andre Lemaire. "Trois tablettes cunéiformes à l'onomastique ouest sémitique." *Transeuphratène* 17 (1999): 17–34.

Kessler, John. "Reconstructing Haggai's Jerusalem: Demographic and Sociological Considerations and the Search for an Adequate Point of Departure." In *"Every City Shall Be Forsaken": Urbanism and Prophecy in Ancient Israel and the Near East*, edited by Lester L. Grabbe and Robert D. Haak, 135–58. Sheffield: Sheffield Academic, 2001.

King, Philip J., and Lawrence E. Stager. *Life in Biblical Israel*. Louisville, KY: Westminster John Knox, 2001.

Klein, Ralph W. *1 Chronicles: A Commentary*. Minneapolis: Fortress, 2006.

Knoppers, Gary N. "An Achaemenid Imperial Authorization of Torah in Yehud?" In *Persia and Torah: The Theory of Imperial Authorization of the Pentateuch*, edited by James W. Watts) 115–34. Atlanta: Society of Biblical Literature, 2001.

Knowles, Melody D. *Centrality Practiced: Jerusalem and the Religious Practice of Yehud in the Diaspora in the Persian Period*. Atlanta: Society of Biblical Literature, 2006.

Kugel, James L. *A Walk through Jubilees: Studies in the Book of Jubilees and the World of Its Creation*. Leiden: Brill, 2012.

———. "Jubilees." In *Outside the Bible: Ancient Jewish Writings Related to Scripture*, vol. 1, edited by Louis H. Feldman et al., 272–465. Philadelphia: Jewish Publication Society, 2013.

———. *The Bible as It Was*. Cambridge, MA: Harvard University Press, 1997.

Kvanvig, Helge. *Primeval History: Babylonian, Biblical, and Enochic: An Intertextual Reading*. Leiden: Brill, 2011.

LaCoque, André. *The Captivity of Innocence: Babel and the Yahwist*. Eugene, OR: Wipf & Stock, 2010.

———. *Onslaught against Innocence: Cain, Abel, and the Yahwist*. Eugene, OR: Cascade, 2008.

Laird, Donna. *Negotiating Power in Ezra–Nehemiah*. Atlanta: Society of Biblical Literature, 2016.

Launderville, Dale F. *Spirit and Reason: The Embodied Character of Ezekiel's Symbolic Thinking*. Waco, TX: Baylor University Press, 2007.

Leach, Edmund. "Anthropological Approaches to the Study of the Bible during the Twentieth Century." In *Structuralist Interpretations of Biblical Myth*, edited by Edmund Leach and D. Alan Aycock, 7–32. Cambridge: Cambridge University Press, 1983.

Lefebvre, Henri. *The Production of Space*. Translated by Donald Nicholson Smith. Oxford: Blackwell, 1991.

Levenson, Jon D. *Creation and the Persistence of Evil: The Jewish Drama of Divine Omnipotence*. San Francisco: Harper & Row, 1988.

———. *Sinai and Zion: An Entry into the Jewish Bible*. San Francisco: Harper & Row, 1985.

Levin, Christoph. "The Yahwist: The Earliest Editor in the Pentateuch." *Journal of Biblical Literature* 126 (2007): 209–30.

Levine, Baruch A. *Numbers 1–20: A New Translation with Introduction and Commentary*. New York: Doubleday, 1993.

Levine, Yigal. "Nimrod the Mighty, King of Kish, King of Sumer and Akkad." *Vetus Testamentum* 52 (2002): 350–66.

Levinson, Bernard M. *A More Perfect Torah: At the Intersection of Philology and Hermeneutics in Deuteronomy and the Temple Scroll*. Winona Lake, IN: Eisenbrauns, 2013.

Linzey, Andrew. *Animal Theology*. Urbana: University of Illinois Press, 1994.

Lipiński, E. "הנק," in the *Theological Dictionary of the Old Testament*, vol. 8, edited by G. Johannes Botterweck et al., 58–65. Grand Rapids: Eerdmans, 2004.

Lipschits, Oded. *The Fall and Rise of Jerusalem*. Winona Lake, IN: Eisenbrauns, 2005.

Livneh, Atar. "With My Sword and Bow: Jacob as Warrior in Jubilees." In *Rewriting and Interpreting the Hebrew Bible: The Biblical Patriarchs in the Light of the Dead Sea Scrolls*, edited by Devorah Dimant and Reinhard G. Kratz, 189–213. Berlin: De Gruyter, 2013.

Lowery, Daniel D. *Toward a Poetics of Genesis 1–11: Reading Genesis 4:17–22 in Its Near Eastern Context*. Winona Lake, IN: Eisenbrauns, 2013.

Luther, Martin. *Luther's Works*, vol. 1, *Lectures on Genesis 1–5*. Trans. George V. Schick. Edited by Jaroslav Pelikan. St. Louis: Concordia Publishing House, 1955.

Marquis, Liane M. "The Composition of Numbers 32: A New Proposal." *Vetus Testamentum* 63 (2013): 408–32.

McDowell, Catherine L. *The "Image of God" in the Garden of Eden: The Creation of Humankind in Genesis 2:5–3:24 in Light of the* mīs pî pīt pî *and* wpt-r *Rituals of Mesopotamia and Ancient Egypt*. Winona Lake, IN: Eisenbrauns, 2015.

McEntire, Mark. "Being Seen and Not Heard: The Interpretation of Genesis 4:8." In *Of Scribes and Sages*, vol. 1, *Ancient Versions and Traditions*, edited by Craig A. Evans, 4–13. New York: T&T Clark, 2004.

———. *The Blood of Abel: The Violent Plot in the Hebrew Bible*. Macon, GA: Mercer University Press, 1999.

———. "From Bound and Gagged to Swimming in the Water of Life: How God Breaks and Heals Ezekiel." *Review and Expositor* 111 (2014): 329–36.

———. "Haggai—Bringing God into the Picture." *Review and Expositor* 97 (2000): 69–78.

———. *Portraits of a Mature God: Choices in Old Testament Theology*. Minneapolis: Fortress, 2013.

McNutt, Paula. "In the Shadow of Cain." *Semeia* 87 (1999): 45–64.

———. *Reconstructing the Society of Ancient Israel*. Louisville, KY: Westminster John Knox, 1999.

Menn, Esther Marie. *Judah and Tamar (Genesis 38) in Ancient Jewish Exegesis: Studies in Literary Form and Hermeneutics*. Leiden: Brill, 1997.

Middlemas, Jill. *The Templeless Age: An Introduction to the History, Literature, and Theology of the "Exile."* Louisville: Westminster John Knox, 2007.

Míguez-Bonino, José. "Genesis 11:1–9: A Latin American Perspective." In *Return to Babel: Global Perspectives on the Bible*, edited by John R. Levison and Priscilla Pope-Levison, 13–16. Louisville, KY: Westminster John Knox, 1999.

Miles, Jack. *God: A Biography*. New York: Vintage, 1996.

Milgrom, Jacob. *Numbers: JPS Torah Commentary*. New York: Jewish Publication Society, 1990.

Mobley, Gregory. *The Return of the Chaos Monsters*. Grand Rapids: Eerdmans, 2012.

Moskowitz, Peter. *How to Kill a City: Gentrification, Inequality, and the Fight for the Neighborhood*. New York: Nation Books, 2017.

Moughtin-Mumby, Sharon. *Sexual and Marital Metaphors in Hosea, Jeremiah, Isaiah, and Ezekiel*. Oxford: Oxford University Press, 2008.

Mroczek, Eva. *The Literary Imagination in Jewish Antiquity*. Oxford: Oxford University Press, 2016.

Mullen, E. Theodore. *Ethnic Myths and Pentateuchal Foundations: A New Approach to the Formation of the Pentateuch*. Atlanta: Scholars Press, 1997.

Na'aman, Nadav. *Canaan in the Second Millennium B.C.E.: Collected Essays, Volume 2*. Winona Lake, IN: Eisenbrauns, 2005.

Nickelsburg, George W. E. *1 Enoch 1: A Commentary on the Book of 1 Enoch, Chapters 1–36; 81–108*. Minneapolis: Fortress, 2001.

Niditch, Susan. *War in the Hebrew Bible: A Study in the Ethics of Violence*. Oxford: Oxford University Press, 1993.

Nissinen, Marti. "City as Lofty as Heaven: Arbela and Other Cities in Neo-Assyrian Prophecy." In *"Every City Shall Be Forsaken": Urbanism ad Prophecy in Ancient Israel and the Near East*, edited by Lester L. Grabbe and Robert D. Haak, 172–209. Sheffield: Sheffield Academic, 2001.

Nogalski, James. *The Book of the Twelve: Hosea–Jonah*. Macon, GA: Smyth & Helwys, 2011.

Noort, Ed. "For the Sake of Righteousness—Abraham's Negotiations with YHWH as Prologue to the Sodom Narrative: Genesis 18:16–33." In *Sodom's Sin: Genesis 18–19 and Its Interpretation*, edited by Ed Noort and Eibert Tigchelaar, 3–16. Leiden: Brill, 2004.

O'Brien, Julia. *Challenging Prophetic Metaphor: Theology and Ideology in the Prophets*. Louisville, KY: Westminster John Knox, 2008.

Odell, Margaret S. *Ezekiel*. Macon, GA: Smyth & Helwys, 2005.

Oduyọye, Modupẹ. *The Sons of God and the Daughters of Men: An Afro-Asiatic Interpretation of Genesis 1–11*. Maryknoll, NY: Orbis Books, 1984.

Pakkala, Juha. *Ezra the Scribe: The Development of Ezra 7–10 and Nehemiah 8*. Berlin: Walter de Gruyter, 2004.

Parker, Simon. *Urban Theory and the Urban Experience: Encountering the City*, 2nd ed. London: Routledge, 2015.

Pat-el, Na'amah. "Israelian Hebrew: A Re-Evaluation." *Vetus Testamentum* 67 (2017): 1–37.

Perdue, Leo, et al. *Israel and Empire: A Postcolonial History of Israel and Early Judaism*. London: Bloomsbury, 2015.

Person, Raymond F., Jr. *The Deuteronomistic History and the Book of Chronicles: Scribal Works in an Oral World*. Atlanta: Society of Biblical Literature, 2010.

Philo. "Questions and Answers on Genesis." In *Outside the Bible: Ancient Jewish Writings Related to Scripture*, vol. 1. Edited by Louis H. Feldman et al. Translated by Aram Topchyan and Gohar Muradyan. Philadelphia: Jewish Publication Society, 2014.

Plaut, W. Gunther. *Genesis*. New York: Union of American Hebrew Congregations, 1974.

Porten, Bezalel, et al. *The Elephantine Papyri in English: Three Millennia of Cross-Cultural Continuity and Change*, 2nd ed. Atlanta: Society of Biblical Literature, 2011.

Propp, William H. C. *Exodus 1–18: A New Translation with Introduction and Commentary*. New York: Doubleday, 1999.

———. *Exodus 19–40: A New Translation with Introduction and Commentary*. New York: Doubleday, 2006.

Quinn, Josephine Crawley. *In Search of the Phoenicians*. Princeton: Princeton University Press, 2018.

Rendtorff, Rolf. "What Happened to the Yahwist? Reflections after Thirty Years: A Collegial Conversation between Rolf Rendtorff, David J. A. Clines, Allan Rosengren, and John van Seters." In *Probing the Frontiers of Biblical Studies*, edited by J. Harold Ellens and John T. Greene, 39–66. Eugene, OR: Pickwick, 2009.

Ricoeur, Paul. *Time and Narrative, Volume 1*. Chicago: University of Chicago Press, 1984.

Roberts, J. J. M. *First Isaiah: A Commentary*. Minneapolis: Fortress, 2015.

Rogerson, J. W., and John Vincent. *The City in Biblical Perspective*. London: Routledge, 2014.

Rollston, Christopher A. "Epigraphic Evidence from Jerusalem and Its Environs at the Dawn of Biblical History: Methodologies and a Long Durèe Perspective." In *New Studies in the Archaeology of Jerusalem and Its Region: Collected Papers, Volume XI*, edited by Yuval Gadot et al., 7–20. Jerusalem: Israeli Antiquities Authority, 2017.

———. *Writing and Literacy in the World of Ancient Israel: Epigraphic Evidence from the Iron Age*. Atlanta: Society of Biblical Literature, 2010.

Römer, Thomas. "Egypt Nostalgia in Exodus 14–Numbers 21." In *Torah and the Book of Numbers*, edited by Christian Frevel et al., 66–86. Tübingen: Mohr Siebeck, 2013.

Rosen, Steven A. "History Does Not Repeat Itself: Cyclicity and Particularism in Nomad-Sedentary Relations in the Negev in the Long Term." In *Nomads, Tribes, and the State in the Ancient Near East: Cross-Disciplinary Perspectives*, edited by Jeffry Szuchman, 57–86. Chicago: Oriental Institute of the University of Chicago, 2009.

Routledge, Carolyn. "Temple as the Center in Ancient Egyptian Urbanism." In *Urbanism and Antiquity: From Mesopotamia to Crete*, edited by Walter E. Aufrecht et al., 221–35. Sheffield: Sheffield Academic, 1997.

Runions, Erin. *The Babylon Complex: Theopolitical Fantasies of War, Sex, and Sovereignty*. New York: Fordham University Press, 2014.

Sals, Ulrike. "'Babylon' Forever, or How to Divinize What You Want to Damn." In *Memory and the City in Ancient Israel*, edited by Diana V. Edelman and Ehud Ben Zvi, 293–308. Winona Lake, IN: Eisenbrauns, 2014.

Sanders, Seth L. *From Adapa to Enoch: Scribal Culture and Religious Vision in Judea and Babylon*. Tübingen: Mohr Siebeck, 2017.

———. *The Invention of Hebrew*. Urbana: University of Illinois Press, 2009.

———. "What If There Aren't Any Empirical Models for Pentateuchal Criticism?" In *Contextualizing Israel's Sacred Writings: Ancient Literacy, Orality, and Literary Production*, edited by Brian B. Schmidt, 281–304. Atlanta: Society of Biblical Literature, 2015.

Satlow, Michael L. *How the Bible Became Holy*. New Haven: Yale University Press, 2014.

Schaefer, Konrad, O.S.B. *Psalms*. Collegeville, MN: Liturgical Press, 2001.

Schama, Simon. *Landscape and Memory*. New York: Vintage, 1995.

Schmid, Konrad. "Nebukadnezars Antritt der Weltherrschaft und der Abbruch der Davidynastie: Innerbiblische Schriftauslegung und universalgeschichtliche Konstruktion im Jeremiabuch." In *Schriftgelehrte Tradtionsliteratur: Fallstudien innerbiblischen Schriftauslegung im Alten Testament*, 224–41. Tübingen: Mohr Siebeck, 2011.

Schmidt, Brian B. *Contextualizing Israel's Sacred Writings: Ancient Literacy, Orality, and Literary Production*. Atlanta: Society of Biblical Literature, 2015.

———. "Memorializing Conflict: Toward an Iron Age 'Shadow' History of Israel's Earliest Literature." In *Contextualizing Israel's Sacred Writings: Ancient Literacy, Orality, and Literary Production*, edited by Brian B. Schmidt, 103–32. Atlanta: Society of Biblical Literature, 2015.

Schneidau, Herbert N. *Sacred Discontent: The Bible and Western Tradition*. Berkeley: University of California Press, 1977.

Schniedewind, William M. *How the Bible Became a Book*. Cambridge: Cambridge University Press, 2004.

———. "Understanding Scribal Education in Ancient Israel: A View from Kuntillet 'Ajrud." *MAARAV: A Journal for the Study of Northwest Semitic Languages and Literatures* 21 (2014): 271–93.

Schwartz, Baruch J. "Does Recent Scholarship's Critique of the Documentary Hypothesis Constitute Grounds for Its Rejection?" In *The Pentateuch: International Perspectives on Current Research*, edited by Thomas P. Dozeman et al., 3–16. Tübingen: Mohr Siebeck, 2011.

Schwartz, Regina M. *The Curse of Cain: The Violent Legacy of Monotheism*. Chicago: University of Chicago Press, 1997.

Scott, James M. *On Earth as in Heaven: The Restoration of Sacred Time and Sacred Space in the Book of Jubilees*. Leiden: Brill, 2004.

Segal, Michael. *The Book of Jubilees: Rewritten Bible, Redaction, Ideology and Theology*. Leiden: Brill, 2007.

Sherr, Lynn. *America the Beautiful: The Stirring True Story behind Our Nation's Favorite Song*. Washington: Public Affairs, 2001.

Sherwood, Yvonne. *The Prostitute and the Prophet: Hosea's Marriage in Literary Perspective*. Sheffield: Sheffield Academic, 2009.

Ska, Jean-Louis. "The Study of the Book of Genesis: The Beginning of Critical Reading." In *The Book of Genesis: Composition, Reception, and Interpretation*, edited by Craig A. Evans et al., 3–26. Leiden: Brill, 2012.

Smith, Mark S. *The Priestly Vision of Genesis 1*. Minneapolis: Fortress, 2010.

———. *Where the Gods Are: Spatial Dimensions of Anthropomorphism in the Biblical World.* New Haven: Yale University Press, 2016.

Speiser, E. A. *Genesis: Introduction, Translation and Notes.* Garden City, NY: Doubleday, 1964.

Spina, Frank A. "The Ground for Cain's Rejection (Gen 4): *"damah"* in the Context of Genesis 1–11." *Zeitschrift für die alttestamentliche Wissenschaft* 104 (1992): 319–32.

Stern, Elsie. "Royal Letters and Torah Scrolls: The Place of Ezra–Nehemiah in Scholarly Narratives of Scripturalization." In *Contextualizing Israel's Sacred Writings: Ancient Literacy, Orality, and Literary Production,* edited by Brian B. Schmidt, 239–62. Atlanta: Society of Biblical Literature, 2015.

Sternberg, Meir. *Hebrews between Cultures: Group Portraits and National Literature.* Bloomington: Indiana University Press, 1998.

Stone, Michael E. *Ancient Judaism: New Visions and Views.* Grand Rapids: Eerdmans.

Stone, Michael E., and Matthias Henze. *4 Ezra and 2 Baruch: Translations, Introductions, and Notes.* Minneapolis: Fortress, 2013.

Stordalen, T. *Echoes of Eden: Genesis 2–3 and Symbolism of the Eden Garden in Biblical Hebrew Literature.* Leuven: Peeters, 2000.

Stuhlman, Louis, and Hyun Chul Paul Kim. *You Are My People: An Introduction to the Prophetic Literature.* Nashville: Abingdon, 2010.

Sulzbach, Carla. "Building Castles on Shifting Sands of Memory: From Dystopian to Utopian Views of Jerusalem in the Persian Period." In *Memory and the City in Ancient Israel,* edited by Diana V. Edelman and Ehud Ben Zvi, 309–20. Winona Lake, IN: Eisenbrauns, 2014.

Sweeney, Marvin A. *The Twelve Prophets,* vol. 1. Collegeville, MN: Liturgical Press, 2000.

Szuchman, Jeffrey. "Integrating Approaches to Nomads, Tribes, and the State in the Ancient Near East." In *Nomads, Tribes, and the State in the Ancient Near East: Cross Disciplinary Perspectives,* edited by Jeffrey Szuchman, 1–14. Chicago: Oriental Institute of the University of Chicago, 2009.

Tappey, Ron E., et al. "An Abecedary of the Mid-Tenth Century B.C.E. from the Judaean Shephelah." *Bulletin of the American Schools of Oriental Research* 344 (2006): 5–46.

Thompson, Thomas L. *Biblical Narrative and Palestine's History.* Sheffield: Equinox, 2013.

Tuell, Steven Shawn. *The Law of the Temple in Ezekiel 40–48.* Atlanta: Scholars Press, 1992.

Van De Mieroop, Marc. *The Ancient Mesopotamian City.* Oxford: Oxford University Press, 1997.

VanderKam, James C. *The Book of Jubilees.* Sheffield: Sheffield Academic, 2001.

———. *The Book of Jubilees, II.* Leuven: Peeters, 1989.

———. "The Manuscript Tradition of Jubilees." In *Enoch and the Mosaic Torah: The Evidence of Jubilees,* edited by Gabriele Boccaccini and Giovanni Ibba, 3–21. Grand Rapids: Eerdmans, 2009.

———. *From Revelation to Canon: Studies in the Hebrew Bible and Second Temple Literature.* Leiden: Brill, 2002

Van Der Toorn, Kael. *Scribal Culture and the Making of the Hebrew Bible.* Cambridge, MA: Harvard University Press, 2007.

Van Hoonacker, A. "La succession chronologique Néhémie–Esdras." *Revue Biblique* 32 (1923): 33–64.

Van Ruiten, J. T. A. G. M. *Abraham in the Book of Jubilees: The Rewriting of Genesis 11:26–25:10 in the Book of Jubilees 11:14–23:8*. Leiden: Brill, 2012.

———. "The Garden of Eden and Jubilees 3:1–31." *Bijdragen, Tijdschrift voor filosofie en theologie* 57 (1996): 305–17.

———. "Lot versus Abraham: The Interpretation of Genesis 18:1–19:38 in Jubilees 16:1–9." In *Sodom's Sin: Genesis 18–19 and Its Interpretation*, edited by Ed Noort and Eibert Tigchelaar, 30–46. Leiden: Brill, 2004.

———. *Primaeval History Interpreted: The Rewriting of Genesis 1–11 in the Book of Jubilees*. Leiden: Brill, 2000.

Waerzeggers, Caroline. "The Babylonian Chronicles: Classification and Provenance." *Journal of Near Eastern Studies* 71 (2012): 285–98.

Watts, James W. *Ritual and Rhetoric in Leviticus: From Sacrifice to Scripture*. Cambridge: Cambridge University Press, 2007.

Westermann, Claus. *Genesis: A Practical Commentary*. Grand Rapids: Eerdmans, 1987.

———. *Genesis 1–11: A Commentary*. Translated by John J. Scullion. Minneapolis: Augsburg, 1984.

Wilder, Amos N. *The Bible and the Literary Critic*. Minneapolis: Fortress, 1991.

Williamson, H. G. M. *Ezra–Nehemiah*. Waco, TX: Word, 1985.

Wilson, Robert. R. "Exegesis, Expansion, and Tradition-Making in the Book of Jeremiah." In *Jeremiah's Scriptures: Production, Reception, Interaction, and Transformation*, edited by Hindy Najman and Konrad Schmid, 3–21. Leiden: Brill, 2017.

Wintermute, O. S. "Jubilees: A New Translation and Introduction." In *The Old Testament Pseudepigrapha*, vol. 2, edited by James H. Charlesworth, 35–142. Garden City, NY: Doubleday, 1985.

Wright, David P. *Inventing God's Law: How the Covenant Code of the Bible Used and Revised the Laws of Hammurabi*. Oxford: Oxford University Press, 2009.

Wright, Jacob L. *David, King of Israel, and Caleb in Biblical Memory*. Cambridge: Cambridge University Press, 2014.

———. "Seeking, Finding, and Writing in Ezra–Nehemiah." In *Unity and Disunity in Ezra–Nehemiah: Redaction, Rhetoric, and Reader*, edited by Mark J. Boda and Paul L. Redditt, 277–305. Sheffield: Sheffield Phoenix, 2008.

———. "Urbicide: The Ritualized Killing of Cities in the Ancient Near East." In *Ritual Violence in the Hebrew Bible: New Perspectives*, edited by Saul M. Olyan, 147–66. Oxford: Oxford University Press, 2015.

Young, Ian M. "Israelite Literacy: Interpreting the Evidence, Part II." *Vetus Testamentum* 48 (1998): 408–22.

Young, Stephen L. "Maximizing Literacy as a Protective Strategy: Redescribing Evangelical Inerrantist Scholarship on Israelite Literacy." *Biblical Interpretation* 25 (2015): 145–73.

Ziemer, Benjamin. *Abram–Abraham: Kompositionsgeschichtliche Untersuchungen zu Genesis 14, 15 und 17*. Berlin: de Gruyter, 2005.

Zobel, H. J. "הדר." In the *Theological Dictionary of the Old Testament*, vol. 8, edited by G. Johannes Botterweck et al., 330–36. Grand Rapids: Eerdmans, 2004.

Index of Scripture and Other Ancient Texts

Index of Modern Authors

Index of Subjects

CPSIA information can be obtained
at www.ICGtesting.com
Printed in the USA
LVHW030302261119
638451LV00011B/899/P